DQM+

DRAGON QUEST MONSTERS

STORY & CHARACTERS

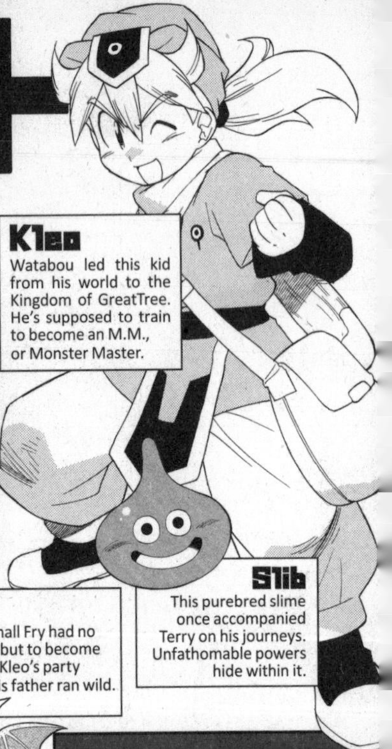

Kleo

Watabou led this kid from his world to the Kingdom of GreatTree. He's supposed to train to become an M.M., or Monster Master.

Story

Though he dreamed of becoming a hero for days on end, Kleo has now instead become a Monster Master, and was tasked with finding Terry, his missing predecessor. Along with the monsters in his party, Slib and Junior, he follows Dragonlord through a traveler's gate and sets off on a big adventure--one filled with hope and uncertainty!! At the same time, an evil presence watches over Kleo from the shadows... What lies in store for Kleo in this world?!

Slib

This purebred slime once accompanied Terry on his journeys. Unfathomable powers hide within it.

Jr.

This Small Fry had no choice but to become one of Kleo's party after his father ran wild.

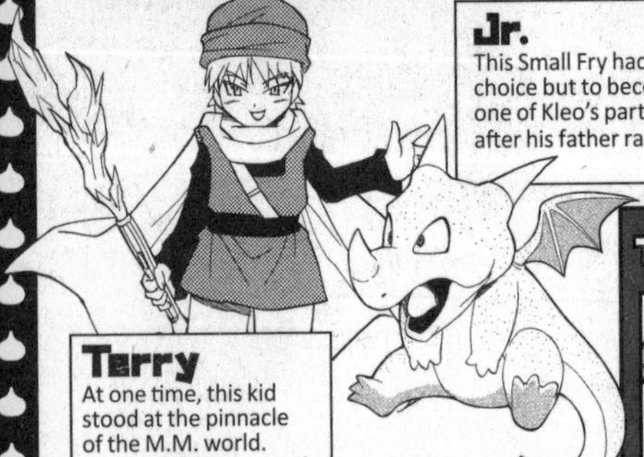

Terry

At one time, this kid stood at the pinnacle of the M.M. world. However, he is currently said to be missing...

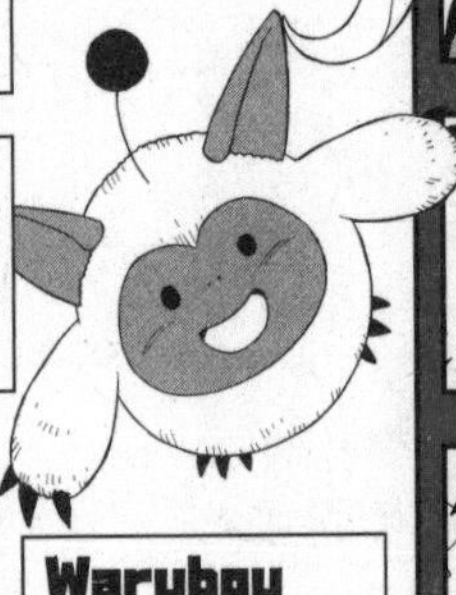

Watabou

It's the spirit of GreatTree. Just like Terry, it's missing at the moment.

The People of GreatTree

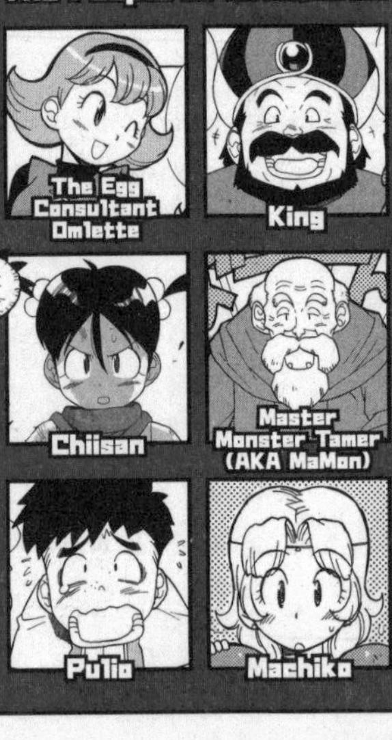
King
The Egg Consultant Omlette
Master Monster Tamer (AKA MaMon)
Chiisan
Machiko
PuTio

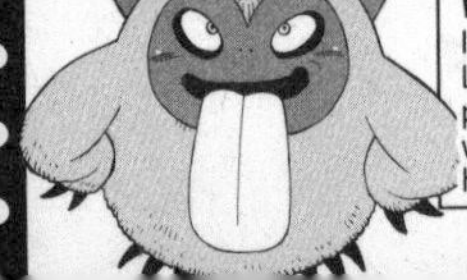

Warubou

It's the spirit of Great-Log, and has a rotten personality. Why is it watching over Kleo and his adventures?!

The 7th Night   Nice Party, Mind if I Join? —————— 005

The 8th Night   So You're the Monster Hunter Everyone's
Talking About?!! ———————————— 029

The 9th Night   Who's That...?! ———————————— 053

The 10th Night   A World Where the Strongest Becomes the Victor!
A World Where Only the Strong Survive! ——— 079

The 11th Night   Where a Journey for "Strength" Leads ——— 103

The 12th Night   *Ooo!* I'm Really Burnin' Up Now!! ———— 119

The 13th Night   If I Could Save the World... ————————— 149

The 14th Night   Welcome Back, Kleo!! ———————————— 173

DQM+

DRAGON QUEST MONSTERS

CONTENTS

2

The 7th Night

Nice Party, Mind if I Join?

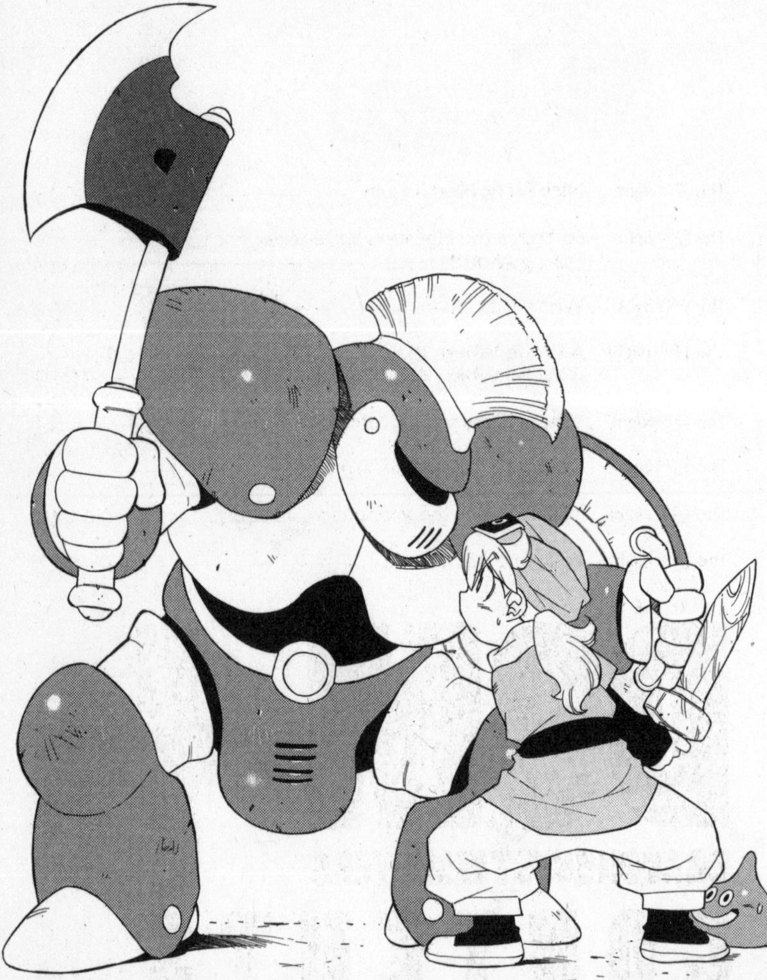

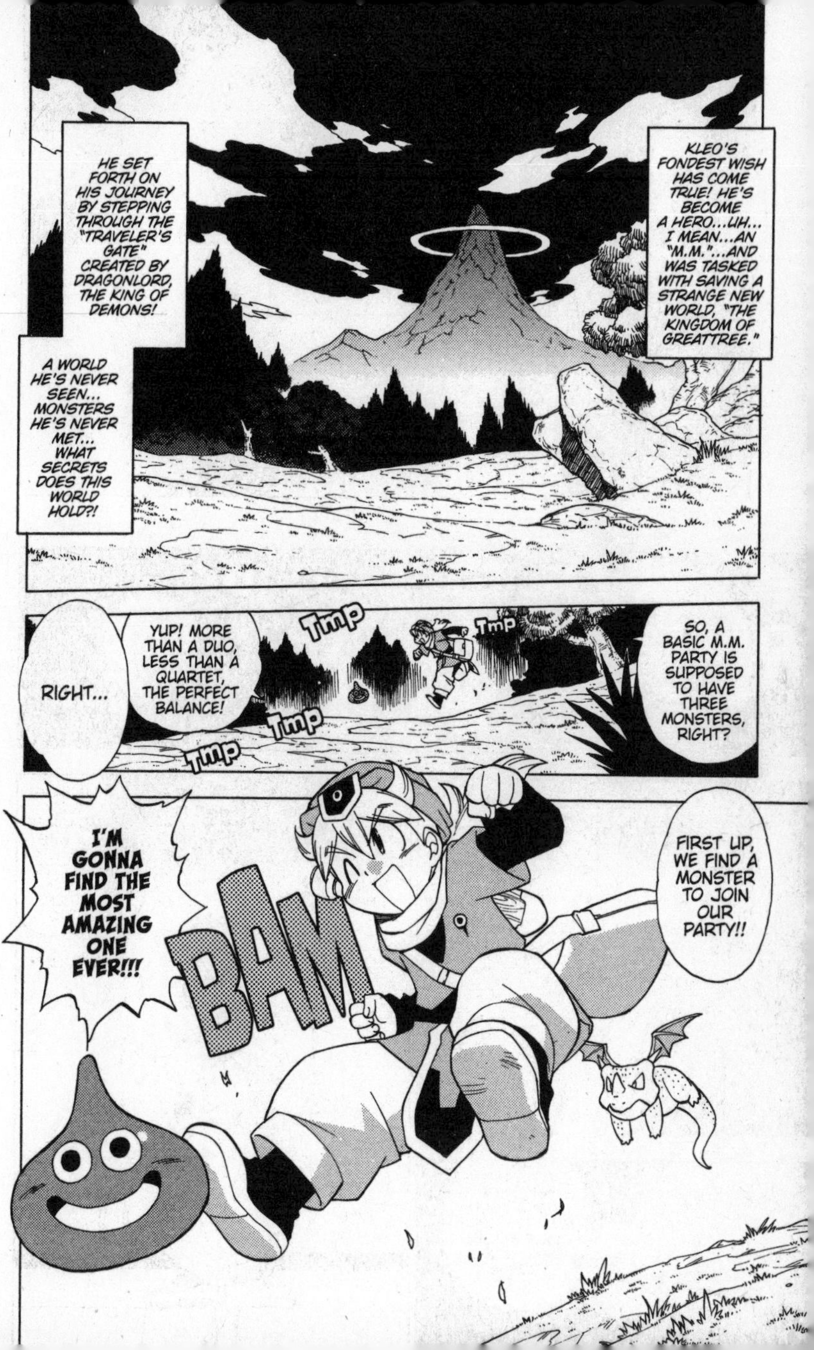
KLEO'S FONDEST WISH HAS COME TRUE! HE'S BECOME A HERO...UH... I MEAN...AN "M.M."...AND WAS TASKED WITH SAVING A STRANGE NEW WORLD, "THE KINGDOM OF GREATTREE."
HE SET FORTH ON HIS JOURNEY BY STEPPING THROUGH THE "TRAVELER'S GATE" CREATED BY DRAGONLORD, THE KING OF DEMONS!
A WORLD HE'S NEVER SEEN... MONSTERS HE'S NEVER MET... WHAT SECRETS DOES THIS WORLD HOLD?!
SO, A BASIC M.M. PARTY IS SUPPOSED TO HAVE THREE MONSTERS, RIGHT?
Tmp
Tmp
YUP! MORE THAN A DUO, LESS THAN A QUARTET, THE PERFECT BALANCE!
Tmp
Tmp
RIGHT...
FIRST UP, WE FIND A MONSTER TO JOIN OUR PARTY!!
BAM
I'M GONNA FIND THE MOST AMAZING ONE EVER!!!

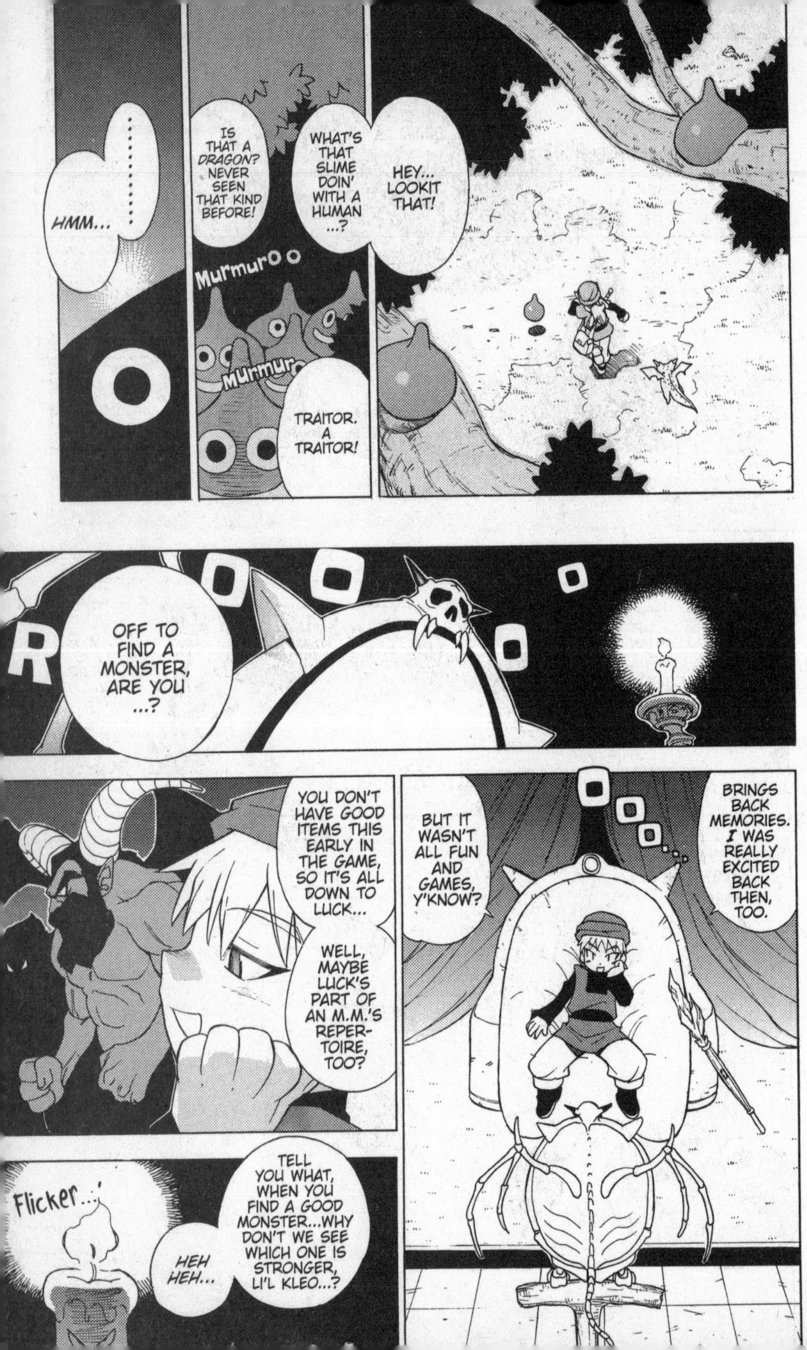
HEY... LOOKIT THAT!
WHAT'S THAT SLIME DOIN' WITH A HUMAN...?
IS THAT A *DRAGON?* NEVER SEEN THAT KIND BEFORE!
Murmur
Murmur
TRAITOR. A TRAITOR!
......
HMM...
OFF TO FIND A MONSTER, ARE YOU...?
BRINGS BACK MEMORIES. *I* WAS REALLY EXCITED BACK THEN, TOO.
BUT IT WASN'T ALL FUN AND GAMES, Y'KNOW?
YOU DON'T HAVE GOOD ITEMS THIS EARLY IN THE GAME, SO IT'S ALL DOWN TO LUCK...
WELL, MAYBE LUCK'S PART OF AN M.M.'S REPERTOIRE, TOO?
TELL YOU WHAT, WHEN YOU FIND A GOOD MONSTER...WHY DON'T WE SEE WHICH ONE IS STRONGER, LI'L KLEO...?
HEH HEH...
Flicker...

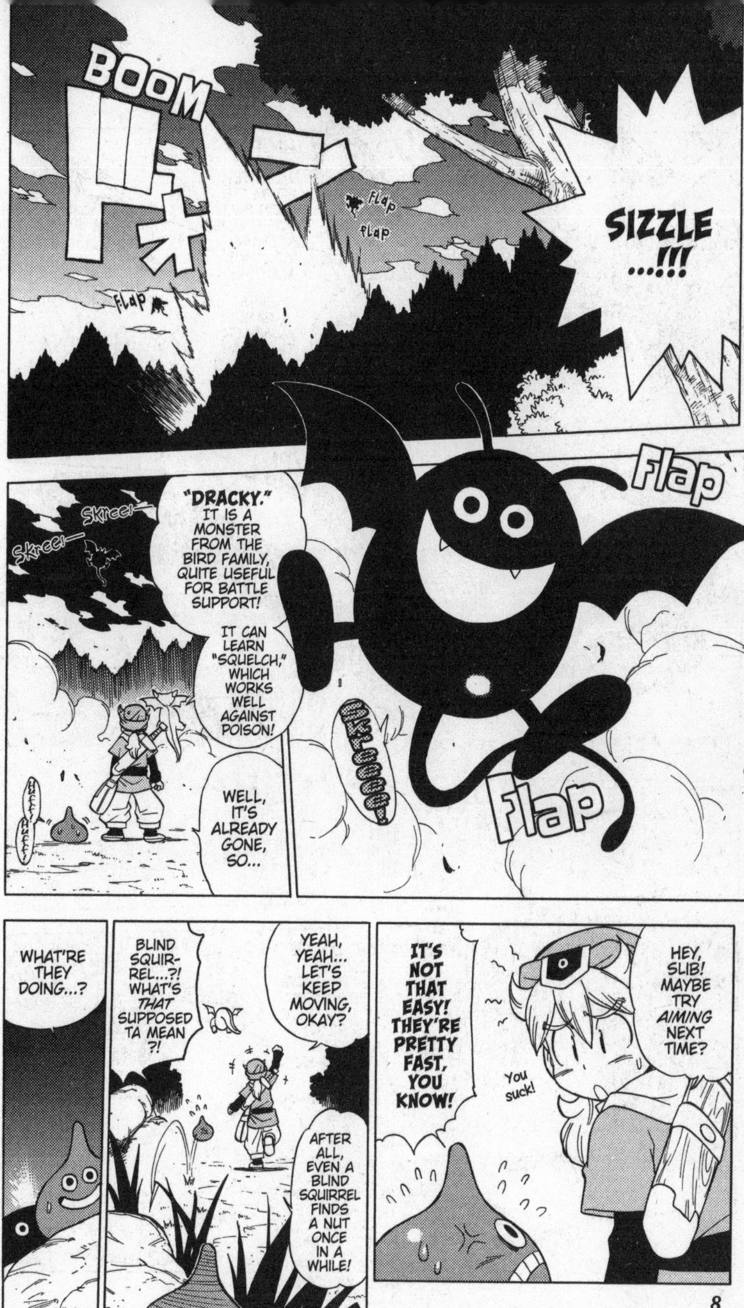
SIZZLE ...!!!
Flap flap
BOOM
Flap
Flap
SKLOOOO!
Flap
WELL, IT'S ALREADY GONE, SO...
"DRACKY." IT IS A MONSTER FROM THE BIRD FAMILY, QUITE USEFUL FOR BATTLE SUPPORT!
IT CAN LEARN "SQUELCH," WHICH WORKS WELL AGAINST POISON!
Skree!
Skree!
Huff! Huff!
HEY, SLIB! MAYBE TRY *AIMING* NEXT TIME?
You suck!
IT'S NOT THAT EASY! THEY'RE PRETTY FAST, YOU KNOW!
YEAH, YEAH... LET'S KEEP MOVING, OKAY?
AFTER ALL, EVEN A BLIND SQUIRREL FINDS A NUT ONCE IN A WHILE!
BLIND SQUIRREL...?! WHAT'S *THAT* SUPPOSED TA MEAN?!
WHAT'RE THEY DOING...?

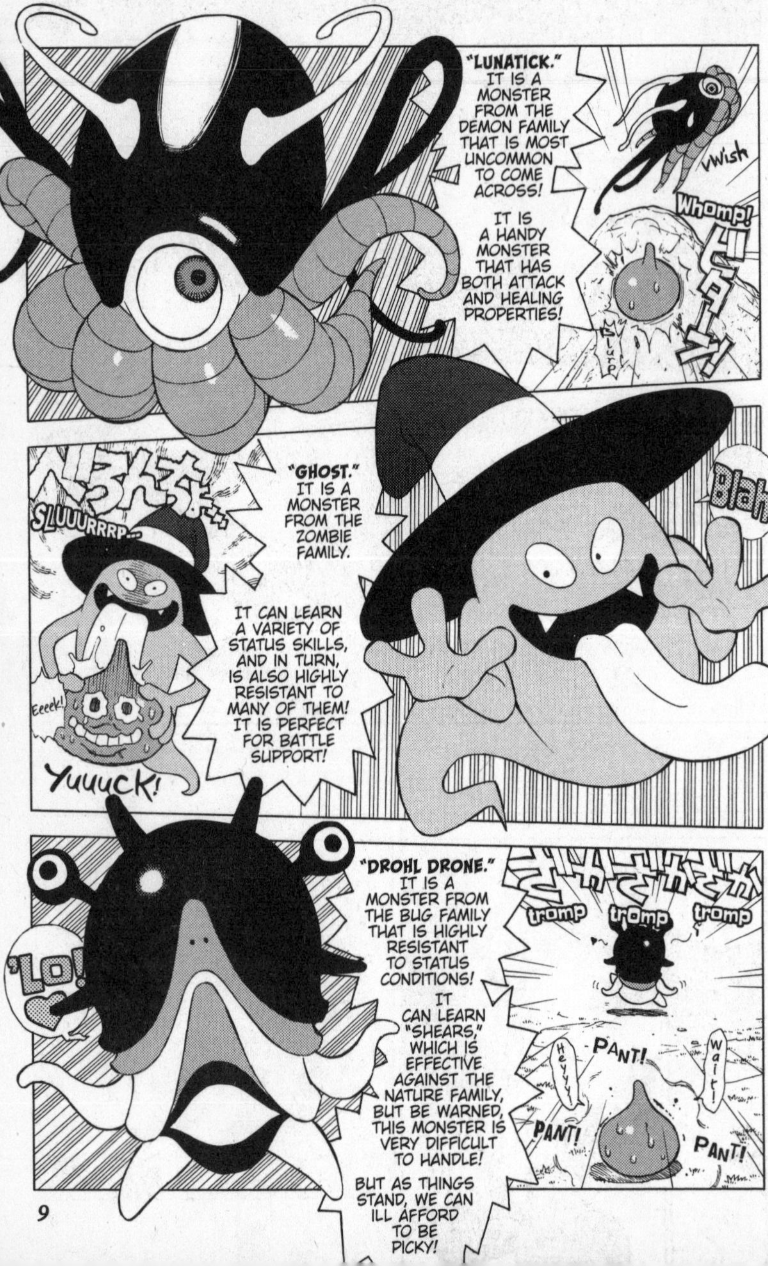
"LUNATICK." IT IS A MONSTER FROM THE DEMON FAMILY THAT IS MOST UNCOMMON TO COME ACROSS!
IT IS A HANDY MONSTER THAT HAS BOTH ATTACK AND HEALING PROPERTIES!
vWish
Whomp!
Slurp
Blah!
"GHOST." IT IS A MONSTER FROM THE ZOMBIE FAMILY.
SLUUURRRP...
IT CAN LEARN A VARIETY OF STATUS SKILLS, AND IN TURN, IS ALSO HIGHLY RESISTANT TO MANY OF THEM! IT IS PERFECT FOR BATTLE SUPPORT!
Eeeek!
Yuuuck!
tromp tromp tromp
"DROHL DRONE." IT IS A MONSTER FROM THE BUG FAMILY THAT IS HIGHLY RESISTANT TO STATUS CONDITIONS!
IT CAN LEARN "SHEARS," WHICH IS EFFECTIVE AGAINST THE NATURE FAMILY, BUT BE WARNED, THIS MONSTER IS VERY DIFFICULT TO HANDLE!
Wait!
PANT!
Heyyy!
PANT!
PANT!
'Lo!
BUT AS THINGS STAND, WE CAN ILL AFFORD TO BE PICKY!

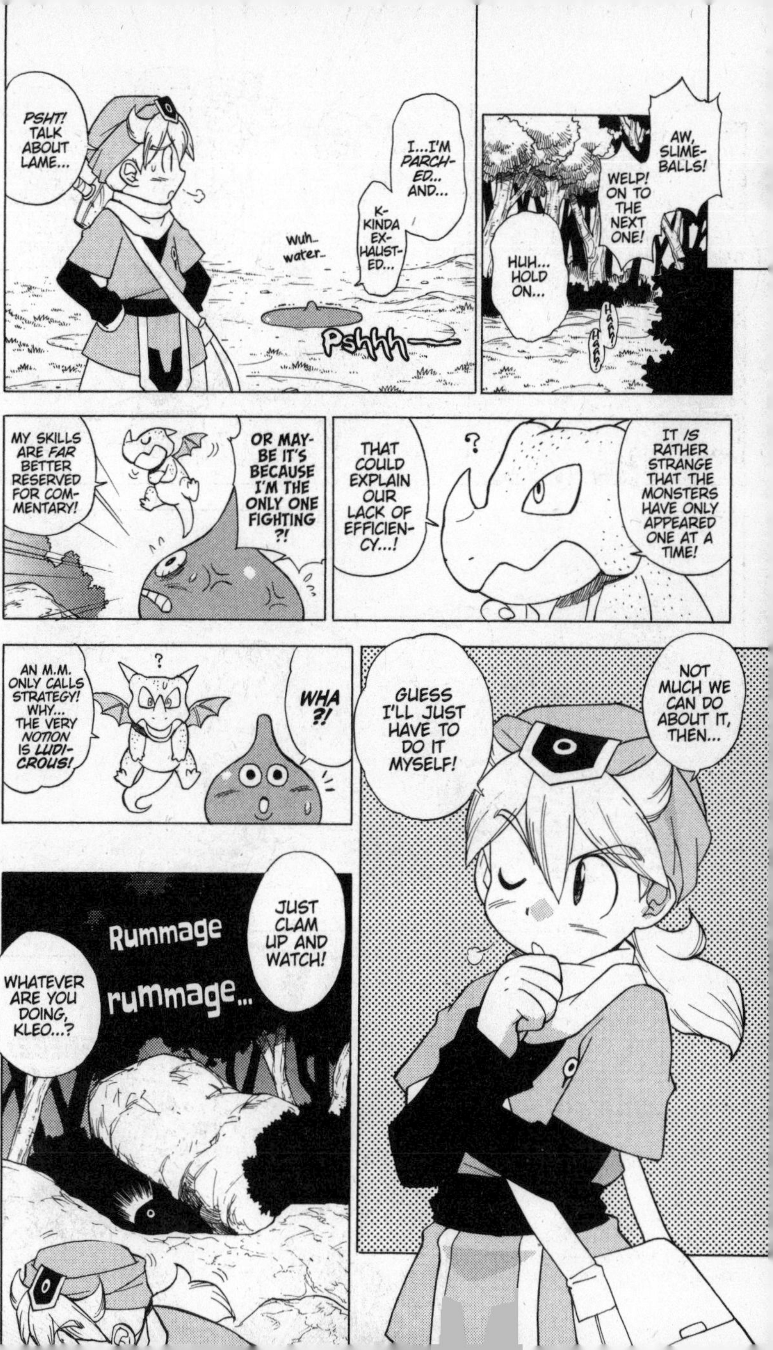
AW, SLIME-BALLS!
WELP! ON TO THE NEXT ONE!
HUH... HOLD ON...
Hah! Hah!
I...I'M PARCHED... AND...
K-KINDA EX-HAUSTED...
Wuh.. water..
Pshhh—
PSHT! TALK ABOUT LAME...
IT IS RATHER STRANGE THAT THE MONSTERS HAVE ONLY APPEARED ONE AT A TIME!
?
THAT COULD EXPLAIN OUR LACK OF EFFICIENCY...!
OR MAYBE IT'S BECAUSE I'M THE ONLY ONE FIGHTING?!
MY SKILLS ARE FAR BETTER RESERVED FOR COMMENTARY!
NOT MUCH WE CAN DO ABOUT IT, THEN...
GUESS I'LL JUST HAVE TO DO IT MYSELF!
WHA?!
?
AN M.M. ONLY CALLS STRATEGY! WHY... THE VERY NOTION IS LUDICROUS!
JUST CLAM UP AND WATCH!
Rummage
rummage...
WHATEVER ARE YOU DOING, KLEO...?

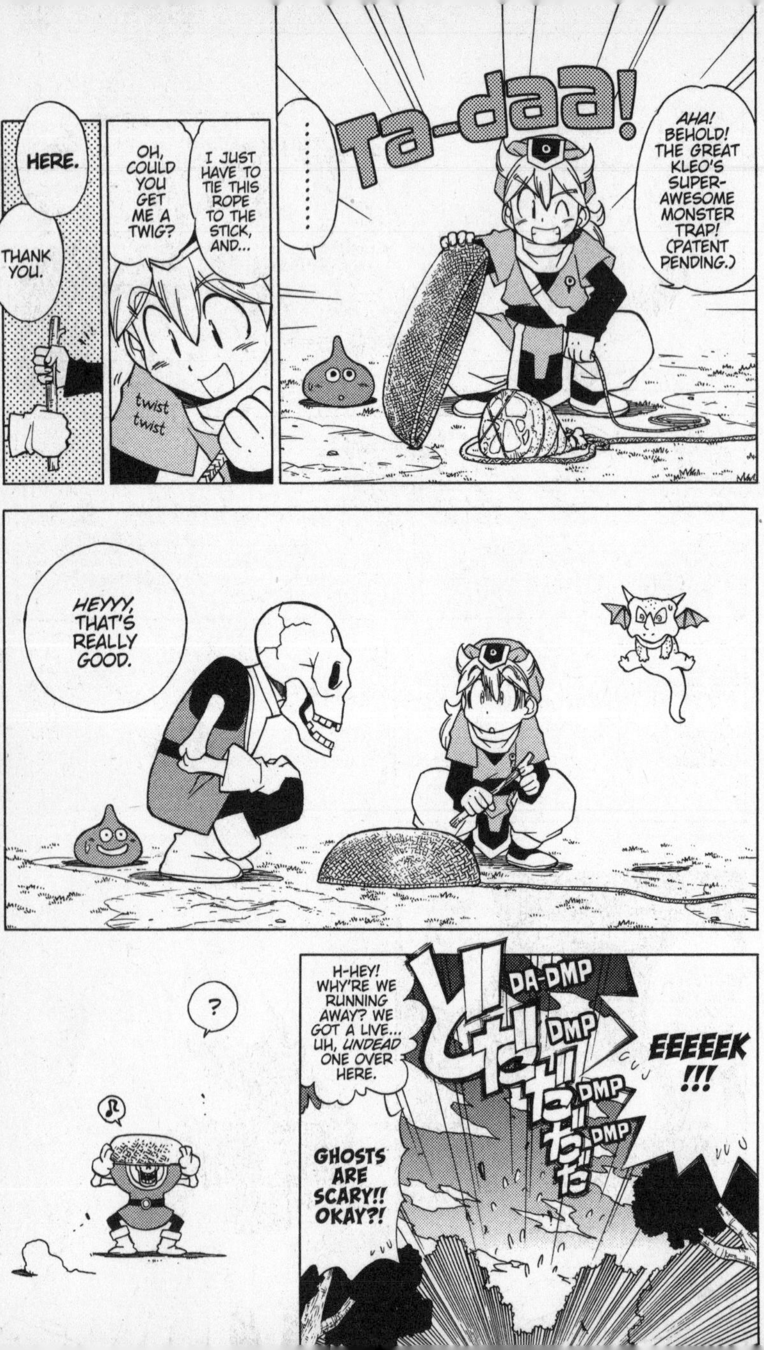
TA-DAAA!
AHA! BEHOLD! THE GREAT KLEO'S SUPER-AWESOME MONSTER TRAP! (PATENT PENDING.)
......
I JUST HAVE TO TIE THIS ROPE TO THE STICK, AND...
OH, COULD YOU GET ME A TWIG?
twist twist
HERE.
THANK YOU.
HEYYY, THAT'S REALLY GOOD.
EEEEEK !!!
DA-DMP
DMP
DMP
DMP
H-HEY! WHY'RE WE RUNNING AWAY? WE GOT A LIVE... UH, *UNDEAD* ONE OVER HERE.
GHOSTS ARE SCARY!! OKAY?!
?

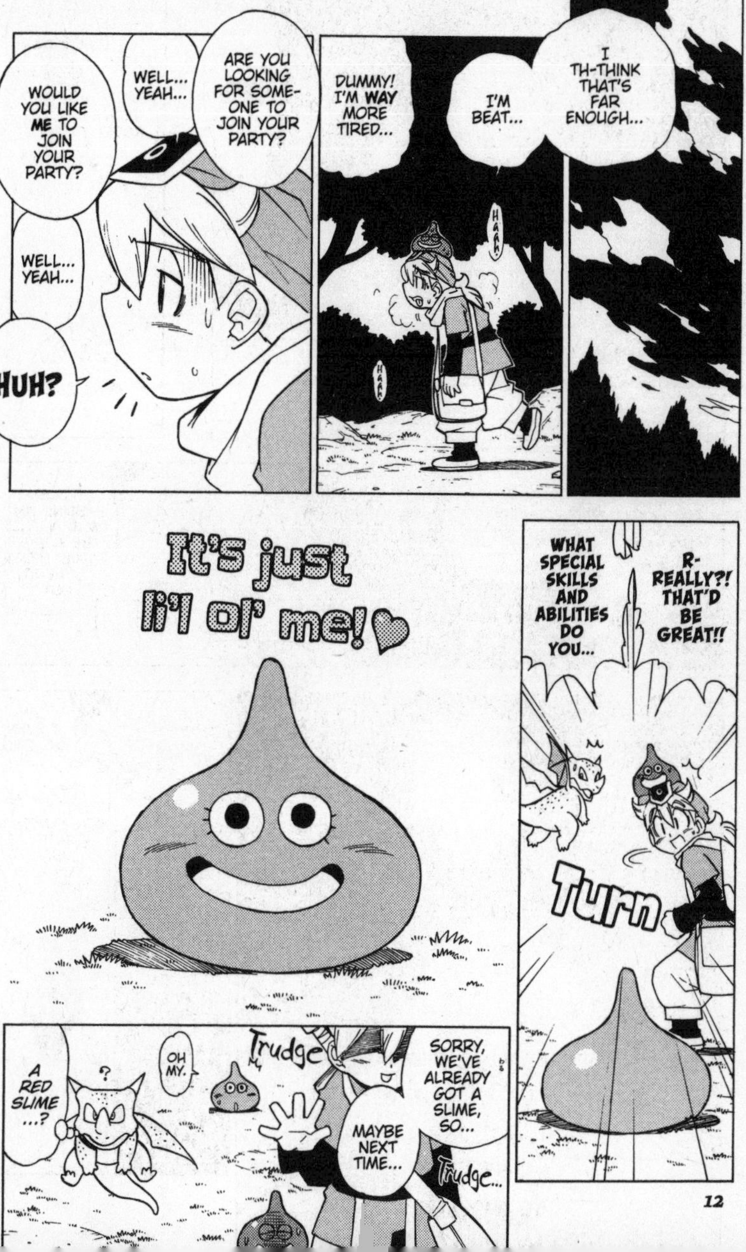

I TH-THINK THAT'S FAR ENOUGH...
I'M BEAT...
DUMMY! I'M WAY MORE TIRED...
HAAH
HAAH
ARE YOU LOOKING FOR SOME-ONE TO JOIN YOUR PARTY?
WELL... YEAH...
WOULD YOU LIKE ME TO JOIN YOUR PARTY?
WELL... YEAH...
HUH?
R-REALLY?! THAT'D BE GREAT!!
WHAT SPECIAL SKILLS AND ABILITIES DO YOU...
Turn
It's just li'l ol' me!
SORRY, WE'VE ALREADY GOT A SLIME, SO...
MAYBE NEXT TIME...
Trudge
OH MY.
A RED SLIME ...?
Trudge...

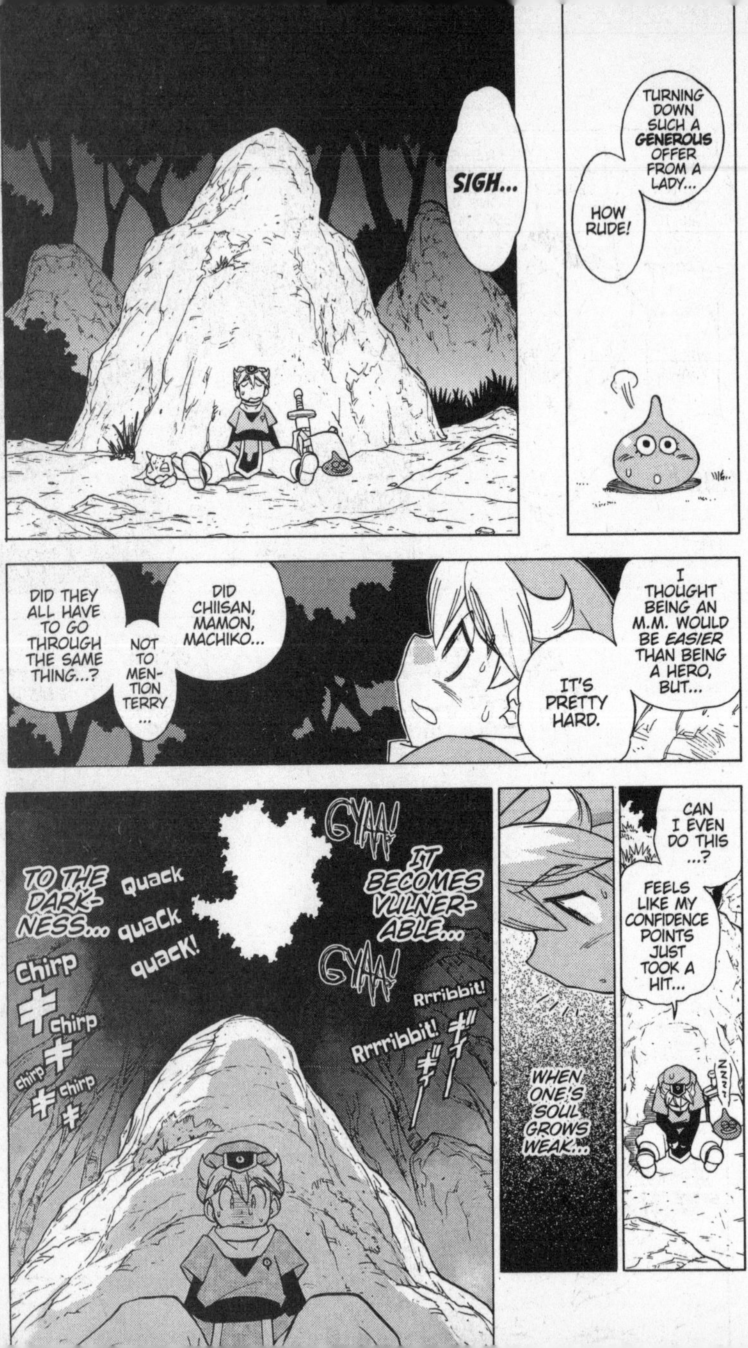
TURNING DOWN SUCH A GENEROUS OFFER FROM A LADY...
HOW RUDE!
SIGH...
I THOUGHT BEING AN M.M. WOULD BE EASIER THAN BEING A HERO, BUT...
IT'S PRETTY HARD.
DID CHIISAN, MAMON, MACHIKO...
NOT TO MENTION TERRY...
DID THEY ALL HAVE TO GO THROUGH THE SAME THING...?
CAN I EVEN DO THIS...?
FEELS LIKE MY CONFIDENCE POINTS JUST TOOK A HIT...
WHEN ONE'S SOUL GROWS WEAK...
IT BECOMES VULNERABLE...
TO THE DARKNESS...
GYAA!
GYAA!
Rrrribbit! ギ
Rrrribbit! ギ
Quack quack quack!
Chirp キ chirp キ chirp キ chirp キ

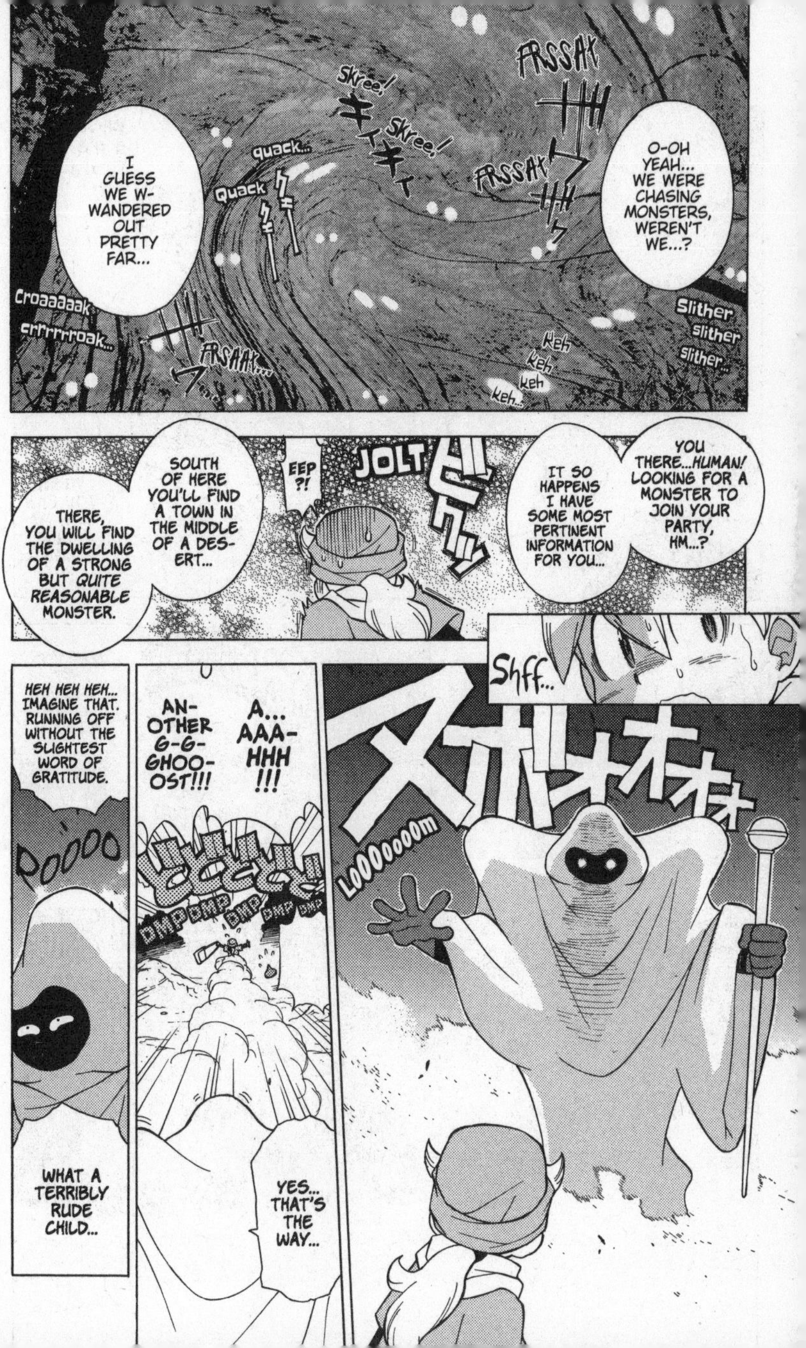
FRSSAK
O-OH YEAH... WE WERE CHASING MONSTERS, WEREN'T WE...?
FRSSAK
Skree!
Skree!
quack...
Quack
I GUESS WE W-WANDERED OUT PRETTY FAR...
Slither slither slither...
keh keh keh keh...
FRSSAK...
Croaaaaak crrrrrroak...
YOU THERE...HUMAN! LOOKING FOR A MONSTER TO JOIN YOUR PARTY, HM...?
IT SO HAPPENS I HAVE SOME MOST PERTINENT INFORMATION FOR YOU...
JOLT
EEP?!
SOUTH OF HERE YOU'LL FIND A TOWN IN THE MIDDLE OF A DESERT...
THERE, YOU WILL FIND THE DWELLING OF A STRONG BUT QUITE REASONABLE MONSTER.
Shff...
LOOOOOOOm
A... AAA-HHH!!!
AN-OTHER G-G-GHOOOST!!!
DMP DMP DMP DMP DMP
YES... THAT'S THE WAY...
HEH HEH HEH... IMAGINE THAT. RUNNING OFF WITHOUT THE SLIGHTEST WORD OF GRATITUDE.
POOOO
WHAT A TERRIBLY RUDE CHILD...

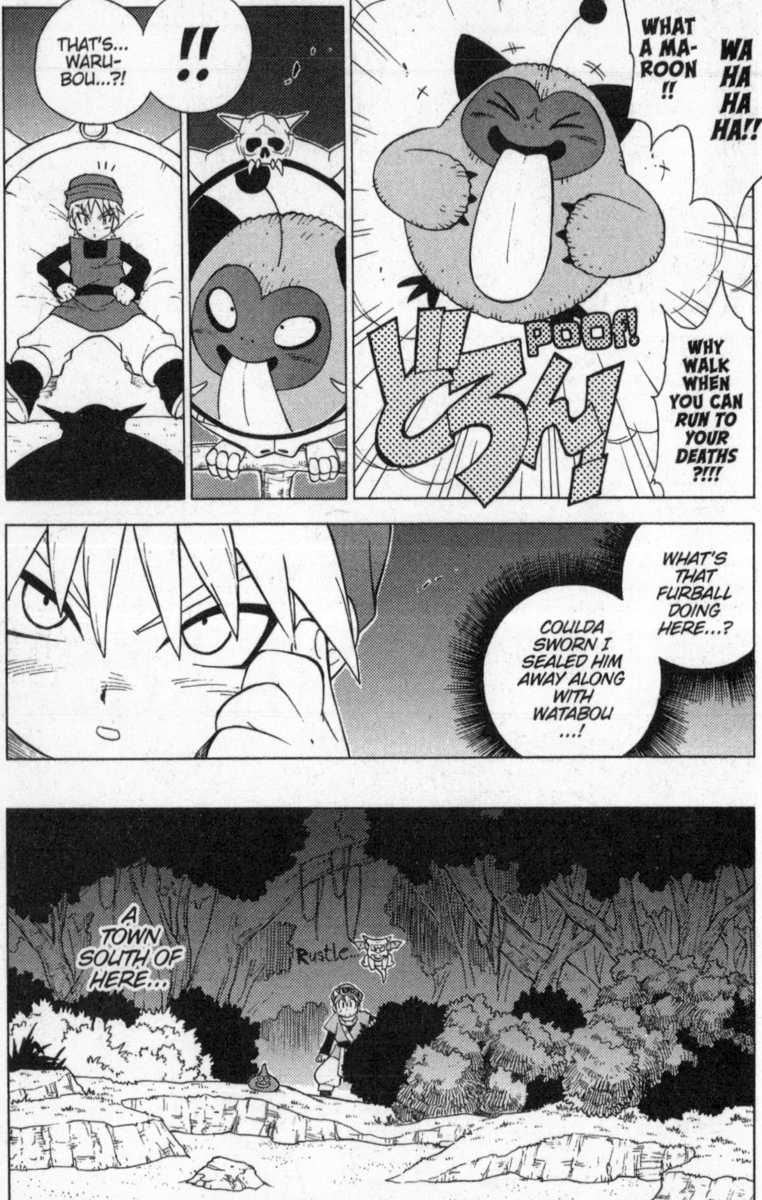
WA HA HA HA!!
WHAT A MA-ROON!!
どろん
POOF!
WHY WALK WHEN YOU CAN RUN TO YOUR DEATHS?!!!
!!
THAT'S... WARU-BOU...?!
WHAT'S THAT FURBALL DOING HERE...?
COULDA SWORN I SEALED HIM AWAY ALONG WITH WATABOU...!
A TOWN SOUTH OF HERE...
Rustle...

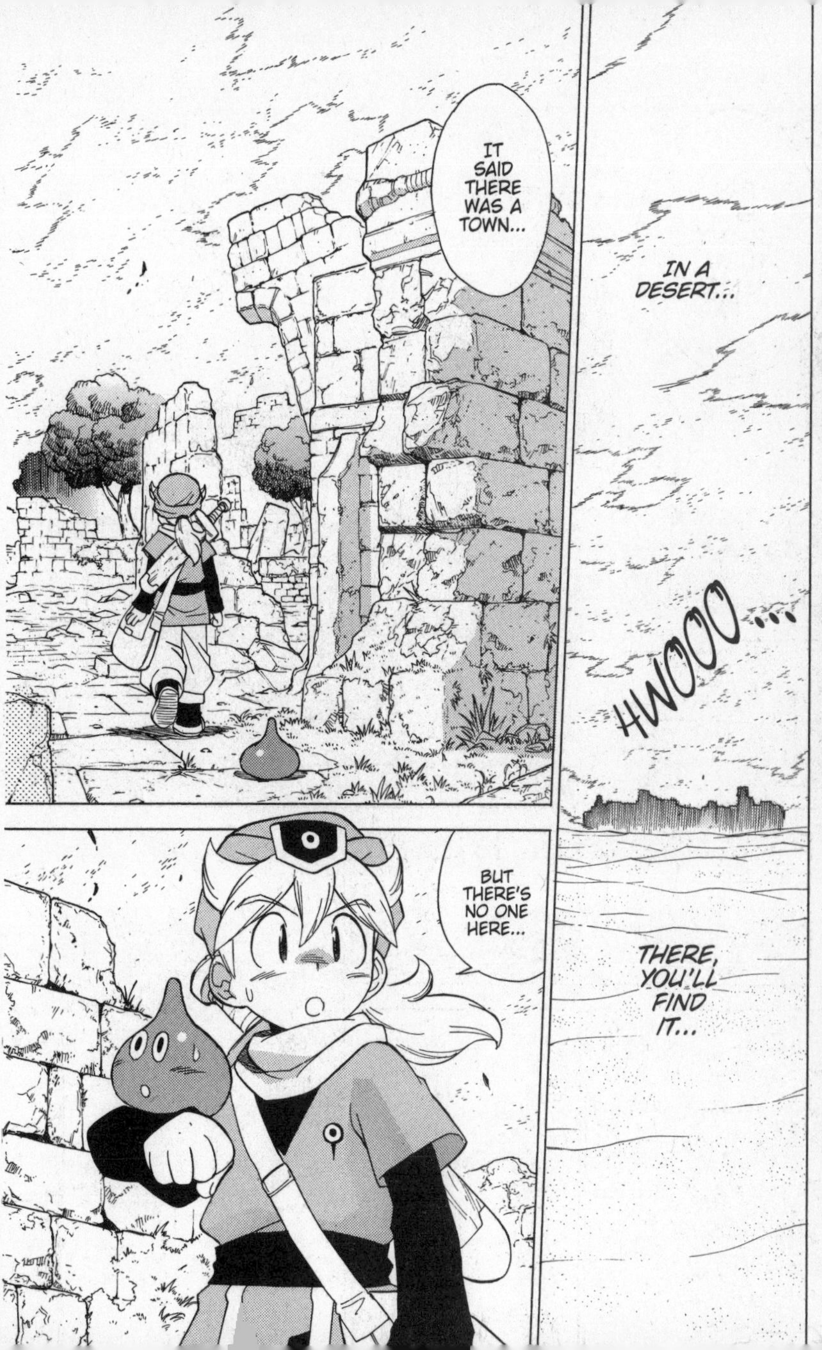
IN A DESERT...
HWOOO...
THERE, YOU'LL FIND IT...
IT SAID THERE WAS A TOWN...
BUT THERE'S NO ONE HERE...

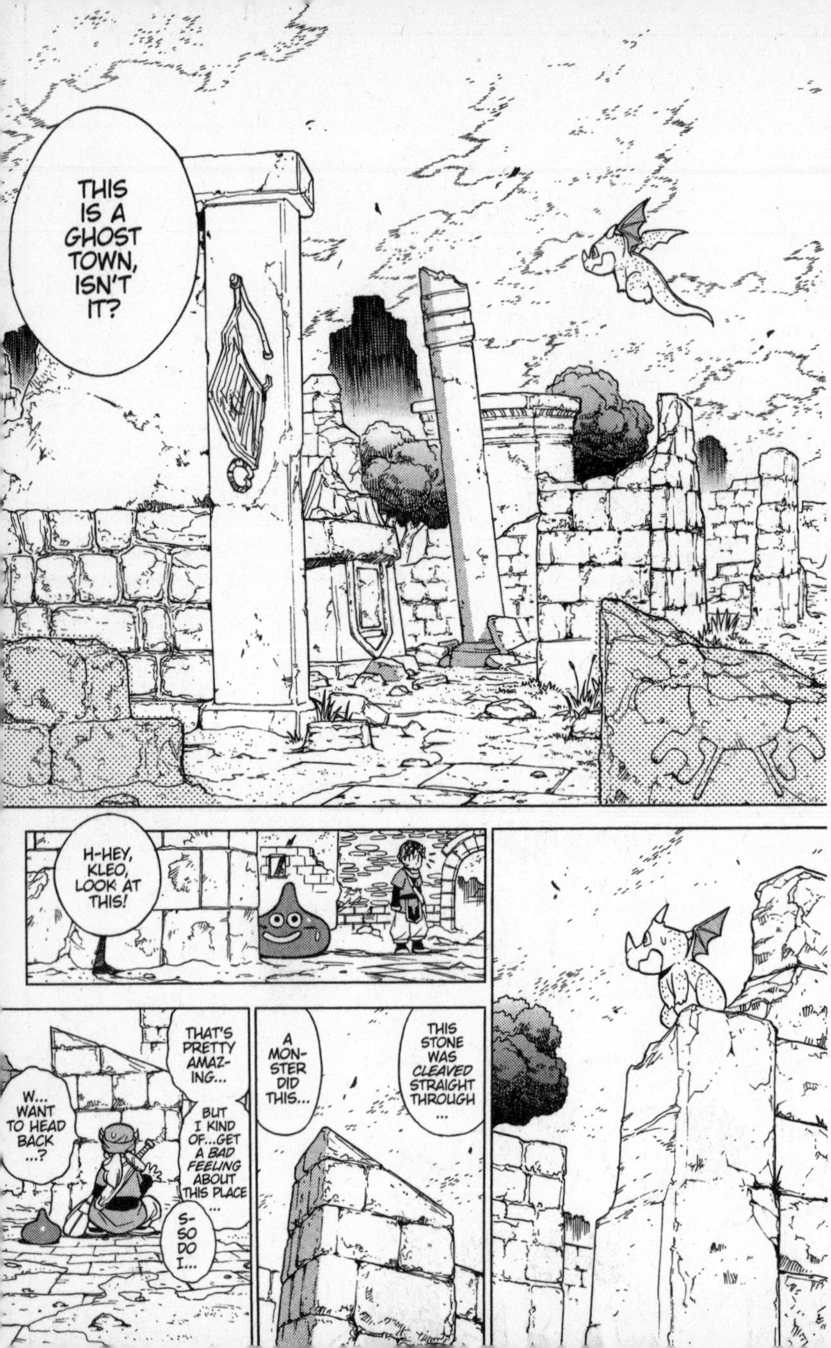
THIS IS A GHOST TOWN, ISN'T IT?
H-HEY, KLEO, LOOK AT THIS!
THIS STONE WAS CLEAVED STRAIGHT THROUGH ...
A MONSTER DID THIS...
THAT'S PRETTY AMAZ-ING...
BUT I KIND OF...GET A BAD FEELING ABOUT THIS PLACE ...
W... WANT TO HEAD BACK ...?
S-SO DO I...

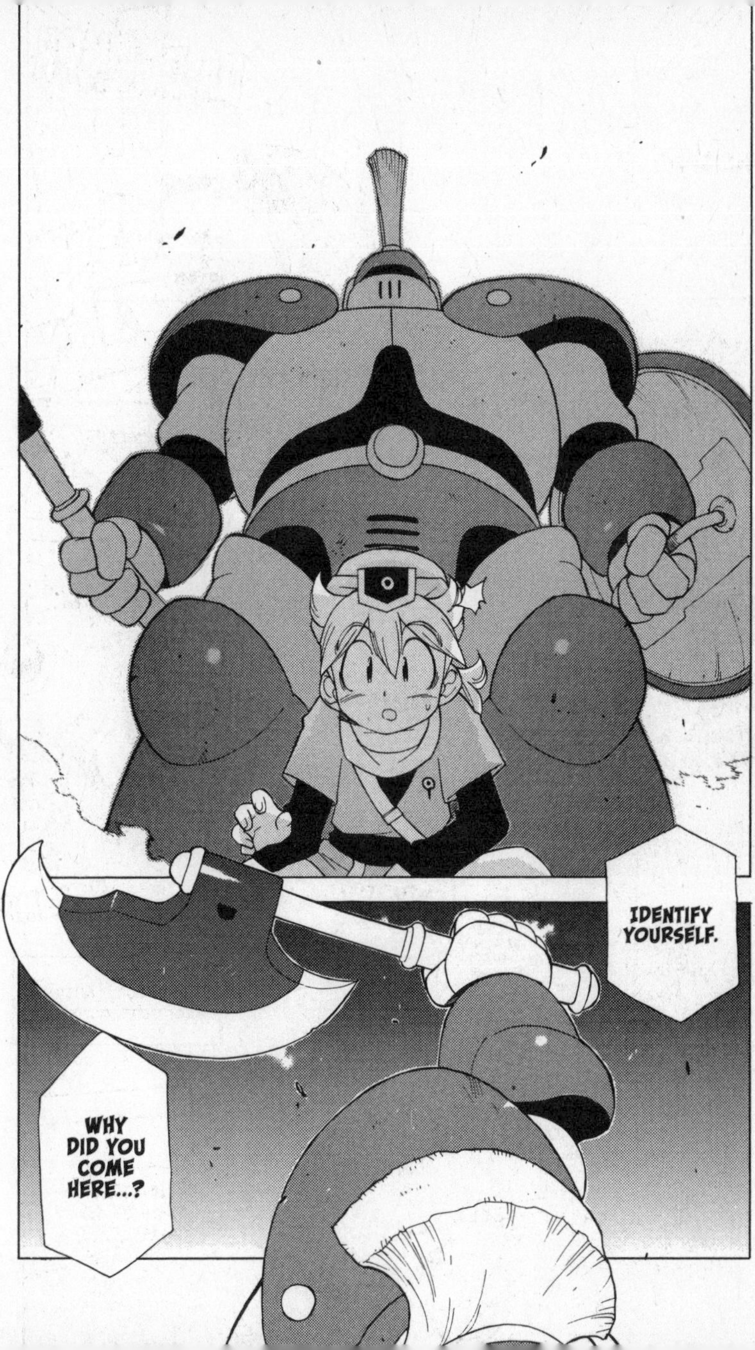
IDENTIFY YOURSELF.
WHY DID YOU COME HERE...?

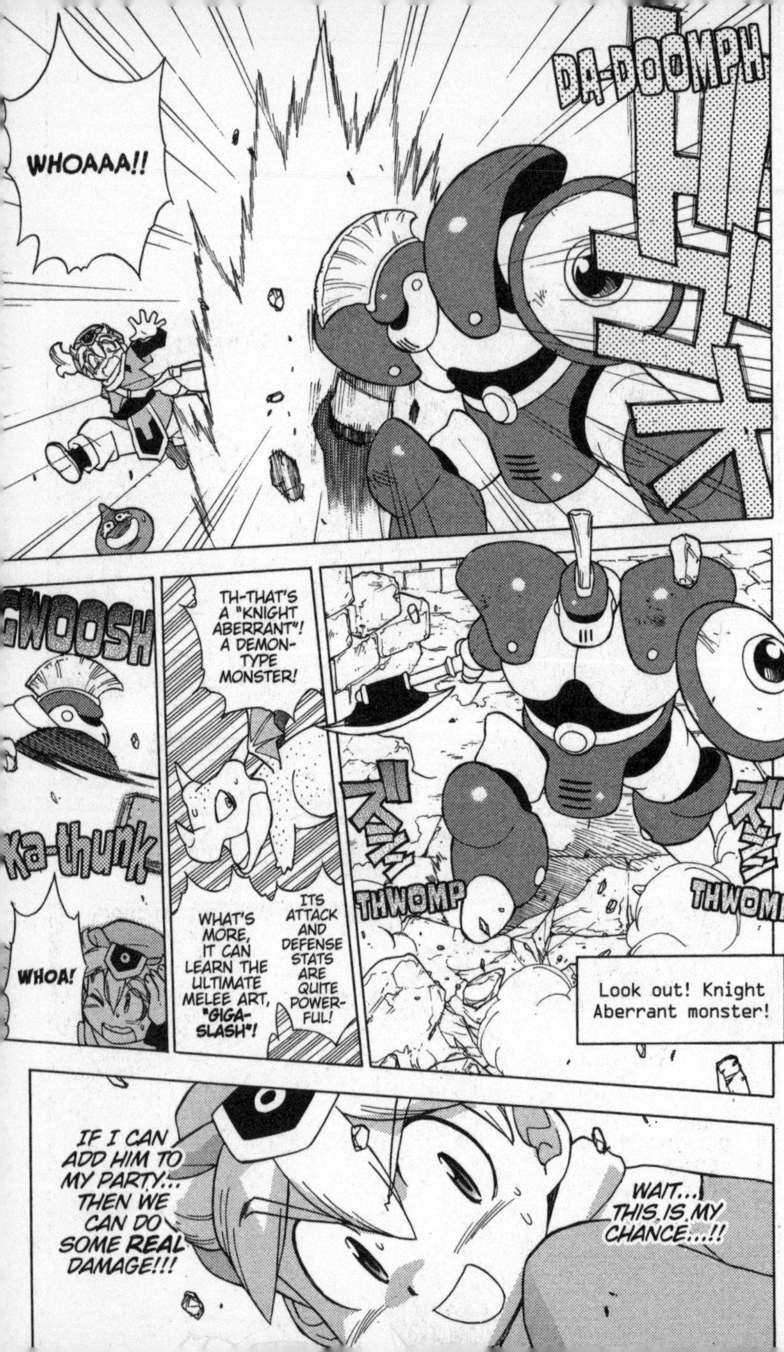
DA-DOOMPH
WHOAAA!!
THWOMP
THWOMP
Look out! Knight Aberrant monster!
TH-THAT'S A "KNIGHT ABERRANT"! A DEMON-TYPE MONSTER!
ITS ATTACK AND DEFENSE STATS ARE QUITE POWERFUL!
WHAT'S MORE, IT CAN LEARN THE ULTIMATE MELEE ART, "GIGA-SLASH"!
GWOOSH
Ka-thunk
WHOA!
WAIT... THIS IS MY CHANCE...!!
IF I CAN ADD HIM TO MY PARTY... THEN WE CAN DO SOME REAL DAMAGE!!!

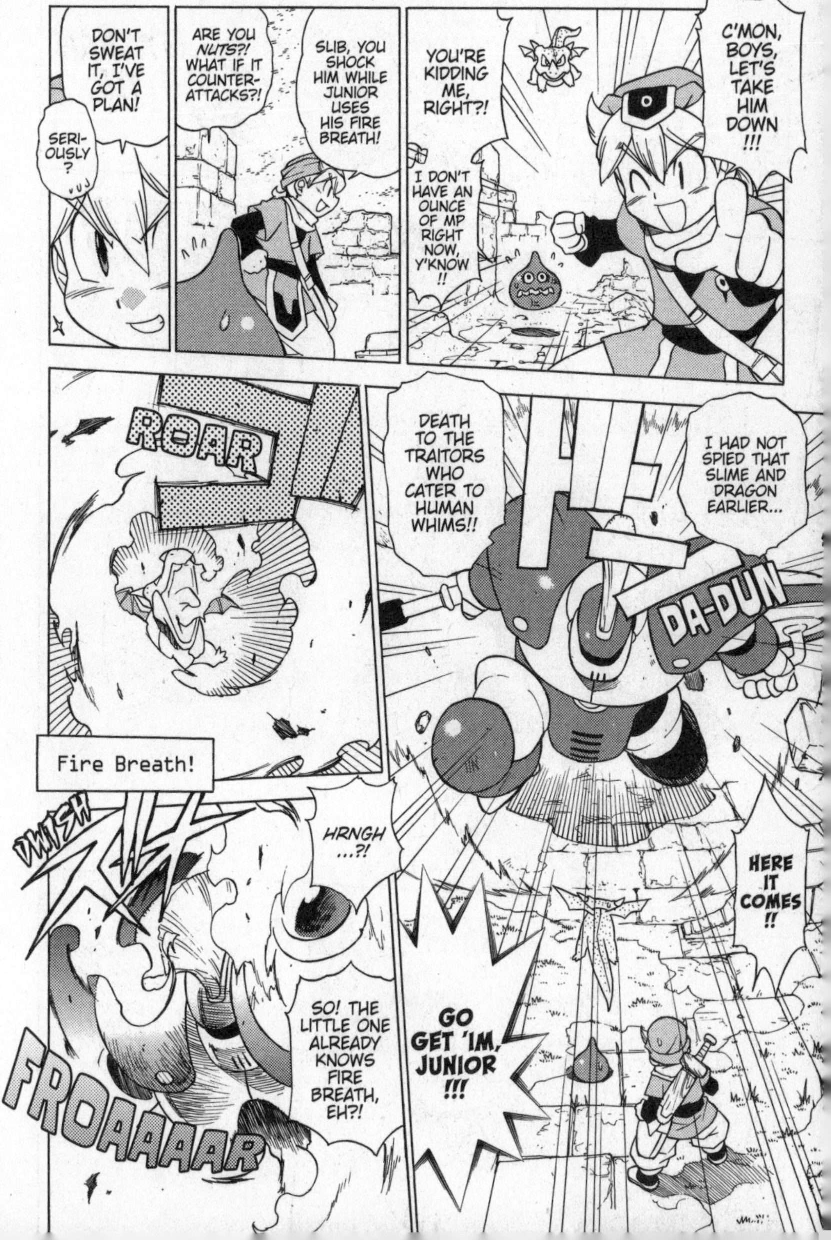

C'MON, BOYS, LET'S TAKE HIM DOWN!!!
YOU'RE KIDDING ME, RIGHT?!
I DON'T HAVE AN OUNCE OF MP RIGHT NOW, Y'KNOW!!
SLIB, YOU SHOCK HIM WHILE JUNIOR USES HIS FIRE BREATH!
ARE YOU *NUTS?!* WHAT IF IT COUNTER-ATTACKS?!
DON'T SWEAT IT, I'VE GOT A PLAN!
SERIOUSLY?
I HAD NOT SPIED THAT SLIME AND DRAGON EARLIER...
DEATH TO THE TRAITORS WHO CATER TO HUMAN WHIMS!!
DA-DUN
HERE IT COMES!!
GO GET 'IM, JUNIOR!!!
ROAR
Fire Breath!
SWISH
HRNGH...?!
SO! THE LITTLE ONE ALREADY KNOWS FIRE BREATH, EH?!
FROAAAAAR

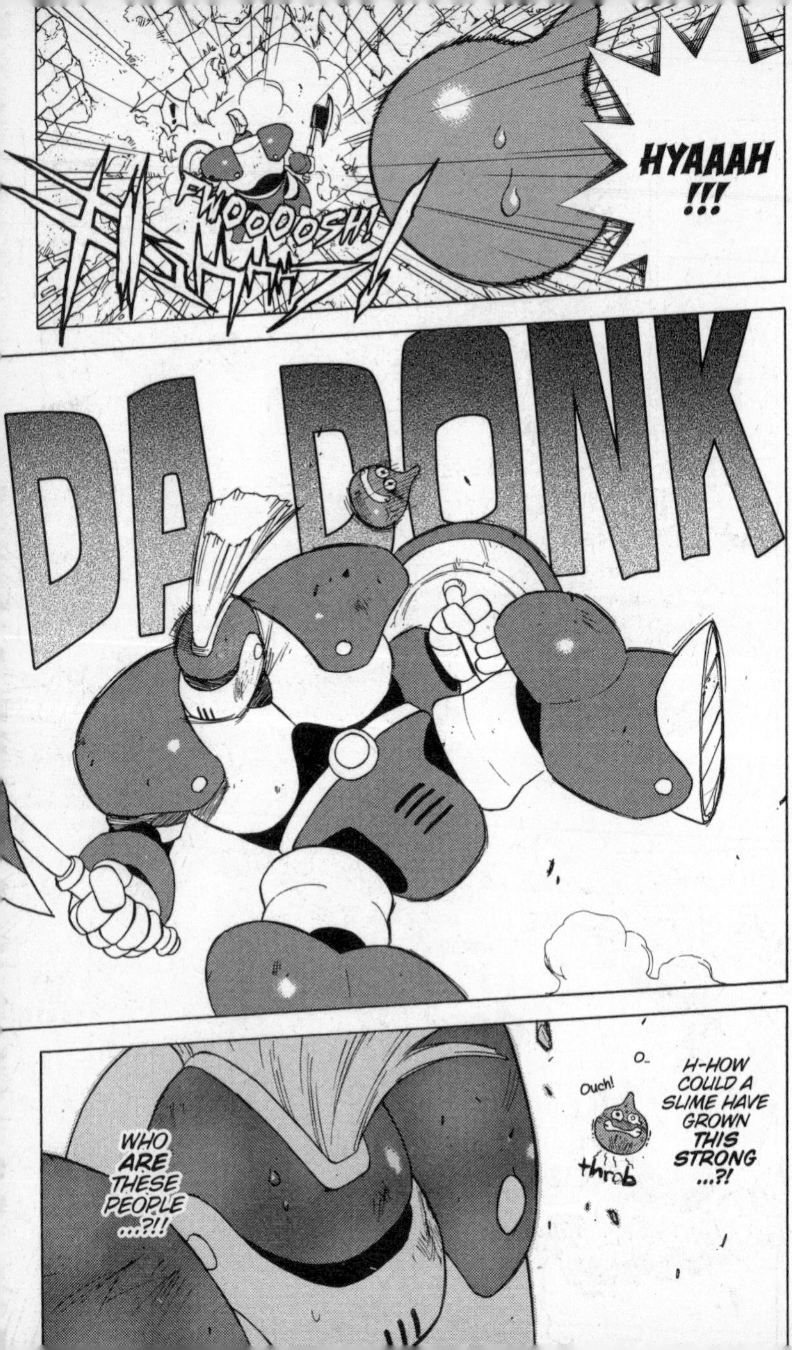
HYAAAH !!!
FWOOOOSH!
DA DONK
H-HOW COULD A SLIME HAVE GROWN THIS STRONG ...?!
O..
Ouch!
throb
WHO ARE THESE PEOPLE ...?!!

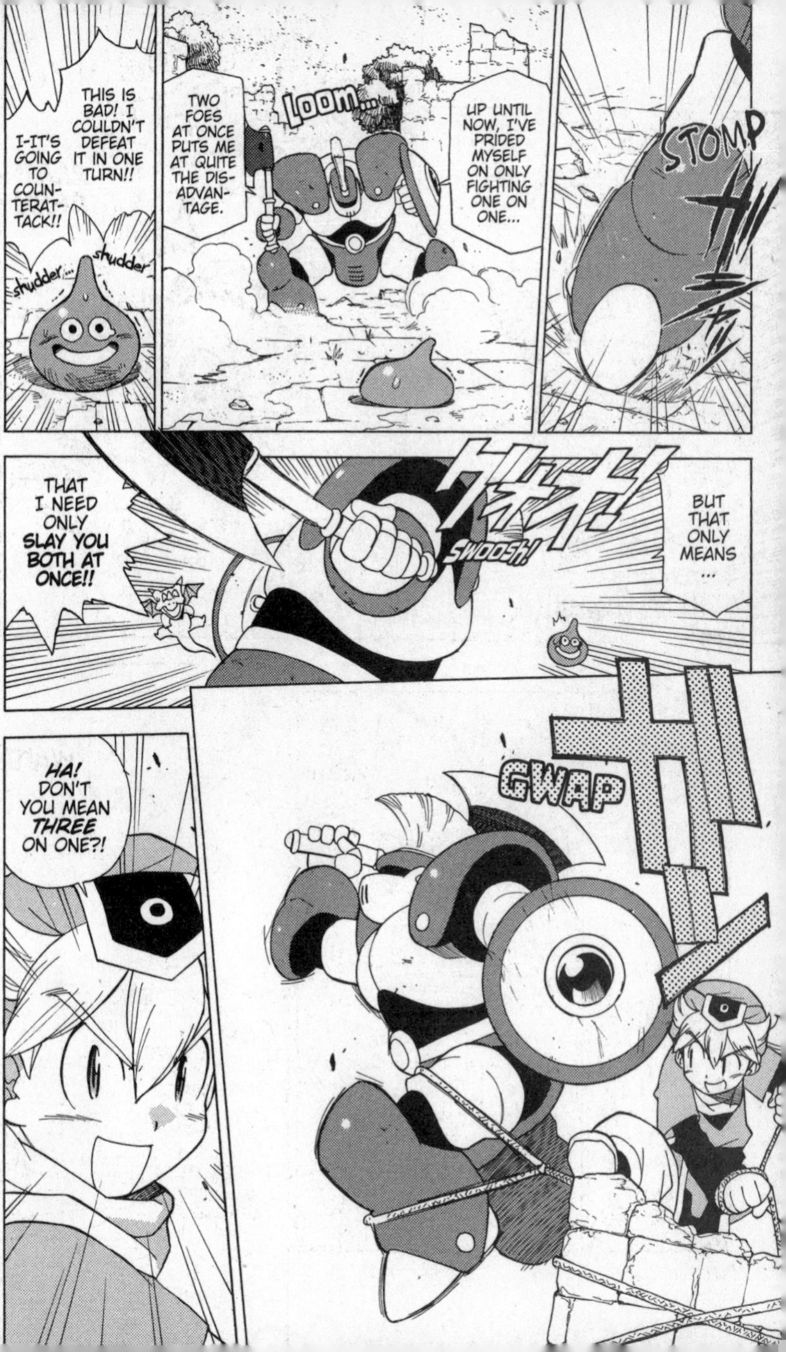
STOMP
UP UNTIL NOW, I'VE PRIDED MYSELF ON ONLY FIGHTING ONE ON ONE...
TWO FOES AT ONCE PUTS ME AT QUITE THE DIS-ADVAN-TAGE.
LOOM...
THIS IS BAD! I COULDN'T DEFEAT IT IN ONE TURN!!
I-IT'S GOING TO COUN-TERAT-TACK!!
shudder
shudder...
BUT THAT ONLY MEANS ...
SWOOSH!
THAT I NEED ONLY **SLAY YOU BOTH AT ONCE!!**
GWAP
HA! DON'T YOU MEAN ***THREE*** ON ONE?!

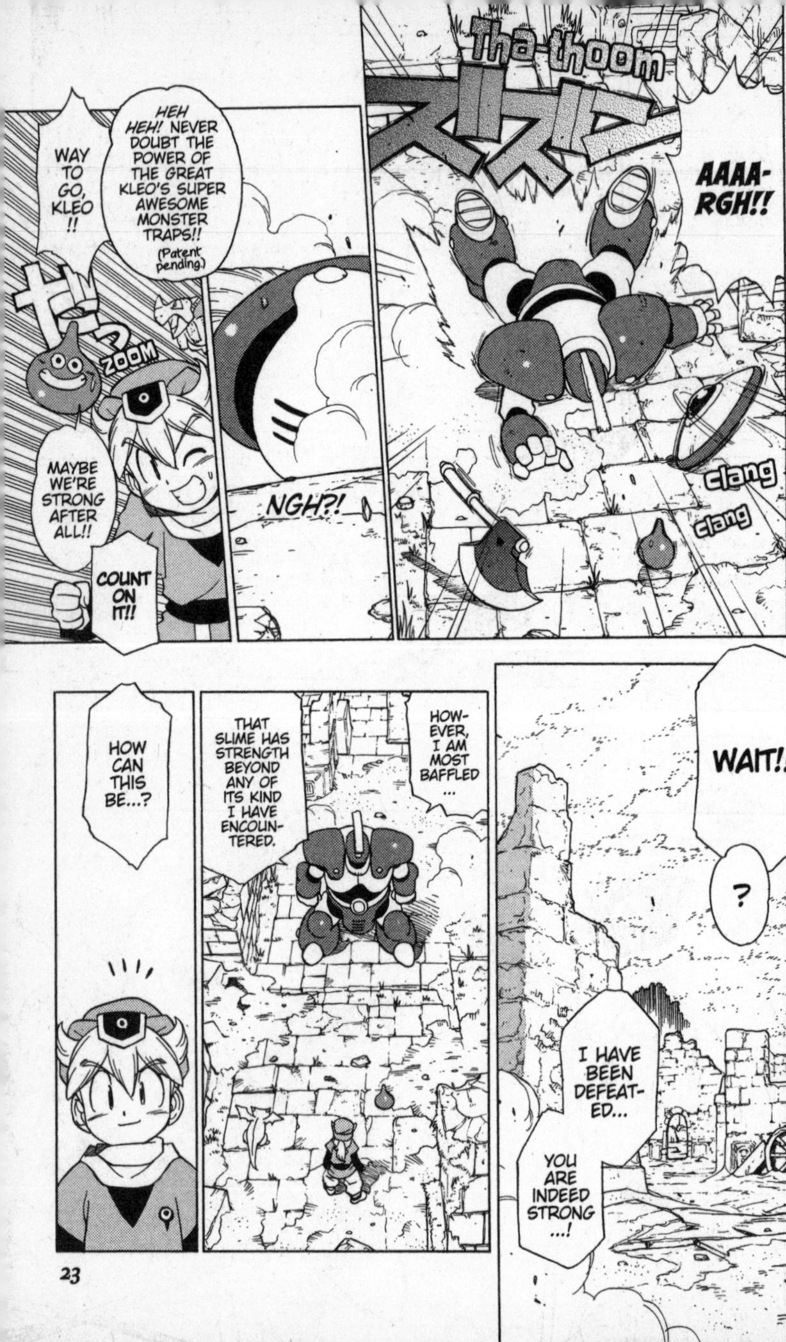
Tha-thoom
AAAA-RGH!!
clang
clang
NGH?!
WAY TO GO, KLEO!!
HEH HEH! NEVER DOUBT THE POWER OF THE GREAT KLEO'S SUPER AWESOME MONSTER TRAPS!!
(Patent pending.)
ZOOM
MAYBE WE'RE STRONG AFTER ALL!!
COUNT ON IT!!
WAIT!!
?
I HAVE BEEN DEFEAT-ED...
YOU ARE INDEED STRONG ...!
HOW-EVER, I AM MOST BAFFLED ...
THAT SLIME HAS STRENGTH BEYOND ANY OF ITS KIND I HAVE ENCOUN-TERED.
HOW CAN THIS BE...?

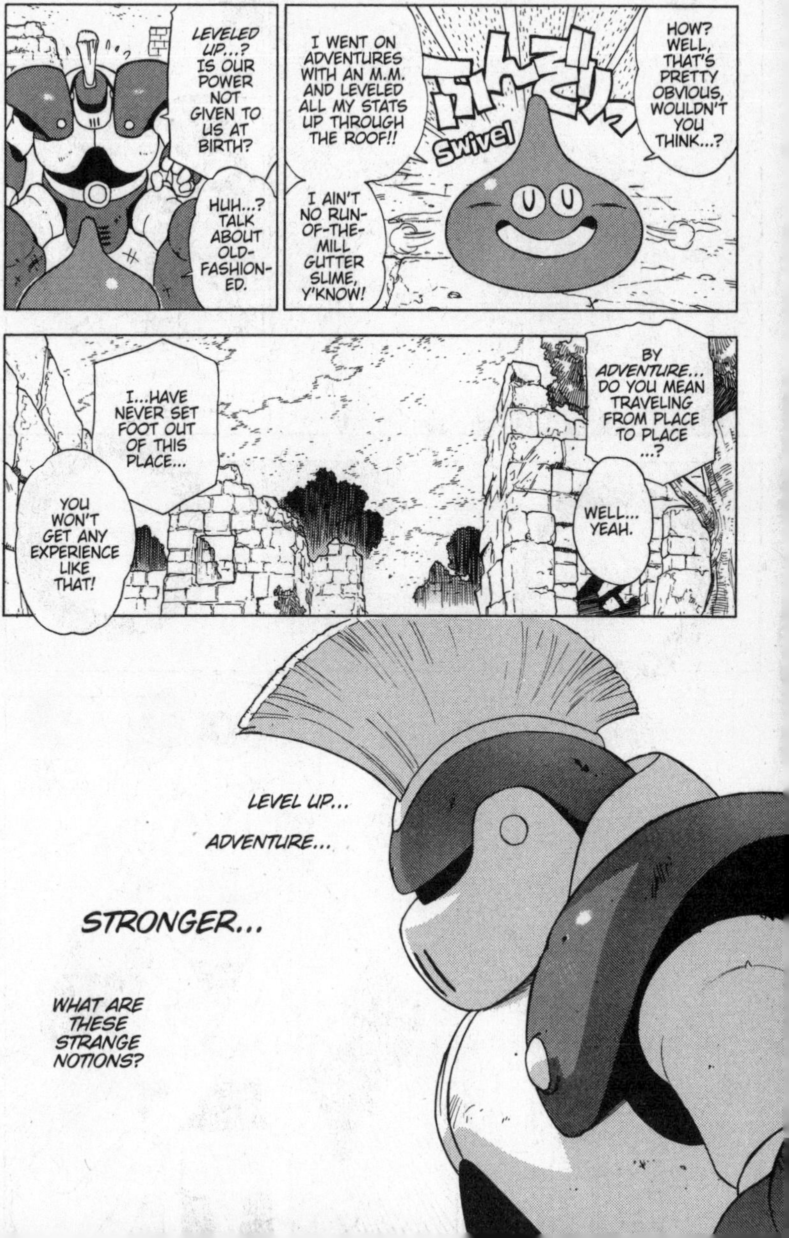
HOW? WELL, THAT'S PRETTY OBVIOUS, WOULDN'T YOU THINK...?
Swivel
I WENT ON ADVENTURES WITH AN M.M. AND LEVELED ALL MY STATS UP THROUGH THE ROOF!!
I AIN'T NO RUN-OF-THE-MILL GUTTER SLIME, Y'KNOW!
LEVELED UP...? IS OUR POWER NOT GIVEN TO US AT BIRTH?
HUH...? TALK ABOUT OLD-FASHION-ED.
BY ADVENTURE... DO YOU MEAN TRAVELING FROM PLACE TO PLACE ...?
WELL... YEAH.
I...HAVE NEVER SET FOOT OUT OF THIS PLACE...
YOU WON'T GET ANY EXPERIENCE LIKE THAT!
LEVEL UP...
ADVENTURE...
STRONGER...
WHAT ARE THESE STRANGE NOTIONS?

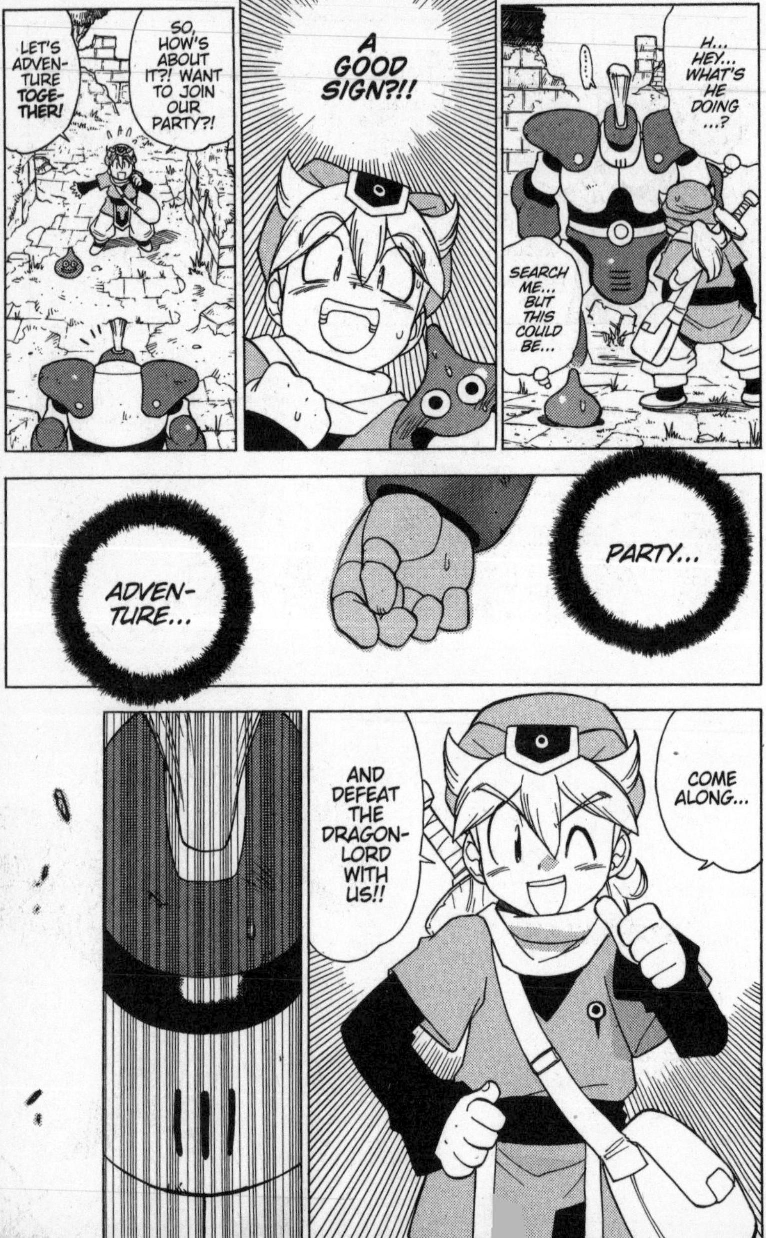
H... HEY... WHAT'S HE DOING ...?
...
SEARCH ME... BUT THIS COULD BE...
A GOOD SIGN?!!
SO, HOW'S ABOUT IT?! WANT TO JOIN OUR PARTY?!
LET'S ADVENTURE TOGETHER!
PARTY...
ADVENTURE...
COME ALONG...
AND DEFEAT THE DRAGONLORD WITH US!!

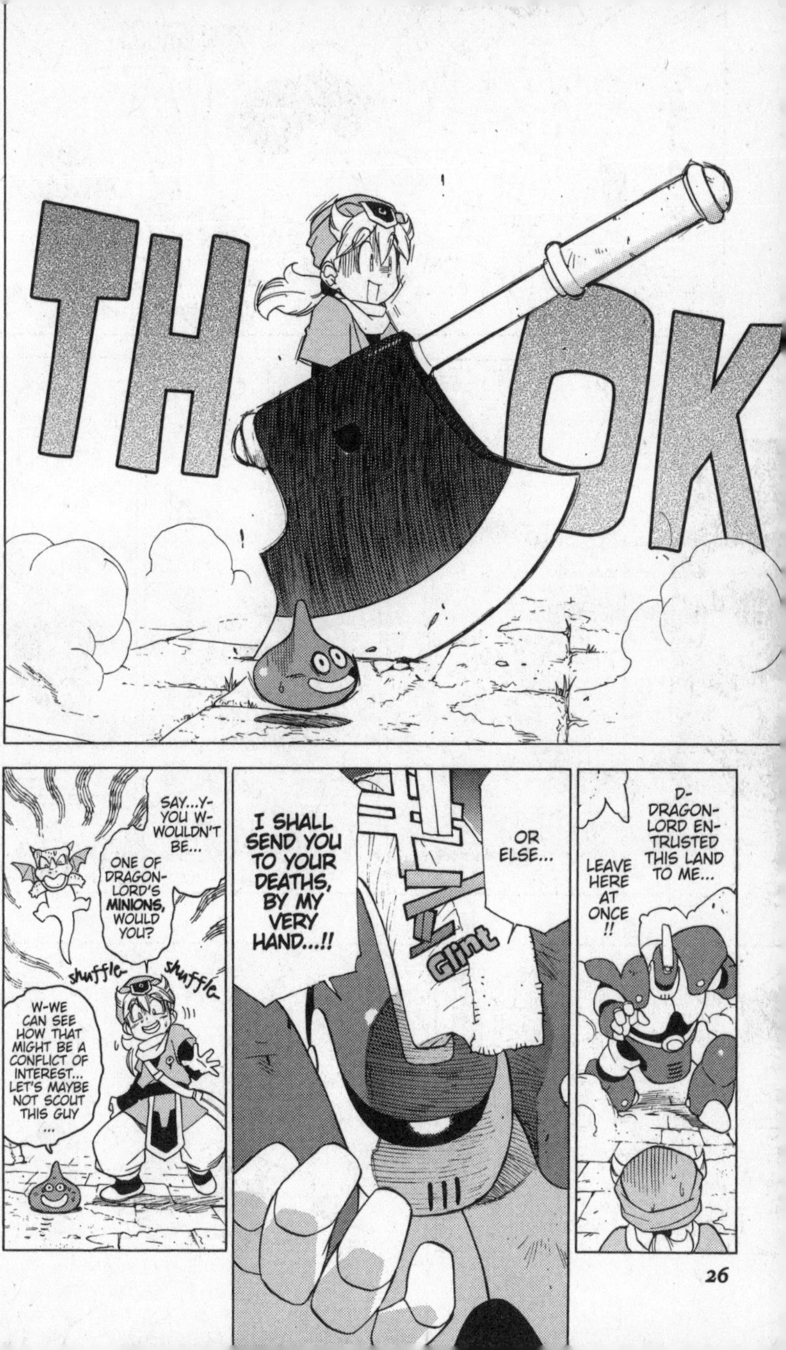
TH
OK
D-DRAGON-LORD EN-TRUSTED THIS LAND TO ME...
LEAVE HERE AT ONCE !!
OR ELSE...
I SHALL SEND YOU TO YOUR DEATHS, BY MY VERY HAND...!!
Glint
SAY...Y-YOU W-WOULDN'T BE...
ONE OF DRAGON-LORD'S MINIONS, WOULD YOU?
shuffle shuffle
W-WE CAN SEE HOW THAT MIGHT BE A CONFLICT OF INTEREST... LET'S MAYBE NOT SCOUT THIS GUY ...

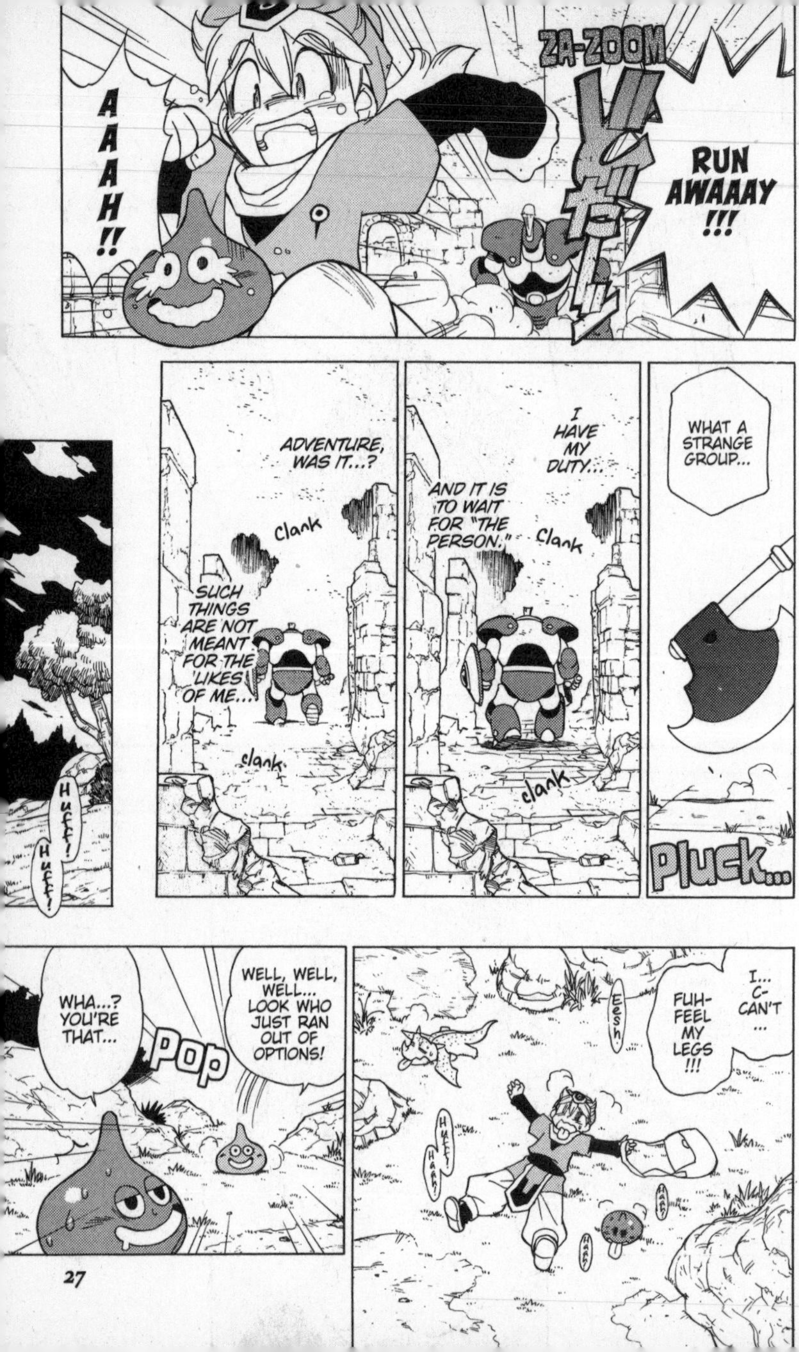
ZA-ZOOM
RUN AWAAAY!!!
AAAAH!!
WHAT A STRANGE GROUP...
Pluck...
I HAVE MY DUTY...
AND IT IS TO WAIT FOR "THE PERSON."
Clank
clank
ADVENTURE, WAS IT...?
Clank
SUCH THINGS ARE NOT MEANT FOR THE LIKES OF ME...
clank
Huff! Huff!
I... C-CAN'T...
FUH-FEEL MY LEGS!!!
Eesh.
WELL, WELL, WELL... LOOK WHO JUST RAN OUT OF OPTIONS!
Pop
WHA...? YOU'RE THAT...

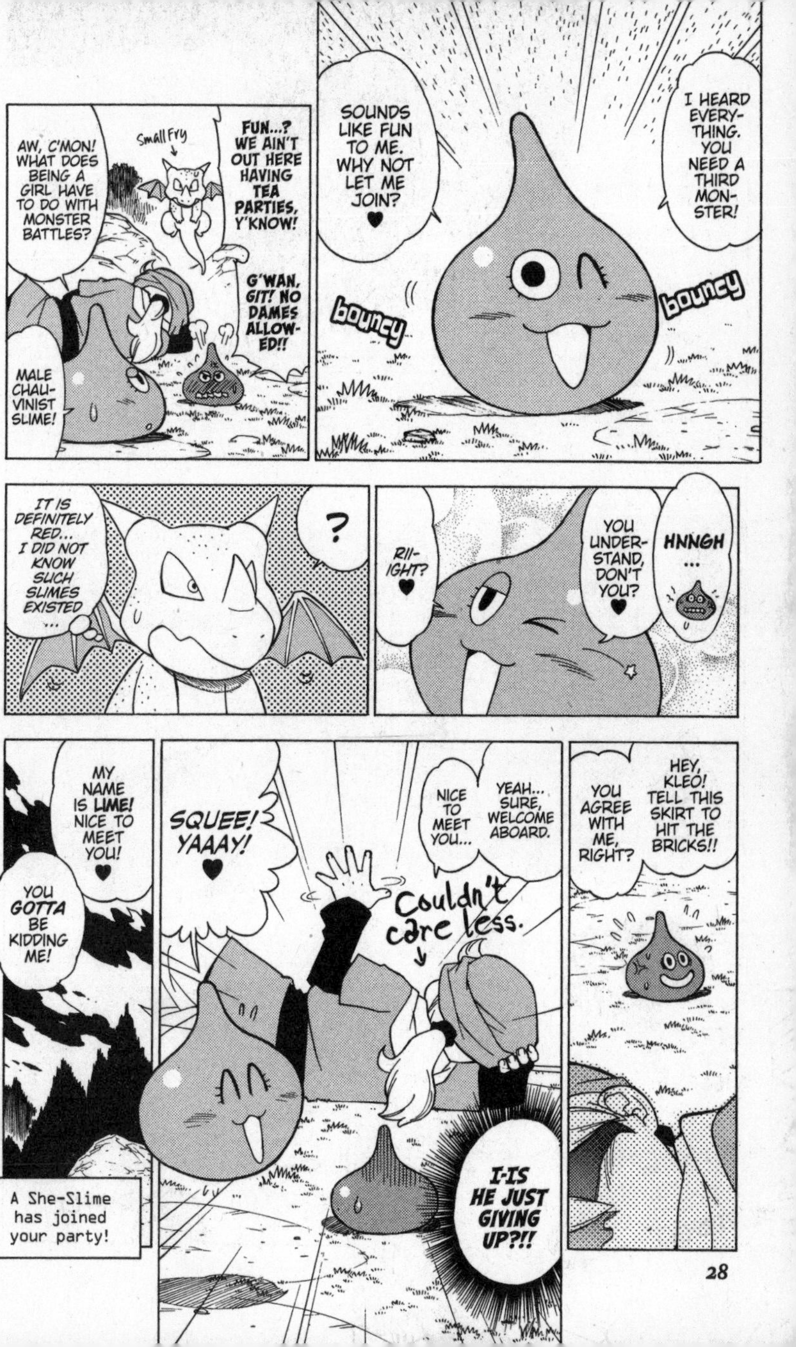
I HEARD EVERYTHING. YOU NEED A THIRD MONSTER!
SOUNDS LIKE FUN TO ME. WHY NOT LET ME JOIN? ♥
bouncy
bouncy
FUN...? WE AIN'T OUT HERE HAVING TEA PARTIES, Y'KNOW!
Small Fry
AW, C'MON! WHAT DOES BEING A GIRL HAVE TO DO WITH MONSTER BATTLES?
G'WAN, GIT! NO DAMES ALLOWED!!
MALE CHAUVINIST SLIME!
HNNGH ...
YOU UNDERSTAND, DON'T YOU? ♥
RII-IGHT? ♥
?
IT IS DEFINITELY RED... I DID NOT KNOW SUCH SLIMES EXISTED ...
HEY, KLEO! TELL THIS SKIRT TO HIT THE BRICKS!!
YOU AGREE WITH ME, RIGHT?
YEAH... SURE, WELCOME ABOARD.
NICE TO MEET YOU...
Couldn't care less.
SQUEE! YAAAY! ♥
I-IS HE JUST GIVING UP?!!
MY NAME IS LIME! NICE TO MEET YOU! ♥
YOU GOTTA BE KIDDING ME!
A She-Slime has joined your party!

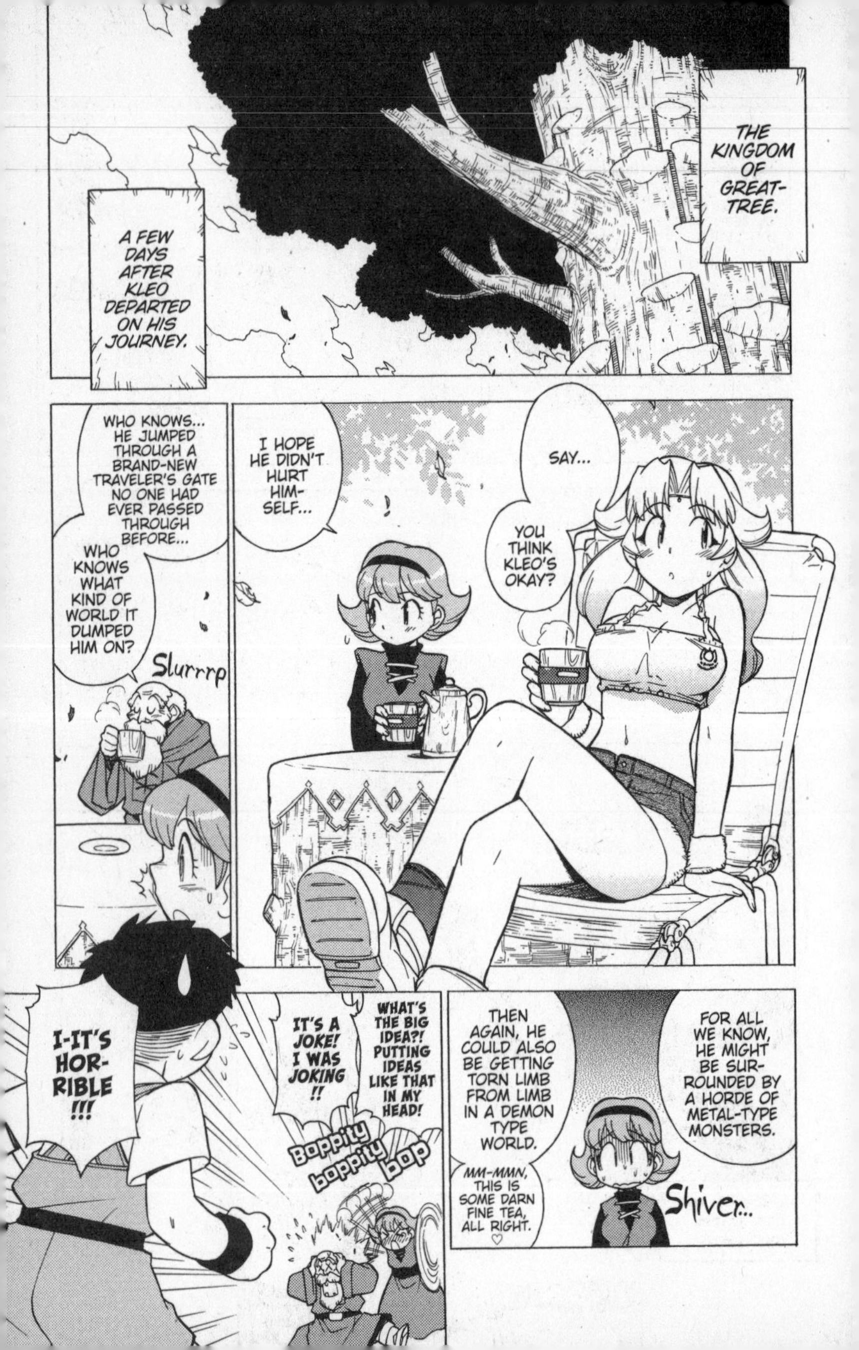
THE KINGDOM OF GREAT-TREE.
A FEW DAYS AFTER KLEO DEPARTED ON HIS JOURNEY.
SAY...
YOU THINK KLEO'S OKAY?
I HOPE HE DIDN'T HURT HIM-SELF...
WHO KNOWS... HE JUMPED THROUGH A BRAND-NEW TRAVELER'S GATE NO ONE HAD EVER PASSED THROUGH BEFORE...
WHO KNOWS WHAT KIND OF WORLD IT DUMPED HIM ON?
Slurrrp
FOR ALL WE KNOW, HE MIGHT BE SUR-ROUNDED BY A HORDE OF METAL-TYPE MONSTERS.
THEN AGAIN, HE COULD ALSO BE GETTING TORN LIMB FROM LIMB IN A DEMON TYPE WORLD.
MM-MMN, THIS IS SOME DARN FINE TEA, ALL RIGHT. ♡
Shiver...
WHAT'S THE BIG IDEA?! PUTTING IDEAS LIKE THAT IN MY HEAD!
IT'S A JOKE! I WAS JOKING!!
I-IT'S HOR-RIBLE!!!
Boppity boppity bop

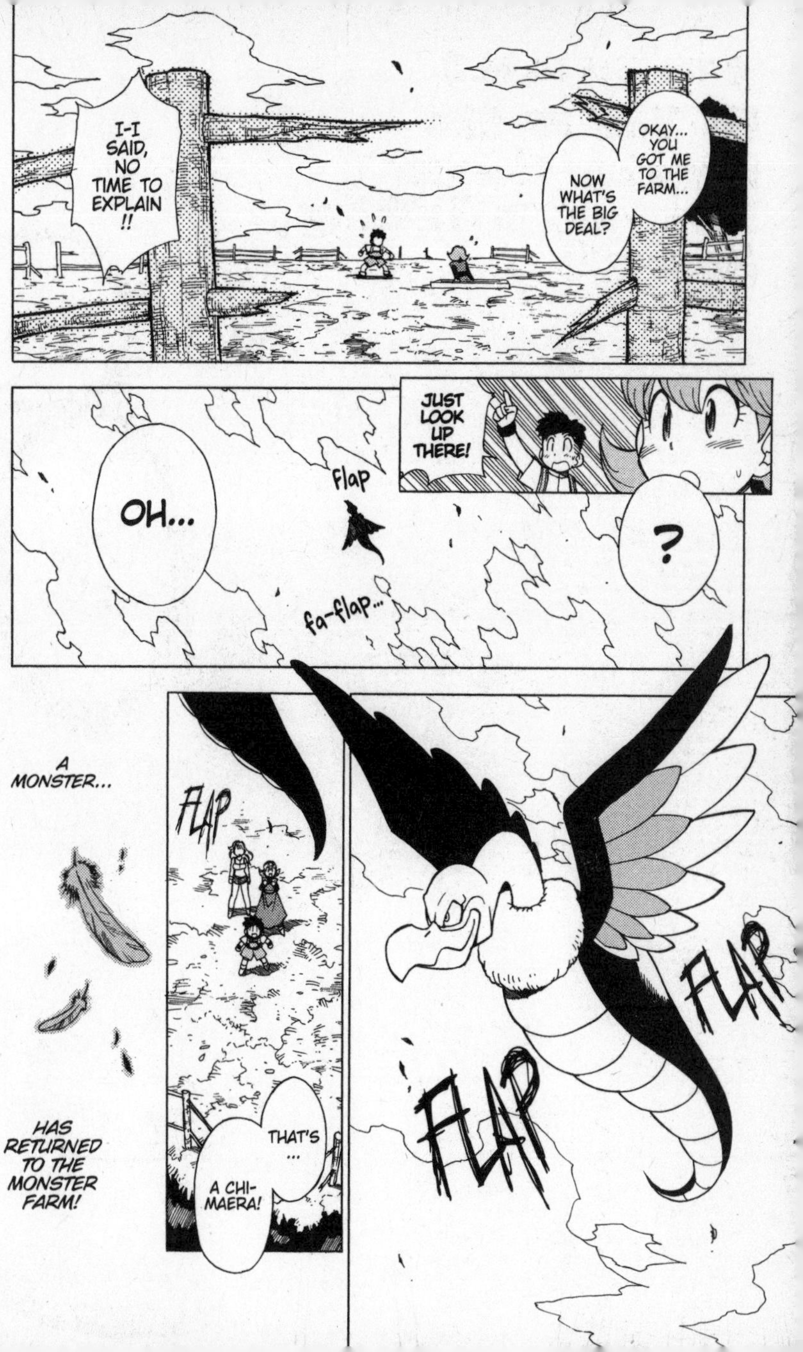
OKAY... YOU GOT ME TO THE FARM...
NOW WHAT'S THE BIG DEAL?
I-I SAID, NO TIME TO EXPLAIN !!
JUST LOOK UP THERE!
?
Flap
fa-flap...
OH...
FLAP
FLAP
FLAP
THAT'S ...
A CHI-MAERA!
A MONSTER...
HAS RETURNED TO THE MONSTER FARM!

The 8th Night
So You're the Monster Hunter Everyone's Talking About?!!

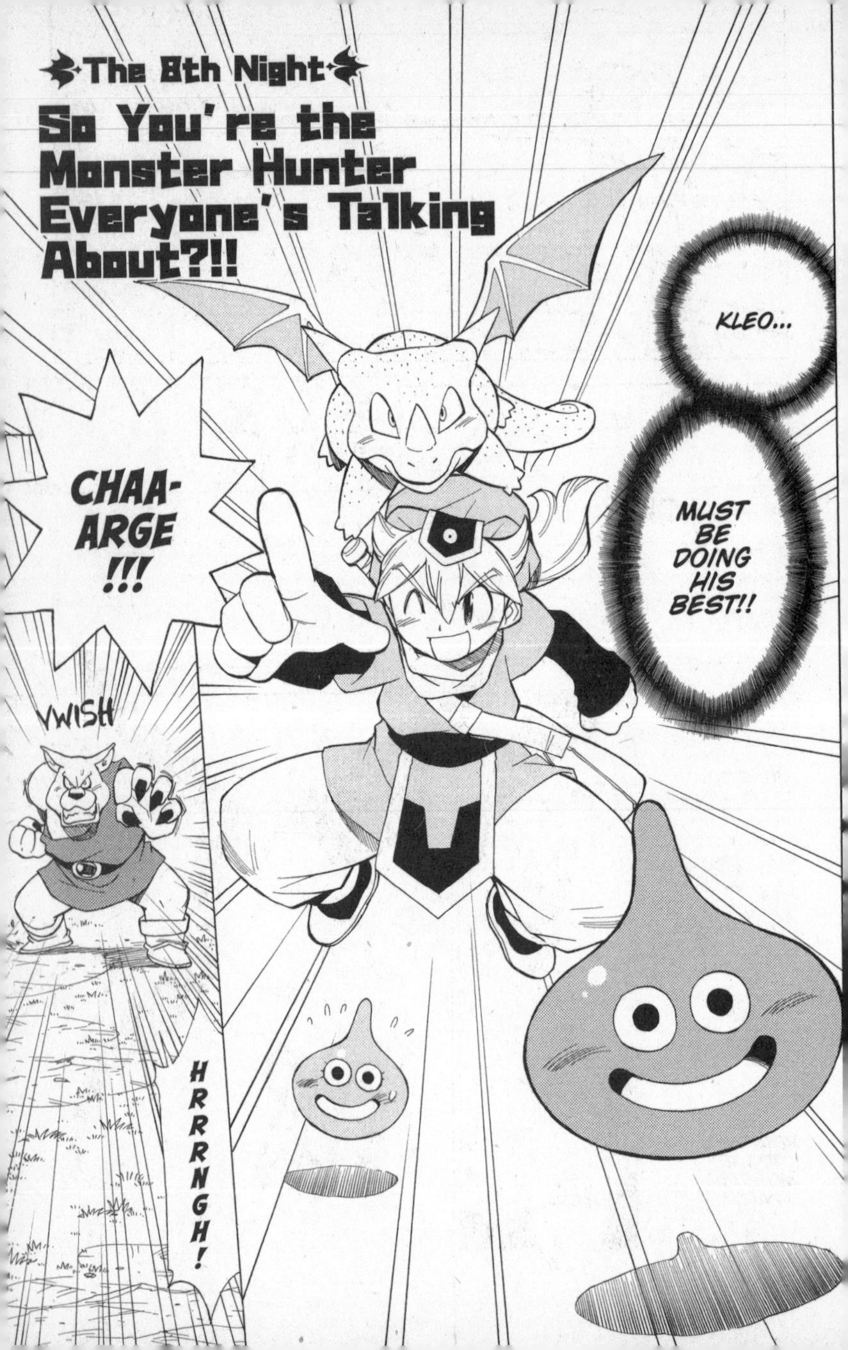
KLEO...
MUST BE DOING HIS BEST!!
CHAA-ARGE!!!
VWISH
HRRRNGH!

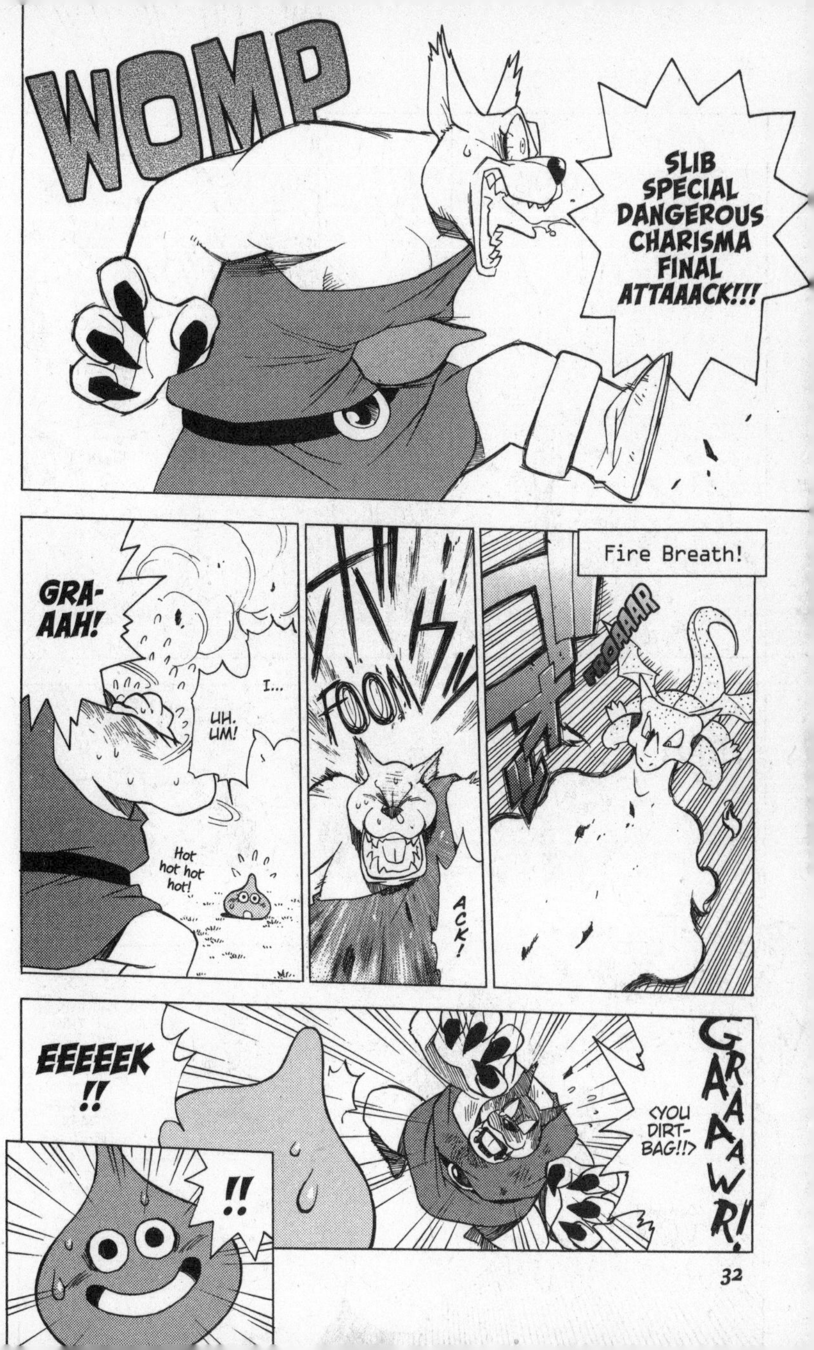
WOMP
SLIB SPECIAL DANGEROUS CHARISMA FINAL ATTAAACK!!!
Fire Breath!
FROAAAR
FOOM
ACK!
GRA-AAH!
I...
UH. UM!
Hot hot hot hot!
GRAAAAWR!
<YOU DIRT-BAG!!>
EEEEEK!!
!!

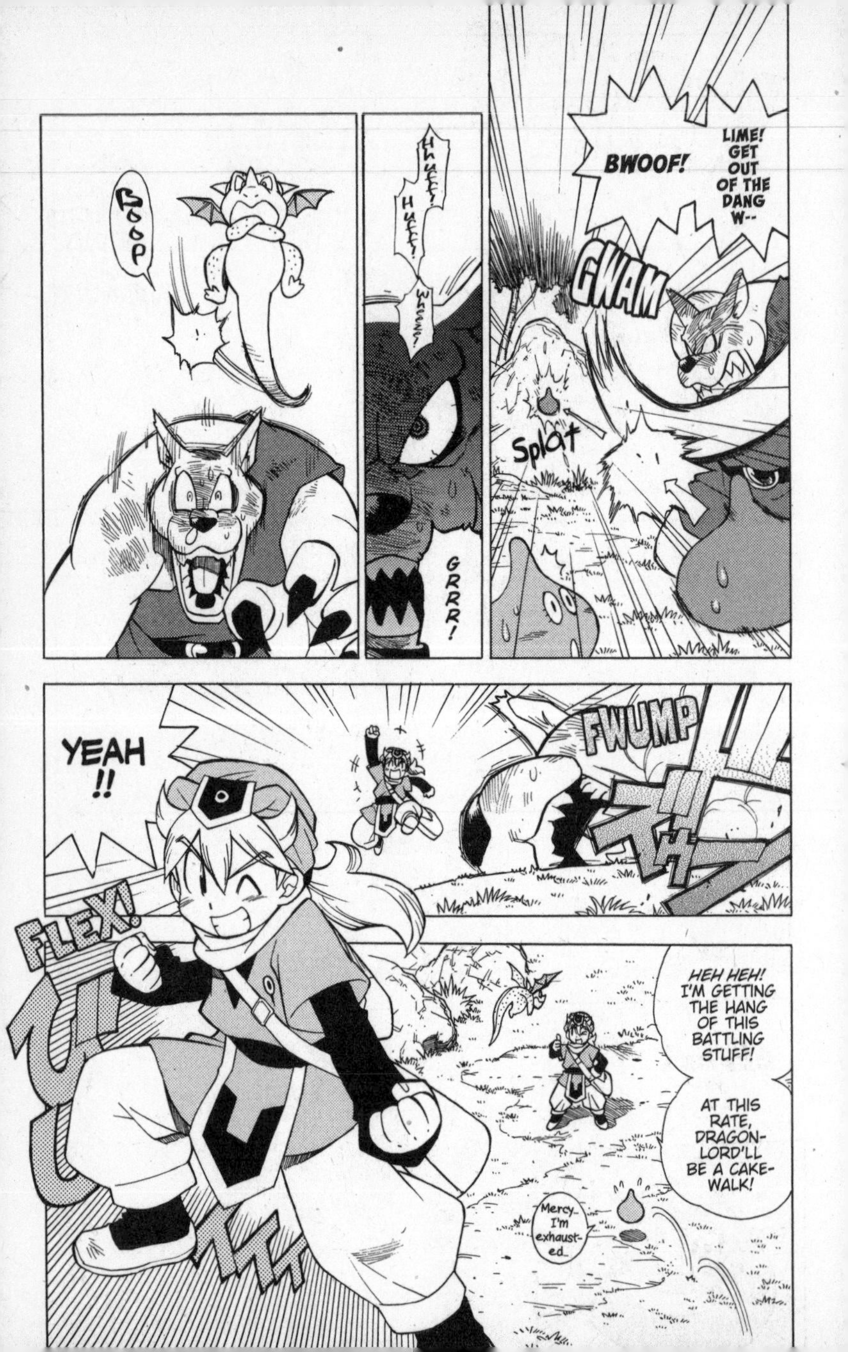
BWOOF!
LIME! GET OUT OF THE DANG W--
GWAM
Splat
Huff! Huff!
Wheeze!
GRRR!
Boop
!
FWUMP
YEAH !!
HEH HEH! I'M GETTING THE HANG OF THIS BATTLING STUFF!
AT THIS RATE, DRAGON-LORD'LL BE A CAKE-WALK!
Mercy... I'm exhaust-ed...
FLEX!

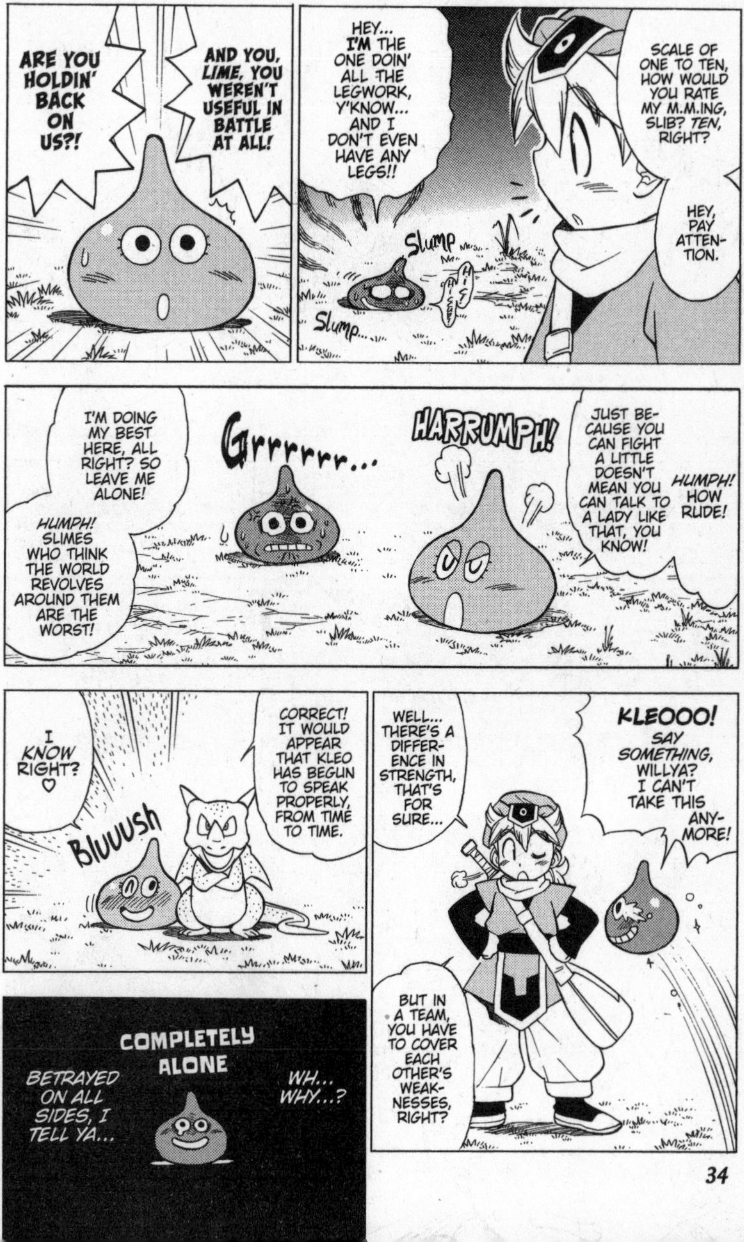
SCALE OF ONE TO TEN, HOW WOULD YOU RATE MY M.M.ING, SLIB? TEN, RIGHT?
HEY, PAY ATTEN-TION.
HEY... I'M THE ONE DOIN' ALL THE LEGWORK, Y'KNOW... AND I DON'T EVEN HAVE ANY LEGS!!
Slump
Slump...
AND YOU, LIME, YOU WEREN'T USEFUL IN BATTLE AT ALL!
ARE YOU HOLDIN' BACK ON US?!
JUST BE-CAUSE YOU CAN FIGHT A LITTLE DOESN'T MEAN YOU CAN TALK TO A LADY LIKE THAT, YOU KNOW!
HUMPH! HOW RUDE!
HARRUMPH!
Grrrrrr...
I'M DOING MY BEST HERE, ALL RIGHT? SO LEAVE ME ALONE!
HUMPH! SLIMES WHO THINK THE WORLD REVOLVES AROUND THEM ARE THE WORST!
KLEOOO! SAY SOMETHING, WILLYA? I CAN'T TAKE THIS ANY-MORE!
WELL... THERE'S A DIFFER-ENCE IN STRENGTH, THAT'S FOR SURE...
BUT IN A TEAM, YOU HAVE TO COVER EACH OTHER'S WEAK-NESSES, RIGHT?
CORRECT! IT WOULD APPEAR THAT KLEO HAS BEGUN TO SPEAK PROPERLY, FROM TIME TO TIME.
Bluuush
I KNOW RIGHT? ♡
COMPLETELY ALONE
WH... WHY...?
BETRAYED ON ALL SIDES, I TELL YA...

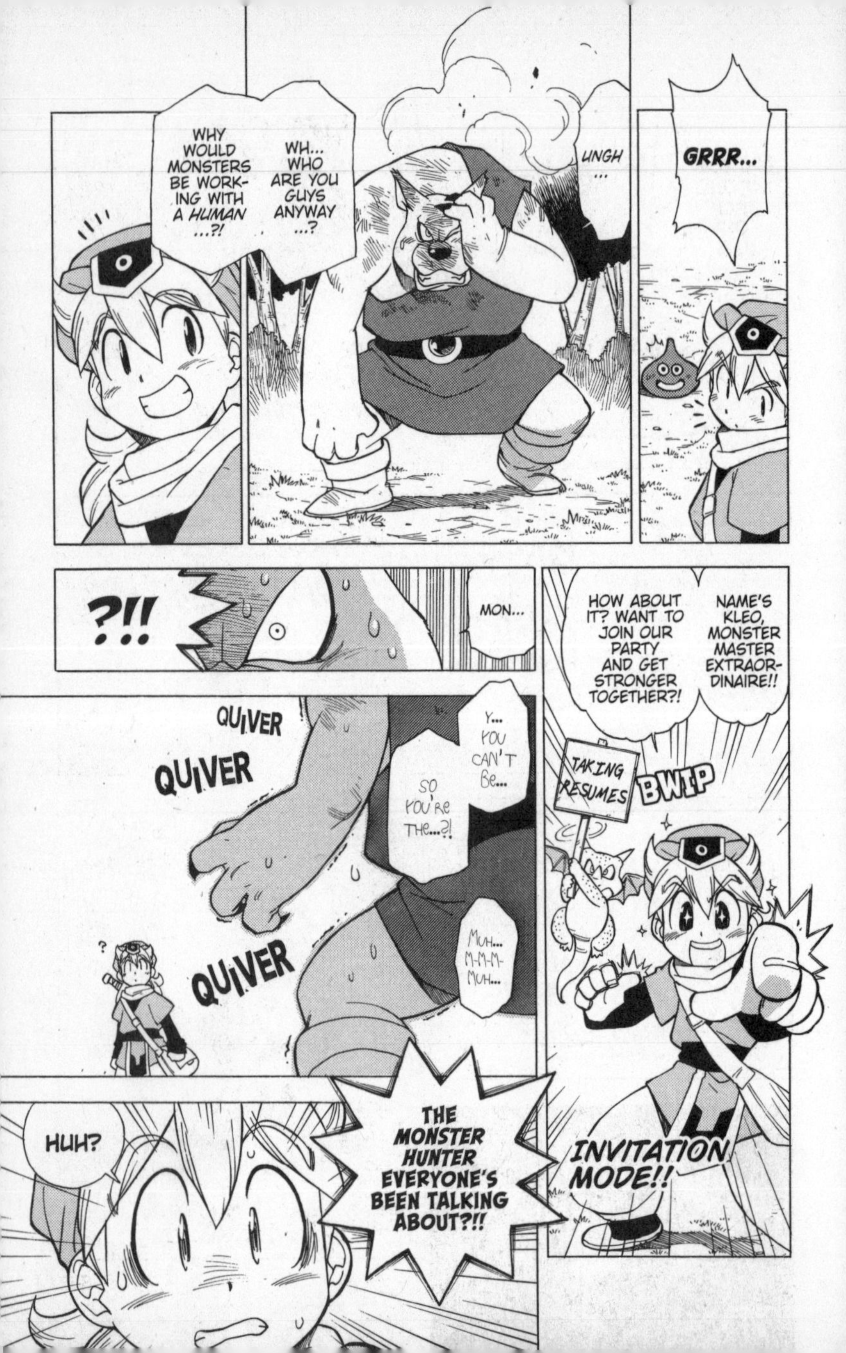
GRRR...
UNGH...
WH... WHO ARE YOU GUYS ANYWAY...?
WHY WOULD MONSTERS BE WORKING WITH A *HUMAN*...?!
NAME'S KLEO, MONSTER MASTER EXTRAORDINAIRE!!
HOW ABOUT IT? WANT TO JOIN OUR PARTY AND GET STRONGER TOGETHER?!
TAKING RESUMES
BWIP
INVITATION MODE!!
MON...
?!!
Y... YOU CAN'T BE...
SO YOU'RE THE...?!
QUIVER
QUIVER
QUIVER
MUH... M-M-M-MUH...
THE MONSTER HUNTER EVERYONE'S BEEN TALKING ABOUT?!!
HUH?

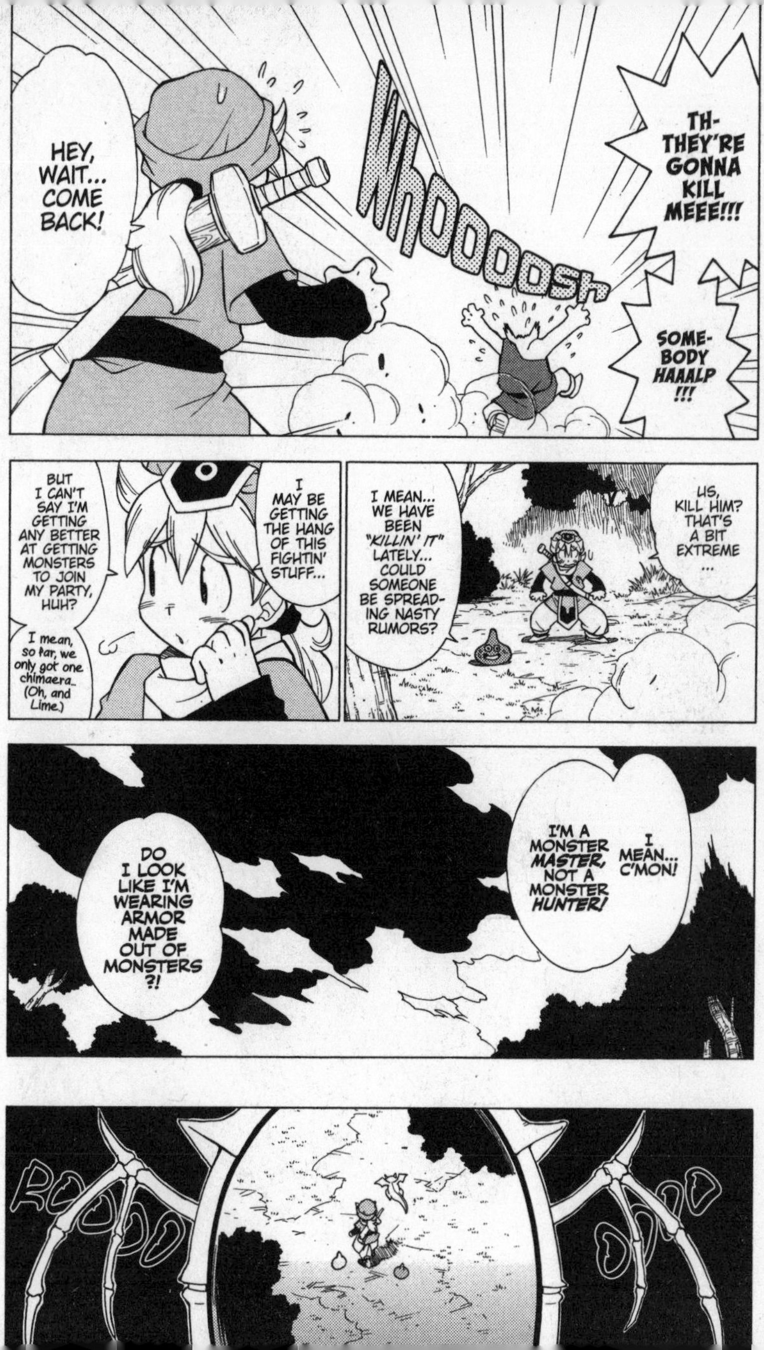
TH-THEY'RE GONNA KILL MEEE!!!
SOME-BODY HAAALP!!!
WHOOOOOSH
HEY, WAIT... COME BACK!
US, KILL HIM? THAT'S A BIT EXTREME...
I MEAN... WE HAVE BEEN "KILLIN' IT" LATELY... COULD SOMEONE BE SPREAD-ING NASTY RUMORS?
I MAY BE GETTING THE HANG OF THIS FIGHTIN' STUFF...
BUT I CAN'T SAY I'M GETTING ANY BETTER AT GETTING MONSTERS TO JOIN MY PARTY, HUH?
I mean, so far, we only got one chimaera.. (Oh, and Lime.)
I MEAN... C'MON!
I'M A MONSTER *MASTER*, NOT A MONSTER *HUNTER*!
DO I LOOK LIKE I'M WEARING ARMOR MADE OUT OF MONSTERS?!

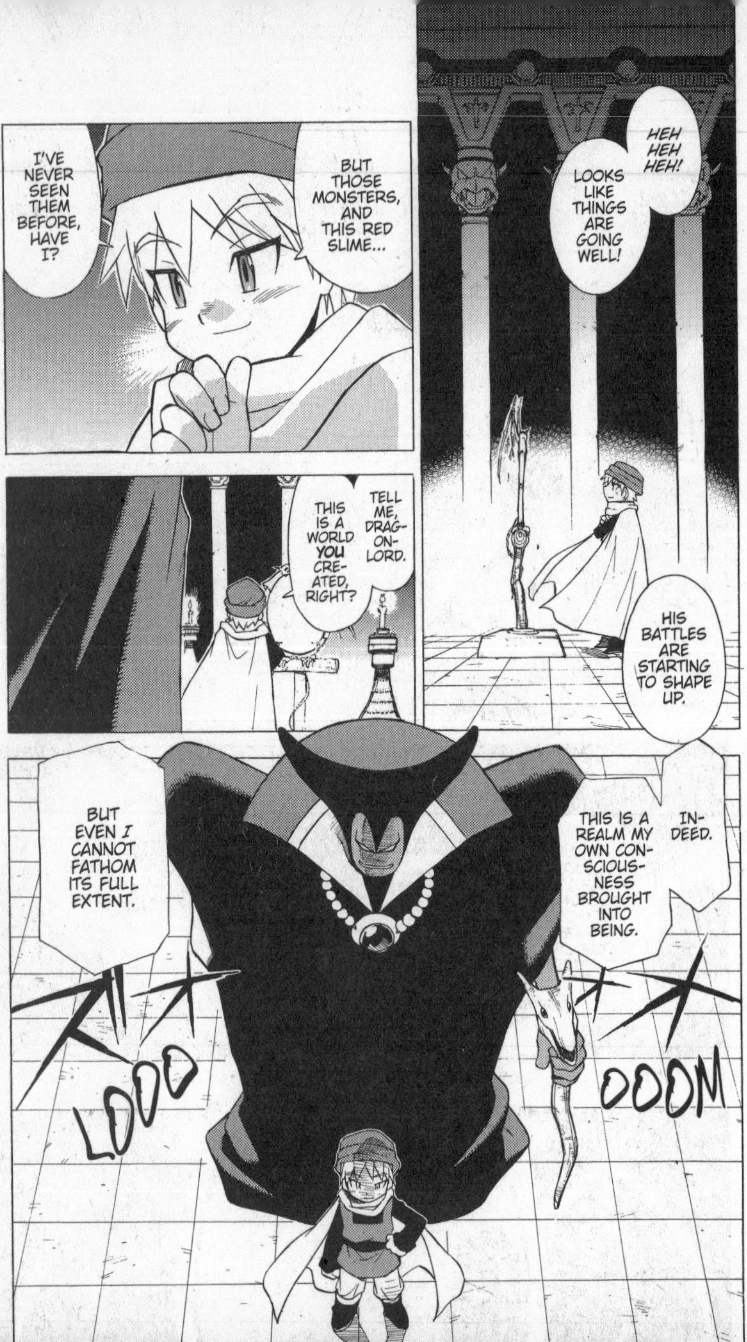
HEH HEH HEH!
LOOKS LIKE THINGS ARE GOING WELL!
HIS BATTLES ARE STARTING TO SHAPE UP.
BUT THOSE MONSTERS, AND THIS RED SLIME...
I'VE NEVER SEEN THEM BEFORE, HAVE I?
TELL ME, DRAG-ON-LORD.
THIS IS A WORLD **YOU** CRE-ATED, RIGHT?
IN-DEED.
THIS IS A REALM MY OWN CON-SCIOUS-NESS BROUGHT INTO BEING.
BUT EVEN I CANNOT FATHOM ITS FULL EXTENT.
LOOO
OOOM

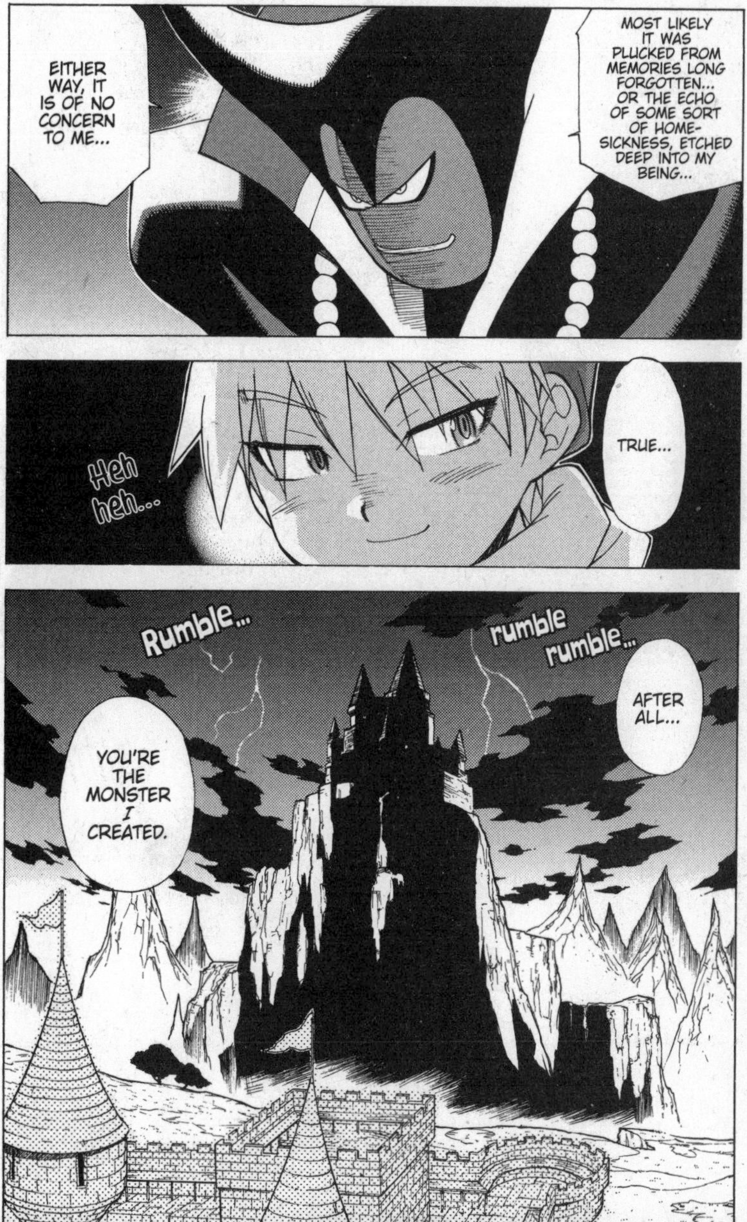
MOST LIKELY IT WAS PLUCKED FROM MEMORIES LONG FORGOTTEN... OR THE ECHO OF SOME SORT OF HOME-SICKNESS, ETCHED DEEP INTO MY BEING...
EITHER WAY, IT IS OF NO CONCERN TO ME...
TRUE...
Heh heh...
rumble rumble...
Rumble...
AFTER ALL...
YOU'RE THE MONSTER I CREATED.

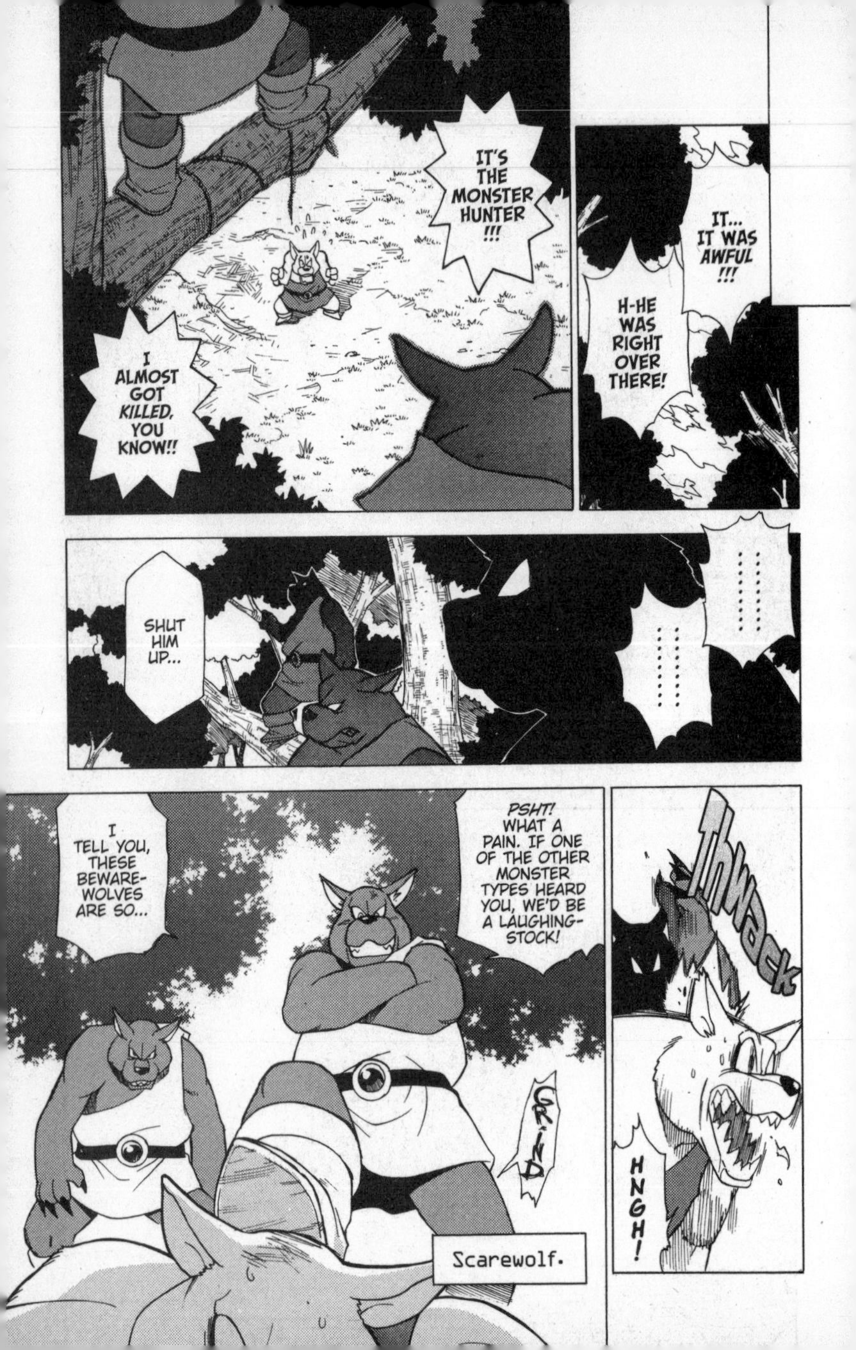
IT... IT WAS AWFUL!!!
H-HE WAS RIGHT OVER THERE!
IT'S THE MONSTER HUNTER!!!
I ALMOST GOT KILLED, YOU KNOW!!
......
......
SHUT HIM UP...
THWACK
HNGH!
PSHT! WHAT A PAIN. IF ONE OF THE OTHER MONSTER TYPES HEARD YOU, WE'D BE A LAUGHING-STOCK!
I TELL YOU, THESE BEWARE-WOLVES ARE SO...
GRIND
Scarewolf.

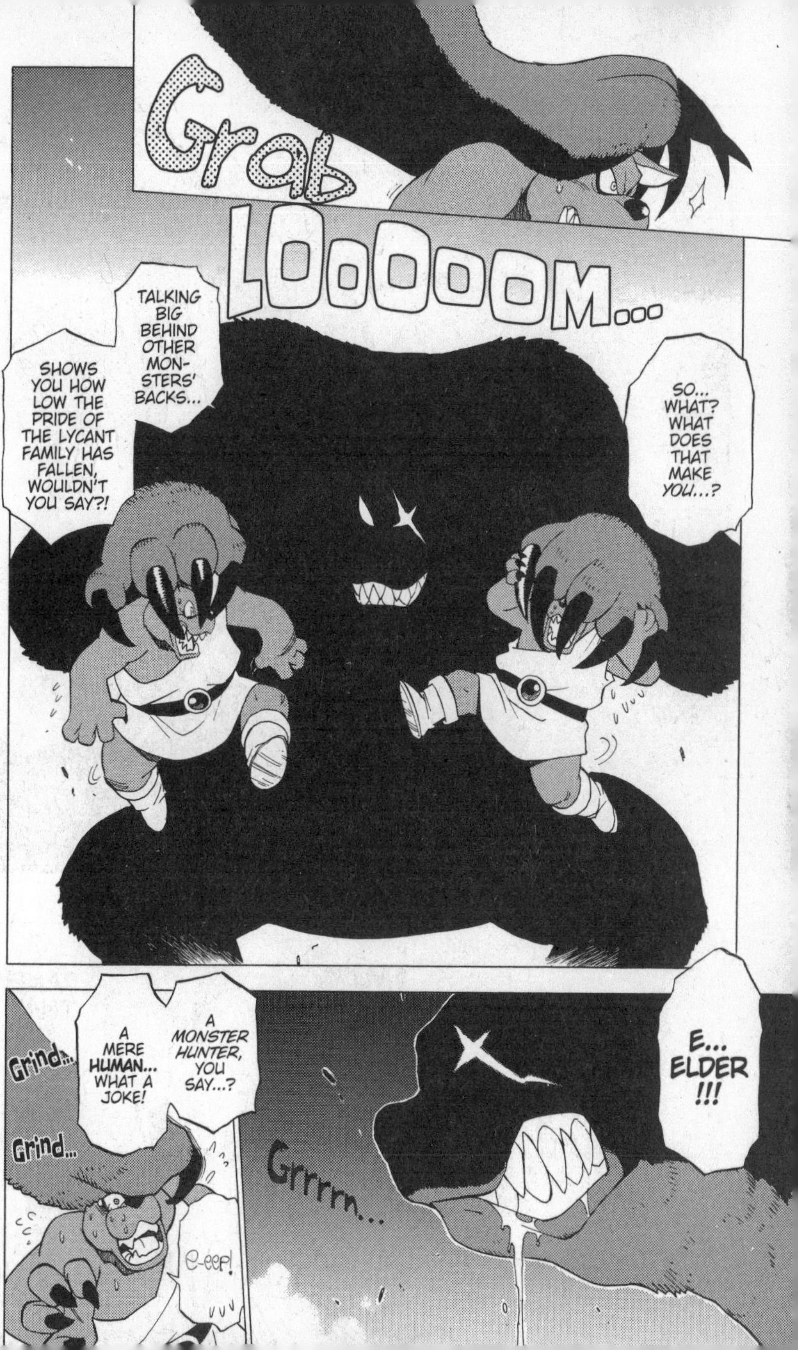
Grab
LOOOOOOM...
SO... WHAT? WHAT DOES THAT MAKE YOU...?
TALKING BIG BEHIND OTHER MONSTERS' BACKS...
SHOWS YOU HOW LOW THE PRIDE OF THE LYCANT FAMILY HAS FALLEN, WOULDN'T YOU SAY?!
E... ELDER!!!
Grrrrn...
A MONSTER HUNTER, YOU SAY...?
A MERE HUMAN... WHAT A JOKE!
Grind...
Grind...
e-eep!

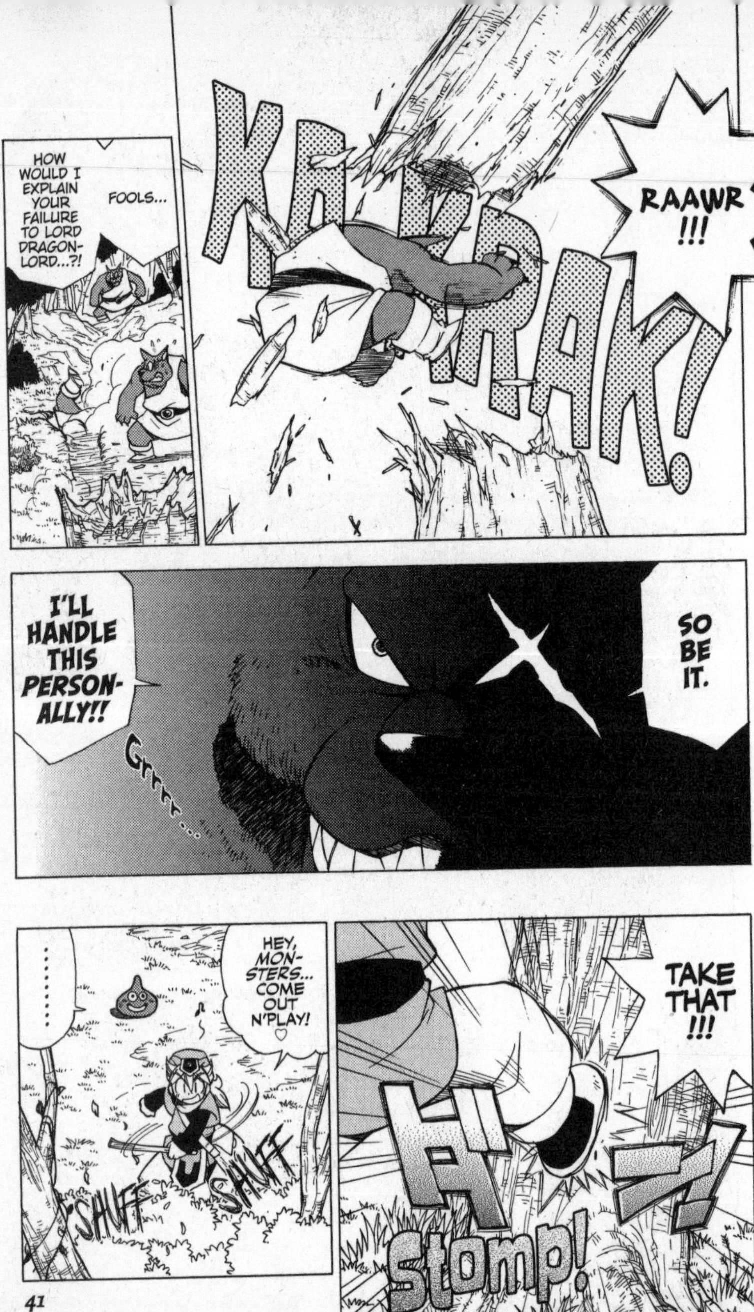
RAAWR!!!
KAKRAK!
FOOLS...
HOW WOULD I EXPLAIN YOUR FAILURE TO LORD DRAGON-LORD...?!
SO BE IT.
I'LL HANDLE THIS PERSON-ALLY!!
Grrrr...
TAKE THAT!!!
Stomp!
HEY, MON-STERS... COME OUT N'PLAY! ♡
......
SHUFF
SHUFF

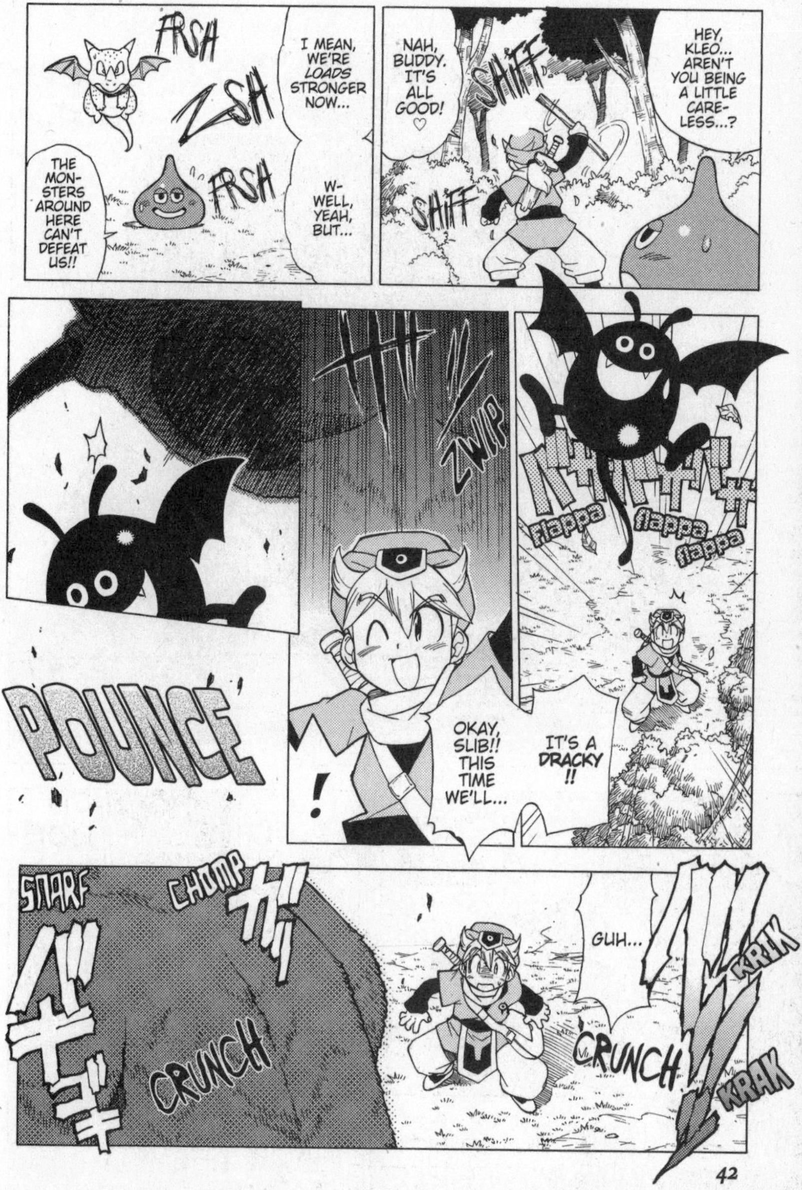
HEY, KLEO... AREN'T YOU BEING A LITTLE CARE-LESS...?
NAH, BUDDY. IT'S ALL GOOD! ♡
SHIFF
SHIFF
I MEAN, WE'RE LOADS STRONGER NOW...
W-WELL, YEAH, BUT...
FRSH
ZSH
FRSH
THE MON-STERS AROUND HERE CAN'T DEFEAT US!!
flappa flappa flappa
IT'S A DRACKY!!
ZWIP
OKAY, SLIB!! THIS TIME WE'LL...
!
POUNCE
KRAK
KRAK
GUH...
CRUNCH
CHOMP
SNARF
CRUNCH

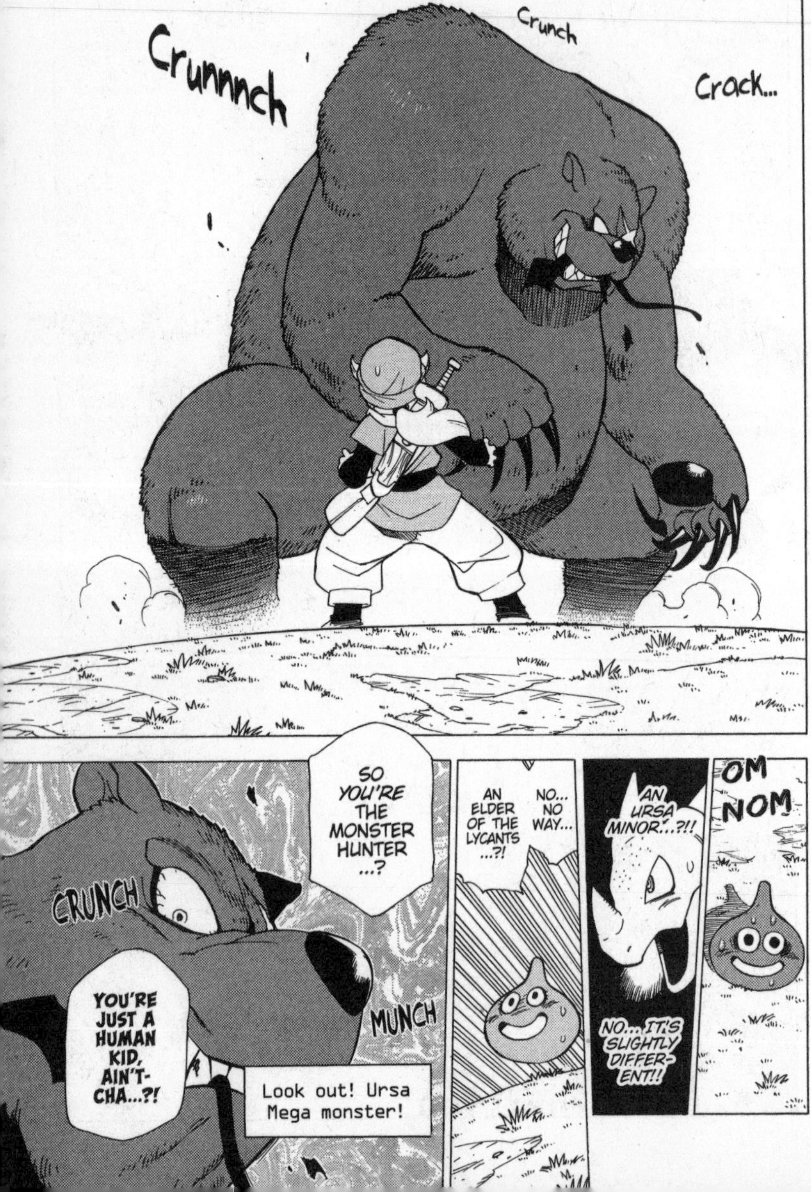
Crunch
Crack...
Crunnnch
OM NOM
AN URSA MINOR...?!!
NO... IT'S SLIGHTLY DIFFER-ENT!!
NO... NO WAY...
AN ELDER OF THE LYCANTS ...?!
SO YOU'RE THE MONSTER HUNTER ...?
CRUNCH
MUNCH
YOU'RE JUST A HUMAN KID, AIN'T-CHA...?!
Look out! Ursa Mega monster!

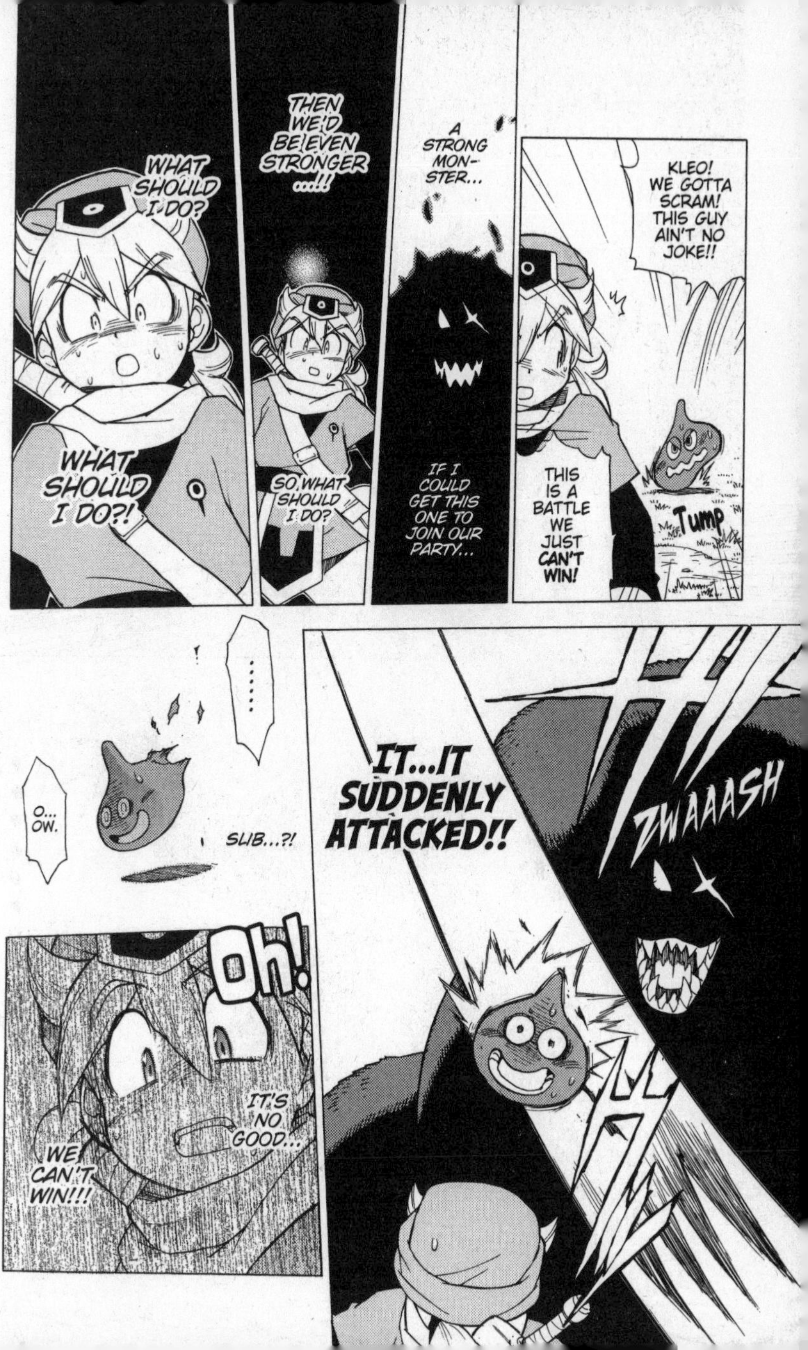
KLEO! WE GOTTA SCRAM! THIS GUY AIN'T NO JOKE!!
THIS IS A BATTLE WE JUST CAN'T WIN!
Tump
A STRONG MONSTER...
IF I COULD GET THIS ONE TO JOIN OUR PARTY...
THEN WE'D BE EVEN STRONGER...!!
SO, WHAT SHOULD I DO?
WHAT SHOULD I DO?
WHAT SHOULD I DO?!
IT...IT SUDDENLY ATTACKED!!
ZWAAASH
......
O... OW.
SUB...?!
Oh!
IT'S NO GOOD...
WE CAN'T WIN!!!

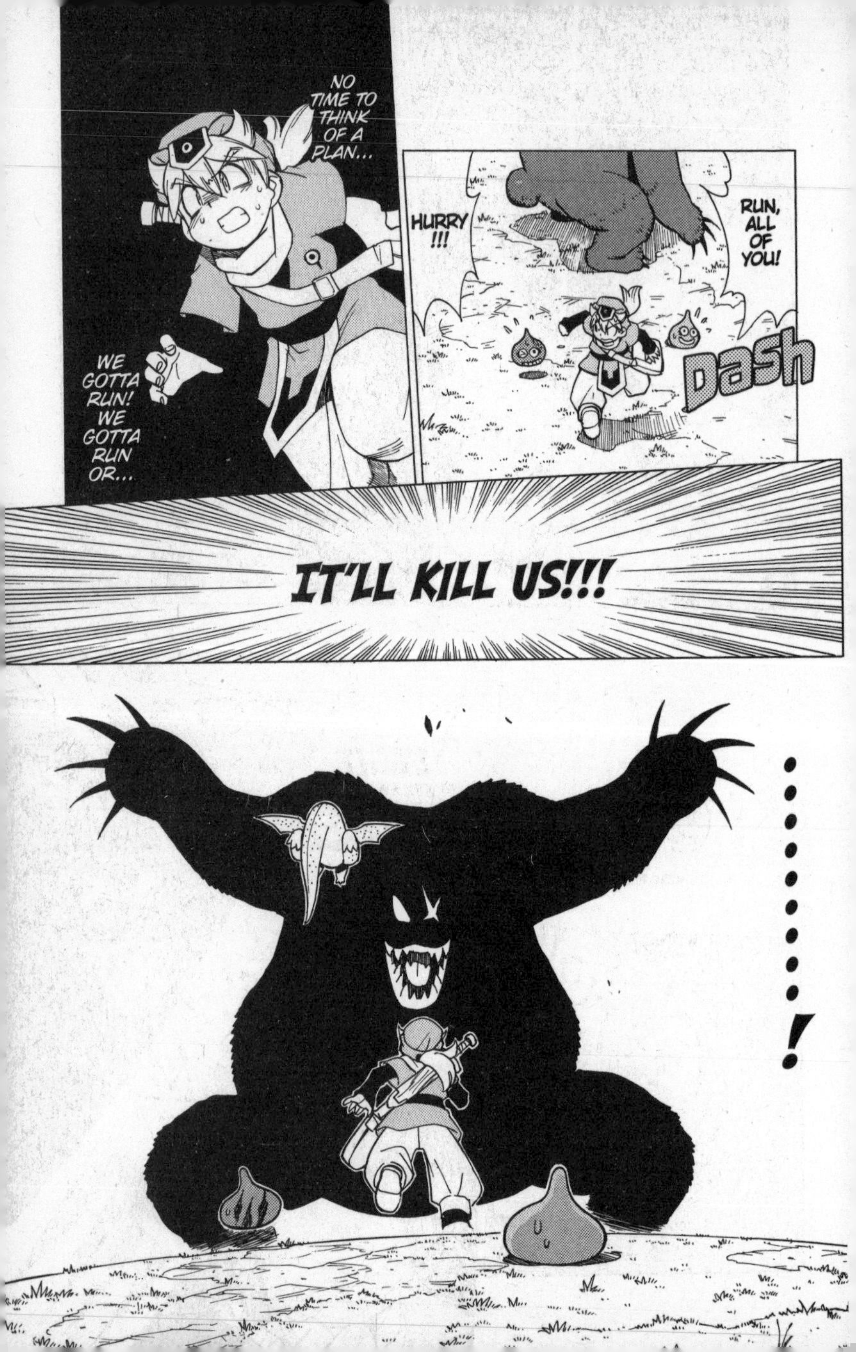
RUN, ALL OF YOU!
HURRY!!!
Dash
NO TIME TO THINK OF A PLAN...
WE GOTTA RUN! WE GOTTA RUN OR...
IT'LL KILL US!!!
.........!

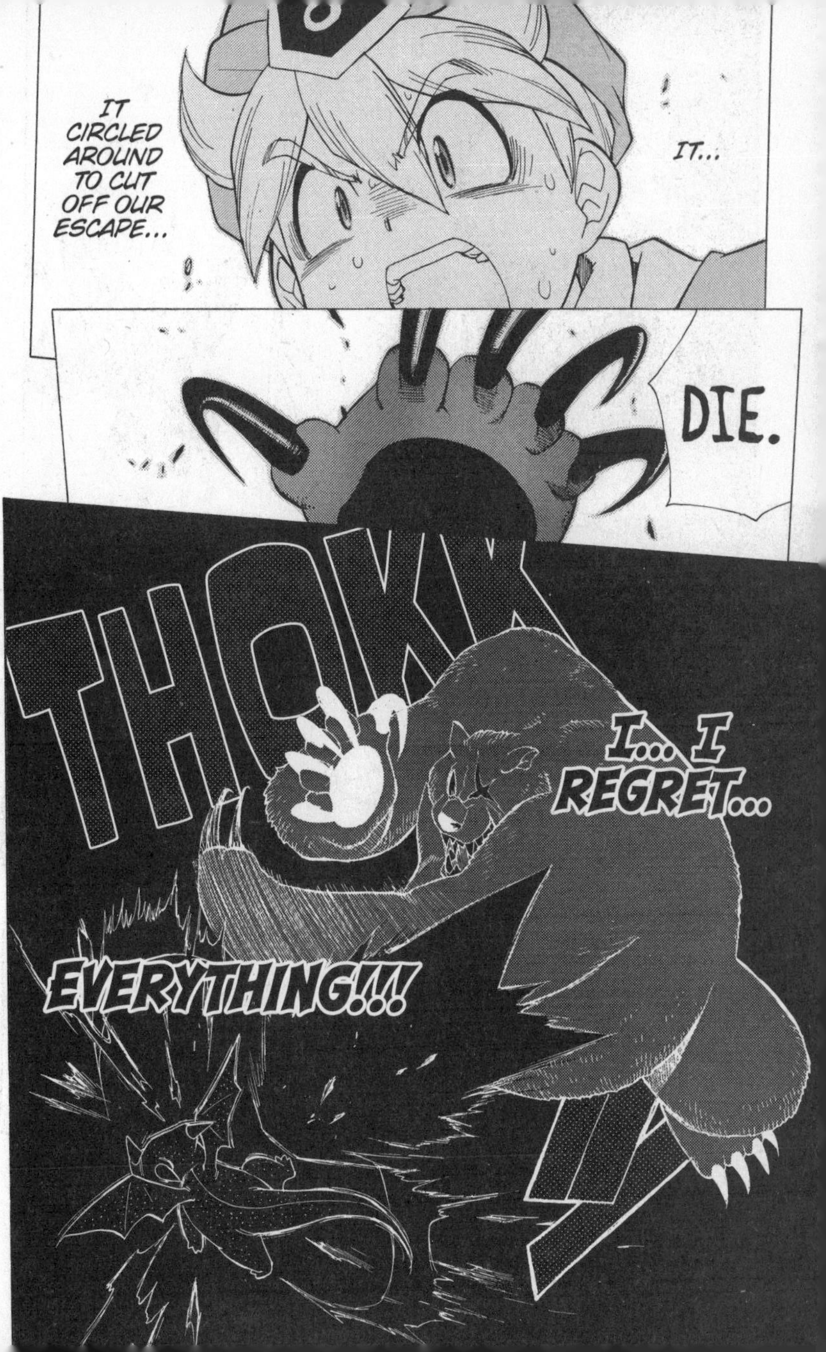
IT...
IT CIRCLED AROUND TO CUT OFF OUR ESCAPE...
DIE.
THOKK
I... I REGRET...
EVERYTHING!!!

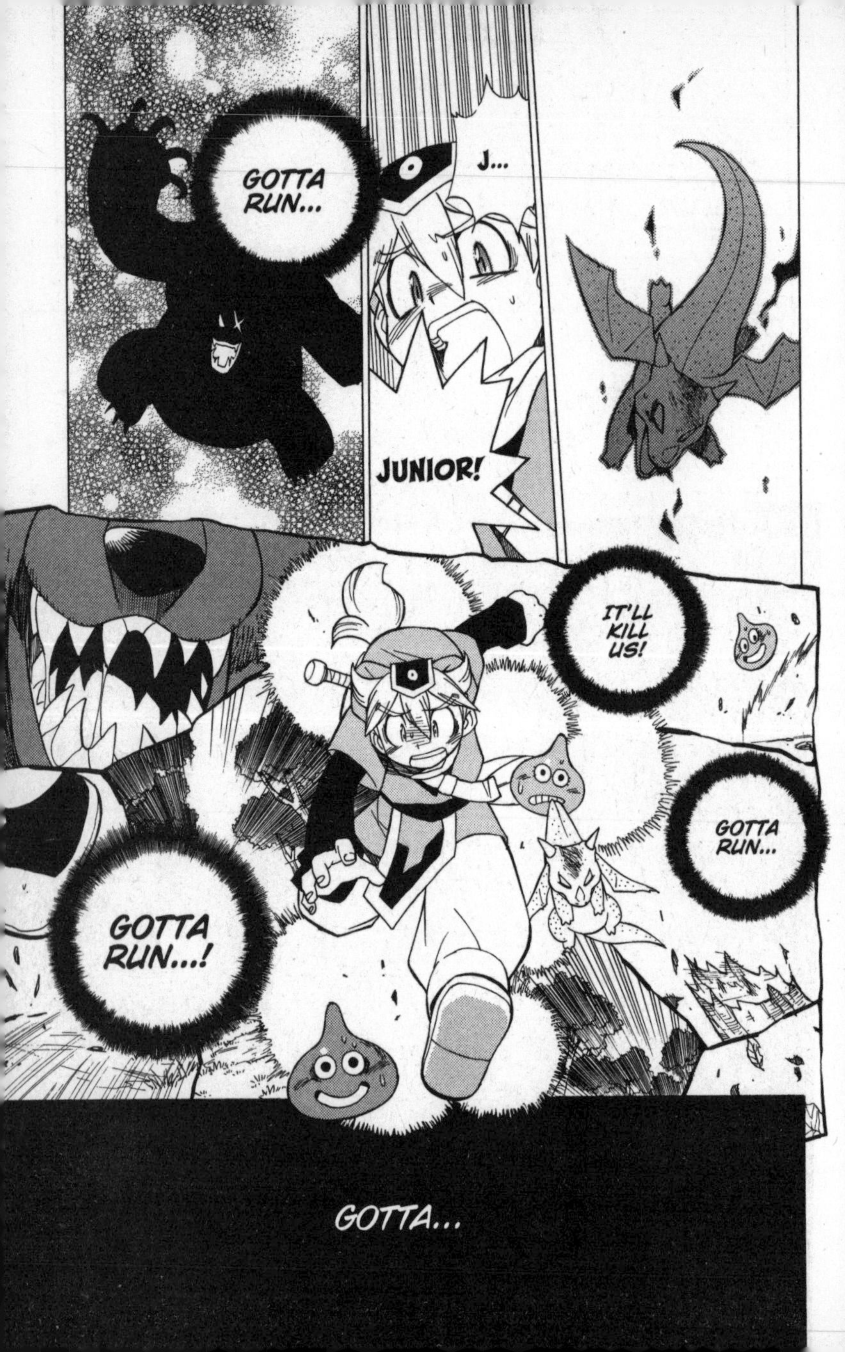
J...
JUNIOR!
GOTTA RUN...
IT'LL KILL US!
GOTTA RUN...
GOTTA RUN...!
GOTTA...

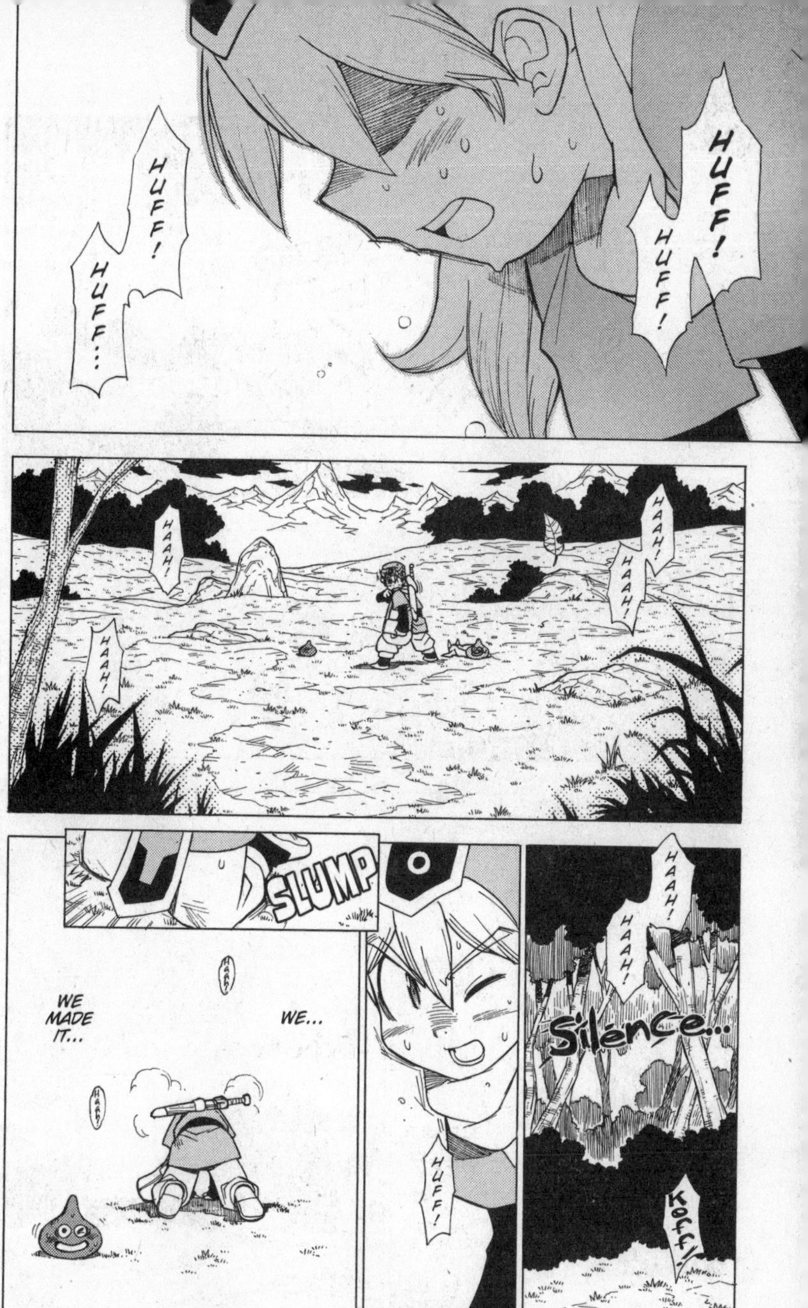
HUFF! HUFF!
HUFF! HUFF...
HAAH! HAAH!
HAAH!
HAAH!
HAAH! HAAH!
Silence...
Koff!
HUFF!
SLUMP
WE...
WE MADE IT...

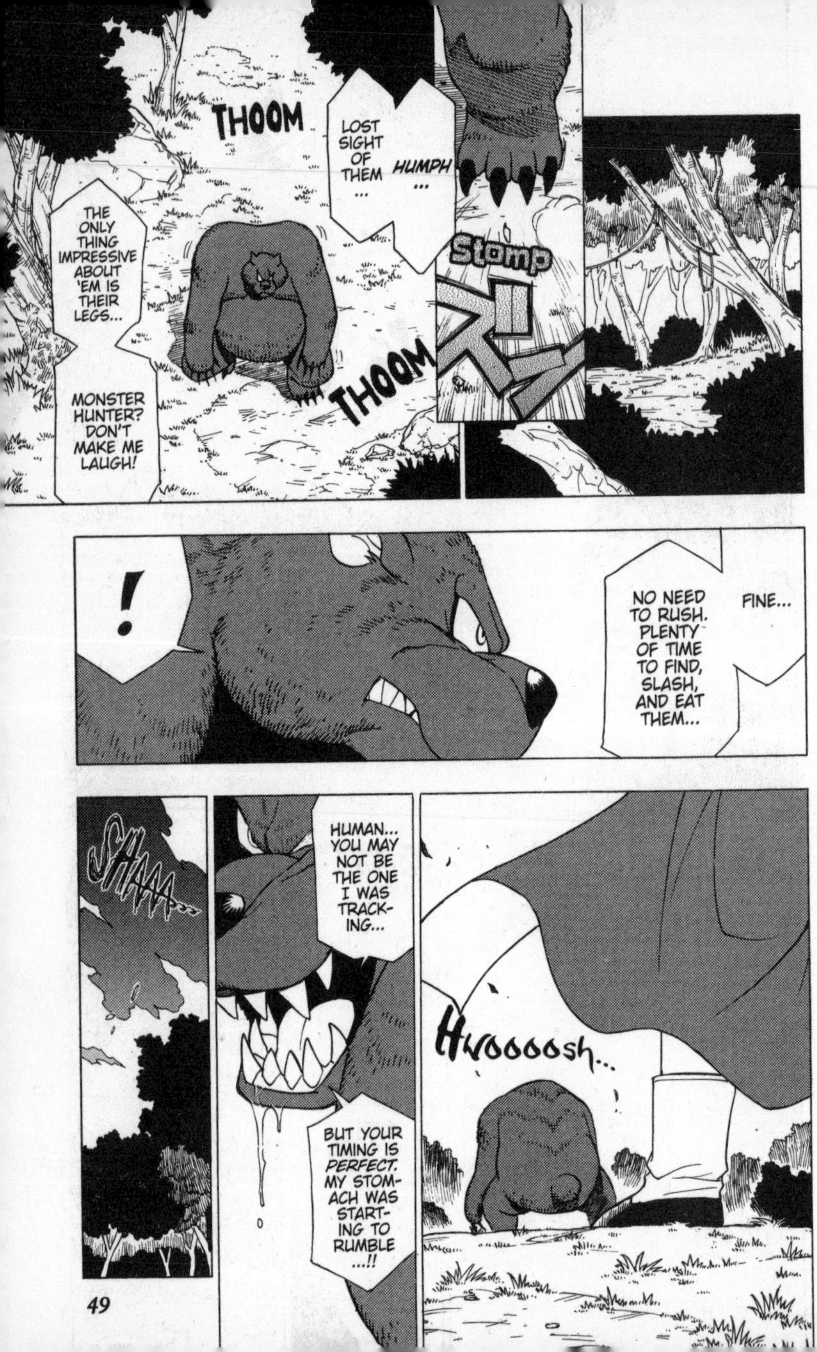

Stomp
LOST SIGHT OF THEM ...
HUMPH ...
THOOM
THOOM
THE ONLY THING IMPRESSIVE ABOUT 'EM IS THEIR LEGS...
MONSTER HUNTER? DON'T MAKE ME LAUGH!
FINE...
NO NEED TO RUSH. PLENTY OF TIME TO FIND, SLASH, AND EAT THEM...
!
Hwoooosh...
HUMAN... YOU MAY NOT BE THE ONE I WAS TRACK-ING...
BUT YOUR TIMING IS *PERFECT*. MY STOM-ACH WAS START-ING TO RUMBLE ...!!
SHAAA...

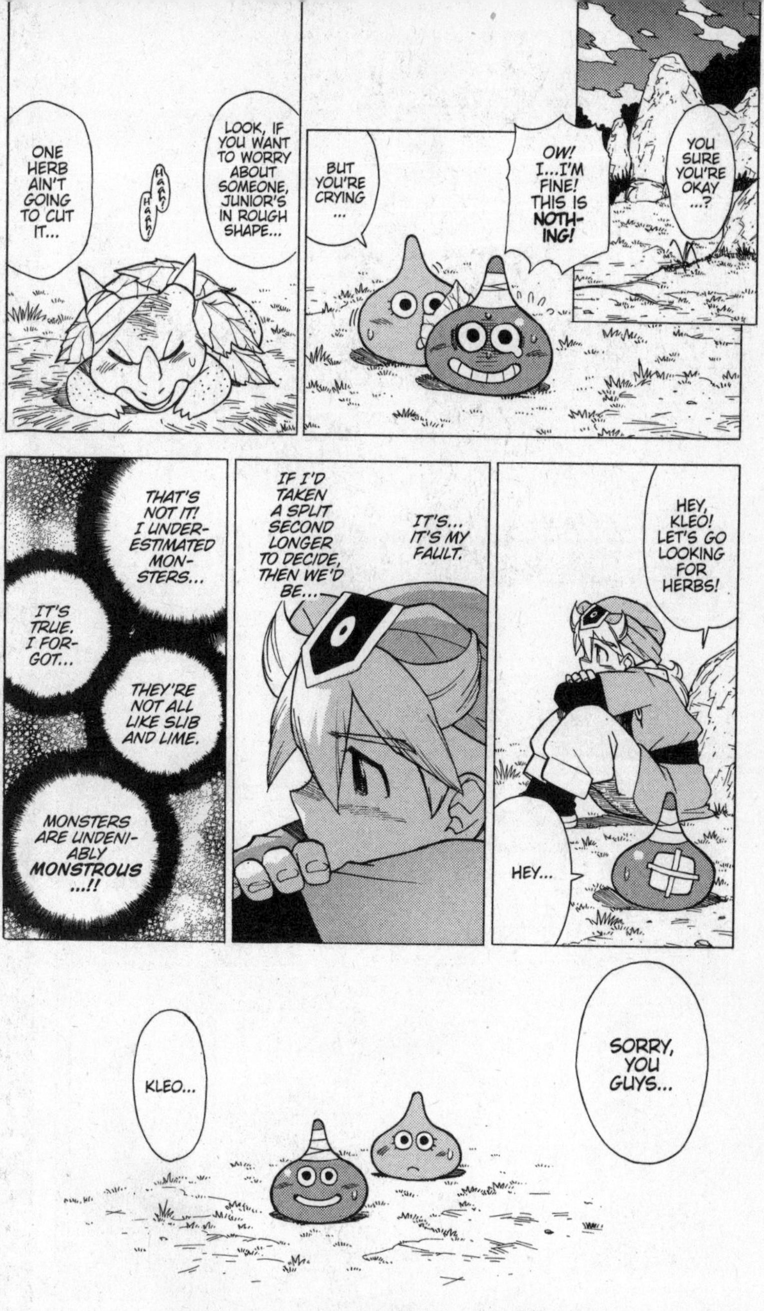
YOU SURE YOU'RE OKAY ...?
OW! I...I'M FINE! THIS IS NOTHING!
BUT YOU'RE CRYING ...
LOOK, IF YOU WANT TO WORRY ABOUT SOMEONE, JUNIOR'S IN ROUGH SHAPE...
HAAH! HAAH!
ONE HERB AIN'T GOING TO CUT IT...
HEY, KLEO! LET'S GO LOOKING FOR HERBS!
HEY...
IT'S... IT'S MY FAULT.
IF I'D TAKEN A SPLIT SECOND LONGER TO DECIDE, THEN WE'D BE...
THAT'S NOT IT! I UNDERESTIMATED MONSTERS...
IT'S TRUE. I FORGOT...
THEY'RE NOT ALL LIKE SLIB AND LIME.
MONSTERS ARE UNDENIABLY MONSTROUS ...!!
SORRY, YOU GUYS...
KLEO...

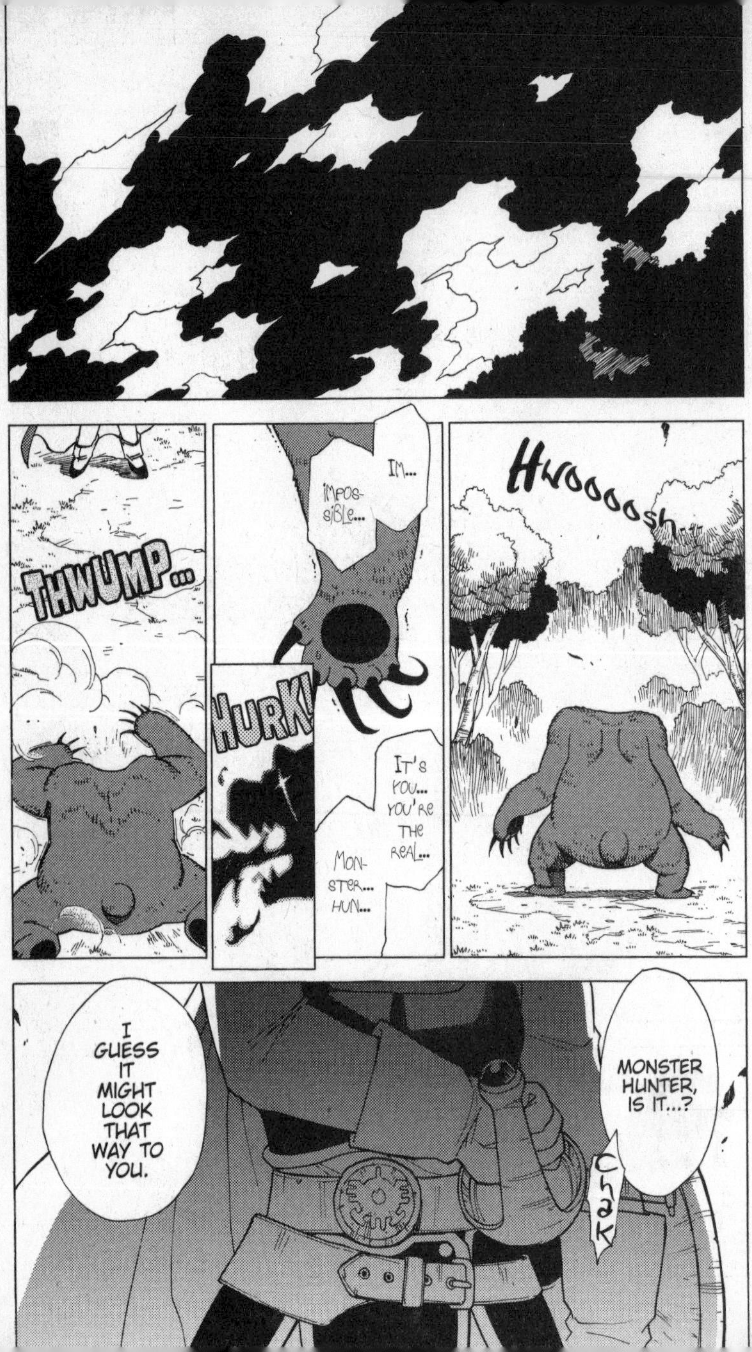
Hwooooosh...
IM... IMPOS-SIBLE...
IT'S YOU... YOU'RE THE REAL...
MON-STER... HUN...
HURK!
THWUMP...
MONSTER HUNTER, IS IT...?
Chak
I GUESS IT MIGHT LOOK THAT WAY TO YOU.

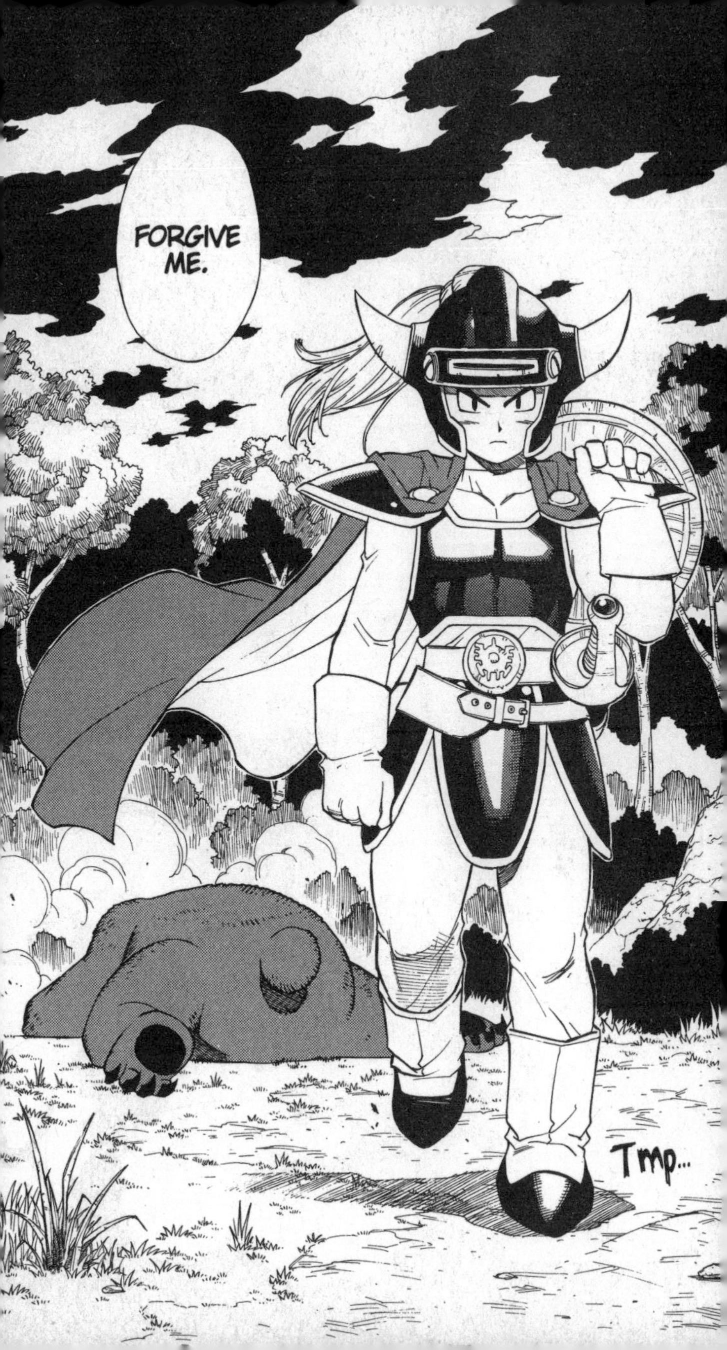
FORGIVE ME.
Tmp...

The 9th Night
Who's That...?!

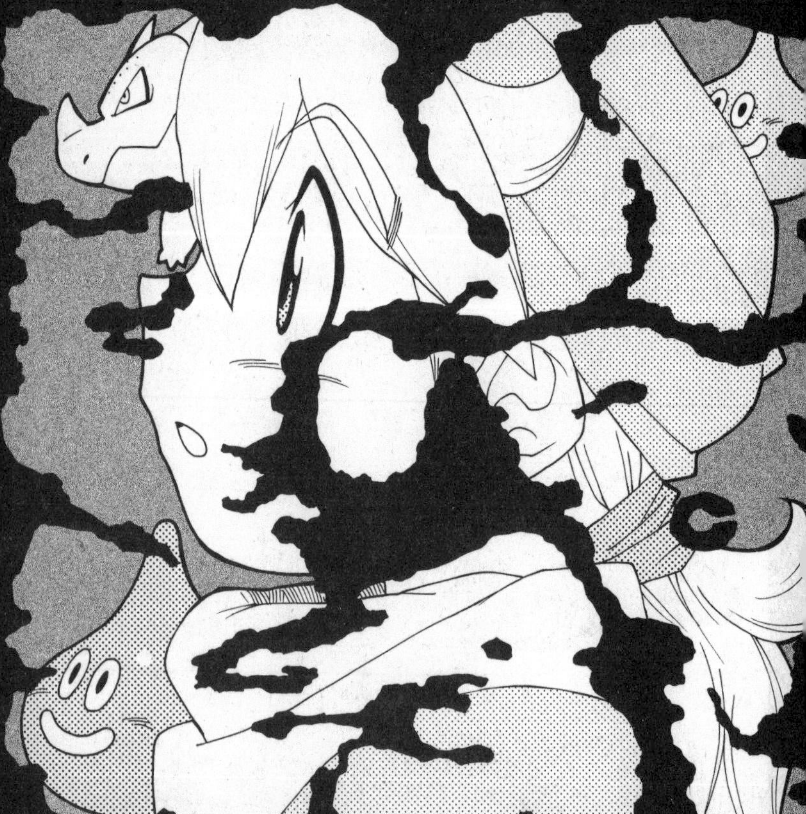

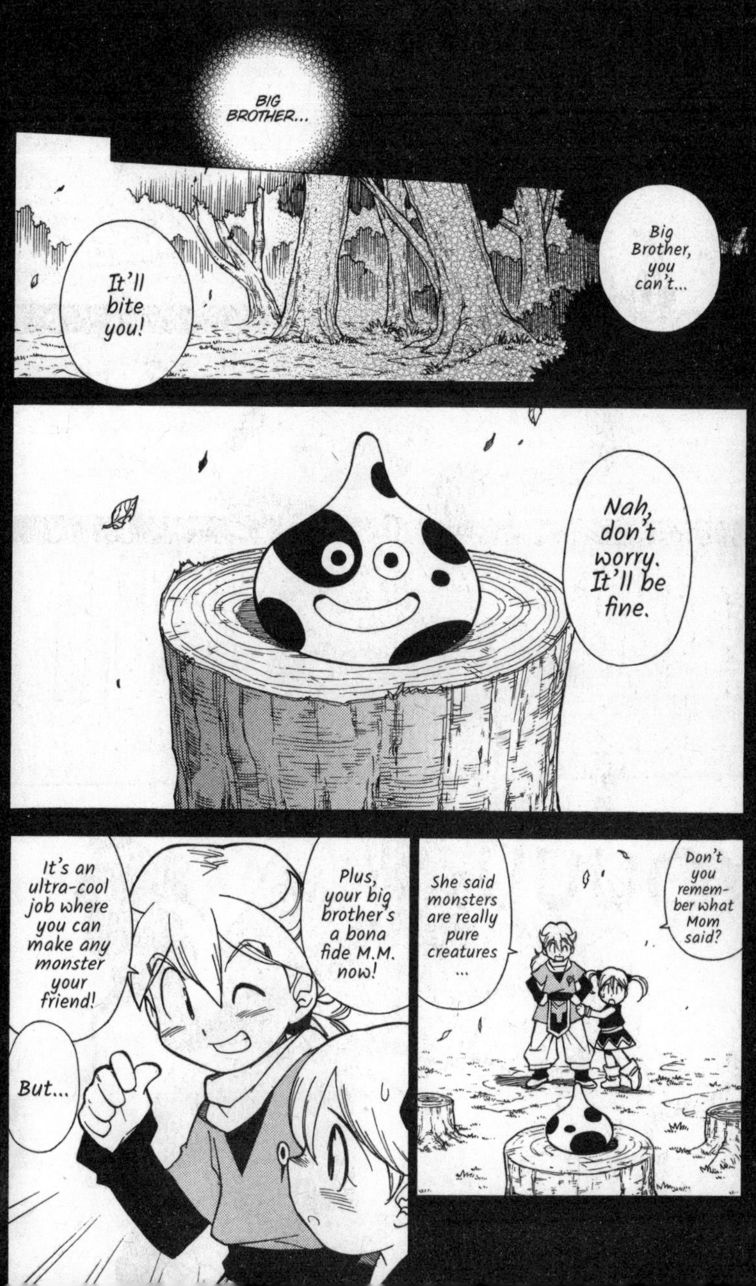
BIG BROTHER...
Big Brother, you can't...
It'll bite you!
Nah, don't worry. It'll be fine.
Don't you remember what Mom said?
She said monsters are really pure creatures ...
Plus, your big brother's a bona fide M.M. now!
It's an ultra-cool job where you can make any monster your friend!
But...

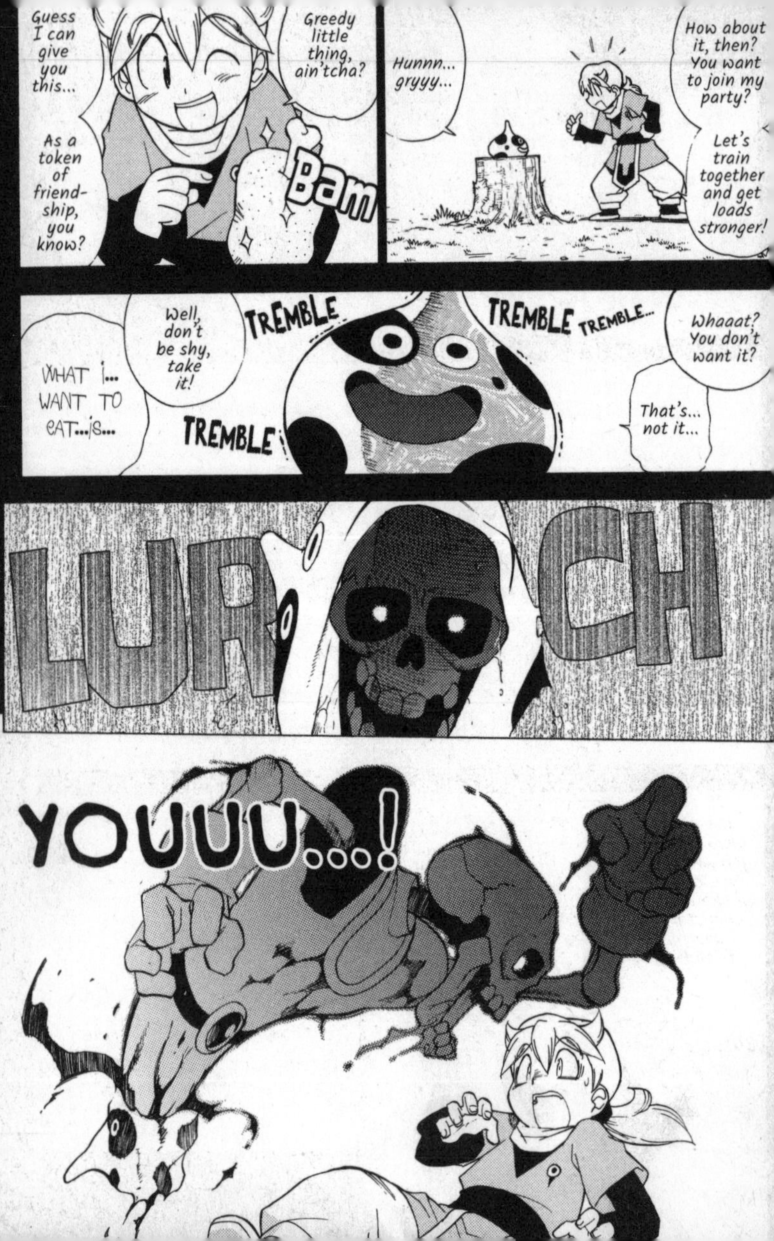
How about it, then? You want to join my party?
Let's train together and get loads stronger!
Hunnn... gryyy...
Greedy little thing, ain'tcha?
Bam
Guess I can give you this...
As a token of friendship, you know?
Whaaat? You don't want it?
That's... not it...
TREMBLE TREMBLE...
TREMBLE
Well, don't be shy, take it!
TREMBLE
WHAT I... WANT TO EAT...IS...
LURCH
YOUUU...!

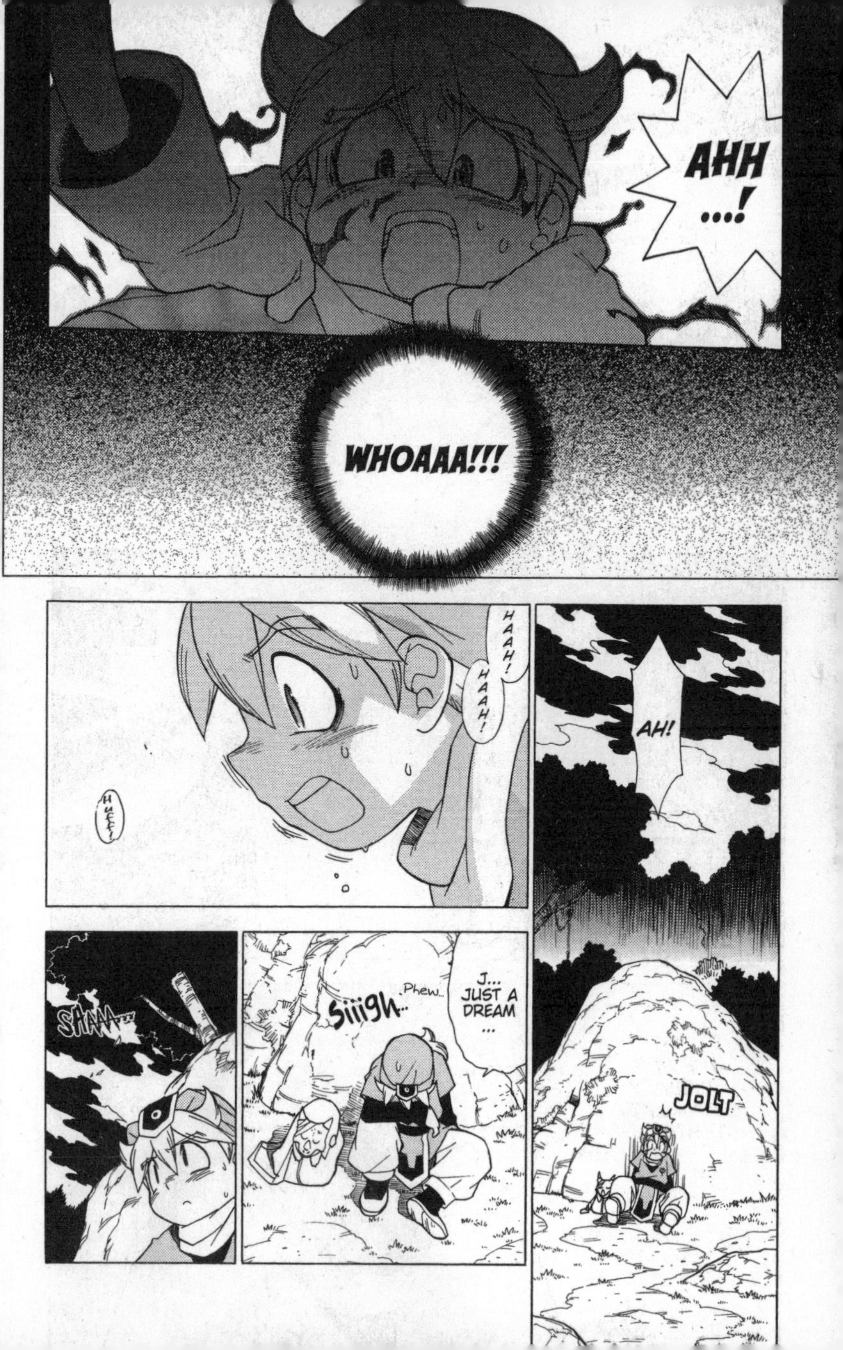
AHH ...!
WHOAAA!!!
AH!
JOLT
HAAH! HAAH!
HUFF!
Siiigh..
Phew...
J... JUST A DREAM ...
SHAAA...

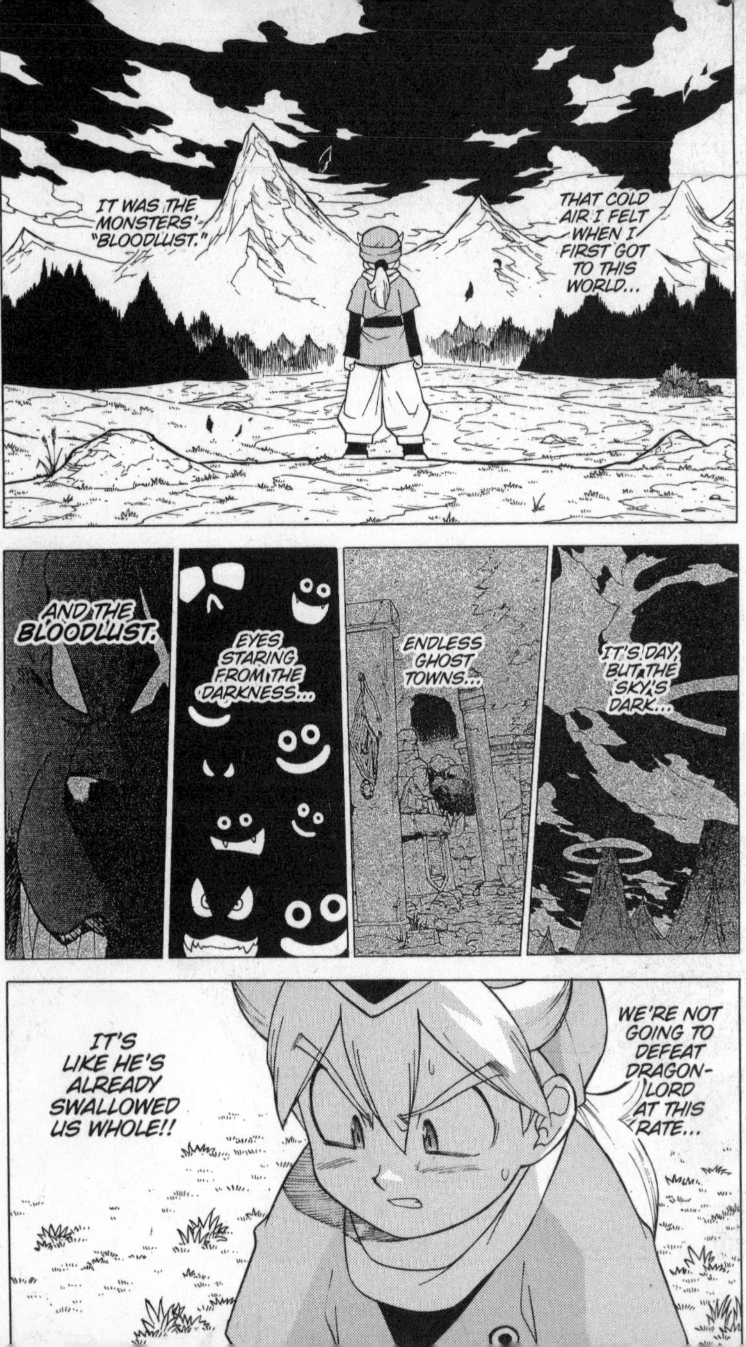
THAT COLD AIR I FELT WHEN I FIRST GOT TO THIS WORLD...
IT WAS THE MONSTERS' "BLOODLUST."
IT'S DAY, BUT THE SKY'S DARK...
ENDLESS GHOST TOWNS...
EYES STARING FROM THE DARKNESS...
AND THE BLOODLUST.
WE'RE NOT GOING TO DEFEAT DRAGON-LORD AT THIS RATE...
IT'S LIKE HE'S ALREADY SWALLOWED US WHOLE!!

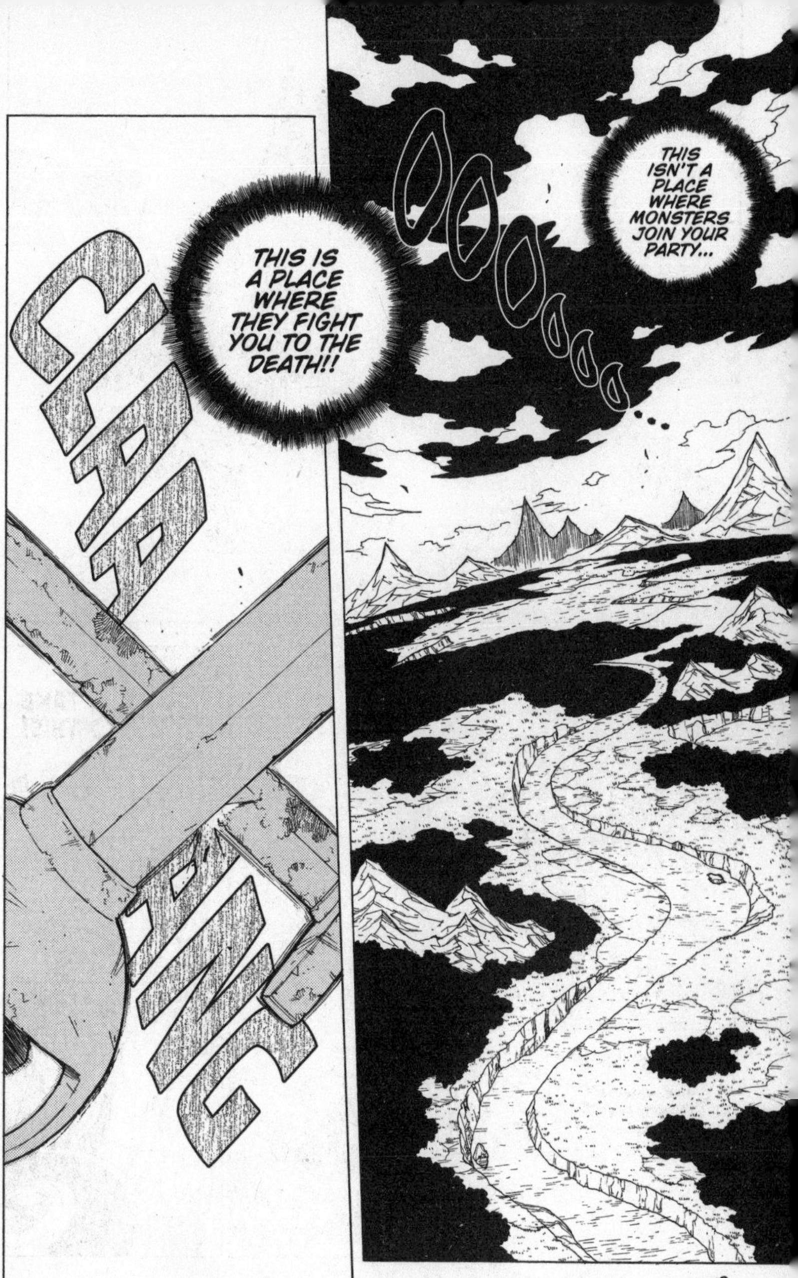
THIS ISN'T A PLACE WHERE MONSTERS JOIN YOUR PARTY...
THIS IS A PLACE WHERE THEY FIGHT YOU TO THE DEATH!!

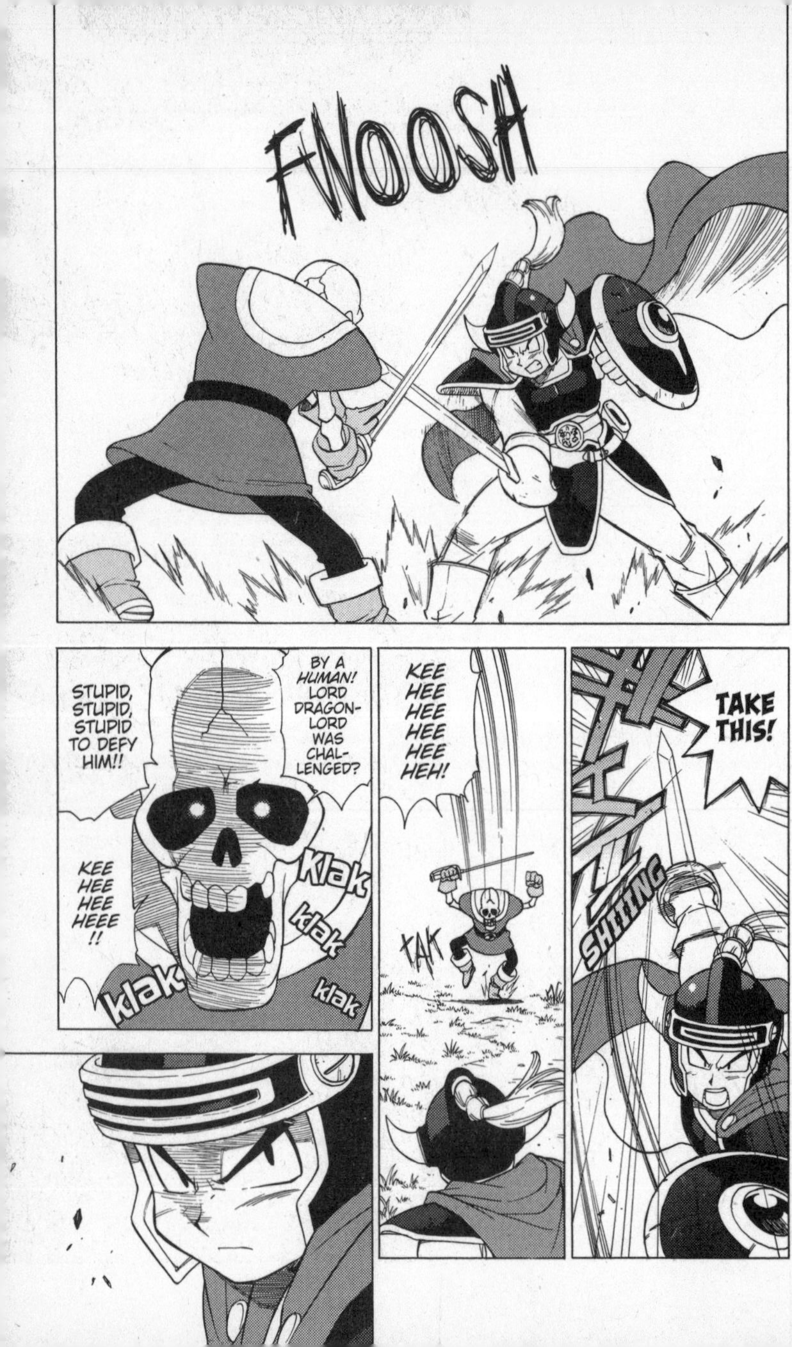
FWOOSH
TAKE THIS!
SHIIING
KEE HEE HEE HEE HEE HEH!
TAK
BY A HUMAN! LORD DRAGON-LORD WAS CHAL-LENGED?
STUPID, STUPID, STUPID TO DEFY HIM!!
KEE HEE HEE HEEE !!
klak
klak
klak
klak

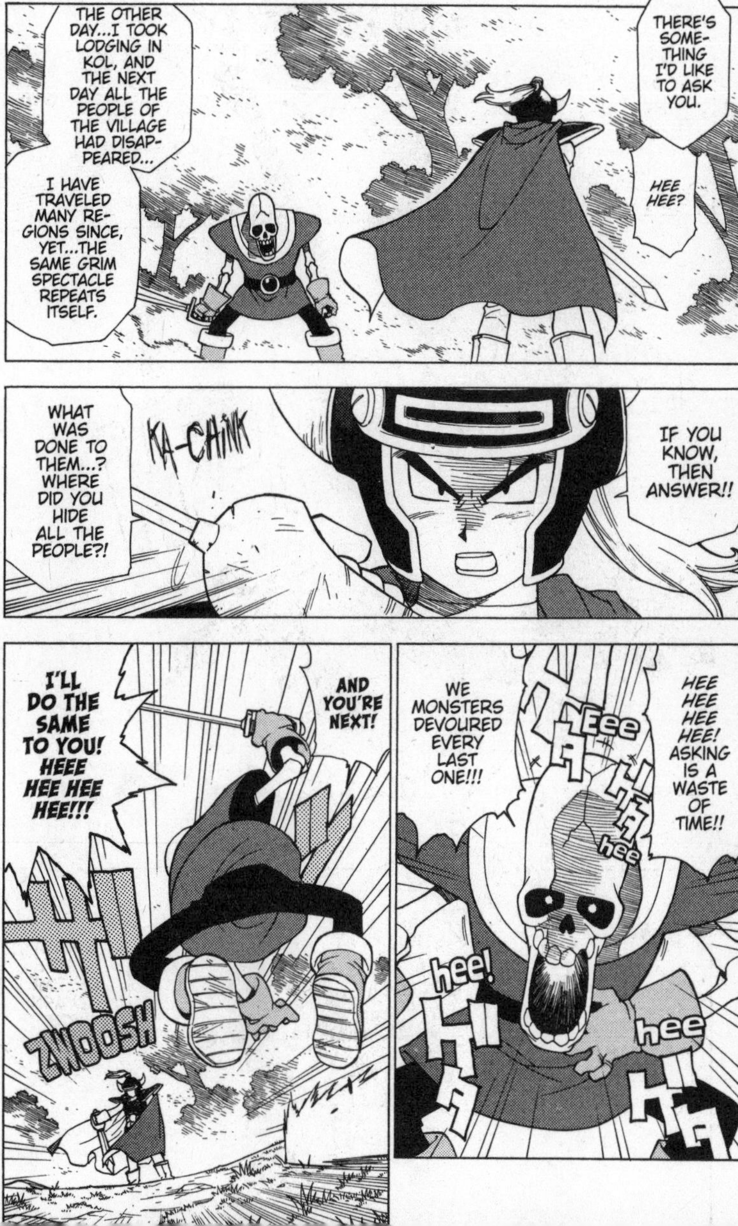
THERE'S SOME-THING I'D LIKE TO ASK YOU.
HEE HEE?
THE OTHER DAY...I TOOK LODGING IN KOL, AND THE NEXT DAY ALL THE PEOPLE OF THE VILLAGE HAD DISAP-PEARED...
I HAVE TRAVELED MANY RE-GIONS SINCE, YET...THE SAME GRIM SPECTACLE REPEATS ITSELF.
IF YOU KNOW, THEN ANSWER!!
KA-CHINK
WHAT WAS DONE TO THEM...? WHERE DID YOU HIDE ALL THE PEOPLE?!
HEE HEE HEE HEE! ASKING IS A WASTE OF TIME!!
WE MONSTERS DEVOURED EVERY LAST ONE!!!
Heee
hee
hee!
hee
AND YOU'RE NEXT!
I'LL DO THE SAME TO YOU! HEEE HEE HEE HEE!!!
ZWOOSH

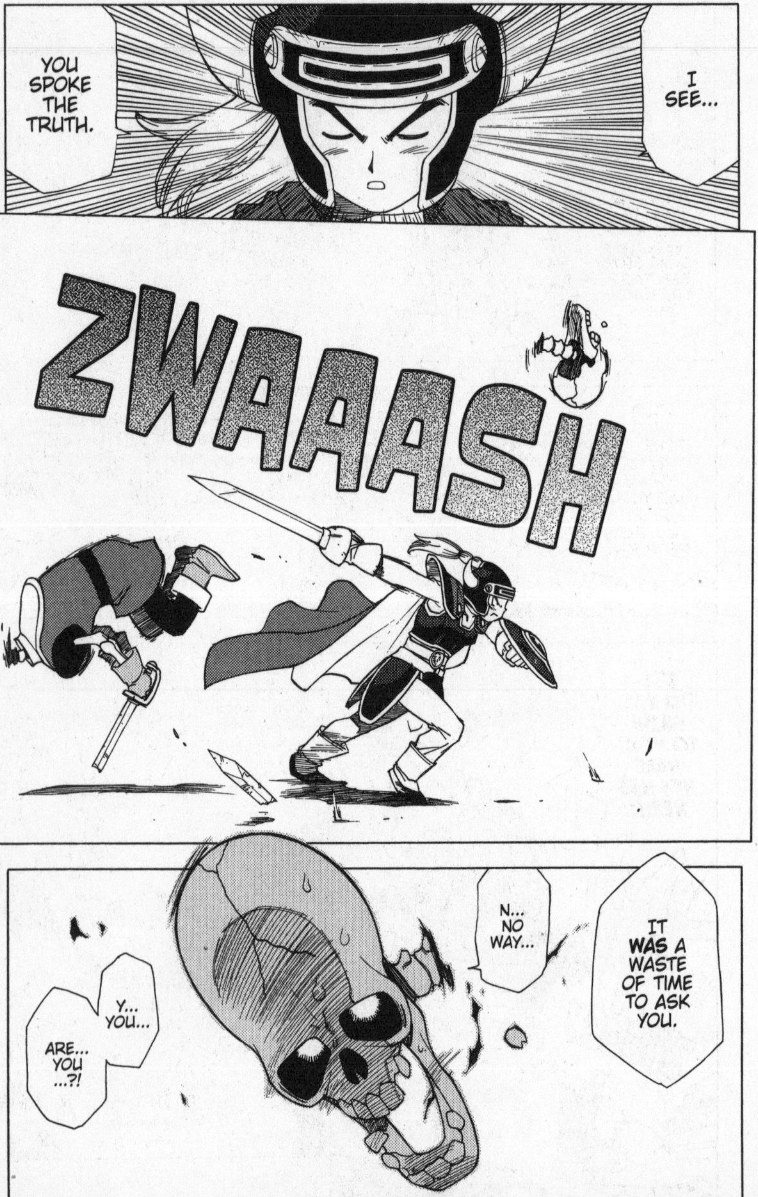
I SEE...
YOU SPOKE THE TRUTH.
ZWAAASH
IT WAS A WASTE OF TIME TO ASK YOU.
N... NO WAY...
Y... YOU...
ARE... YOU ...?!

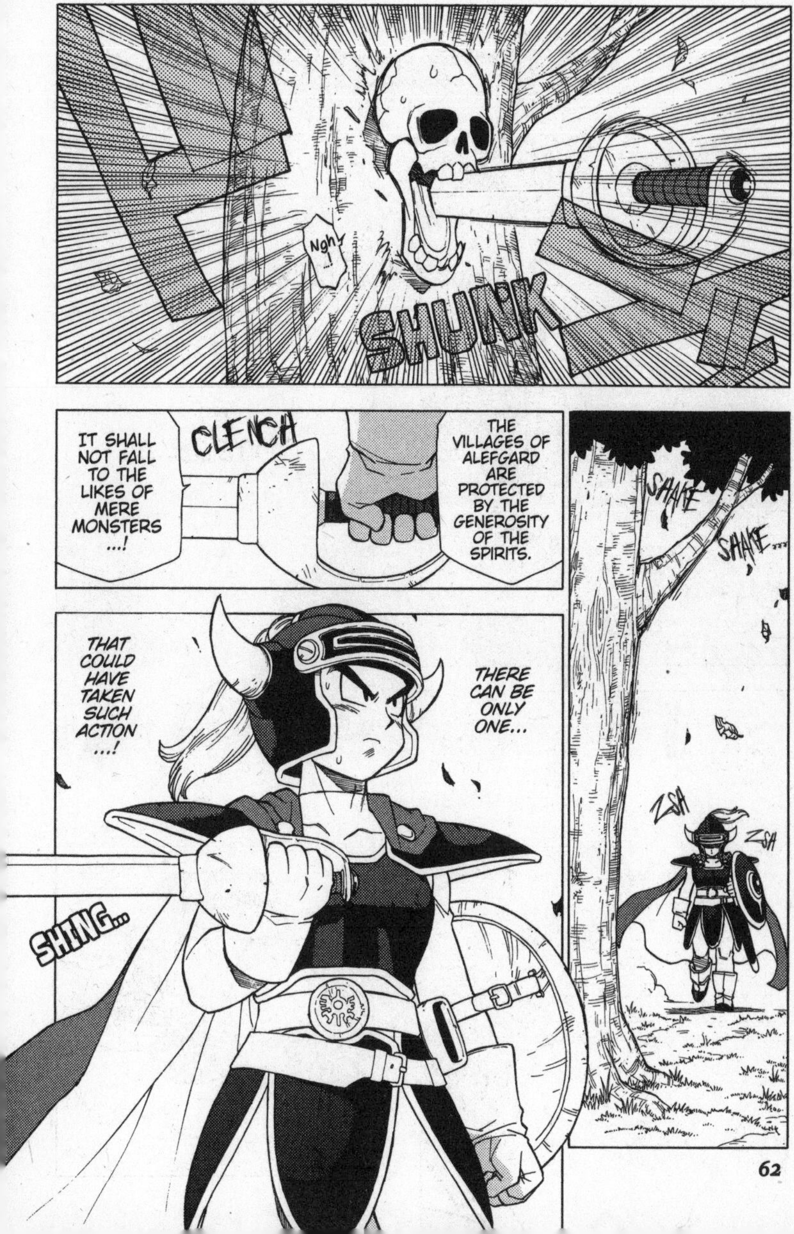
Ngh!
SHUNK
SHAKE
SHAKE...
ZSA
ZSA
THE VILLAGES OF ALEFGARD ARE PROTECTED BY THE GENEROSITY OF THE SPIRITS.
CLENCH
IT SHALL NOT FALL TO THE LIKES OF MERE MONSTERS ...!
THERE CAN BE ONLY ONE...
THAT COULD HAVE TAKEN SUCH ACTION ...!
SHING...

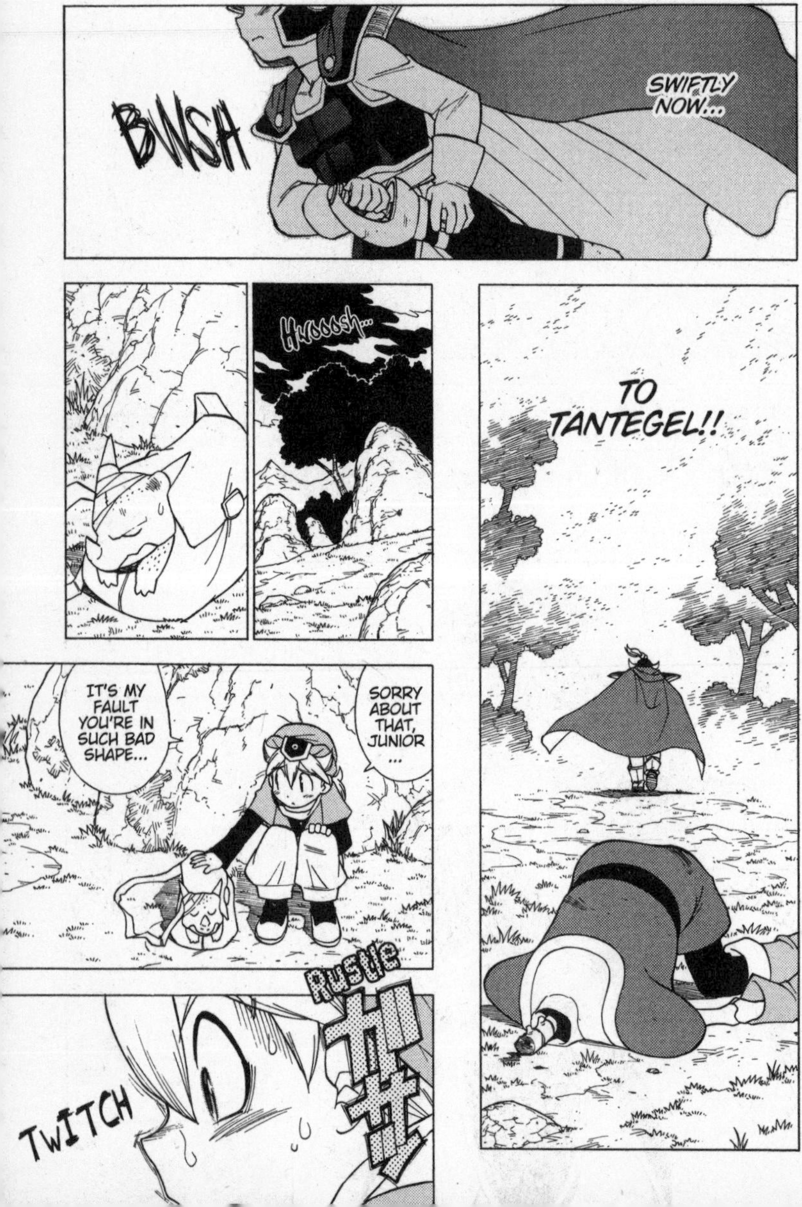
SWIFTLY NOW...
BWSH
TO TANTEGEL!!
Hwooosh...
SORRY ABOUT THAT, JUNIOR ...
IT'S MY FAULT YOU'RE IN SUCH BAD SHAPE...
RUSTLE
TWITCH

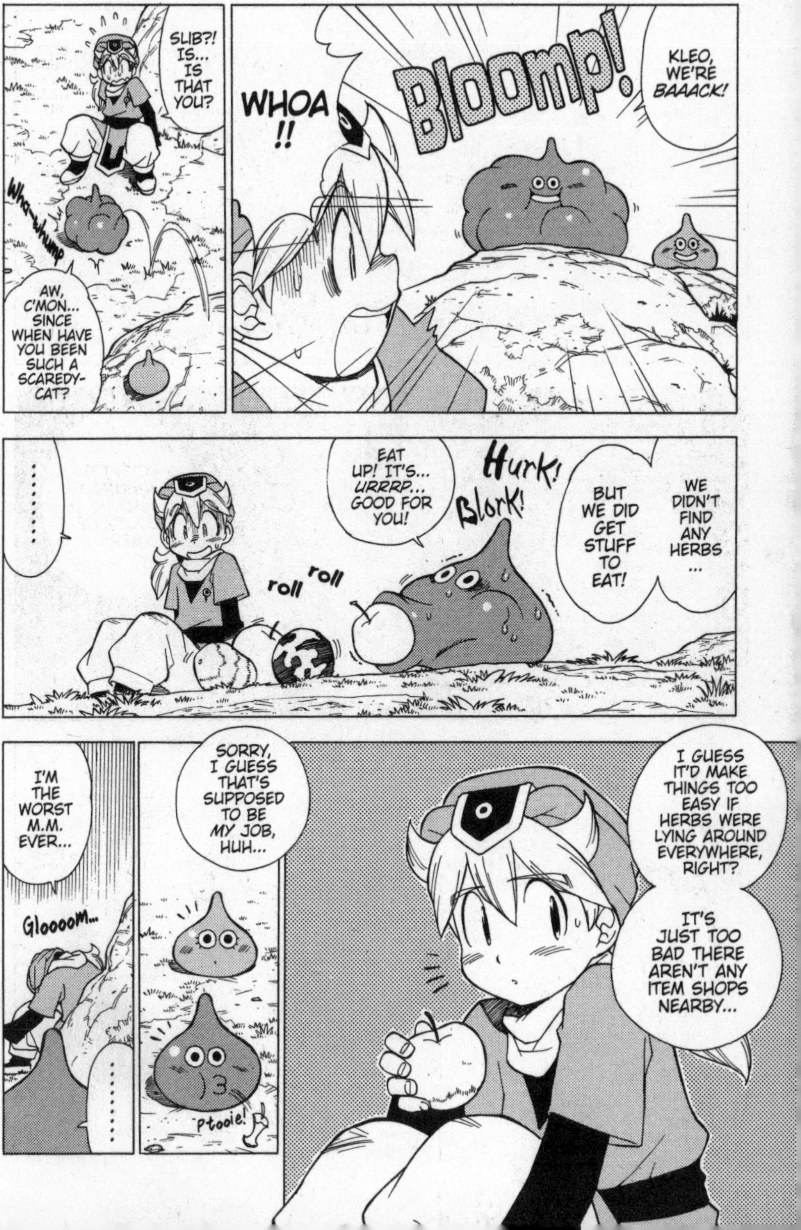
KLEO, WE'RE *BAAACK!*
Bloomp!
WHOA !!
SLIB?! IS... IS THAT YOU?
Wha-whump
AW, C'MON... SINCE WHEN HAVE YOU BEEN SUCH A SCAREDY-CAT?
WE DIDN'T FIND ANY HERBS ...
BUT WE DID GET STUFF TO EAT!
Hurk!
Blork!
EAT UP! IT'S... *URRRP*... GOOD FOR YOU!
roll
roll
....
I GUESS IT'D MAKE THINGS TOO EASY IF HERBS WERE LYING AROUND EVERYWHERE, RIGHT?
IT'S JUST TOO BAD THERE AREN'T ANY ITEM SHOPS NEARBY...
SORRY, I GUESS THAT'S SUPPOSED TO BE *MY* JOB, HUH...
ptooie!
I'M THE WORST M.M. EVER...
Gloooom...
....

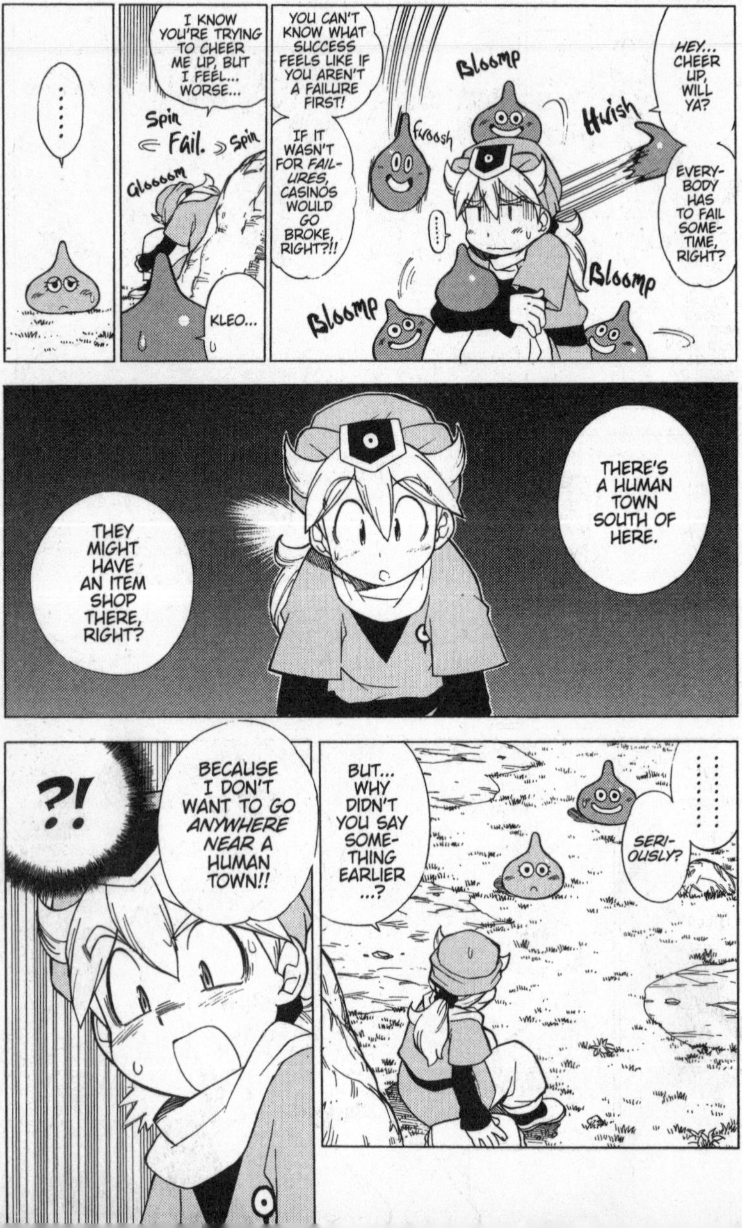
HEY... CHEER UP, WILL YA?
EVERYBODY HAS TO FAIL SOMETIME, RIGHT?
Hwish
Bloomp
YOU CAN'T KNOW WHAT SUCCESS FEELS LIKE IF YOU AREN'T A FAILURE FIRST!
IF IT WASN'T FOR FAILURES, CASINOS WOULD GO BROKE, RIGHT?!!
Froosh
...
Bloomp
Bloomp
I KNOW YOU'RE TRYING TO CHEER ME UP, BUT I FEEL... WORSE...
Spin
Fail.
Spin
Gloooom
KLEO...
......
THERE'S A HUMAN TOWN SOUTH OF HERE.
THEY MIGHT HAVE AN ITEM SHOP THERE, RIGHT?
......
SERIOUSLY?
BUT... WHY DIDN'T YOU SAY SOMETHING EARLIER...?
BECAUSE I DON'T WANT TO GO ANYWHERE NEAR A HUMAN TOWN!!
?!

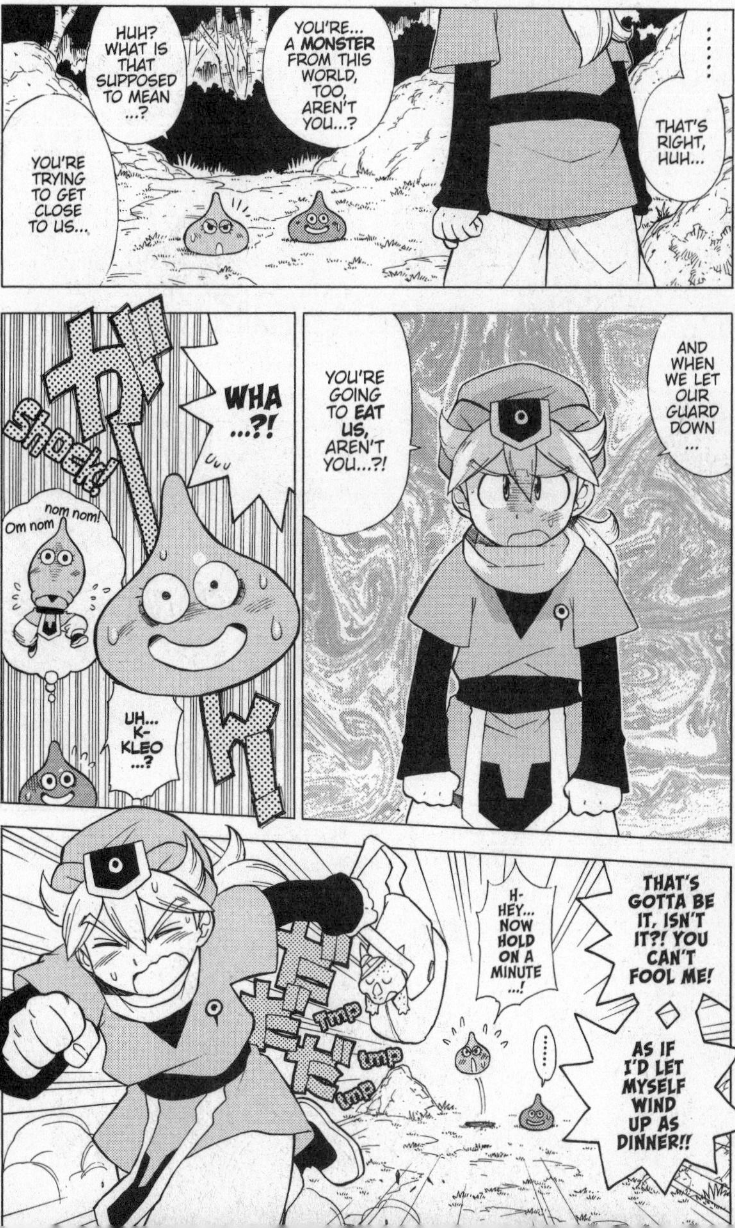
......
THAT'S RIGHT, HUH...
YOU'RE... A MONSTER FROM THIS WORLD, TOO, AREN'T YOU...?
HUH? WHAT IS THAT SUPPOSED TO MEAN...?
YOU'RE TRYING TO GET CLOSE TO US...
AND WHEN WE LET OUR GUARD DOWN...
YOU'RE GOING TO EAT US, AREN'T YOU...?!
WHA...?!
Shock!
Om nom
nom nom!
UH... K-KLEO...?
THAT'S GOTTA BE IT, ISN'T IT?! YOU CAN'T FOOL ME!
H-HEY... NOW HOLD ON A MINUTE...!
AS IF I'D LET MYSELF WIND UP AS DINNER!!
......
tmp
tmp
tmp

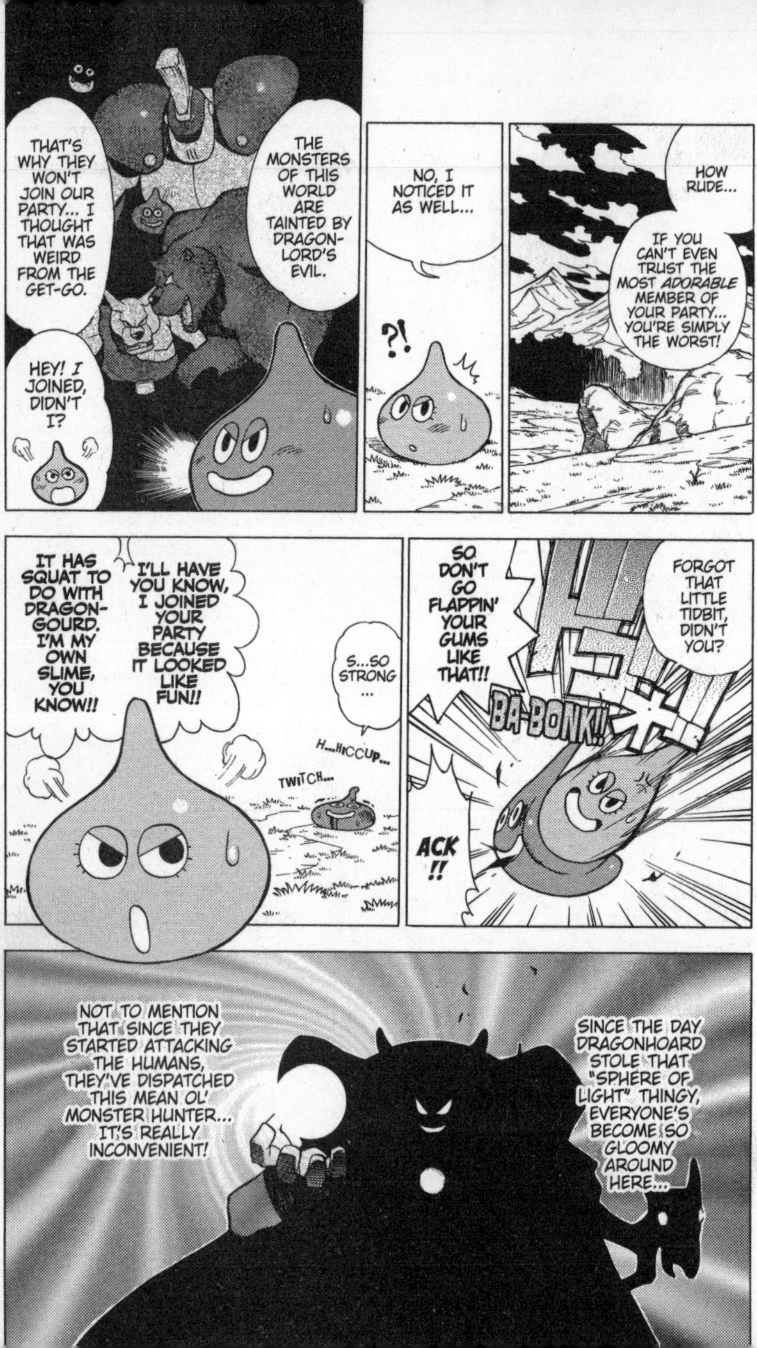
HOW RUDE...
IF YOU CAN'T EVEN TRUST THE MOST *ADORABLE* MEMBER OF YOUR PARTY... YOU'RE SIMPLY THE WORST!
NO, I NOTICED IT AS WELL...
?!
THE MONSTERS OF THIS WORLD ARE TAINTED BY DRAGONLORD'S EVIL.
THAT'S WHY THEY WON'T JOIN OUR PARTY... I THOUGHT THAT WAS WEIRD FROM THE GET-GO.
HEY! *I* JOINED, DIDN'T I?
FORGOT THAT LITTLE TIDBIT, DIDN'T YOU?
SO DON'T GO FLAPPIN' YOUR GUMS LIKE THAT!!
BA-BONK!!
ACK!!
I'LL HAVE YOU KNOW, I JOINED YOUR PARTY BECAUSE IT LOOKED LIKE FUN!!
IT HAS SQUAT TO DO WITH DRAGONGOURD. I'M MY OWN SLIME, YOU KNOW!!
S...SO STRONG...
H...HICCUP...
TWITCH...
SINCE THE DAY DRAGONHOARD STOLE THAT "SPHERE OF LIGHT" THINGY, EVERYONE'S BECOME SO GLOOMY AROUND HERE...
NOT TO MENTION THAT SINCE THEY STARTED ATTACKING THE HUMANS, THEY'VE DISPATCHED THIS MEAN OL' MONSTER HUNTER... IT'S REALLY INCONVENIENT!

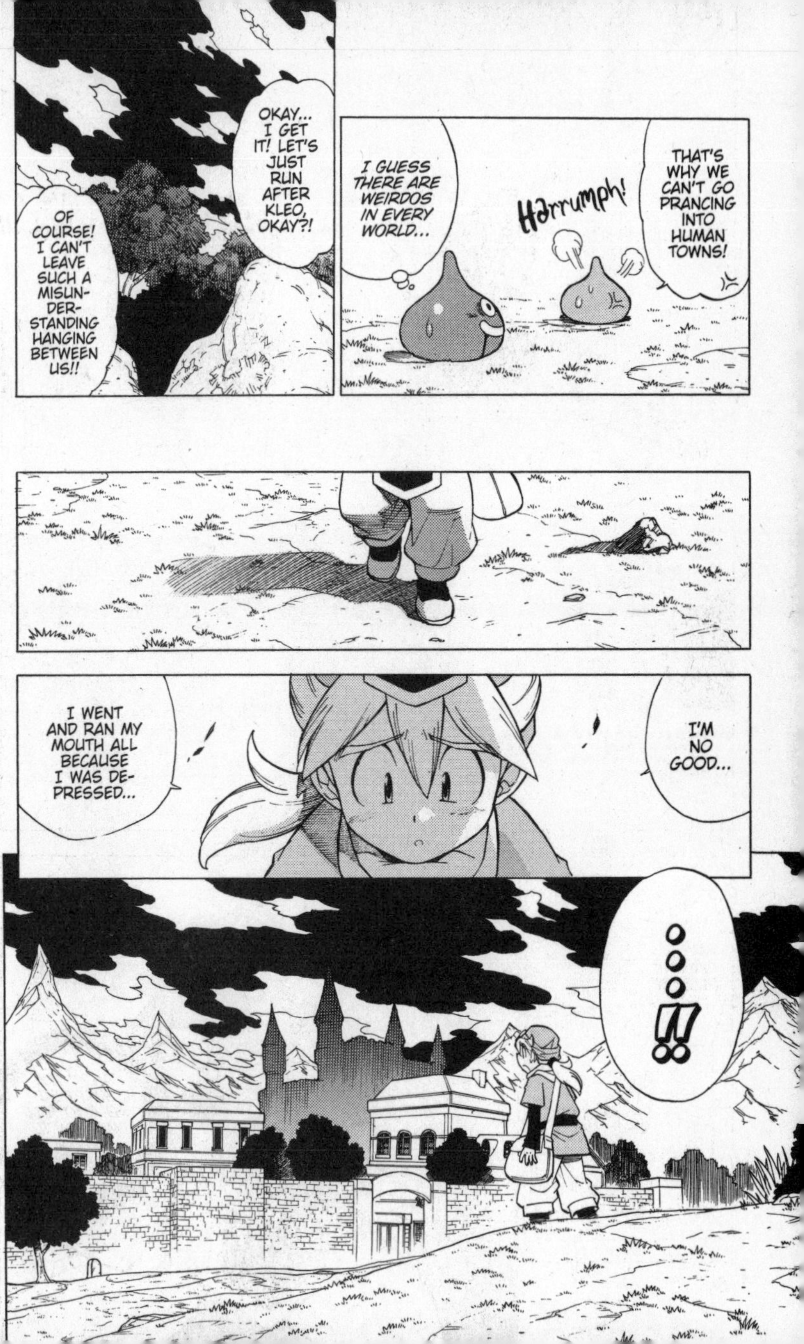
THAT'S WHY WE CAN'T GO PRANCING INTO HUMAN TOWNS!
Harrumph!
I GUESS THERE ARE WEIRDOS IN EVERY WORLD...
OKAY... I GET IT! LET'S JUST RUN AFTER KLEO, OKAY?!
OF COURSE! I CAN'T LEAVE SUCH A MISUNDERSTANDING HANGING BETWEEN US!!
I'M NO GOOD...
I WENT AND RAN MY MOUTH ALL BECAUSE I WAS DEPRESSED...
...?!

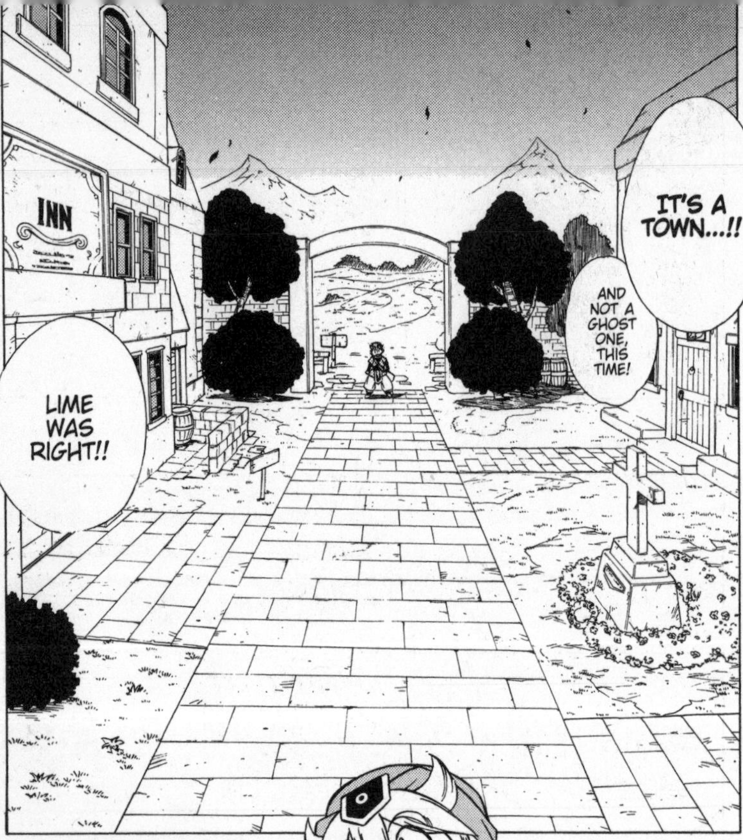
IT'S A TOWN...!!
AND NOT A GHOST ONE, THIS TIME!
LIME WAS RIGHT!!
INN

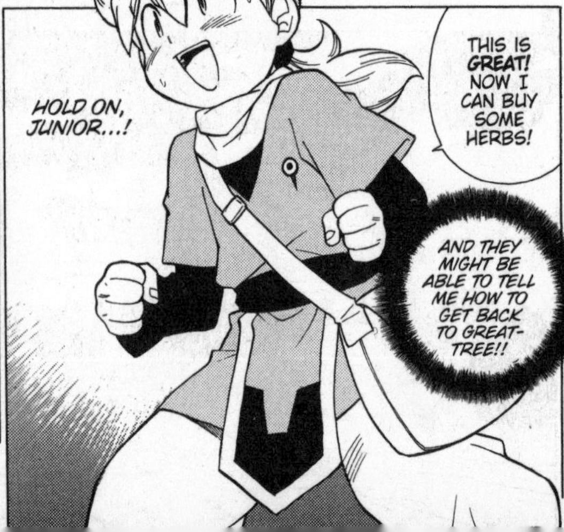
THIS IS GREAT! NOW I CAN BUY SOME HERBS!
AND THEY MIGHT BE ABLE TO TELL ME HOW TO GET BACK TO GREAT-TREE!!
HOLD ON, JUNIOR...!

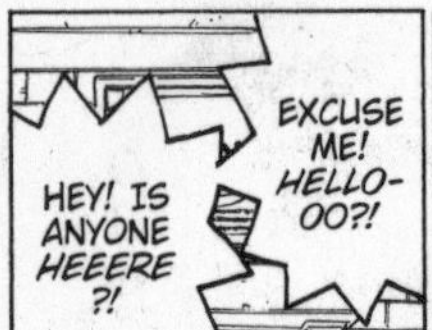
EXCUSE ME! HELLO-OO?!
HEY! IS ANYONE HEEERE?!

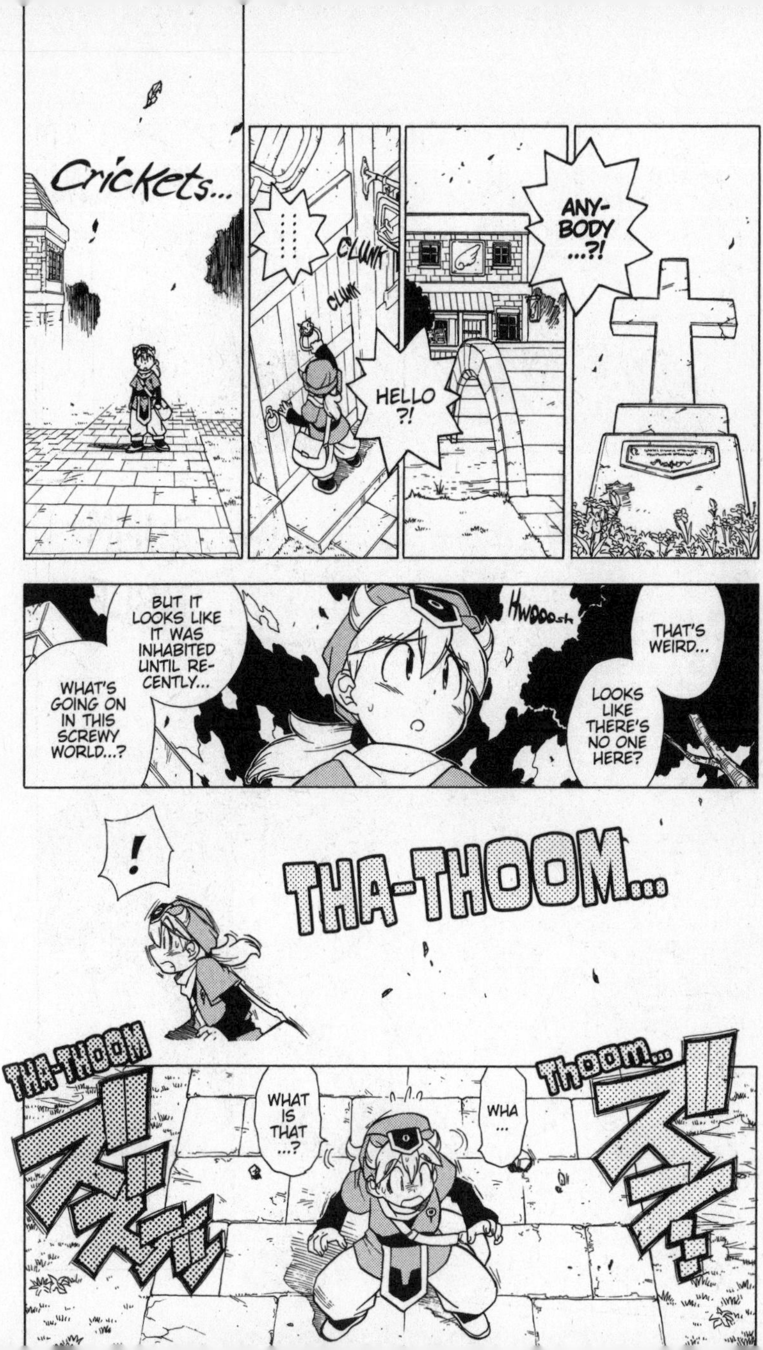
ANY-BODY ...?!
HELLO ?!
......
CLUNK
CLUNK
Crickets...
THAT'S WEIRD...
LOOKS LIKE THERE'S NO ONE HERE?
HWOOOsh
BUT IT LOOKS LIKE IT WAS INHABITED UNTIL RE-CENTLY...
WHAT'S GOING ON IN THIS SCREWY WORLD...?
THA-THOOM...
!
Thoom...
WHA ...
WHAT IS THAT ...?
THA-THOOM

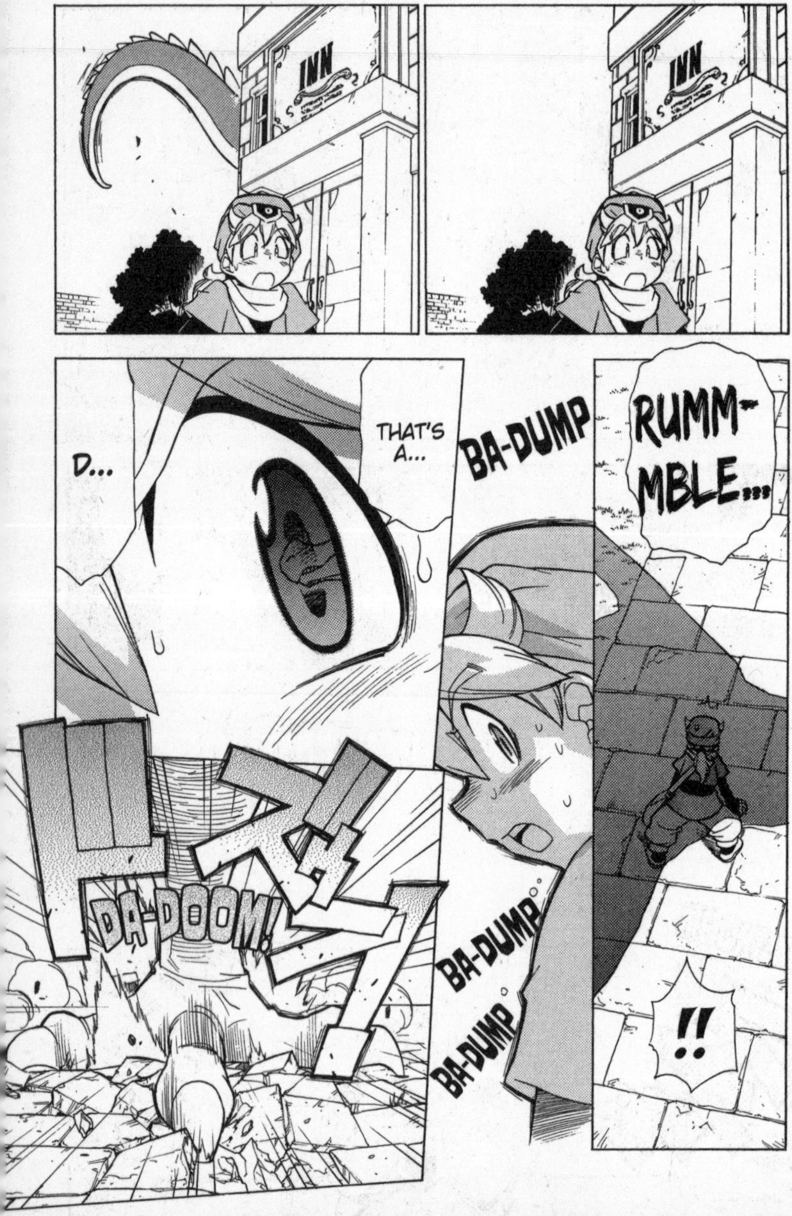
INN
INN
RUMM-
MBLE...
!!
BA-DUMP
THAT'S A...
D...
BA-DUMP
BA-DUMP
DA-DOOM!

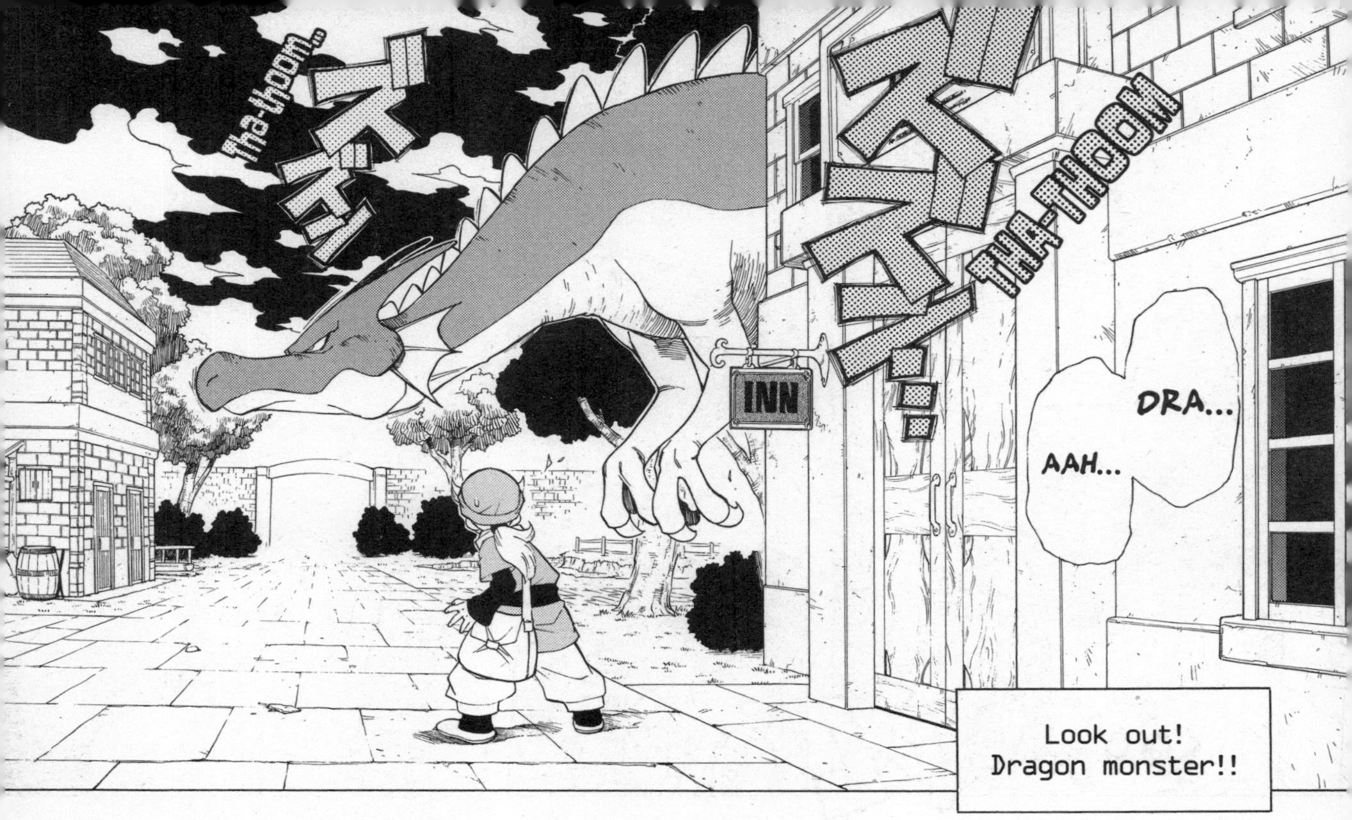
THA-THOOM
AAH... DRA...
Look out! Dragon monster!!
INN
Tha-thoom...

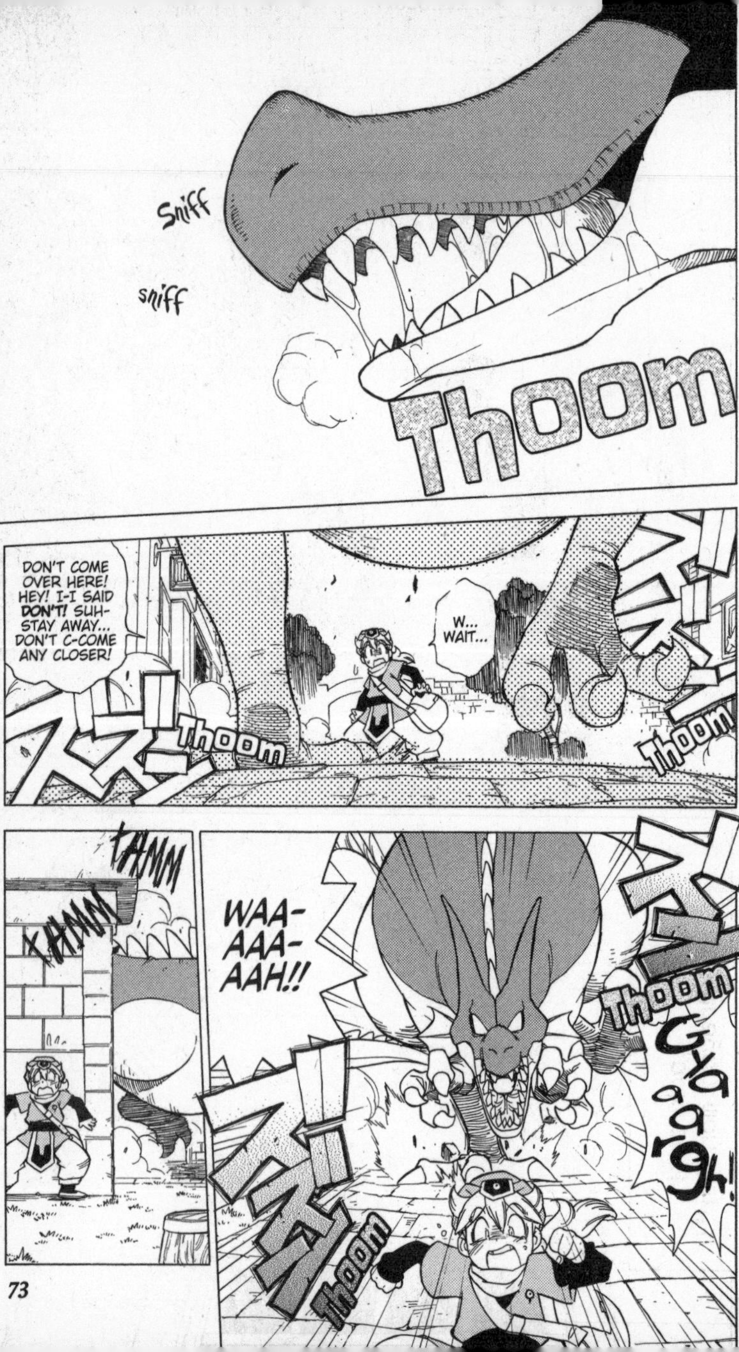
Sniff
sniff
Thoom
W... WAIT...
Thoom
DON'T COME OVER HERE! HEY! I-I SAID **DON'T!** SUH-STAY AWAY... DON'T C-COME ANY CLOSER!
Thoom
WAA-AAA-AAH!!
Thoom
Gyaaaargh!
Thoom
TAMM
TAMM

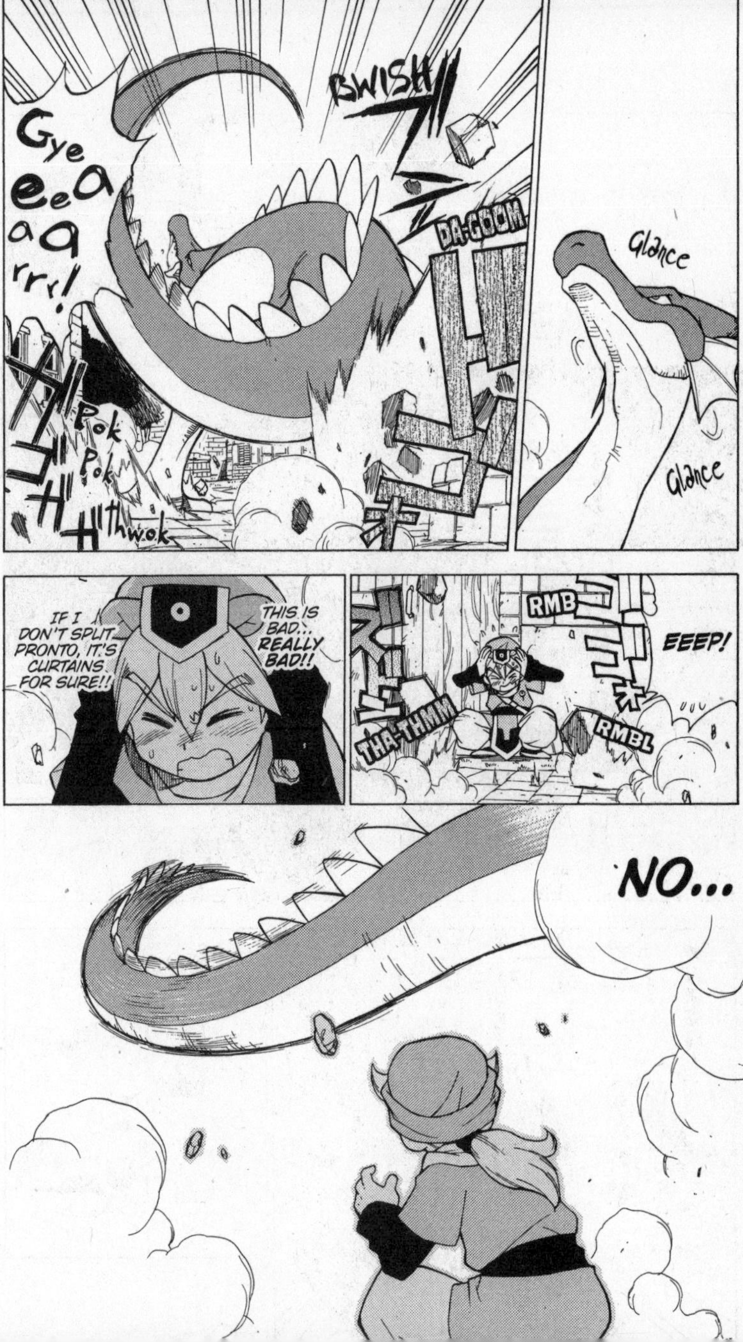
Glance
Glance
BWISH
DA-GOOM
Gyeeeaaarrr!
Pok
Pok
Thwok
RMB
EEEP!
THA-THMM
RMBL
THIS IS BAD... REALLY BAD!!
IF I DON'T SPLIT PRONTO, IT'S CURTAINS FOR SURE!!
NO...

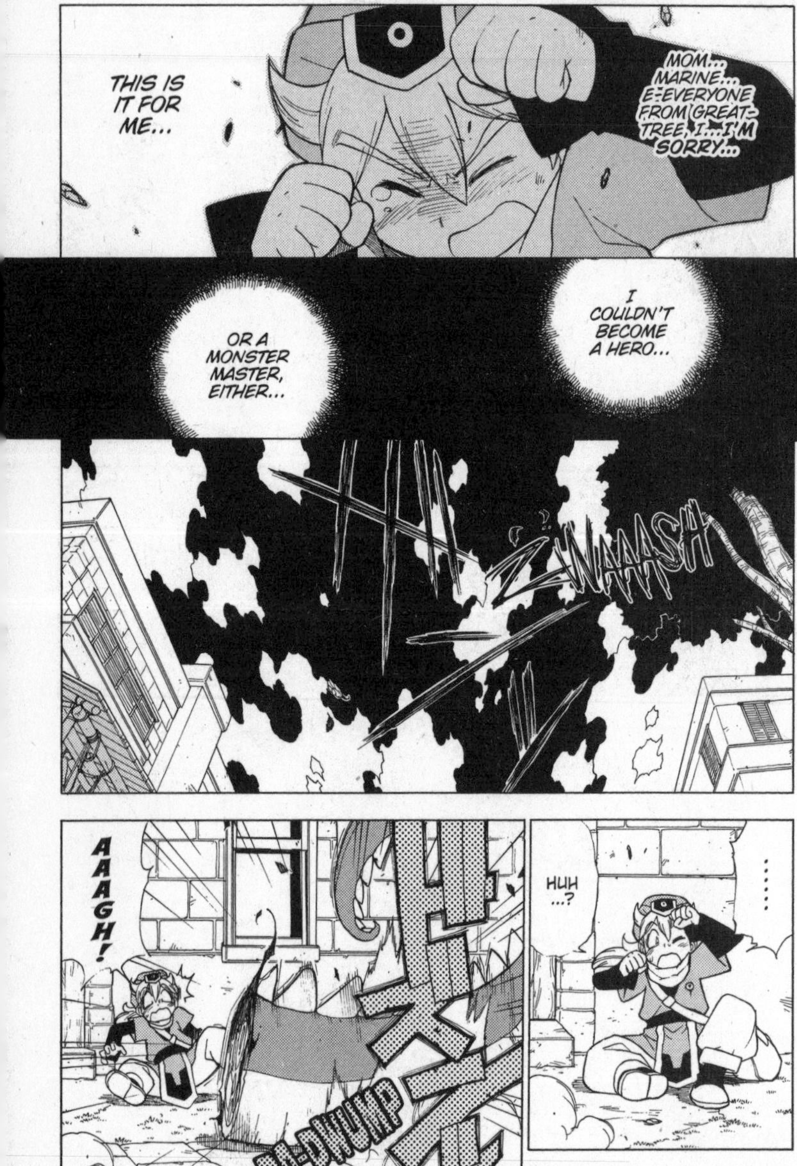
MOM... MARINE... E-EVERYONE FROM GREAT-TREE, I...I'M SORRY...
THIS IS IT FOR ME...
I COULDN'T BECOME A HERO...
OR A MONSTER MASTER, EITHER...
ZWAAASH
......
HUH ...?
DA-DWUMP
AAAGH!

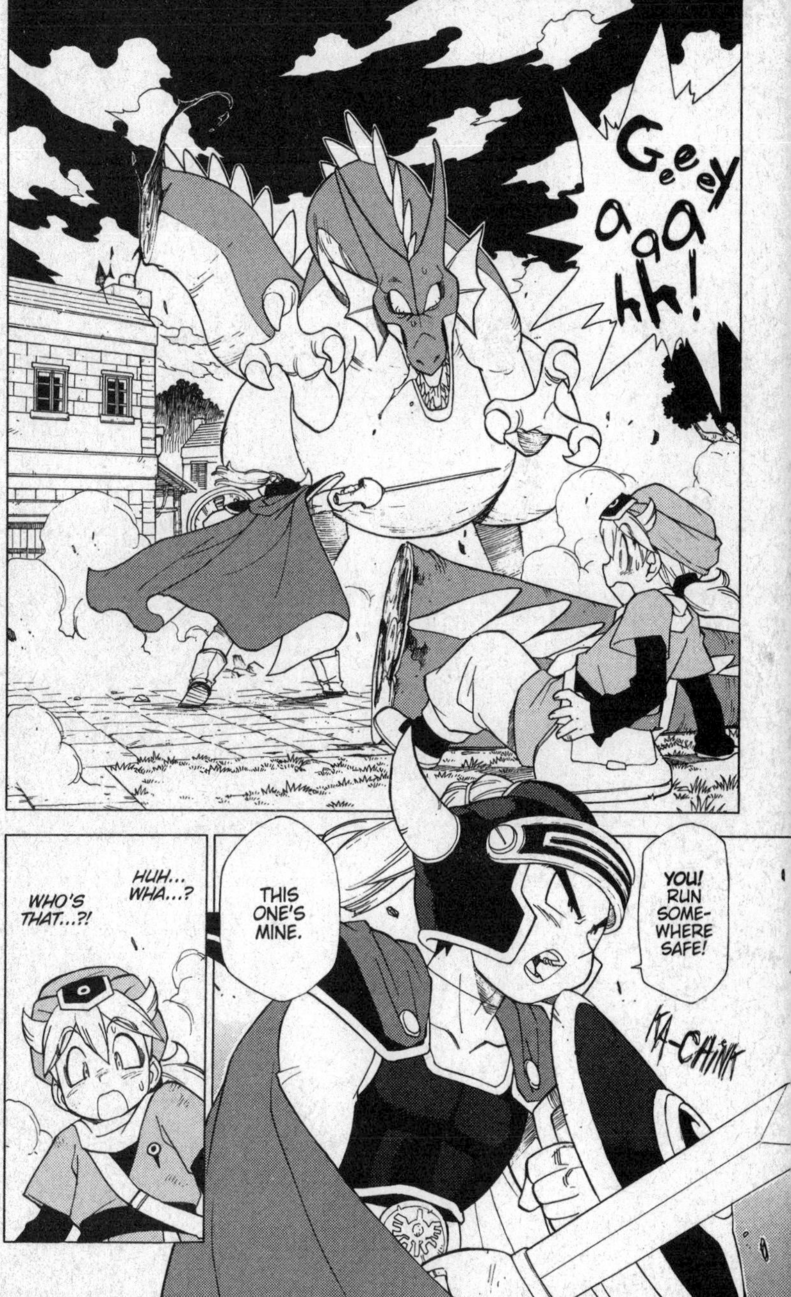
Geeeyaaahh!
YOU! RUN SOMEWHERE SAFE!
THIS ONE'S MINE.
KA-CHINK
HUH... WHA...?
WHO'S THAT...?!

DRAGON QUEST MONSTERS +

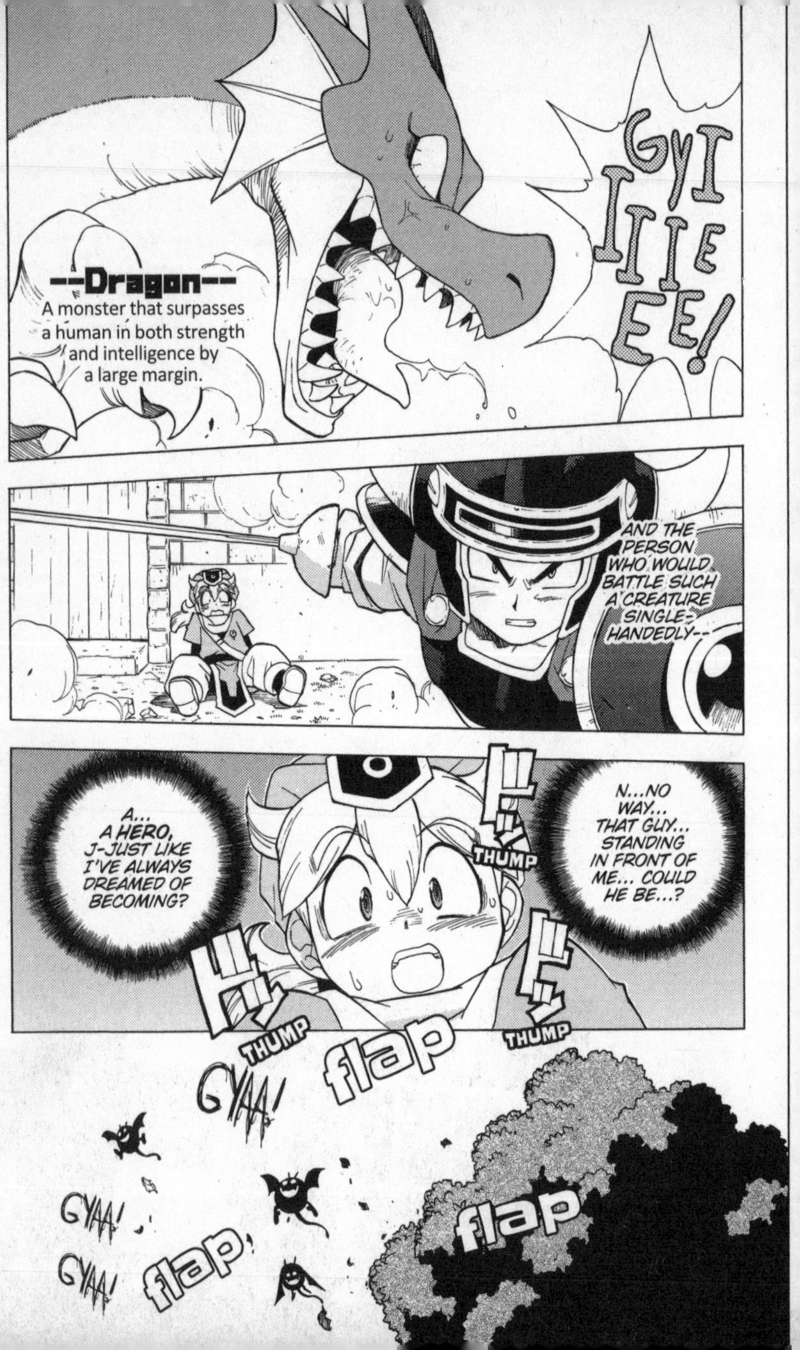
GYIIIEEE!
--Dragon--
A monster that surpasses a human in both strength and intelligence by a large margin.
AND THE PERSON WHO WOULD BATTLE SUCH A CREATURE SINGLE-HANDEDLY--
N...NO WAY... THAT GUY... STANDING IN FRONT OF ME... COULD HE BE...?
THUMP
A... A HERO, J-JUST LIKE I'VE ALWAYS DREAMED OF BECOMING?
THUMP
THUMP
flap
GYAA!
flap
GYAA!
GYAA!
flap

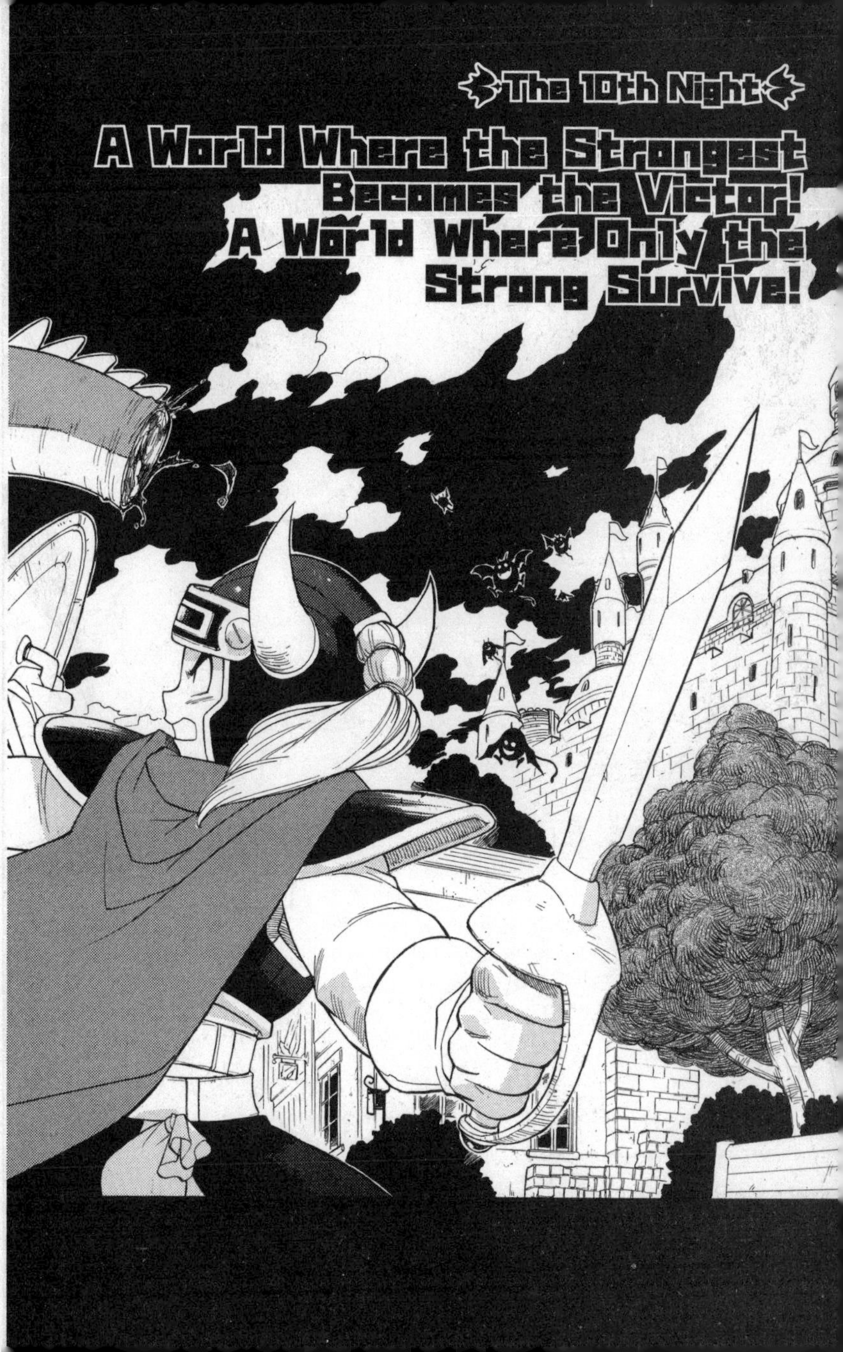
The 10th Night
A World Where the Strongest Becomes the Victor! A World Where Only the Strong Survive!

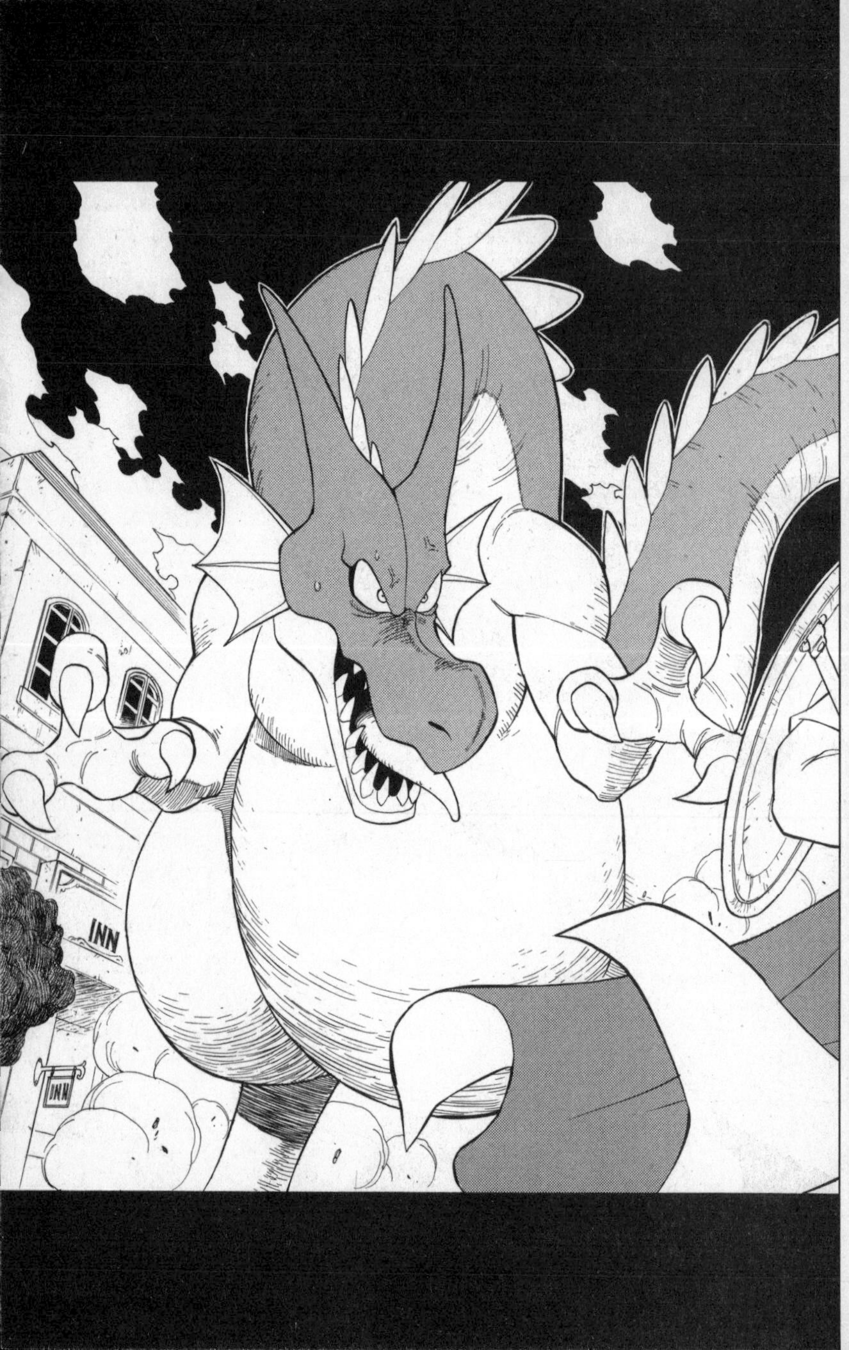
INN
INN

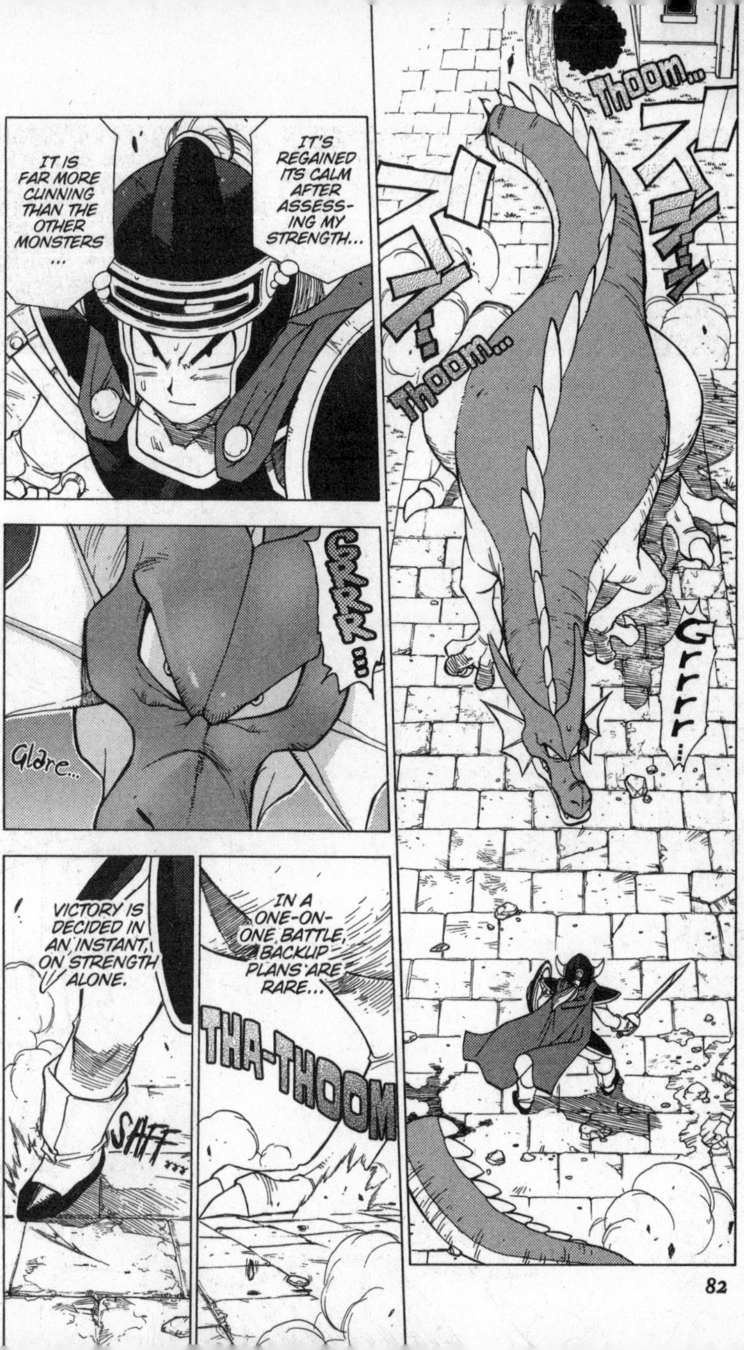
Thoom...
Thoom...
Grrrr...
IT'S REGAINED ITS CALM AFTER ASSESSING MY STRENGTH...
IT IS FAR MORE CUNNING THAN THE OTHER MONSTERS ...
GRRR...
Glare...
IN A ONE-ON-ONE BATTLE, BACKUP PLANS ARE RARE...
THA-THOOM
VICTORY IS DECIDED IN AN INSTANT, ON STRENGTH ALONE.
SAFF

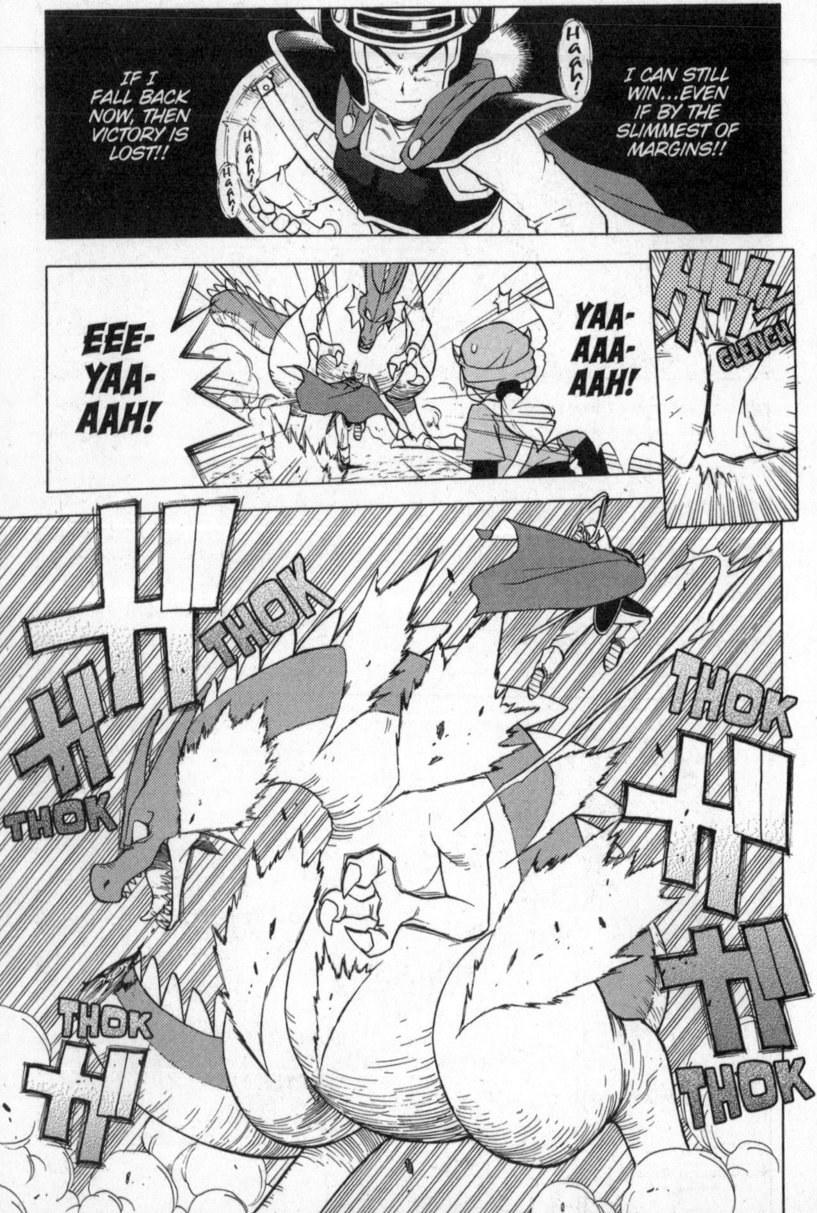

Haah!
I CAN STILL WIN...EVEN IF BY THE SLIMMEST OF MARGINS!!
Haah!
Haah!
IF I FALL BACK NOW, THEN VICTORY IS LOST!!
CLENCH
YAA-AAA-AAH!
EEE-YAA-AAH!
THOK
THOK
THOK
THOK
THOK

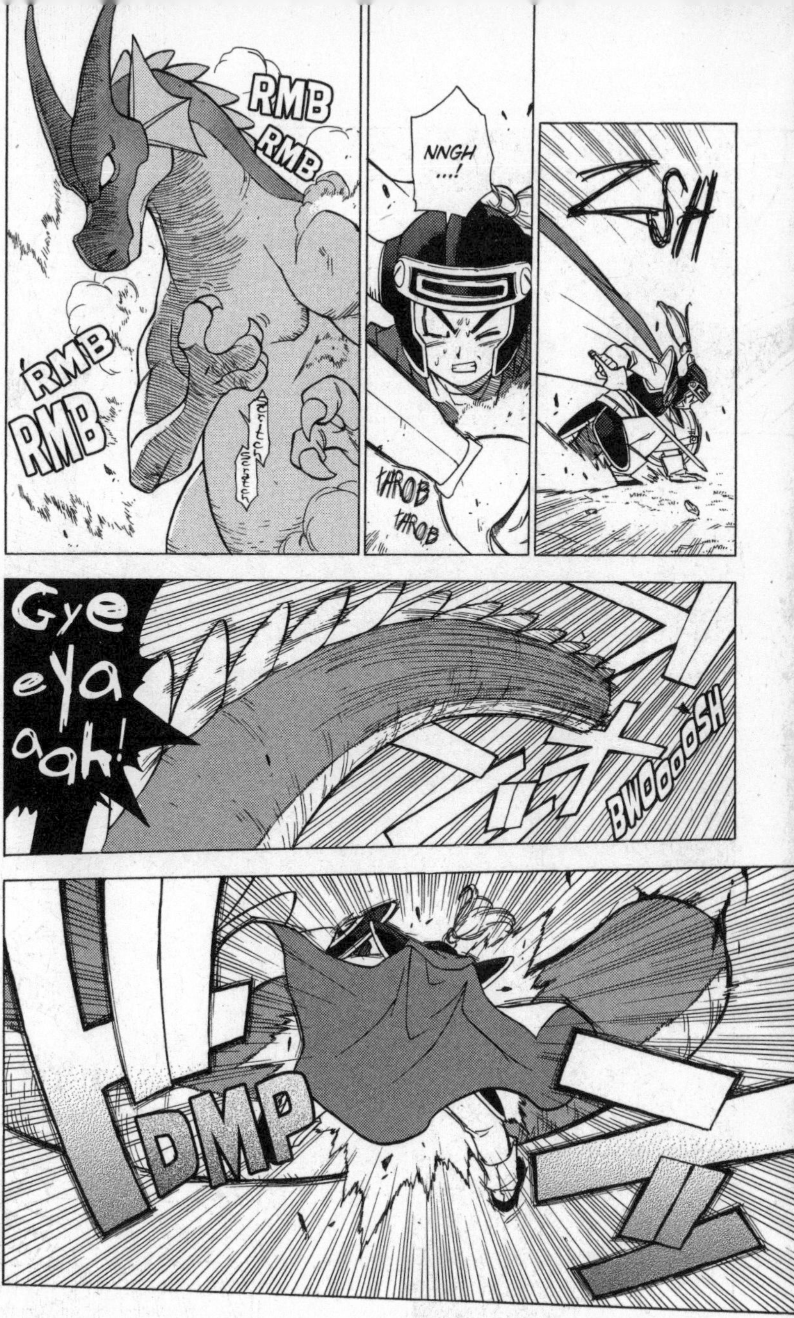
ZSH
NNGH ...!
THROB THROB
RMB RMB
RMB RMB
Gye eya aah!
BWOoooSH
DMP

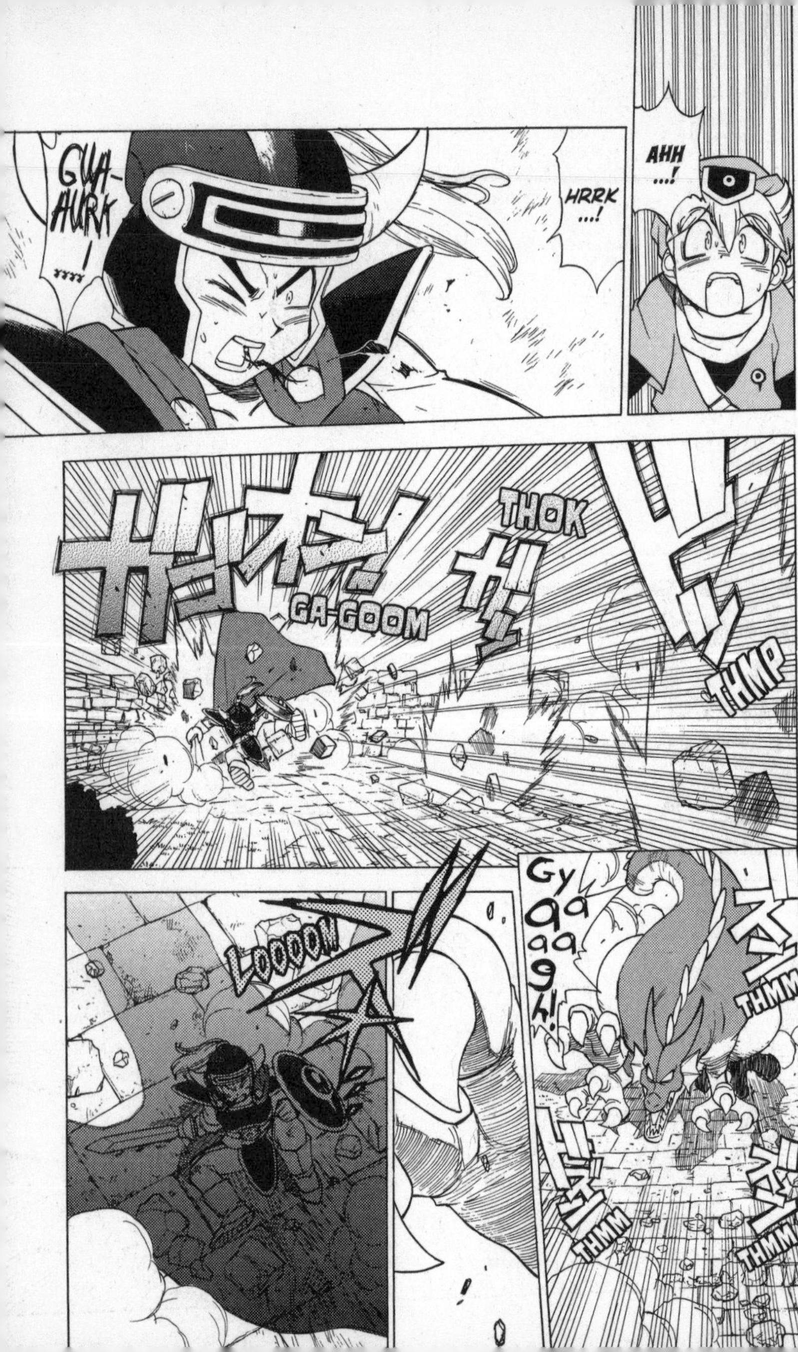
AHH ...!
HRRK ...!
GUA-HURK!
THOK
THMP
GA-GOOM
Gyaaaaaagh!
THMM
THMM
THMM
LOOOOM

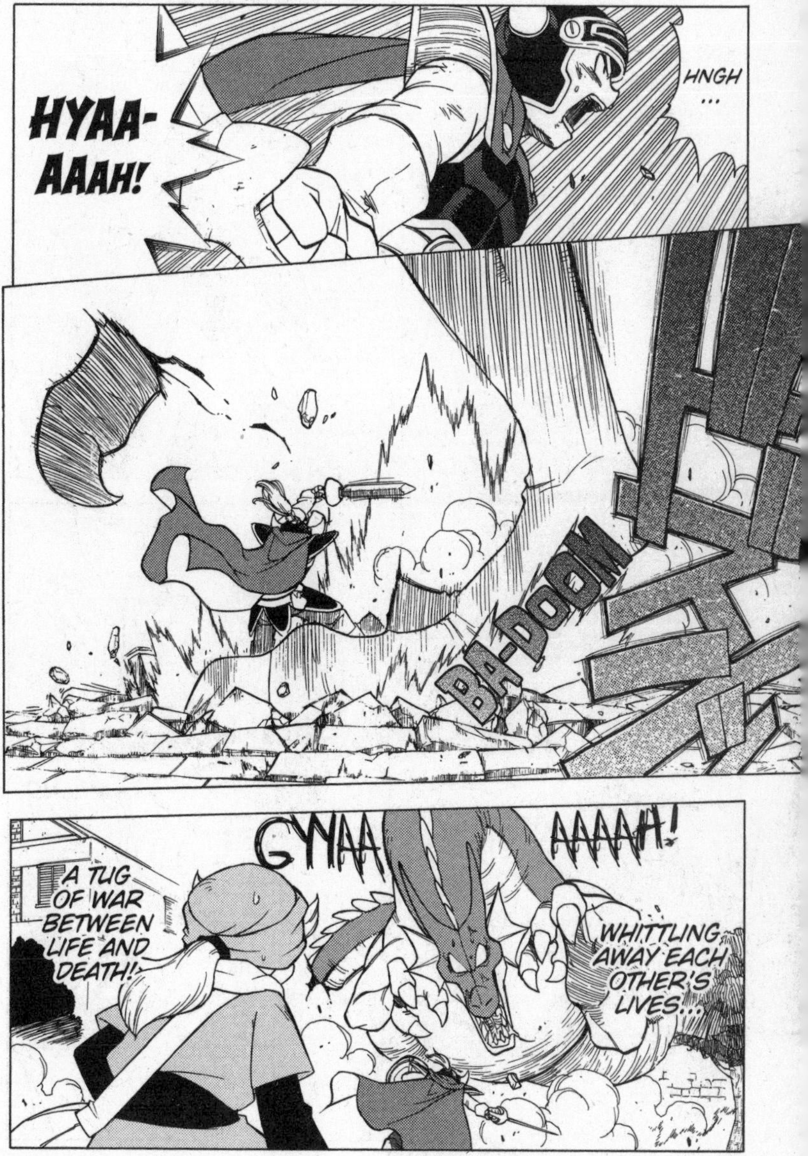
HNGH ...
HYAA-AAAH!
BA-DOOM
GYAA AAAAH!
WHITTLING AWAY EACH OTHER'S LIVES...
A TUG OF WAR BETWEEN LIFE AND DEATH!

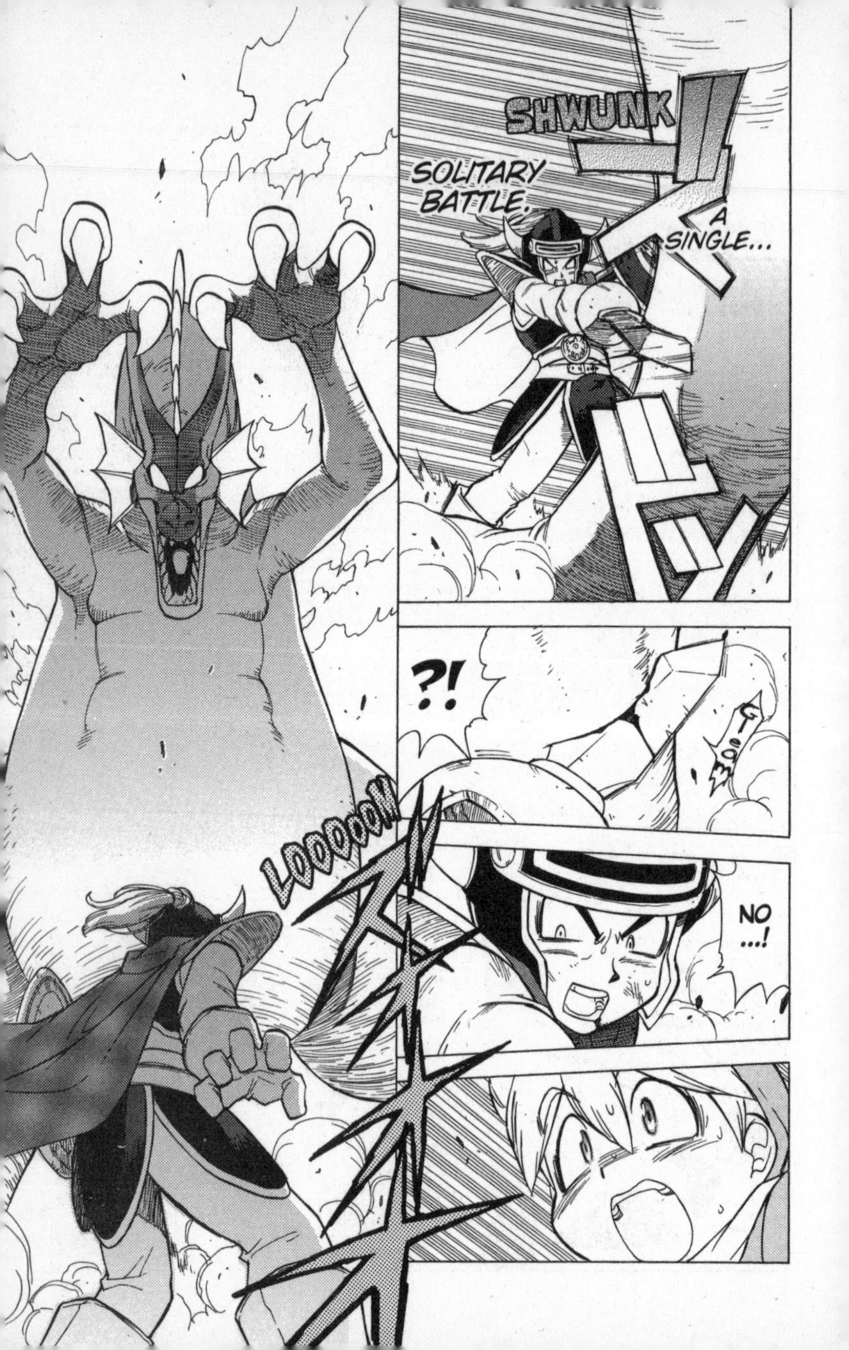
SHWUNK
A SINGLE...
SOLITARY BATTLE.
?!
NO ...!
LOOOOOM!!

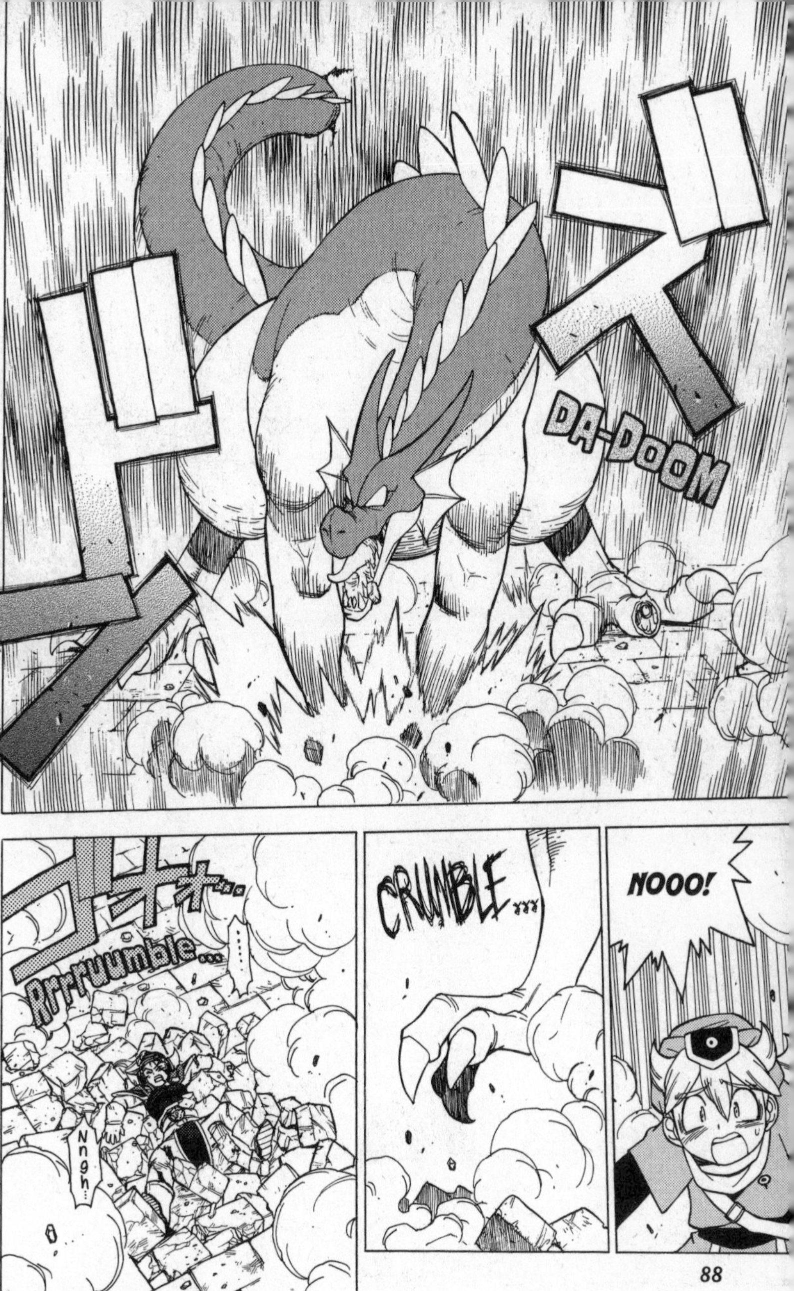
DA-DOOM
NOOO!
CRUMBLE...
Rrrruumble...
Nngh...

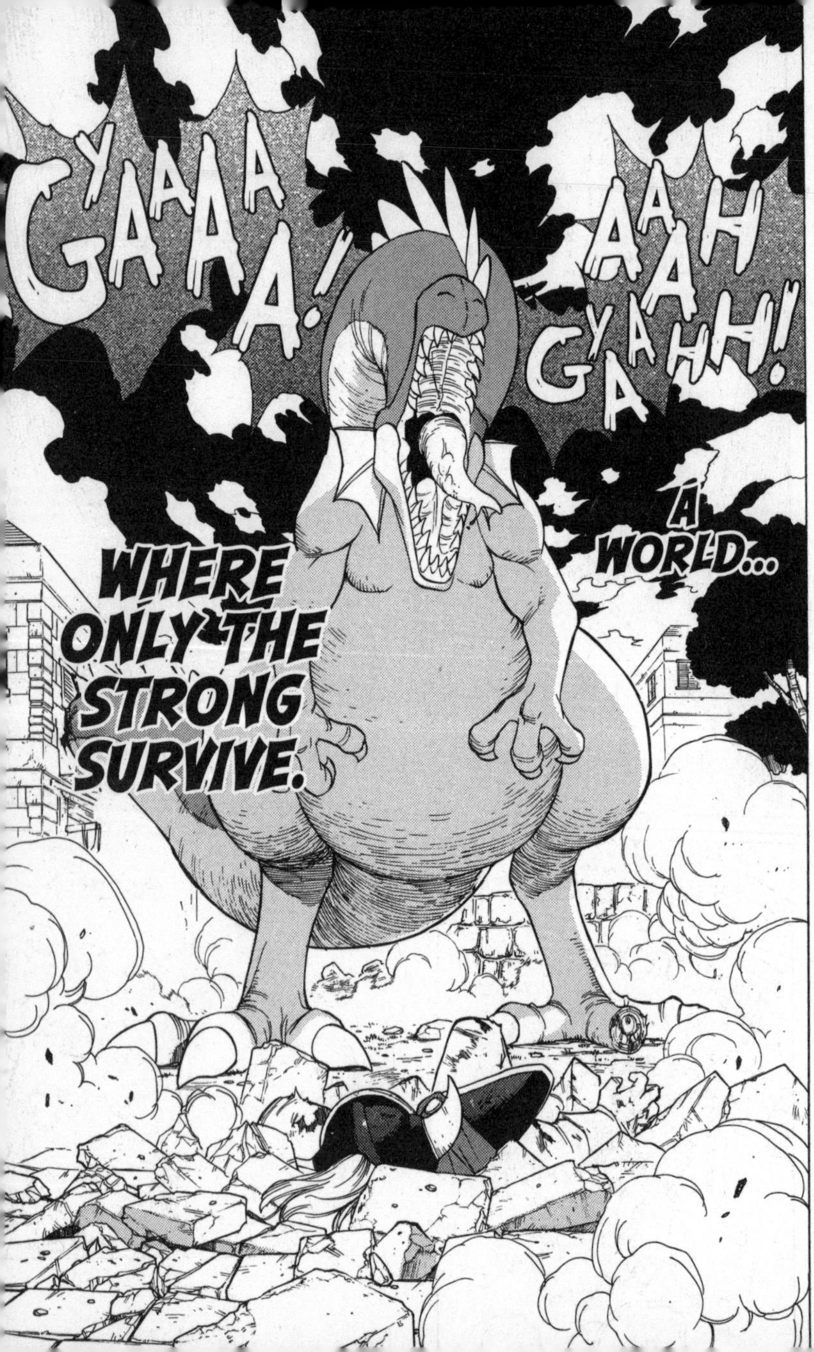
AAH AAH GYAHH! A
A WORLD...
GYAAAA AAA!
WHERE ONLY THE STRONG SURVIVE.

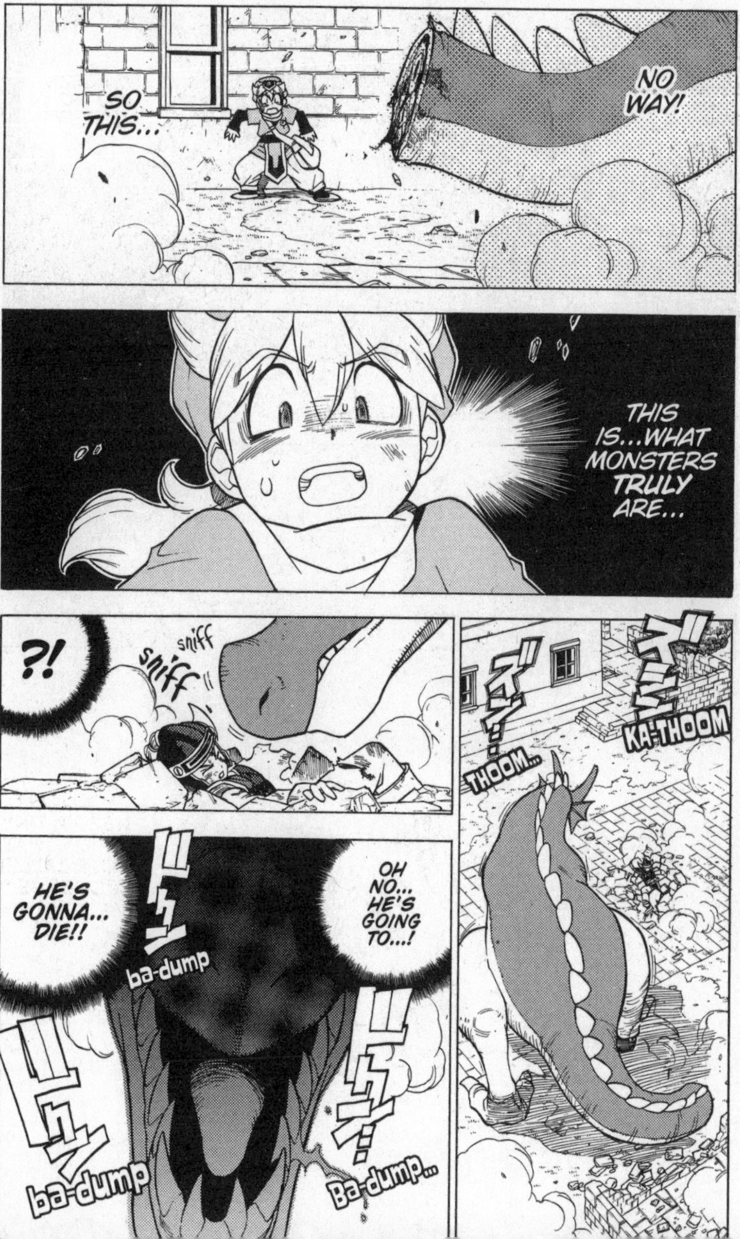
NO WAY!
SO THIS...
THIS IS...WHAT MONSTERS TRULY ARE...
KA-THOOM
THOOM...
sniff
sniff
?!
OH NO... HE'S GOING TO...!
HE'S GONNA... DIE!!
ba-dump
Ba-dump...
ba-dump

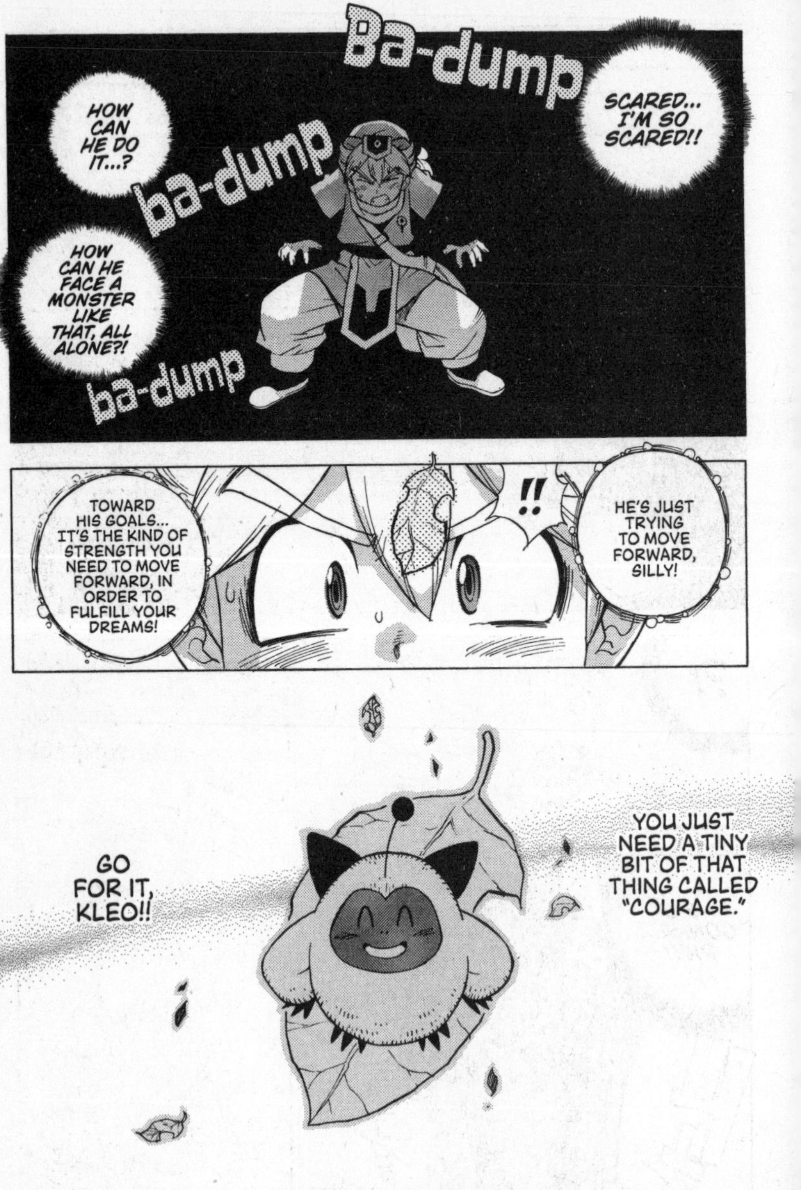

SCARED... I'M SO SCARED!!
Ba-dump
HOW CAN HE DO IT...?
ba-dump
HOW CAN HE FACE A MONSTER LIKE THAT, ALL ALONE?!
ba-dump
HE'S JUST TRYING TO MOVE FORWARD, SILLY!
!!
TOWARD HIS GOALS... IT'S THE KIND OF STRENGTH YOU NEED TO MOVE FORWARD, IN ORDER TO FULFILL YOUR DREAMS!
YOU JUST NEED A TINY BIT OF THAT THING CALLED "COURAGE."
GO FOR IT, KLEO!!

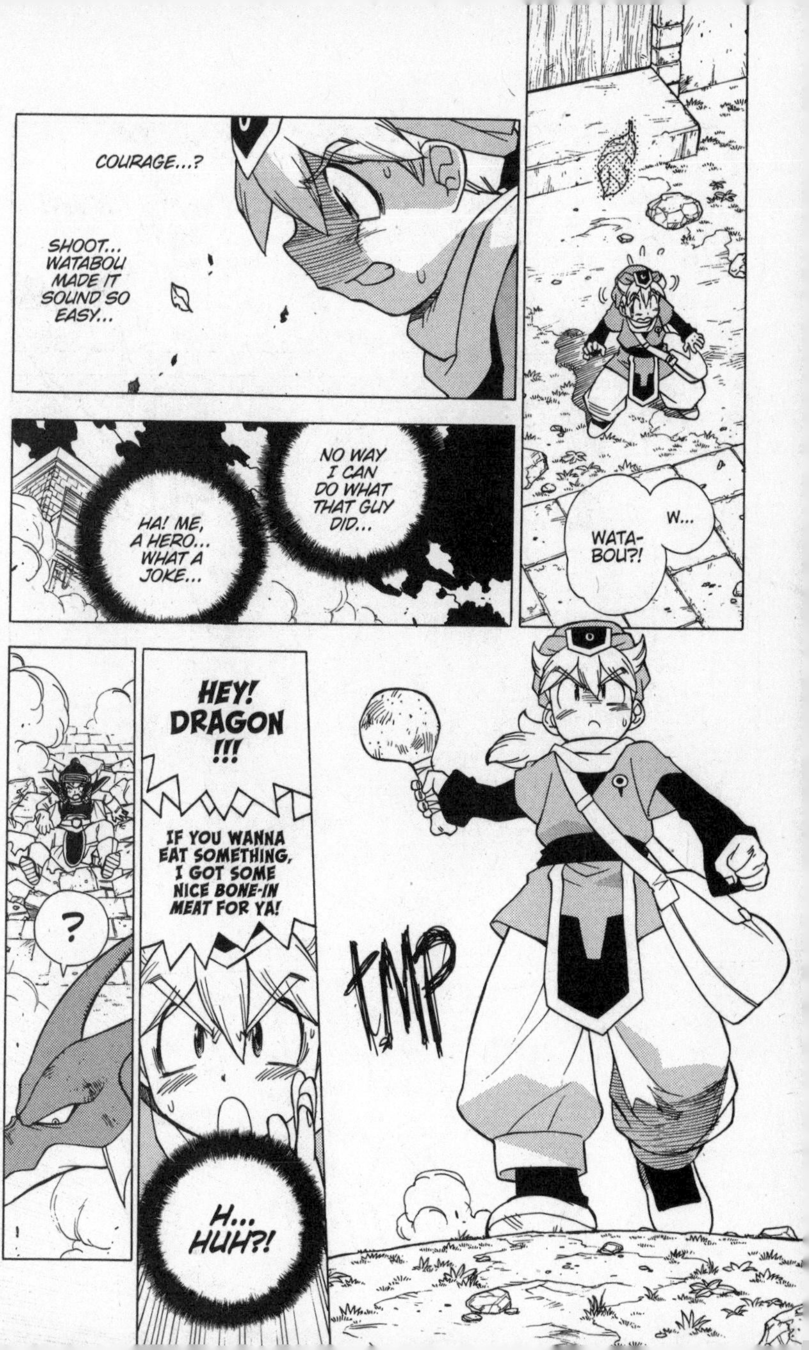
W... WATA-BOU?!
COURAGE...?
SHOOT... WATABOU MADE IT SOUND SO EASY...
NO WAY I CAN DO WHAT THAT GUY DID...
HA! ME, A HERO... WHAT A JOKE...
TMP
HEY! DRAGON!!!
IF YOU WANNA EAT SOMETHING, I GOT SOME NICE BONE-IN MEAT FOR YA!
H... HUH?!
?

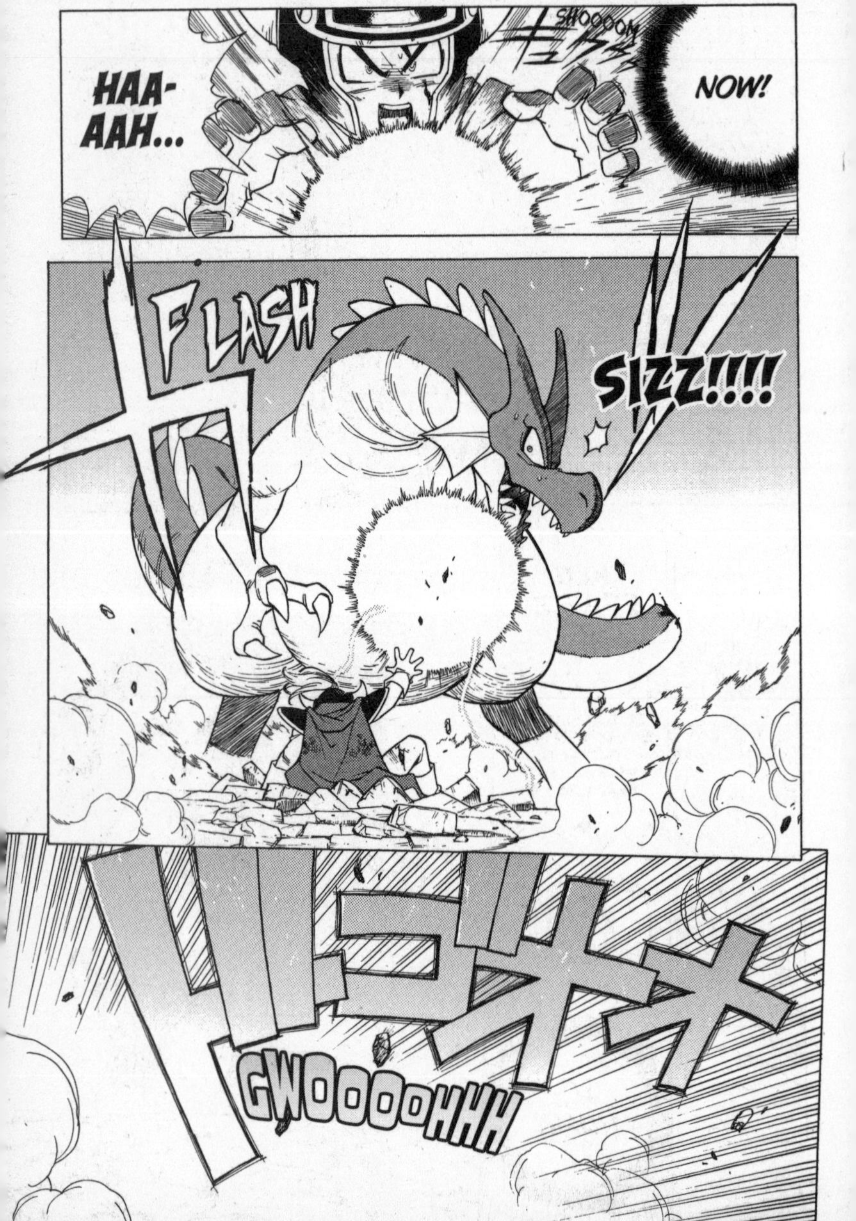
NOW!
SHOOOOM
HAA-
AAH...
SIZZ!!!!
FLASH
GWOOOOOHHH

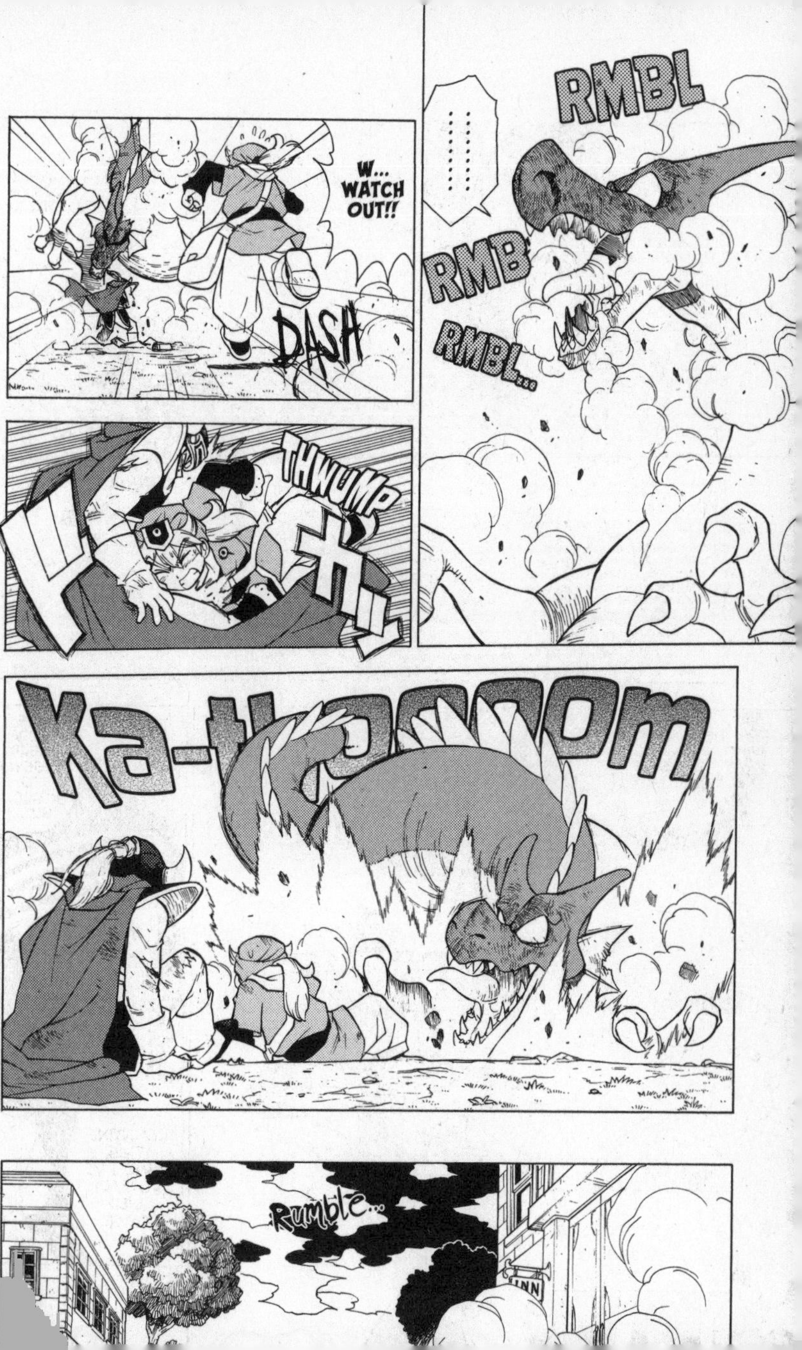
......
RMBL
RMB
RMBL...
W... WATCH OUT!!
DASH
THWUMP
Ka-t oooom
Rumble...
INN

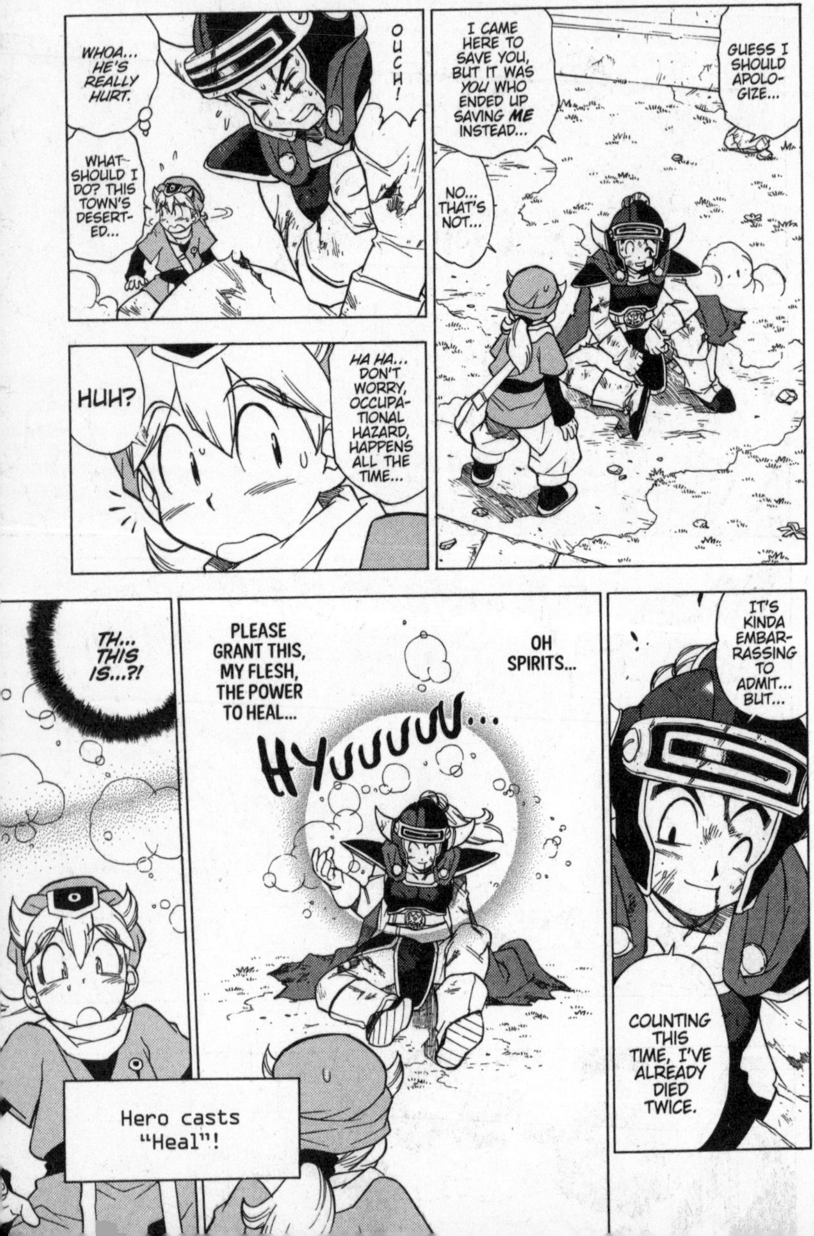
GUESS I SHOULD APOLO-GIZE...
I CAME HERE TO SAVE YOU, BUT IT WAS YOU WHO ENDED UP SAVING ME INSTEAD...
NO... THAT'S NOT...
OUCH!
WHOA... HE'S REALLY HURT.
WHAT-SHOULD I DO? THIS TOWN'S DESERT-ED...
HA HA... DON'T WORRY, OCCUPA-TIONAL HAZARD, HAPPENS ALL THE TIME...
HUH?
IT'S KINDA EMBAR-RASSING TO ADMIT... BUT...
COUNTING THIS TIME, I'VE ALREADY DIED TWICE.
OH SPIRITS...
PLEASE GRANT THIS, MY FLESH, THE POWER TO HEAL...
HYUUUUN...
TH... THIS IS...?!
Hero casts "Heal"!

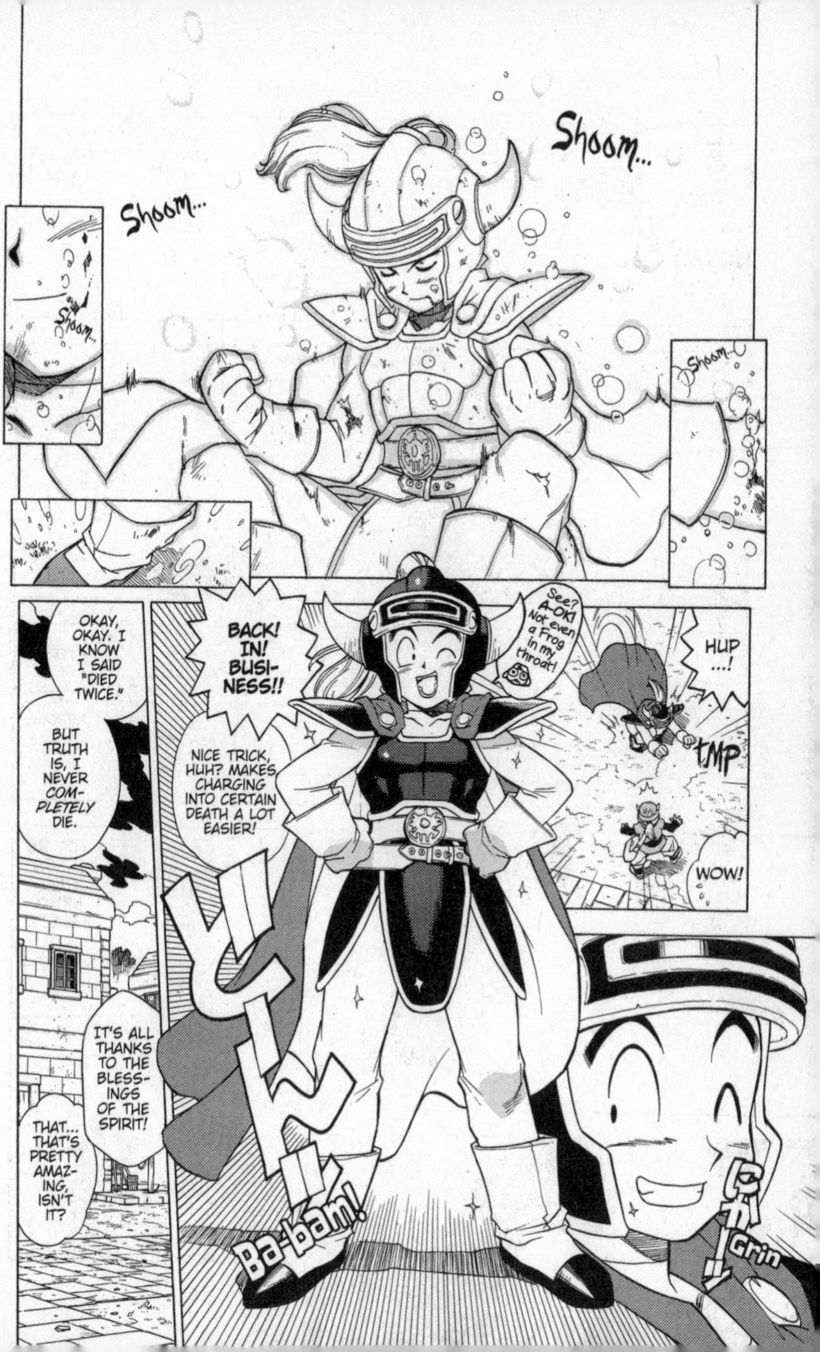

Shoom...
Shoom...
Shoom...
Shoom...
See? A-OK! Not even a Frog in my throat!
HUP ...!
TMP
WOW!
Grin
BACK! IN! BUSI-NESS!!
NICE TRICK, HUH? MAKES CHARGING INTO CERTAIN DEATH A LOT EASIER!
Ba-bam!
OKAY, OKAY. I KNOW I SAID "DIED TWICE."
BUT TRUTH IS, I NEVER COM-PLETELY DIE.
IT'S ALL THANKS TO THE BLESS-INGS OF THE SPIRIT!
THAT... THAT'S PRETTY AMAZ-ING, ISN'T IT?

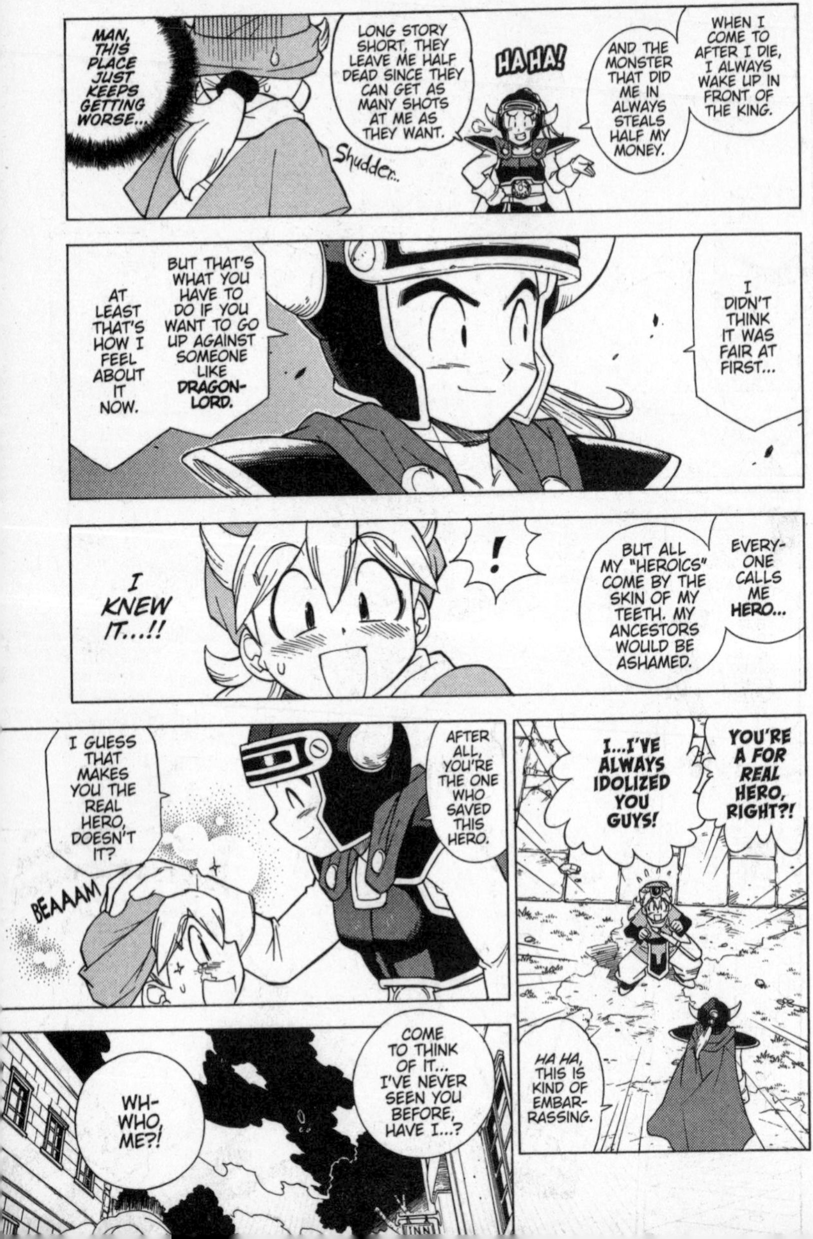
WHEN I COME TO AFTER I DIE, I ALWAYS WAKE UP IN FRONT OF THE KING.
AND THE MONSTER THAT DID ME IN ALWAYS STEALS HALF MY MONEY.
HA HA!
LONG STORY SHORT, THEY LEAVE ME HALF DEAD SINCE THEY CAN GET AS MANY SHOTS AT ME AS THEY WANT.
Shudder..
MAN, THIS PLACE JUST KEEPS GETTING WORSE...
I DIDN'T THINK IT WAS FAIR AT FIRST...
BUT THAT'S WHAT YOU HAVE TO DO IF YOU WANT TO GO UP AGAINST SOMEONE LIKE DRAGONLORD.
AT LEAST THAT'S HOW I FEEL ABOUT IT NOW.
EVERYONE CALLS ME HERO...
BUT ALL MY "HEROICS" COME BY THE SKIN OF MY TEETH. MY ANCESTORS WOULD BE ASHAMED.
!
I KNEW IT...!!
YOU'RE A FOR REAL HERO, RIGHT?!
I...I'VE ALWAYS IDOLIZED YOU GUYS!
HA HA, THIS IS KIND OF EMBARRASSING.
AFTER ALL, YOU'RE THE ONE WHO SAVED THIS HERO.
I GUESS THAT MAKES YOU THE REAL HERO, DOESN'T IT?
BEAAAM
COME TO THINK OF IT... I'VE NEVER SEEN YOU BEFORE, HAVE I...?
WH-WHO, ME?!
INN

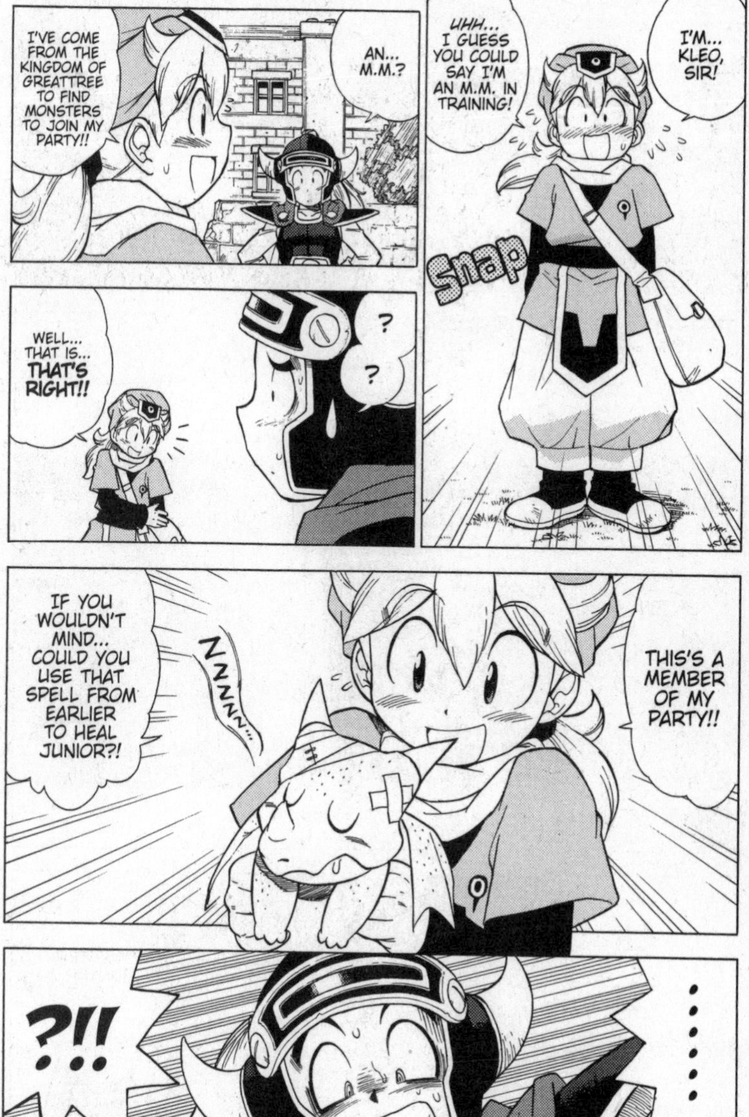
I'M... KLEO, SIR!
UHH... I GUESS YOU COULD SAY I'M AN M.M. IN TRAINING!
Snap
AN... M.M.?
I'VE COME FROM THE KINGDOM OF GREATTREE TO FIND MONSTERS TO JOIN MY PARTY!!
?
?
WELL... THAT IS... **THAT'S RIGHT!!**
THIS'S A MEMBER OF MY PARTY!!
NZZZZ...
IF YOU WOULDN'T MIND... COULD YOU USE THAT SPELL FROM EARLIER TO HEAL JUNIOR?!
......
?!!

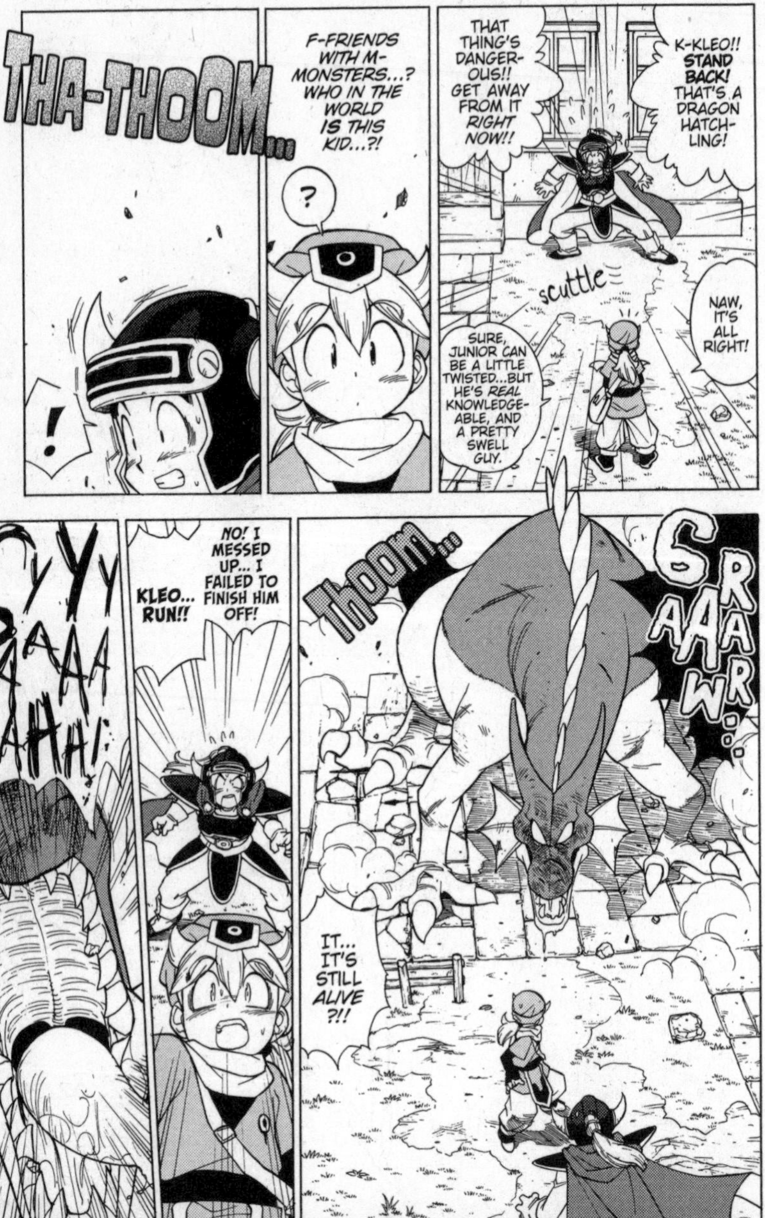
K-KLEO!! STAND BACK! THAT'S A DRAGON HATCHLING!
THAT THING'S DANGER-OUS!! GET AWAY FROM IT RIGHT NOW!!
scuttle
NAW, IT'S ALL RIGHT!
SURE, JUNIOR CAN BE A LITTLE TWISTED...BUT HE'S REAL KNOWLEDGE-ABLE, AND A PRETTY SWELL GUY.
F-FRIENDS WITH M-MONSTERS...? WHO IN THE WORLD IS THIS KID...?!
?
THA-THOOM...
!
GRAAAWR..
Thoom...
IT... IT'S STILL ALIVE?!!
NO! I MESSED UP... I FAILED TO FINISH HIM OFF!
KLEO... RUN!!
GYYYAAAAAAHH!

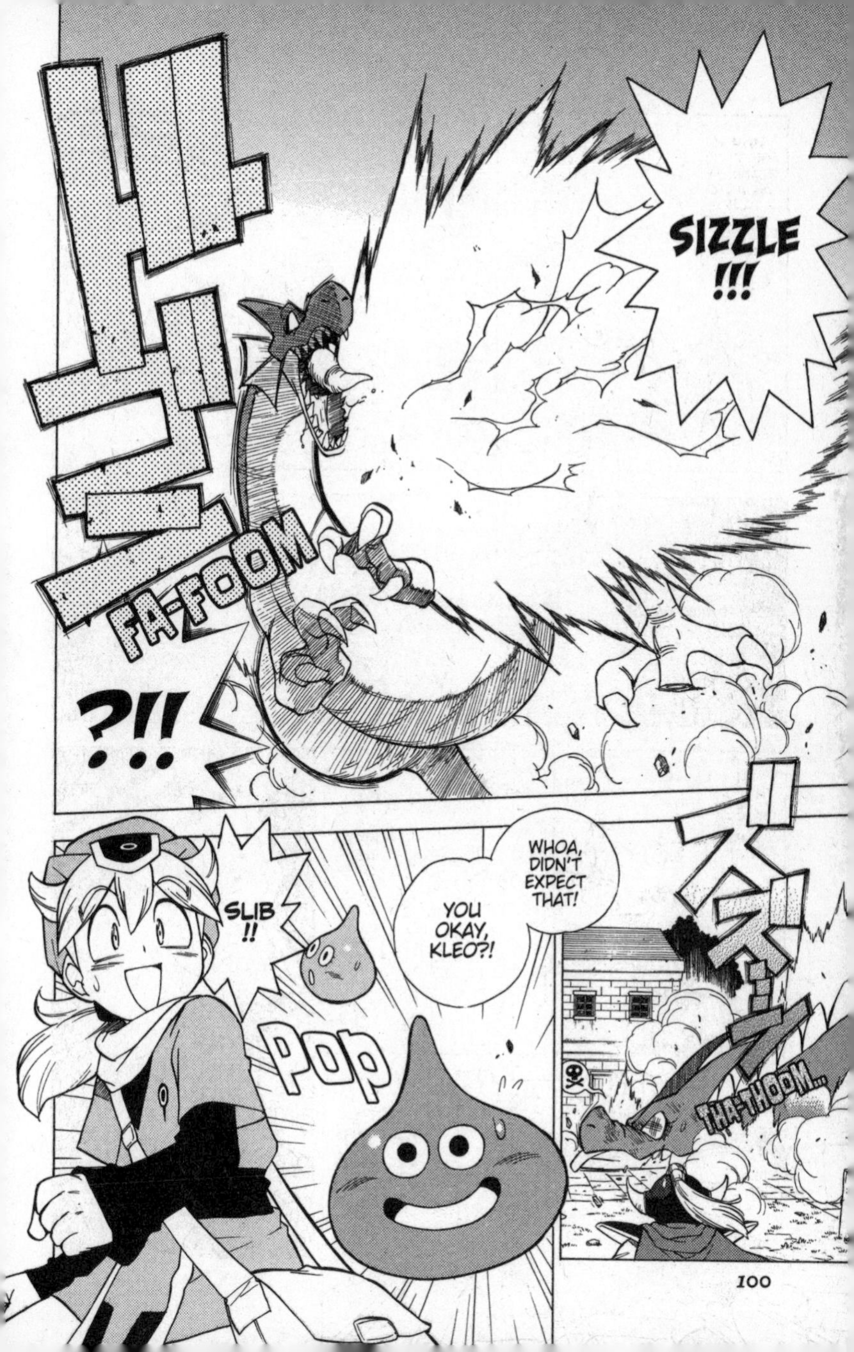
SIZZLE !!!
FA-FOOM
?!!
THA-THOOM...
WHOA, DIDN'T EXPECT THAT!
YOU OKAY, KLEO?!
SLIB !!
POP

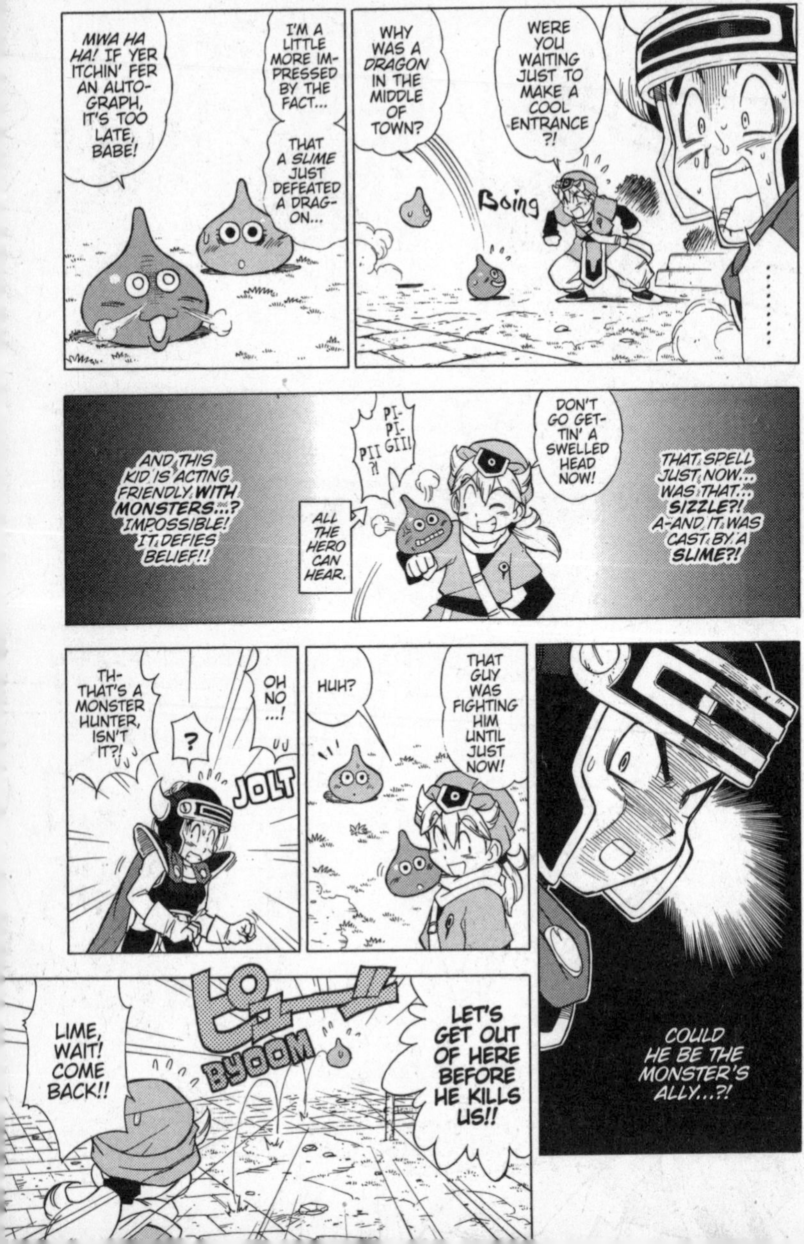
WERE YOU WAITING JUST TO MAKE A COOL ENTRANCE?!
WHY WAS A *DRAGON* IN THE MIDDLE OF TOWN?
Boing
......
I'M A LITTLE MORE IMPRESSED BY THE FACT...
THAT A *SLIME* JUST DEFEATED A DRAGON...
MWA HA HA! IF YER ITCHIN' FER AN AUTOGRAPH, IT'S TOO LATE, BABE!
THAT SPELL JUST NOW... WAS THAT... **SIZZLE?!** A-AND IT WAS CAST BY A **SLIME?!**
DON'T GO GETTIN' A SWELLED HEAD NOW!
PI-PI-GII!
PII?!
ALL THE HERO CAN HEAR.
AND THIS KID IS ACTING FRIENDLY **WITH MONSTERS...?** IMPOSSIBLE! IT DEFIES BELIEF!!
COULD HE BE THE MONSTER'S ALLY...?!
THAT GUY WAS FIGHTING HIM UNTIL JUST NOW!
HUH?
OH NO...!
TH-THAT'S A MONSTER HUNTER, ISN'T IT?!
?
JOLT
LET'S GET OUT OF HERE BEFORE HE KILLS US!!
BYOOM
LIME, WAIT! COME BACK!!

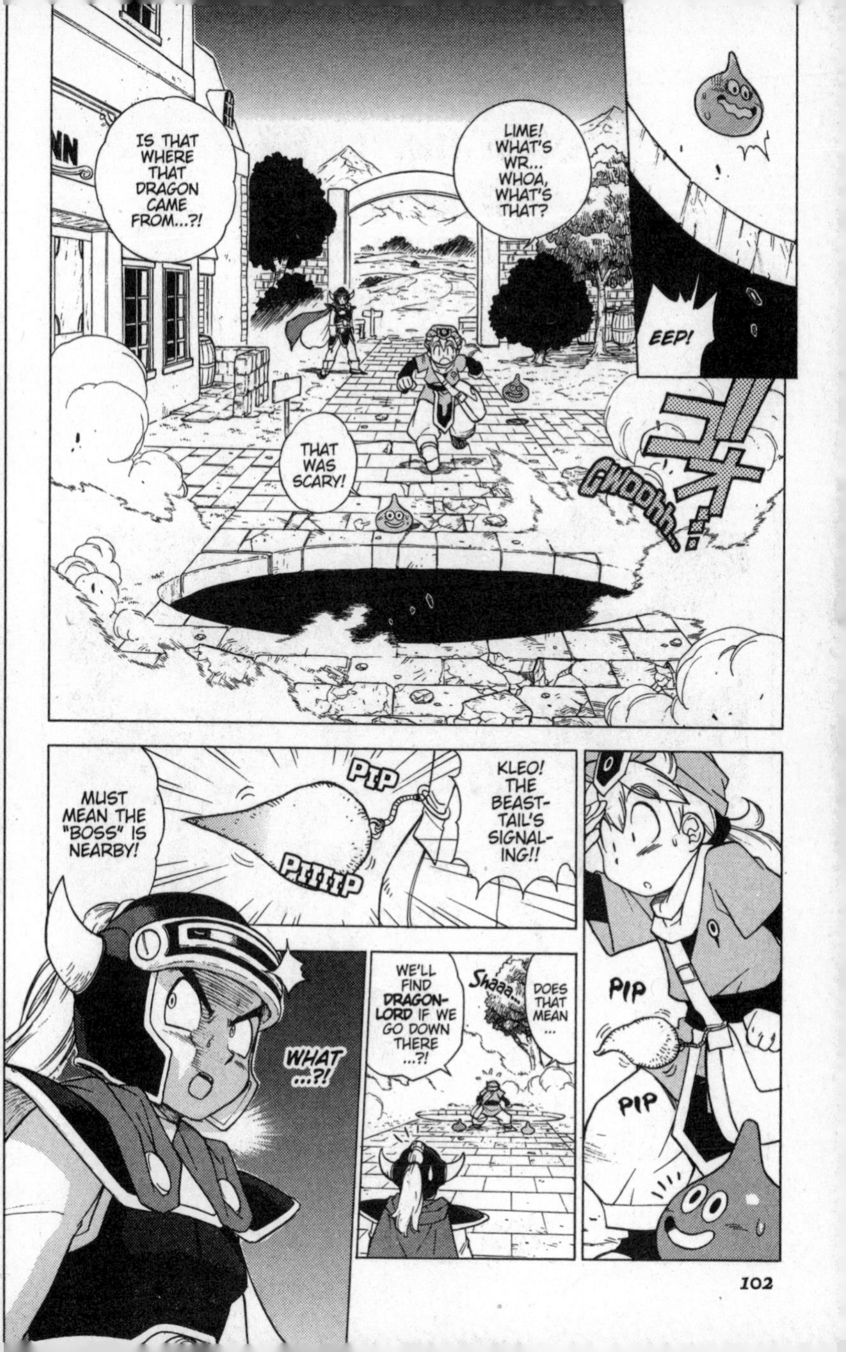
EEP!
GWOOHH...!!
LIME! WHAT'S WR... WHOA, WHAT'S THAT?
IS THAT WHERE THAT DRAGON CAME FROM...?!
THAT WAS SCARY!
PIP
PIP
KLEO! THE BEAST-TAIL'S SIGNAL-ING!!
PIP
PIIIIP
MUST MEAN THE "BOSS" IS NEARBY!
DOES THAT MEAN ...
Shaaa...
WE'LL FIND DRAGON-LORD IF WE GO DOWN THERE ...?!
WHAT ...?!

The 11th Night

Where a Journey for "Strength" Leads

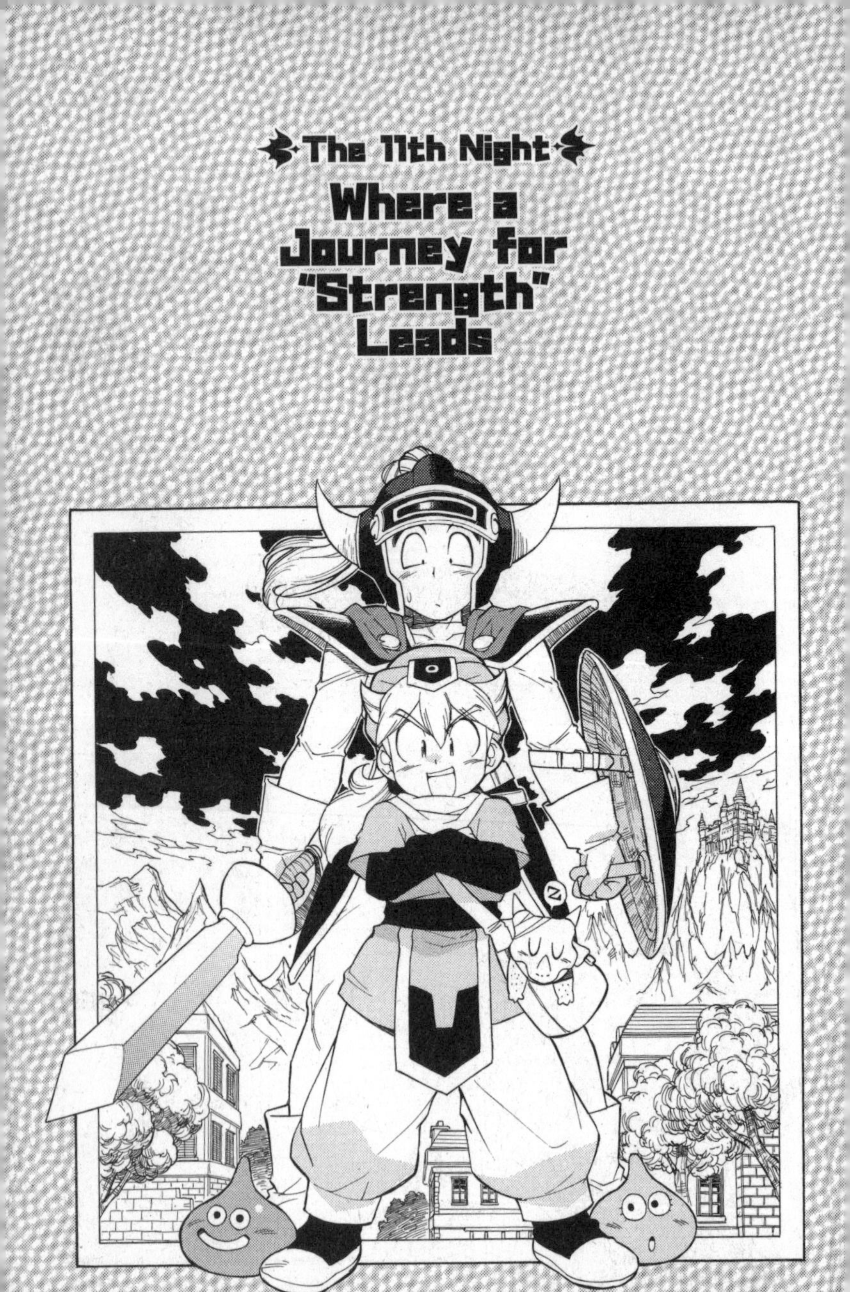

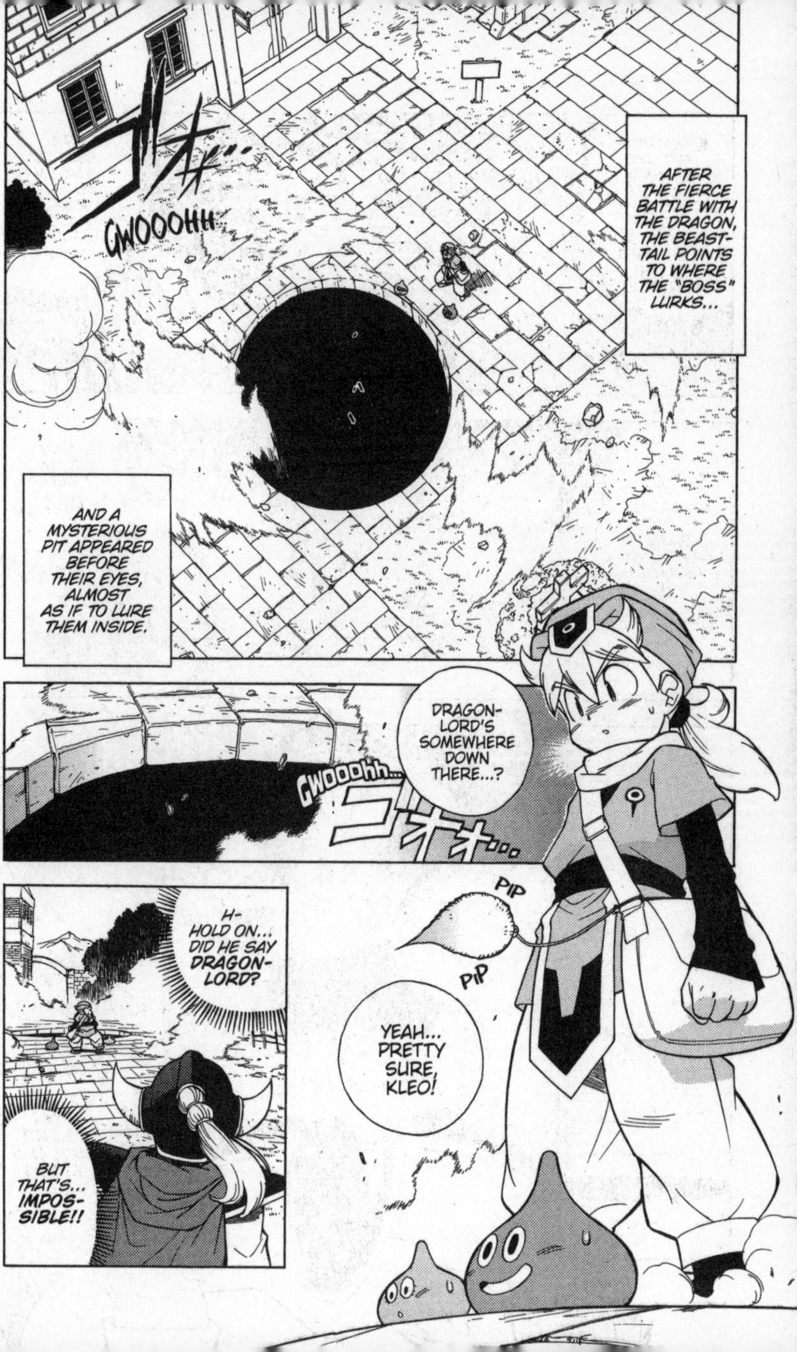
AFTER THE FIERCE BATTLE WITH THE DRAGON, THE BEAST-TAIL POINTS TO WHERE THE "BOSS" LURKS...
GWOOOHH...
AND A MYSTERIOUS PIT APPEARED BEFORE THEIR EYES, ALMOST AS IF TO LURE THEM INSIDE.
DRAGON-LORD'S SOMEWHERE DOWN THERE...?
GWOOOhh...
PIP
PIP
YEAH... PRETTY SURE, KLEO!
H-HOLD ON... DID HE SAY DRAGON-LORD?
BUT THAT'S... IMPOS-SIBLE!!

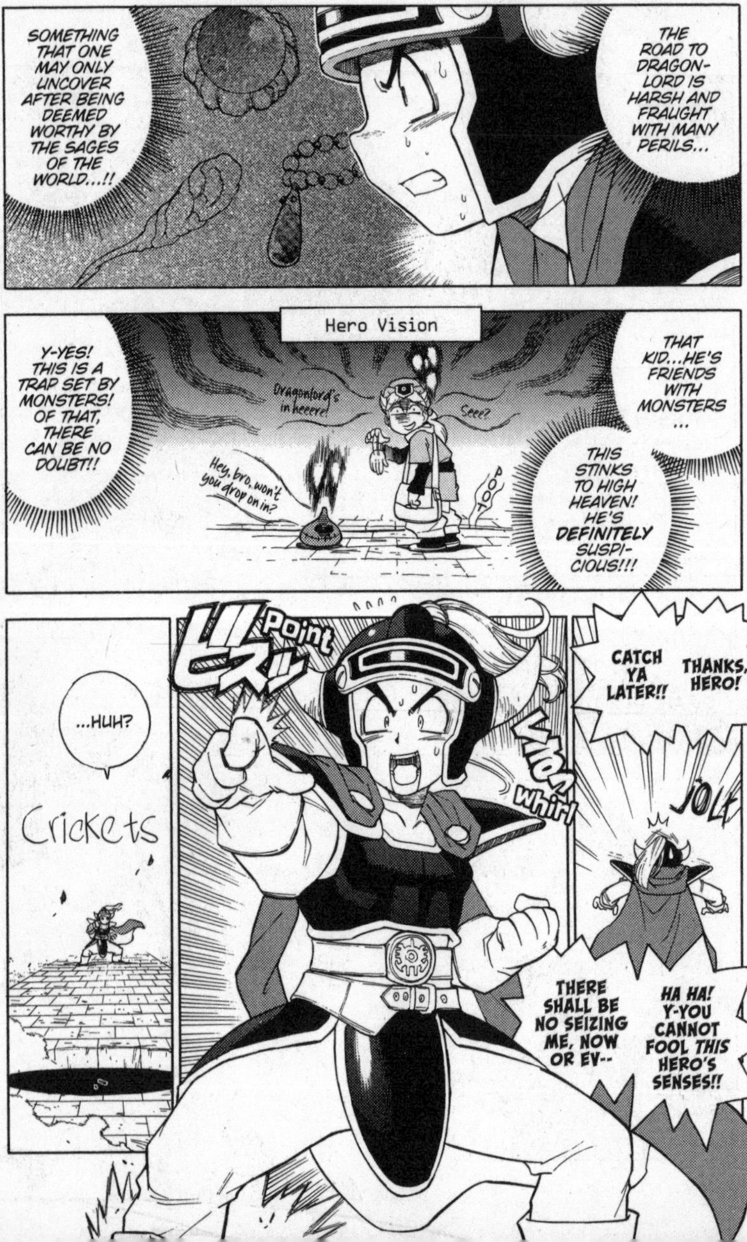
THE ROAD TO DRAGON-LORD IS HARSH AND FRAUGHT WITH MANY PERILS...
SOMETHING THAT ONE MAY ONLY UNCOVER AFTER BEING DEEMED WORTHY BY THE SAGES OF THE WORLD...!!
Hero Vision
THAT KID...HE'S FRIENDS WITH MONSTERS ...
THIS STINKS TO HIGH HEAVEN! HE'S DEFINITELY SUSPICIOUS!!!
See?
Dragonlord's in heeere!
POOT
Hey, bro, won't you drop on in?
Y-YES! THIS IS A TRAP SET BY MONSTERS! OF THAT, THERE CAN BE NO DOUBT!!
THANKS, HERO!
CATCH YA LATER!!
HA HA! Y-YOU CANNOT FOOL THIS HERO'S SENSES!!
THERE SHALL BE NO SEIZING ME, NOW OR EV--
Whirl
Point
...HUH?
Crickets

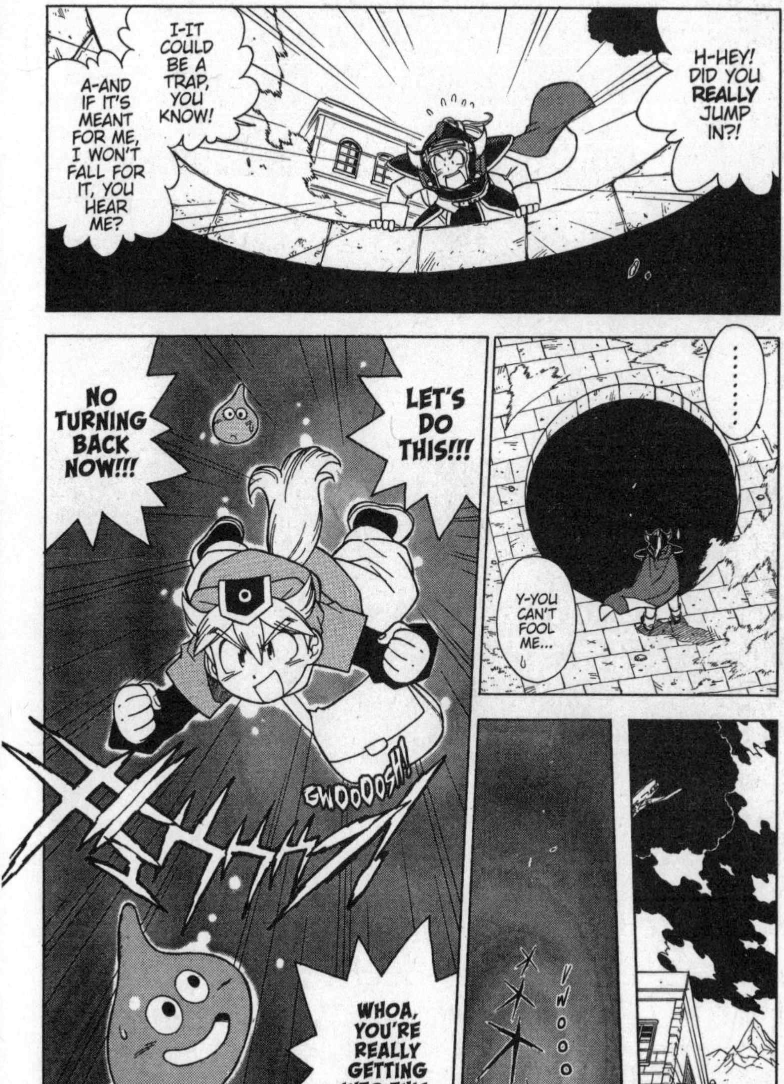
H-HEY! DID YOU REALLY JUMP IN?!
I-IT COULD BE A TRAP, YOU KNOW!
A-AND IF IT'S MEANT FOR ME, I WON'T FALL FOR IT, YOU HEAR ME?
......
Y-YOU CAN'T FOOL ME...
WOOOOOOO....
LET'S DO THIS!!!
NO TURNING BACK NOW!!!
GWOOOOSH!
WHOA, YOU'RE REALLY GETTING INTO THIS, AREN'T YOU, KLEO?!!!

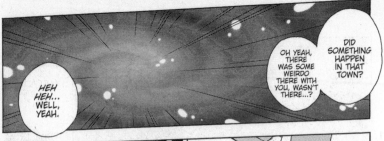

DID SOMETHING HAPPEN IN THAT TOWN?

OH YEAH, THERE WAS SOME WEIRDO THERE WITH YOU, WASN'T THERE...?

HEH HEH... WELL, YEAH.

WHOA, WHAT'S THAT FACE? THAT'S CREEPY!

Grin

THANK YOU, HERO!

FWAAAA...

I FEEL LIKE I'M STARTING TO GET MY COURAGE BACK!

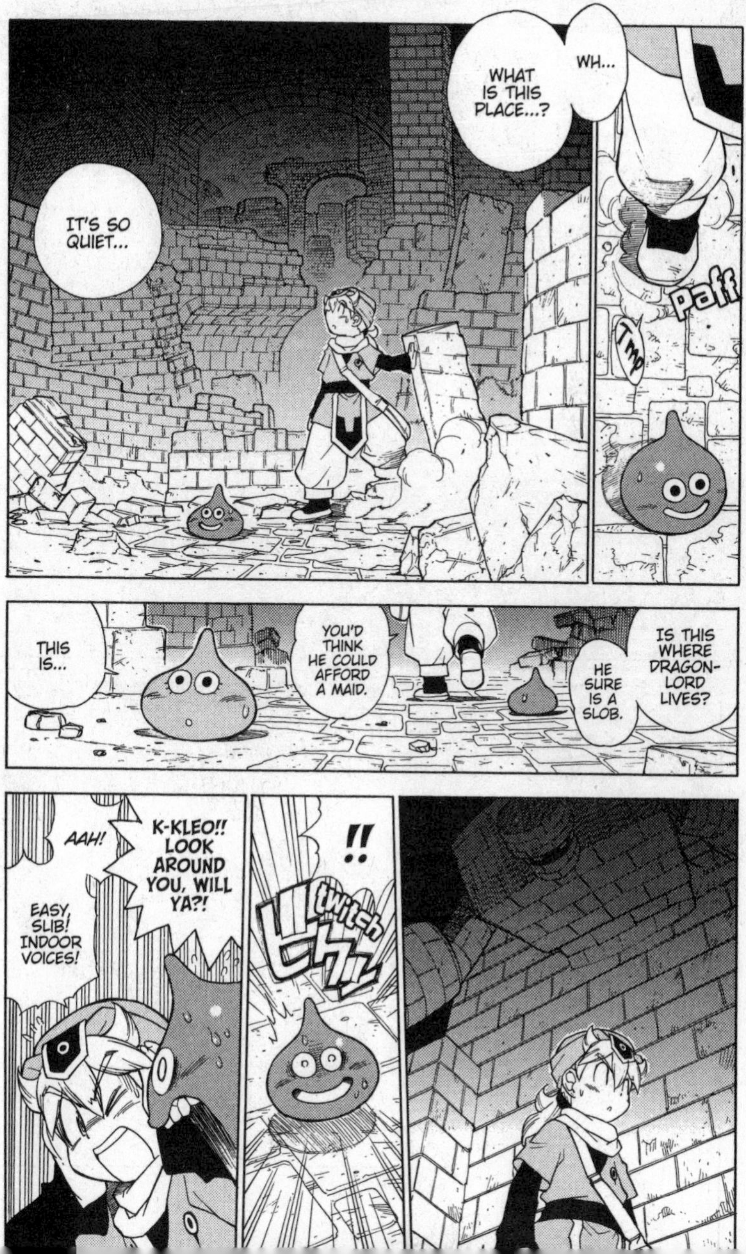
WH...
paff
Tmp
WHAT IS THIS PLACE...?
IT'S SO QUIET...
IS THIS WHERE DRAGON-LORD LIVES?
HE SURE IS A SLOB.
YOU'D THINK HE COULD AFFORD A MAID.
THIS IS...
!!
twitch
K-KLEO!! LOOK AROUND YOU, WILL YA?!
AAH!
EASY, SLIB! INDOOR VOICES!

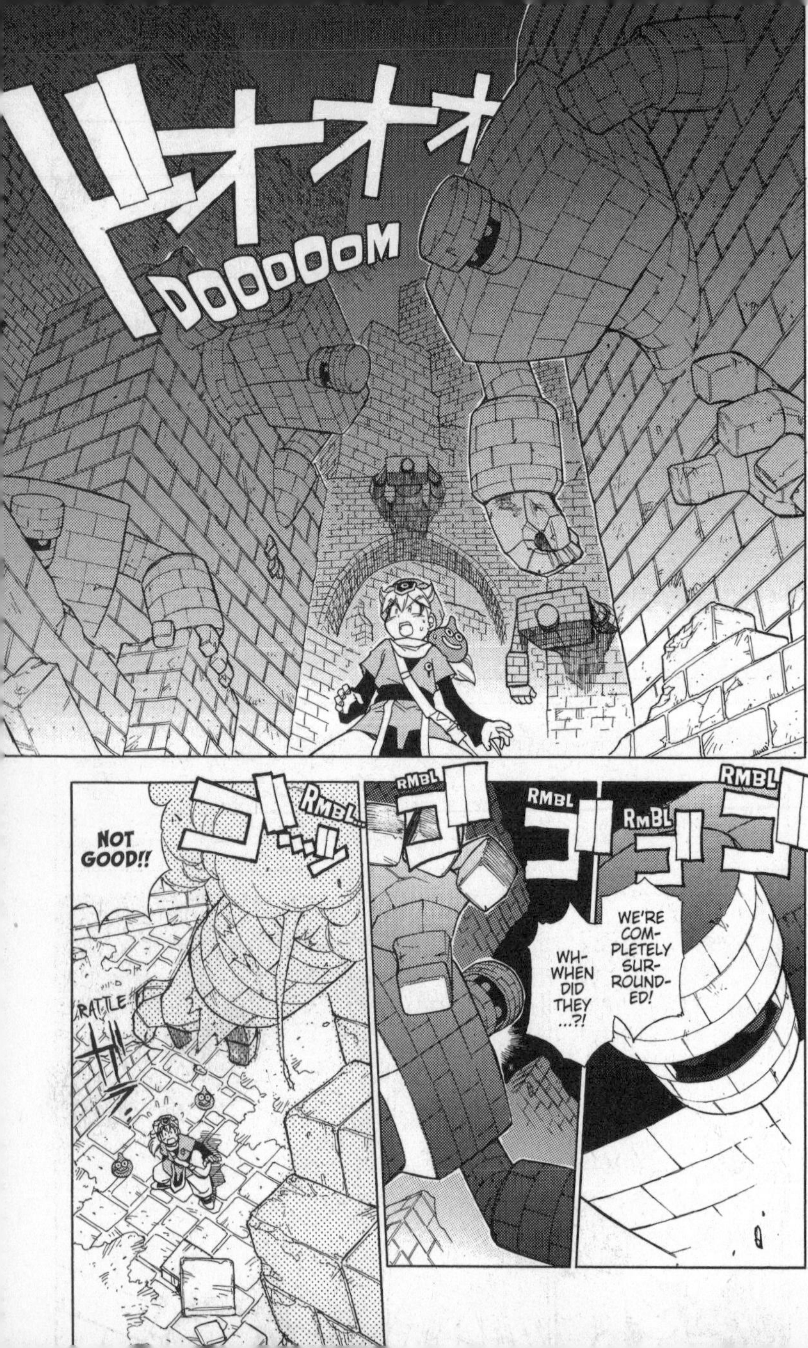
DOOOOOM
RMBL
RMBL
WE'RE COMPLETELY SURROUNDED!
RMBL
RMBL
WH-WHEN DID THEY ...?!
RMBL...
NOT GOOD!!
RATTLE

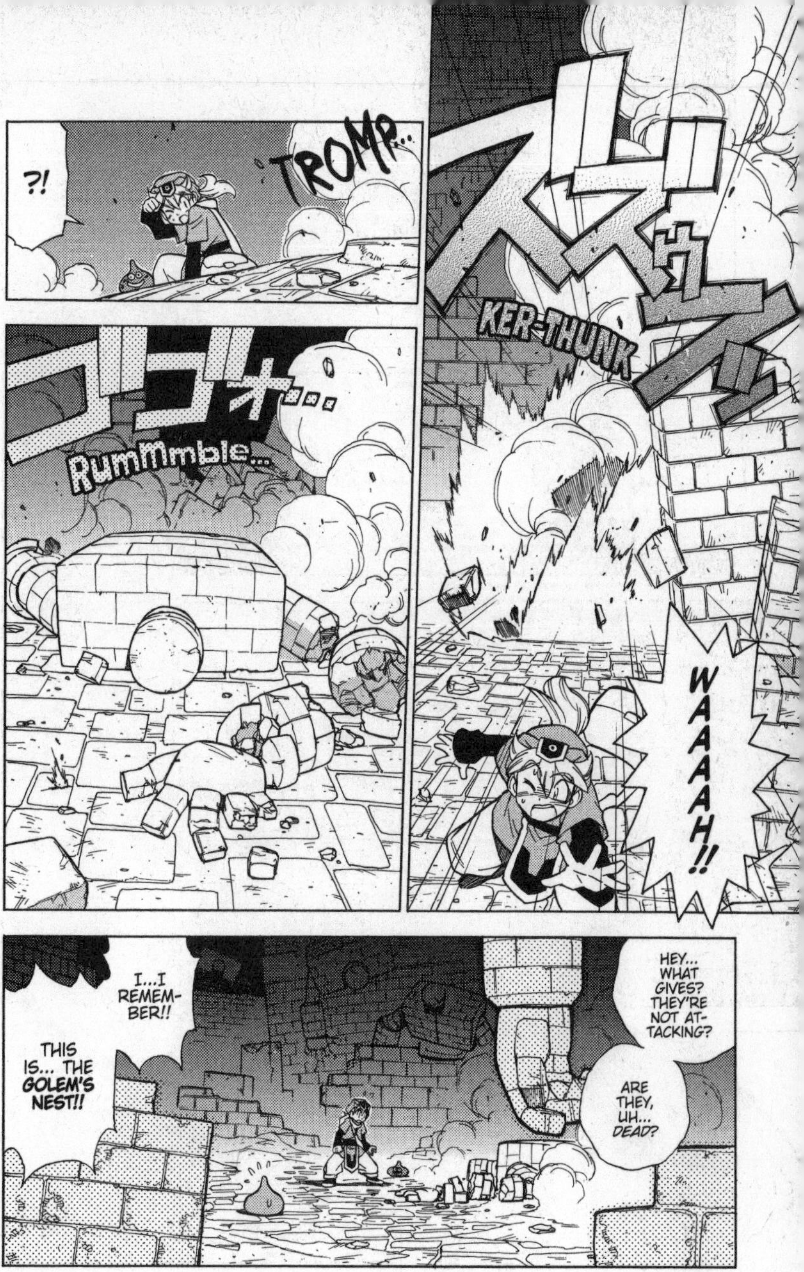
KER-THUNK
WAAAAAH!!
?!
TROMP...
RumMmble...
HEY... WHAT GIVES? THEY'RE NOT AT-TACKING?
ARE THEY, UH... DEAD?
I...I REMEMBER!!
THIS IS... THE GOLEM'S NEST!!

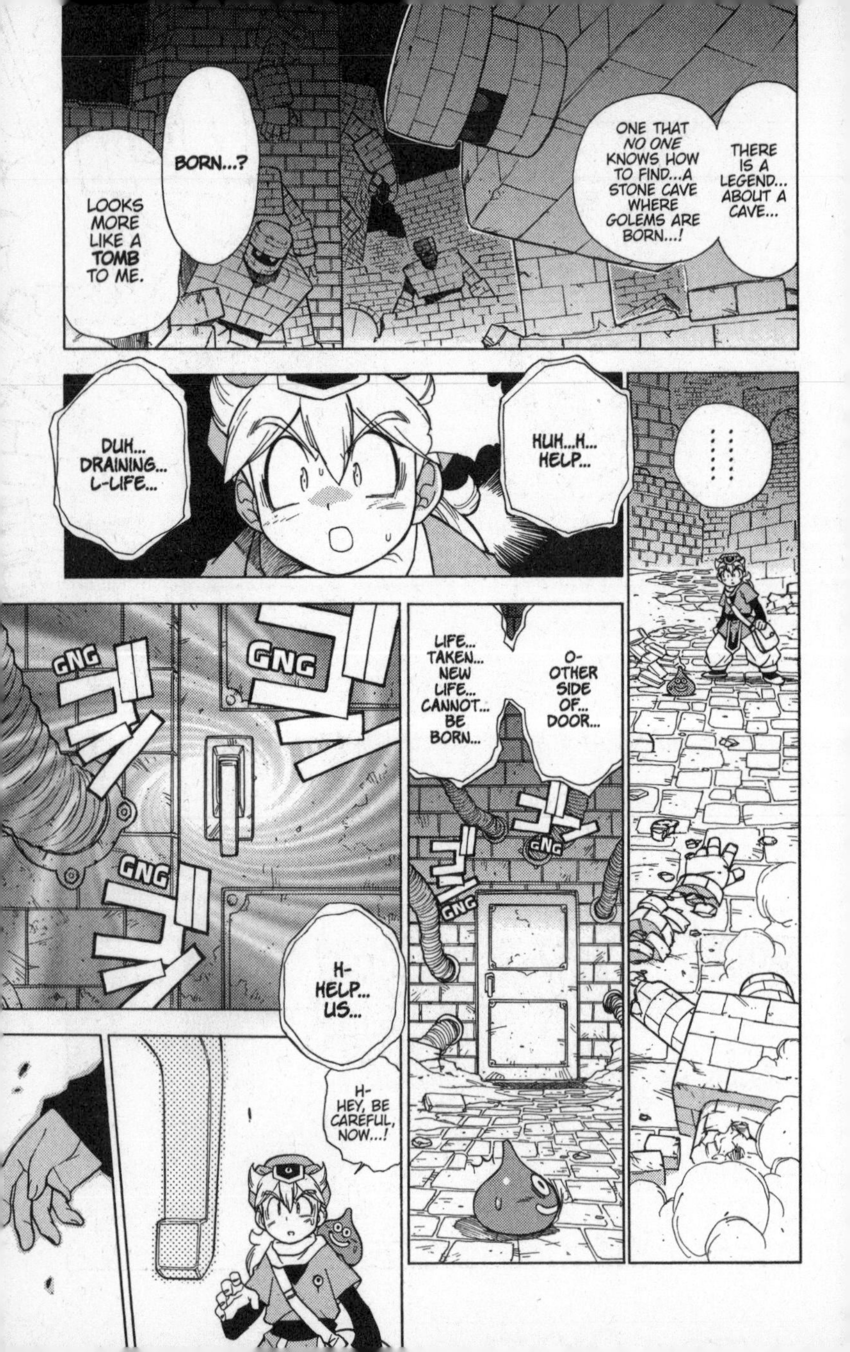
THERE IS A LEGEND... ABOUT A CAVE...
ONE THAT *NO ONE* KNOWS HOW TO FIND...A STONE CAVE WHERE GOLEMS ARE BORN...!
BORN...?
LOOKS MORE LIKE A **TOMB** TO ME.
......
HUH...H... HELP...
DUH... DRAINING... L-LIFE...
O- OTHER SIDE OF... DOOR...
LIFE... TAKEN... NEW LIFE... CANNOT... BE BORN...
GNG
GNG
GNG
GNG
GNG
GNG
H- HELP... US...
H- HEY, BE CAREFUL, NOW...!

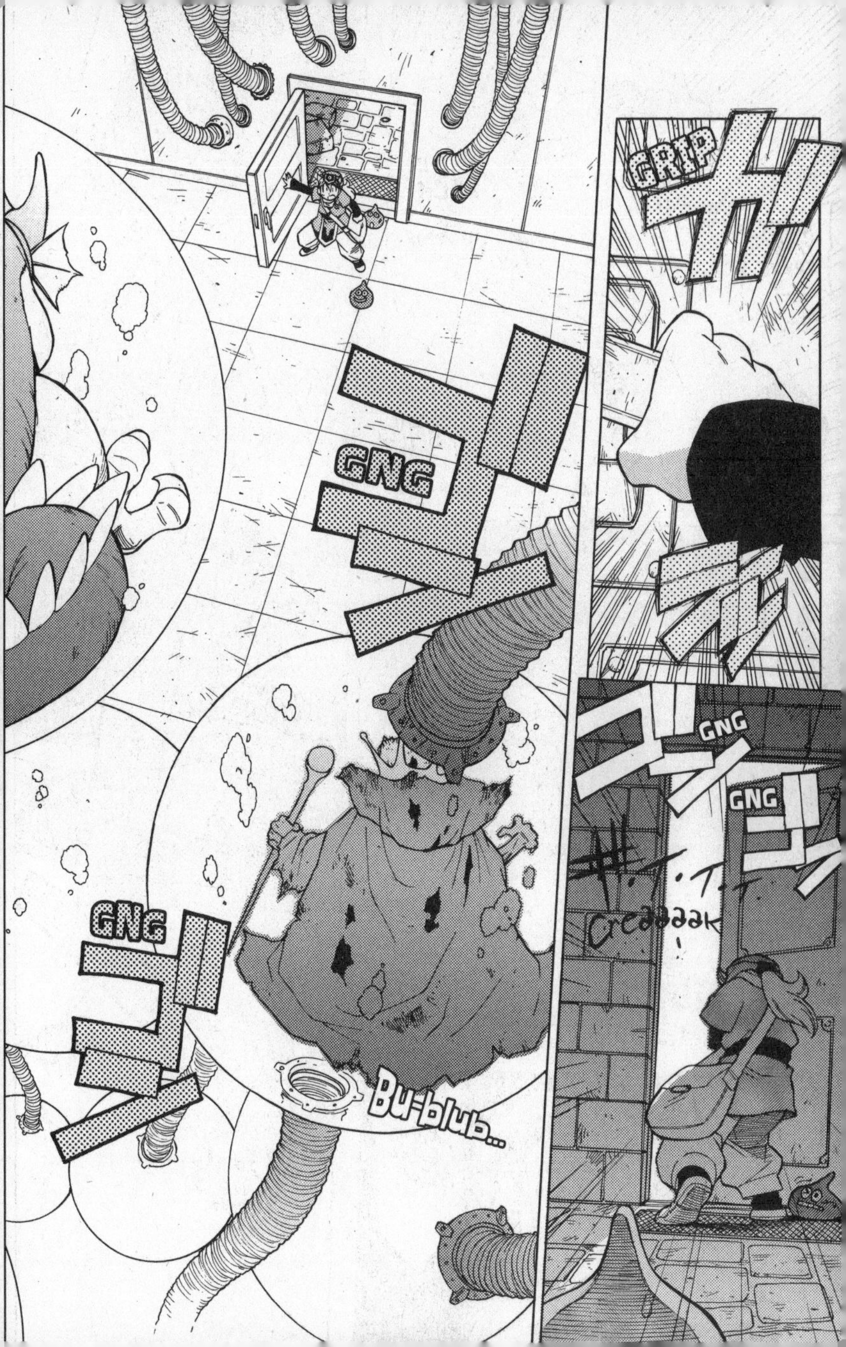
GRIP
GNG
GNG
Creaaak
GNG
GNG
Bu-blub...

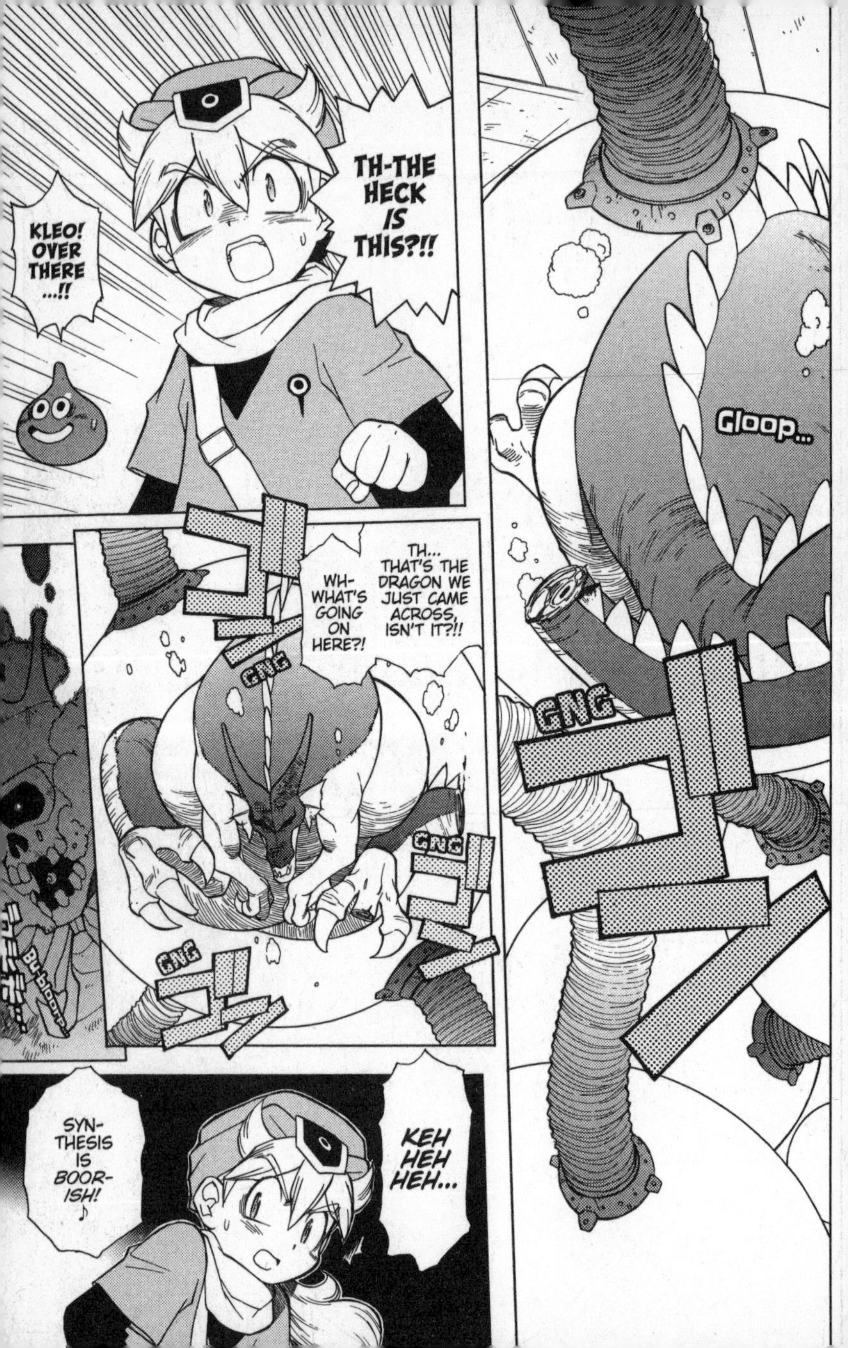
Gloop...
GNG
TH-THE HECK IS THIS?!!
KLEO! OVER THERE ...!!
TH... THAT'S THE DRAGON WE JUST CAME ACROSS, ISN'T IT?!!
WH- WHAT'S GOING ON HERE?!
GNG
GNG
GNG
Bu-bloop...
KEH HEH HEH...
SYN- THESIS IS BOOR- ISH! ♪

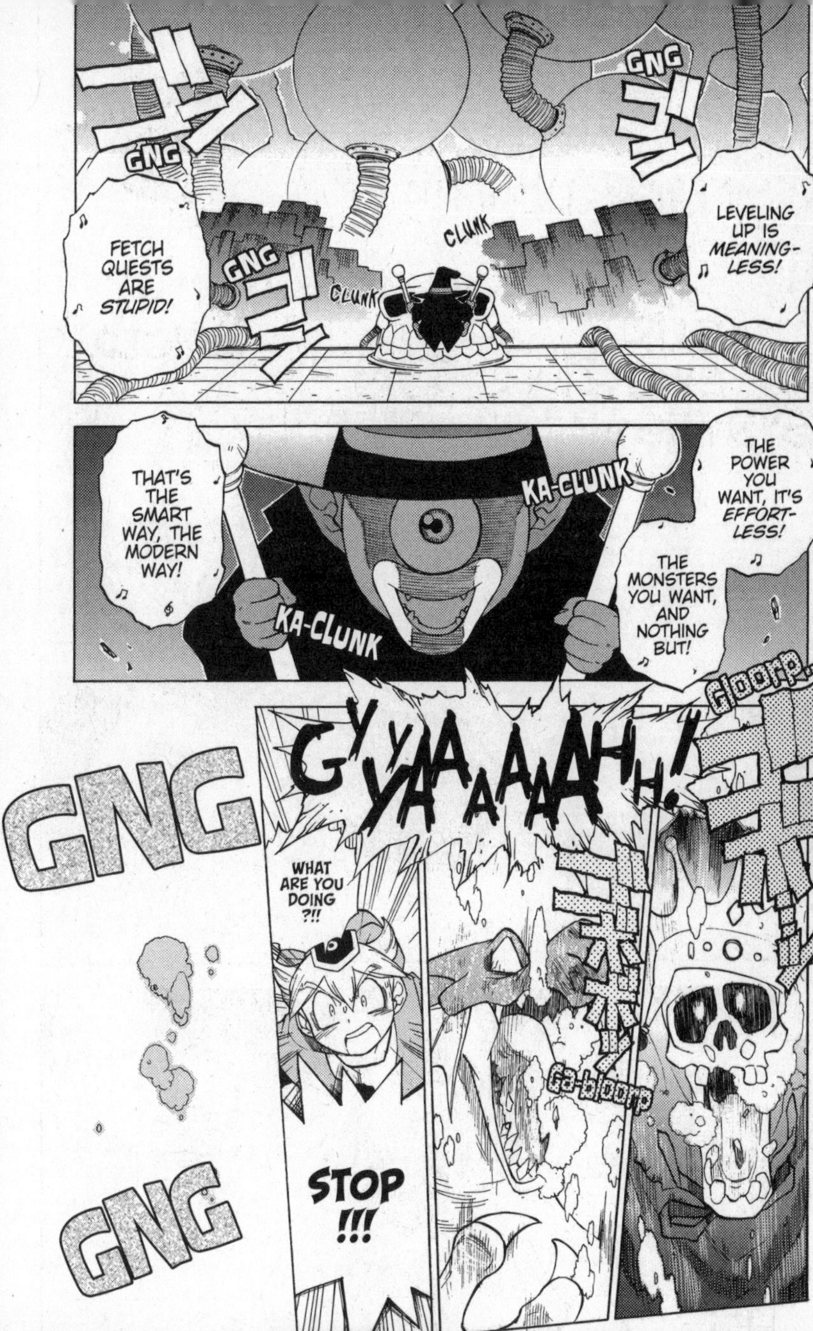
GNG
LEVELING UP IS MEANINGLESS!
CLUNK
CLUNK
GNG
GNG
FETCH QUESTS ARE STUPID!
THE POWER YOU WANT, IT'S EFFORTLESS!
THE MONSTERS YOU WANT, AND NOTHING BUT!
KA-CLUNK
KA-CLUNK
THAT'S THE SMART WAY, THE MODERN WAY!
Gloorp...
GYYAAAAAHH!
ga-bloorp
WHAT ARE YOU DOING?!!
STOP!!!
GNG
GNG

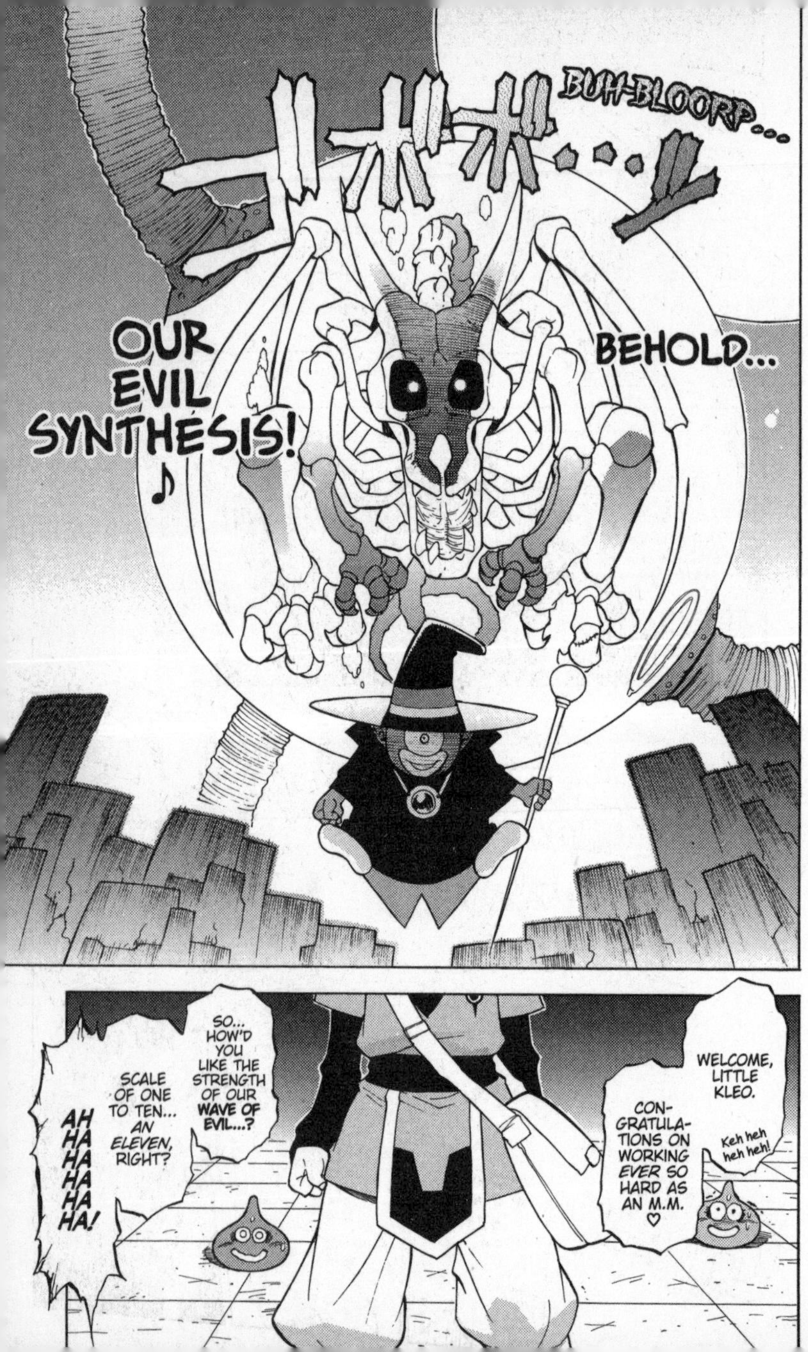
BUH-BLOORP...
BEHOLD...
OUR EVIL SYNTHESIS! ♪
WELCOME, LITTLE KLEO.
CON-GRATULA-TIONS ON WORKING EVER SO HARD AS AN M.M. ♡
Keh heh heh heh!
SO... HOW'D YOU LIKE THE STRENGTH OF OUR WAVE OF EVIL...?
SCALE OF ONE TO TEN... AN ELEVEN, RIGHT?
AH HA HA HA HA HA!

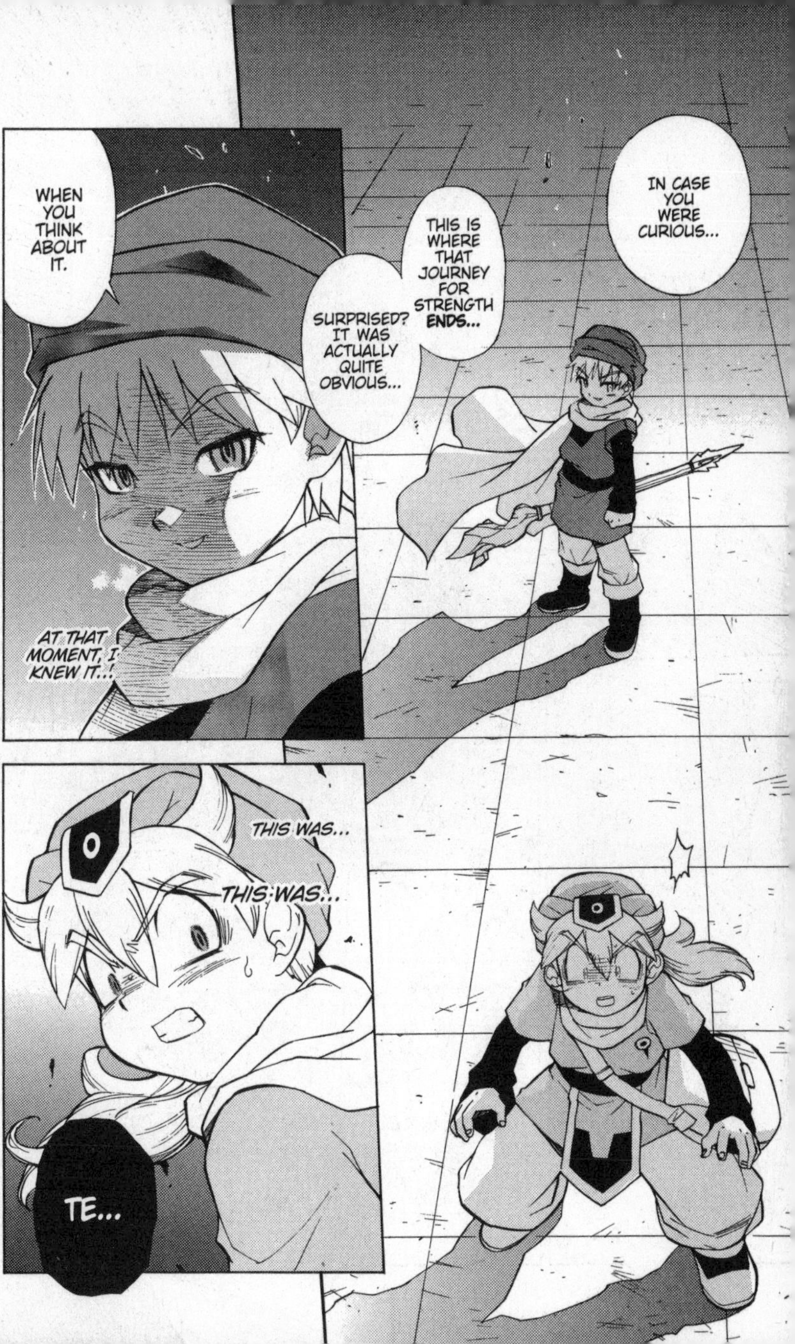
IN CASE YOU WERE CURIOUS...
THIS IS WHERE THAT JOURNEY FOR STRENGTH **ENDS...**
SURPRISED? IT WAS ACTUALLY QUITE OBVIOUS...
WHEN YOU THINK ABOUT IT.
AT THAT MOMENT, I KNEW IT...!
THIS WAS...
THIS WAS...
TE...

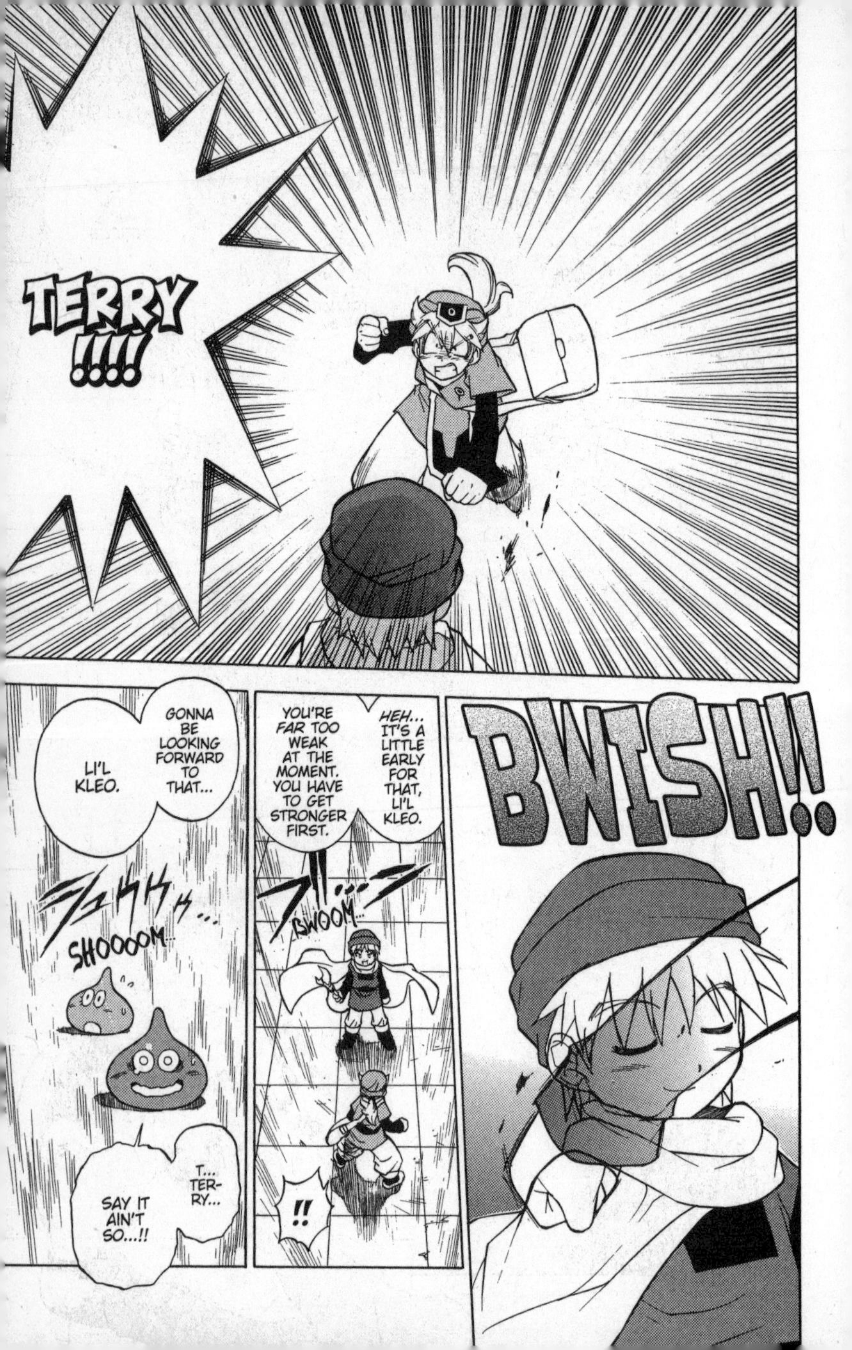
TERRY!!!!
BWISH!!
HEH... IT'S A LITTLE EARLY FOR THAT, LI'L KLEO.
YOU'RE FAR TOO WEAK AT THE MOMENT. YOU HAVE TO GET STRONGER FIRST.
BWOOM...
!!
GONNA BE LOOKING FORWARD TO THAT...
LI'L KLEO.
SHOOOOM...
T... TER-RY...
SAY IT AIN'T SO...!!

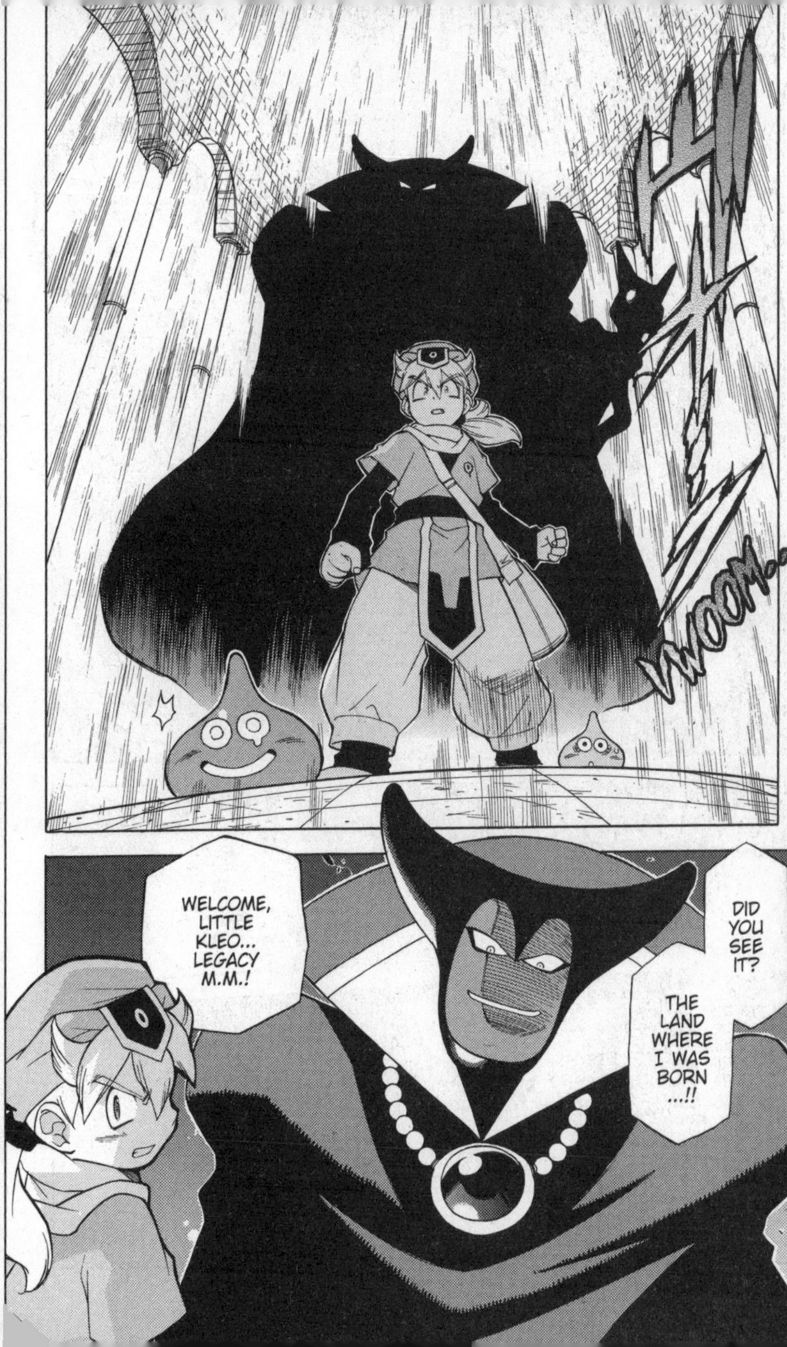
VWOOM...
DID YOU SEE IT?
THE LAND WHERE I WAS BORN ...!!
WELCOME, LITTLE KLEO... LEGACY M.M.!

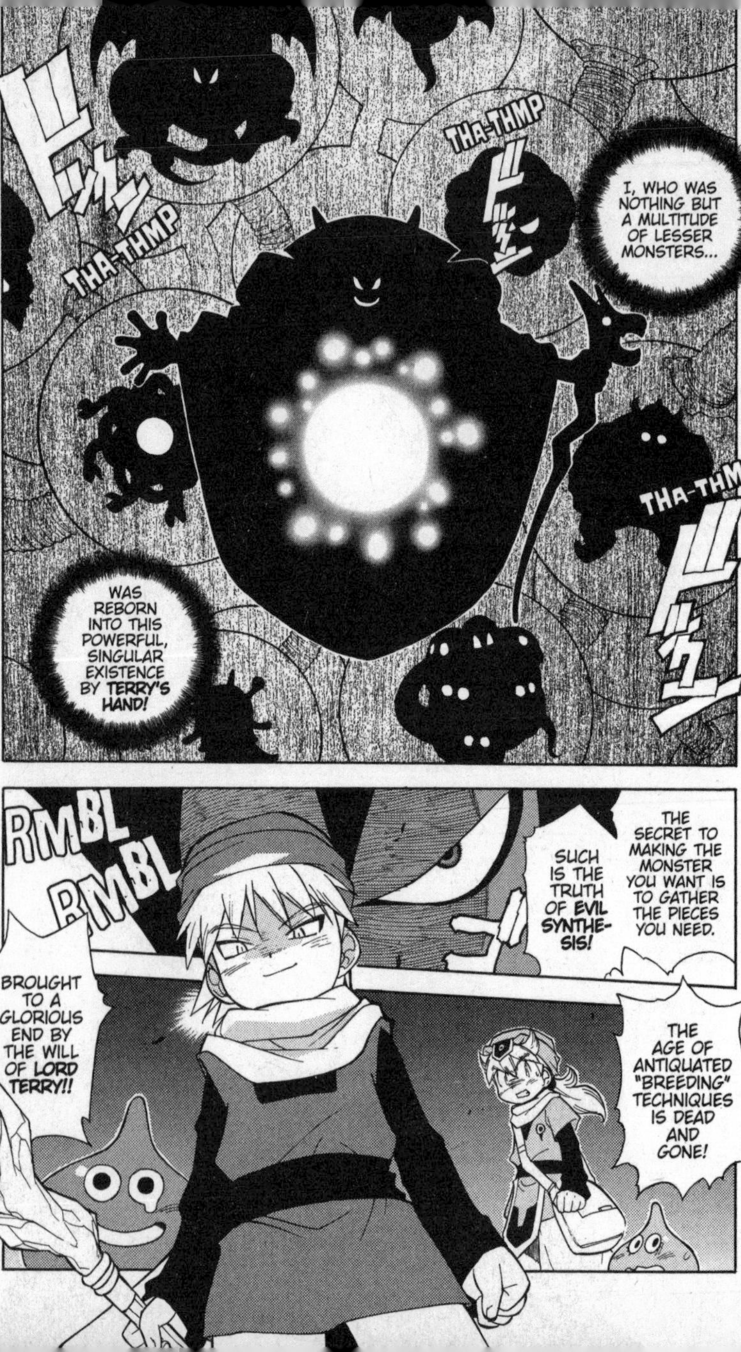
THA-THMP
I, WHO WAS NOTHING BUT A MULTITUDE OF LESSER MONSTERS...
THA-THMP
THA-THMP
WAS REBORN INTO THIS POWERFUL, SINGULAR EXISTENCE BY TERRY'S HAND!
THE SECRET TO MAKING THE MONSTER YOU WANT IS TO GATHER THE PIECES YOU NEED.
SUCH IS THE TRUTH OF EVIL SYNTHE-SIS!
RMBL RMBL
THE AGE OF ANTIQUATED "BREEDING" TECHNIQUES IS DEAD AND GONE!
BROUGHT TO A GLORIOUS END BY THE WILL OF LORD TERRY!!

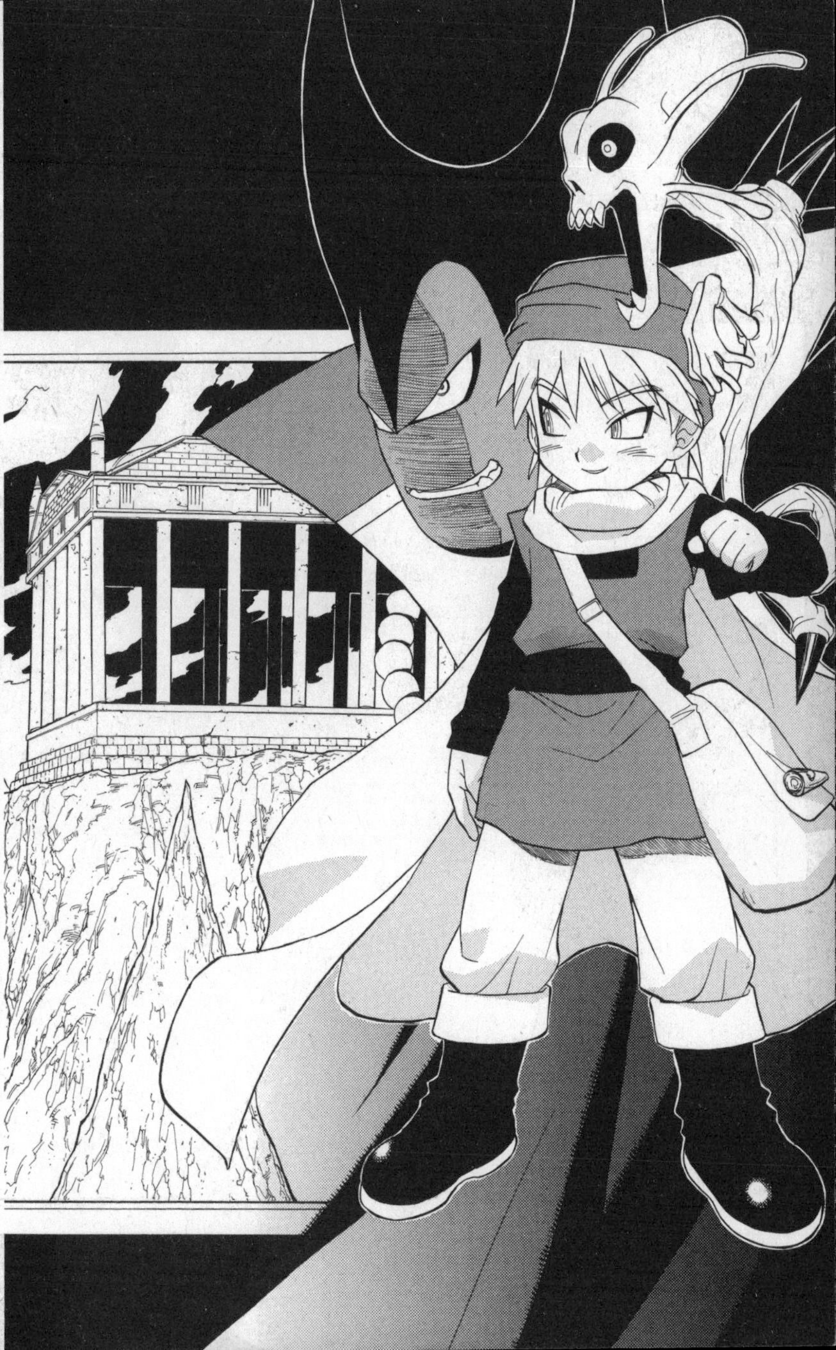

The 12th Night

Ooo! I'm Really Burnin' Up Now!!

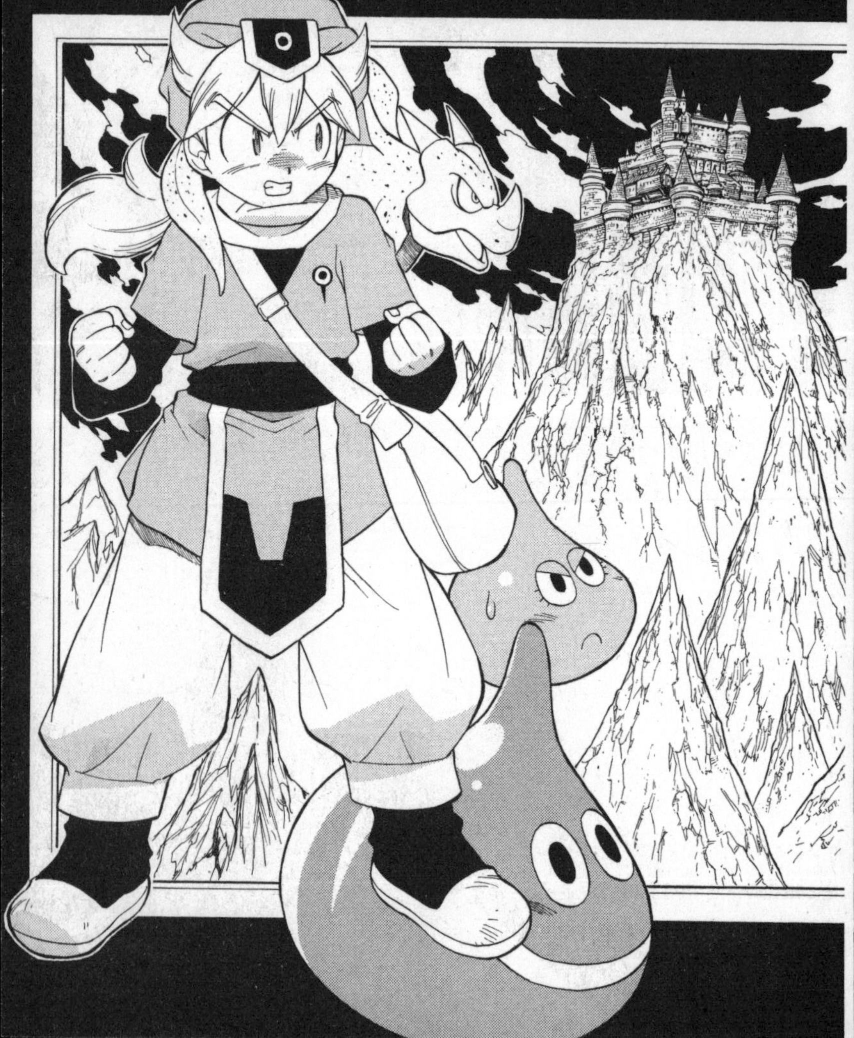

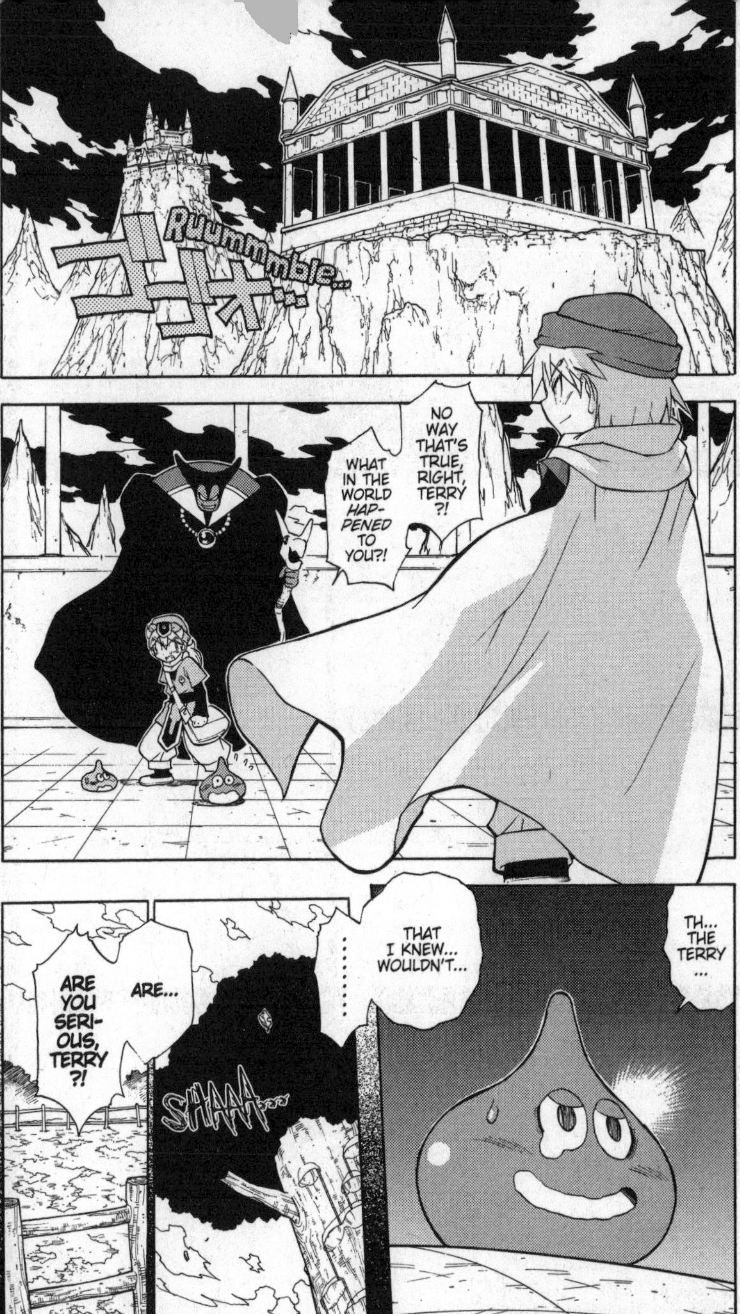
Ruummmble...
NO WAY THAT'S TRUE, RIGHT, TERRY?!
WHAT IN THE WORLD HAPPENED TO YOU?!
TH... THE TERRY...
THAT I KNEW... WOULDN'T...
......
SHAAA...
ARE...
ARE YOU SERIOUS, TERRY?!

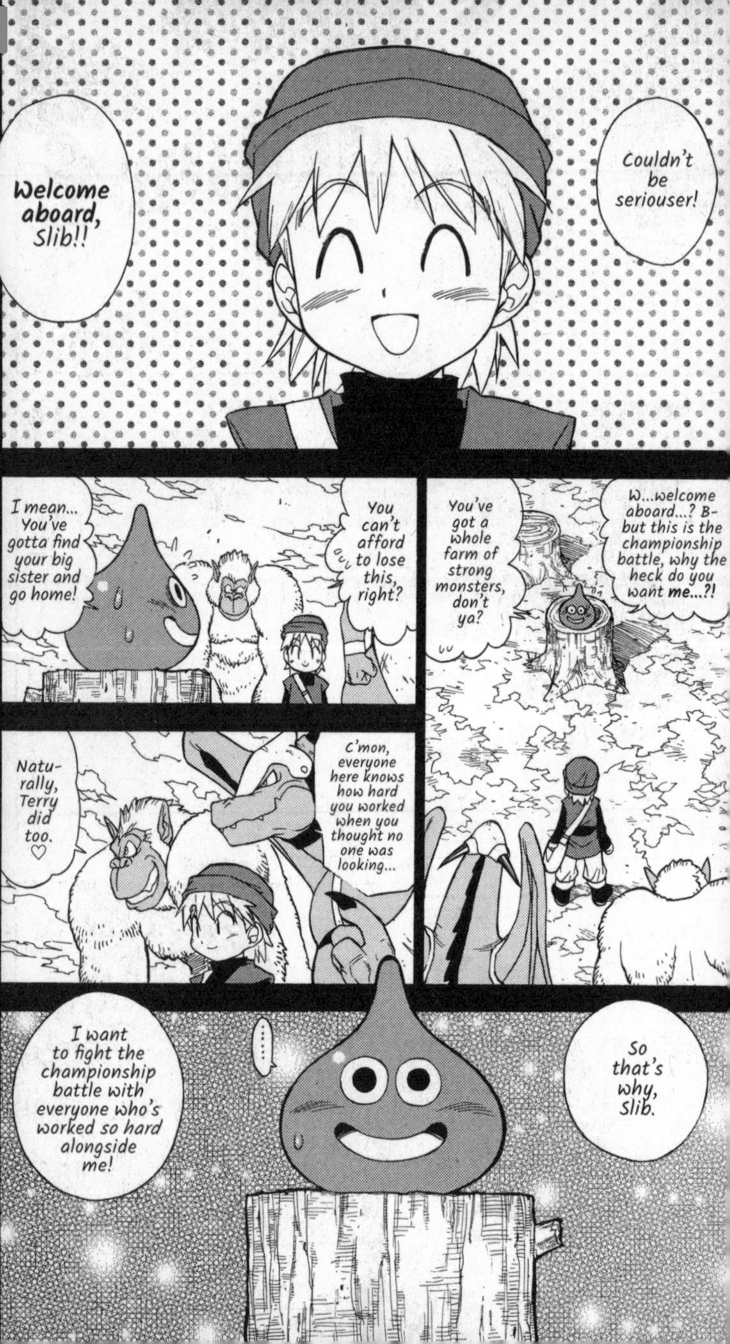
Couldn't be seriouser!
Welcome aboard, Slib!!
W...welcome aboard...? B-but this is the championship battle, why the heck do you want **me**...?!
You've got a whole farm of strong monsters, don't ya?
You can't afford to lose this, right?
I mean... You've gotta find your big sister and go home!
C'mon, everyone here knows how hard you worked when you thought no one was looking...
Natu-rally, Terry did too. ♡
So that's why, Slib.
I want to fight the championship battle with everyone who's worked so hard alongside me!
......

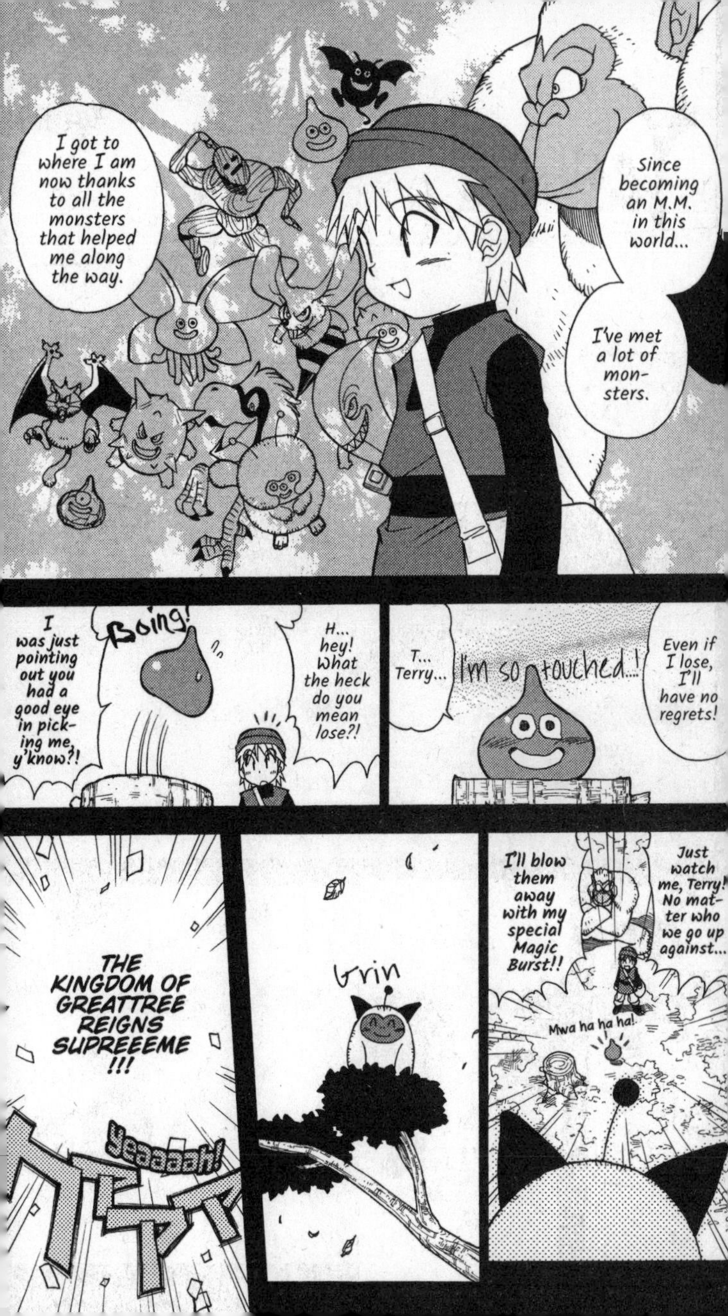
Since becoming an M.M. in this world...
I've met a lot of monsters.
I got to where I am now thanks to all the monsters that helped me along the way.
Even if I lose, I'll have no regrets!
I'm so touched...!
T... Terry...
H... hey! What the heck do you mean lose?!
Boing!
I was just pointing out you had a good eye in picking me, y'know?!
Just watch me, Terry! No matter who we go up against...
I'll blow them away with my special Magic Burst!!
Mwa ha ha ha!
Grin
THE KINGDOM OF GREATTREE REIGNS SUPREEEME!!!
Yeaaaaah!

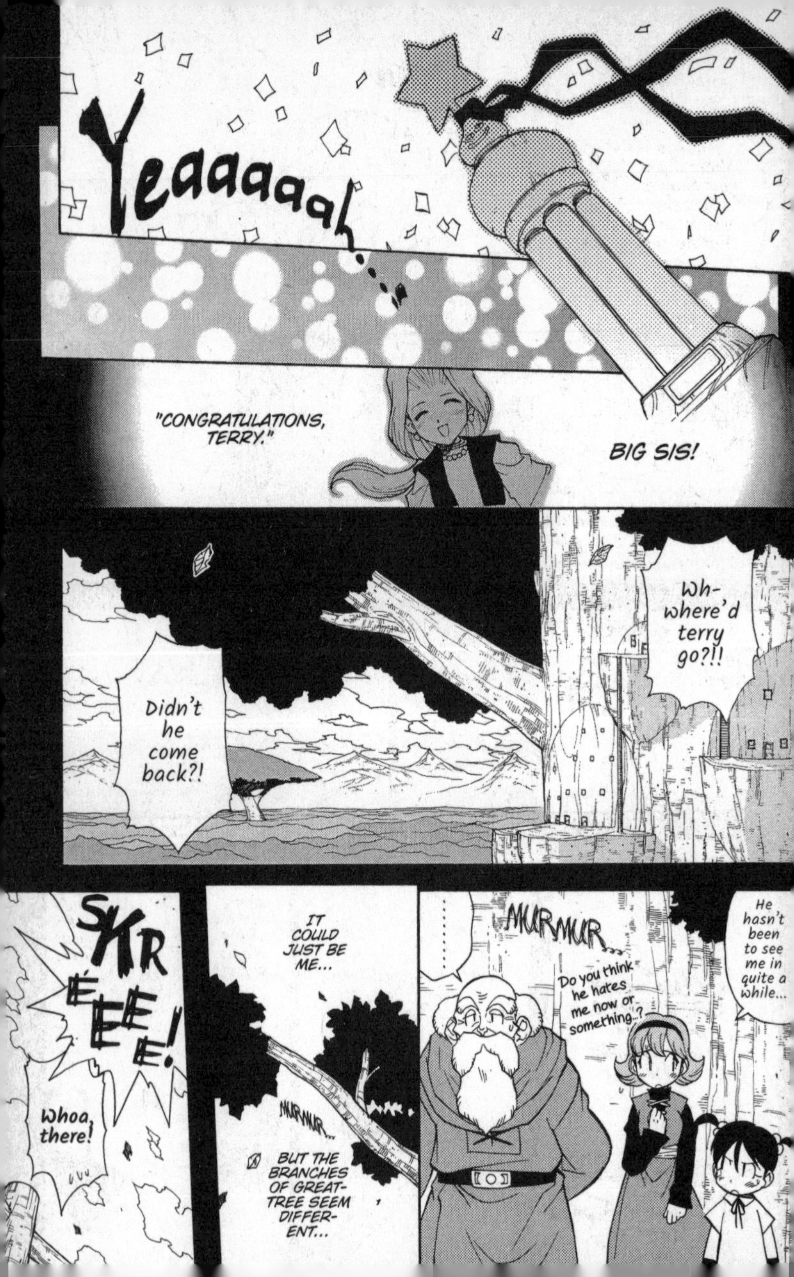
Yeaaaaah...
"CONGRATULATIONS, TERRY."
BIG SIS!
Wh- where'd terry go?!!
Didn't he come back?!
He hasn't been to see me in quite a while...
Do you think he hates me now or something...?
MURMUR...
...
IT COULD JUST BE ME...
MURMUR...
BUT THE BRANCHES OF GREAT-TREE SEEM DIFFERENT...
SKRÉEEEE!
Whoa, there!

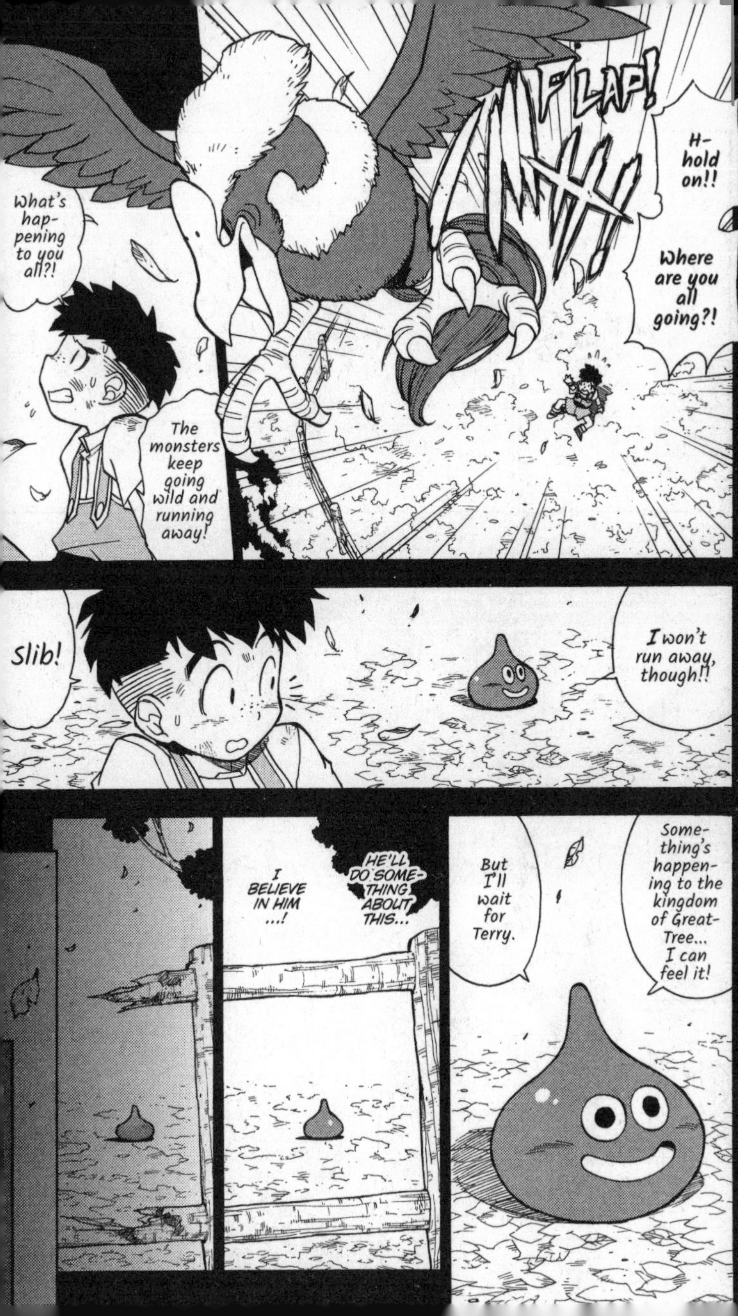
FLAP!
H-hold on!!
Where are you all going?!
What's hap-pening to you all?!
The monsters keep going wild and running away!
I won't run away, though!!
Slib!
Some-thing's happen-ing to the kingdom of Great-Tree... I can feel it!
But I'll wait for Terry.
HE'LL DO SOME-THING ABOUT THIS...
I BELIEVE IN HIM...!

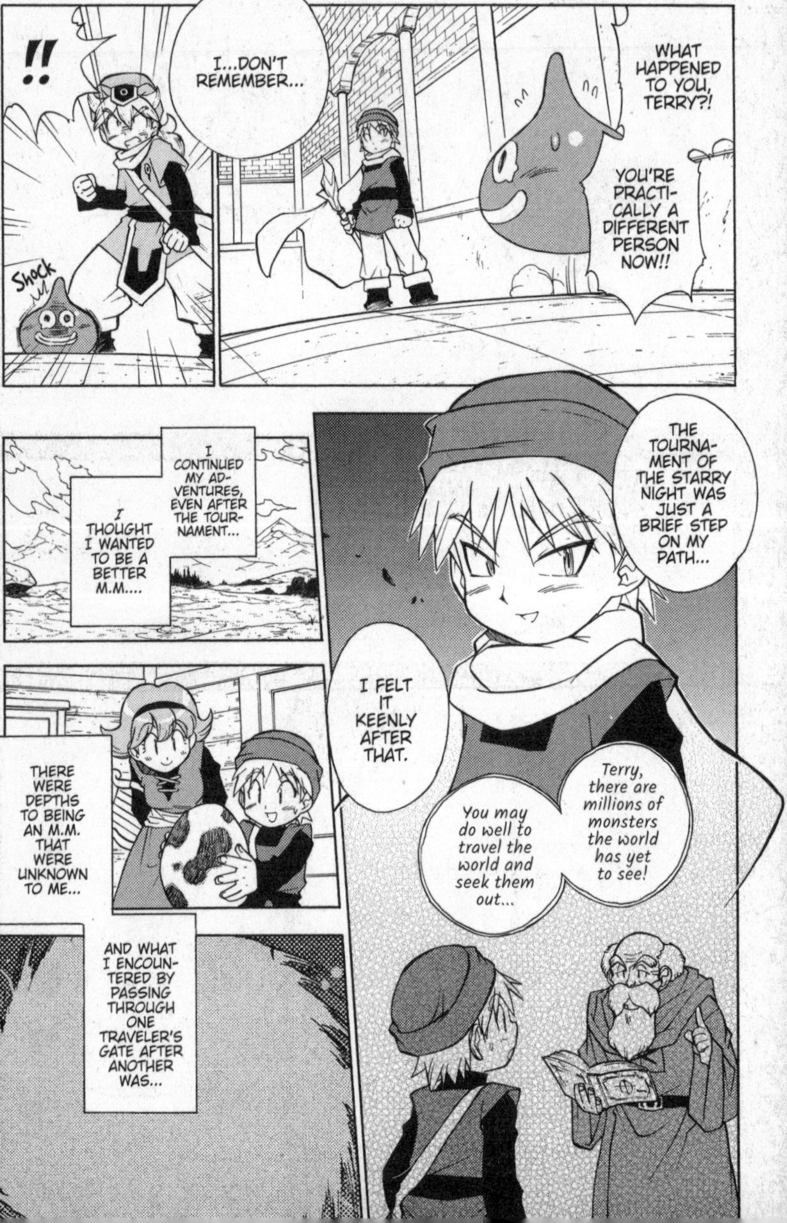
WHAT HAPPENED TO YOU, TERRY?!
YOU'RE PRACTICALLY A DIFFERENT PERSON NOW!!
I...DON'T REMEMBER...
!!
Shock
THE TOURNAMENT OF THE STARRY NIGHT WAS JUST A BRIEF STEP ON MY PATH...
I FELT IT KEENLY AFTER THAT.
Terry, there are millions of monsters the world has yet to see!
You may do well to travel the world and seek them out...
I CONTINUED MY ADVENTURES, EVEN AFTER THE TOURNAMENT...
I THOUGHT I WANTED TO BE A BETTER M.M....
THERE WERE DEPTHS TO BEING AN M.M. THAT WERE UNKNOWN TO ME...
AND WHAT I ENCOUNTERED BY PASSING THROUGH ONE TRAVELER'S GATE AFTER ANOTHER WAS...

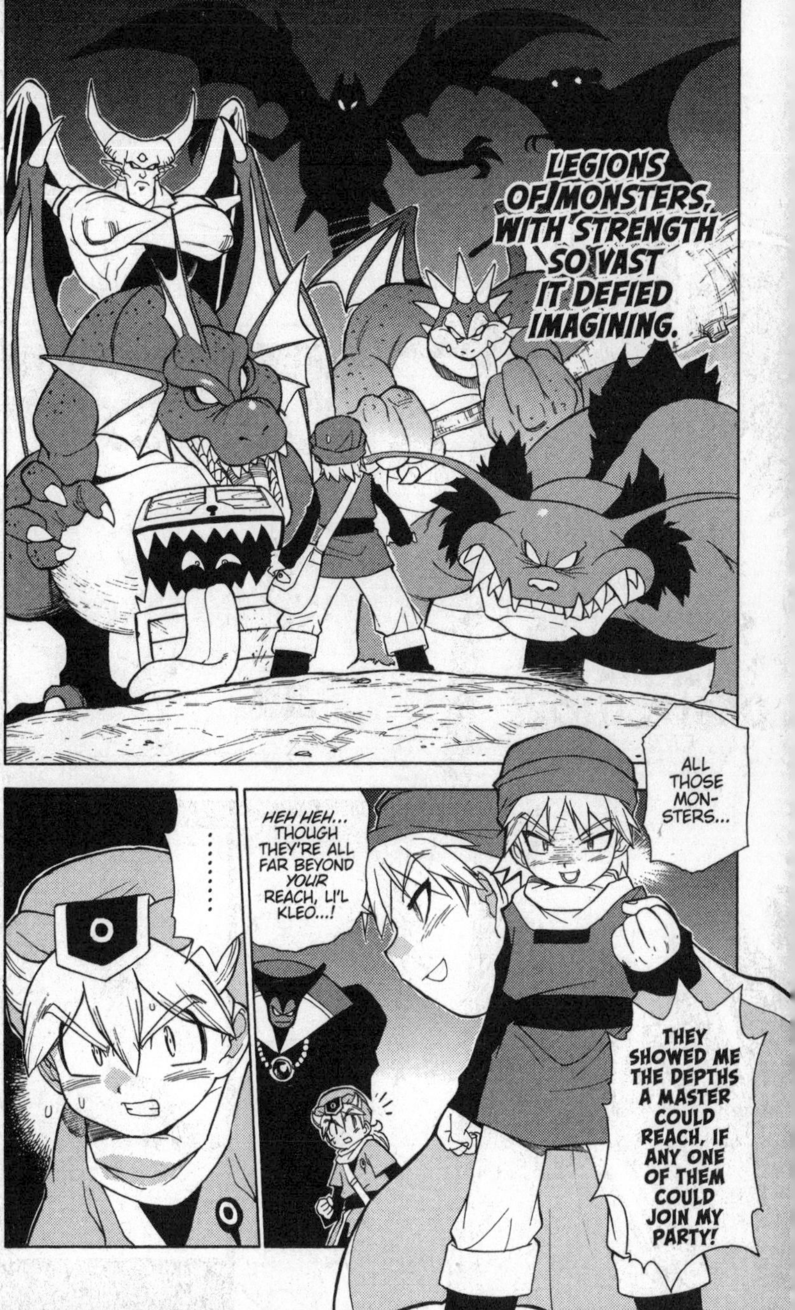
LEGIONS OF MONSTERS, WITH STRENGTH SO VAST IT DEFIED IMAGINING.
ALL THOSE MONSTERS...
THEY SHOWED ME THE DEPTHS A MASTER COULD REACH, IF ANY ONE OF THEM COULD JOIN MY PARTY!
HEH HEH... THOUGH THEY'RE ALL FAR BEYOND *YOUR* REACH, LI'L KLEO...!
......

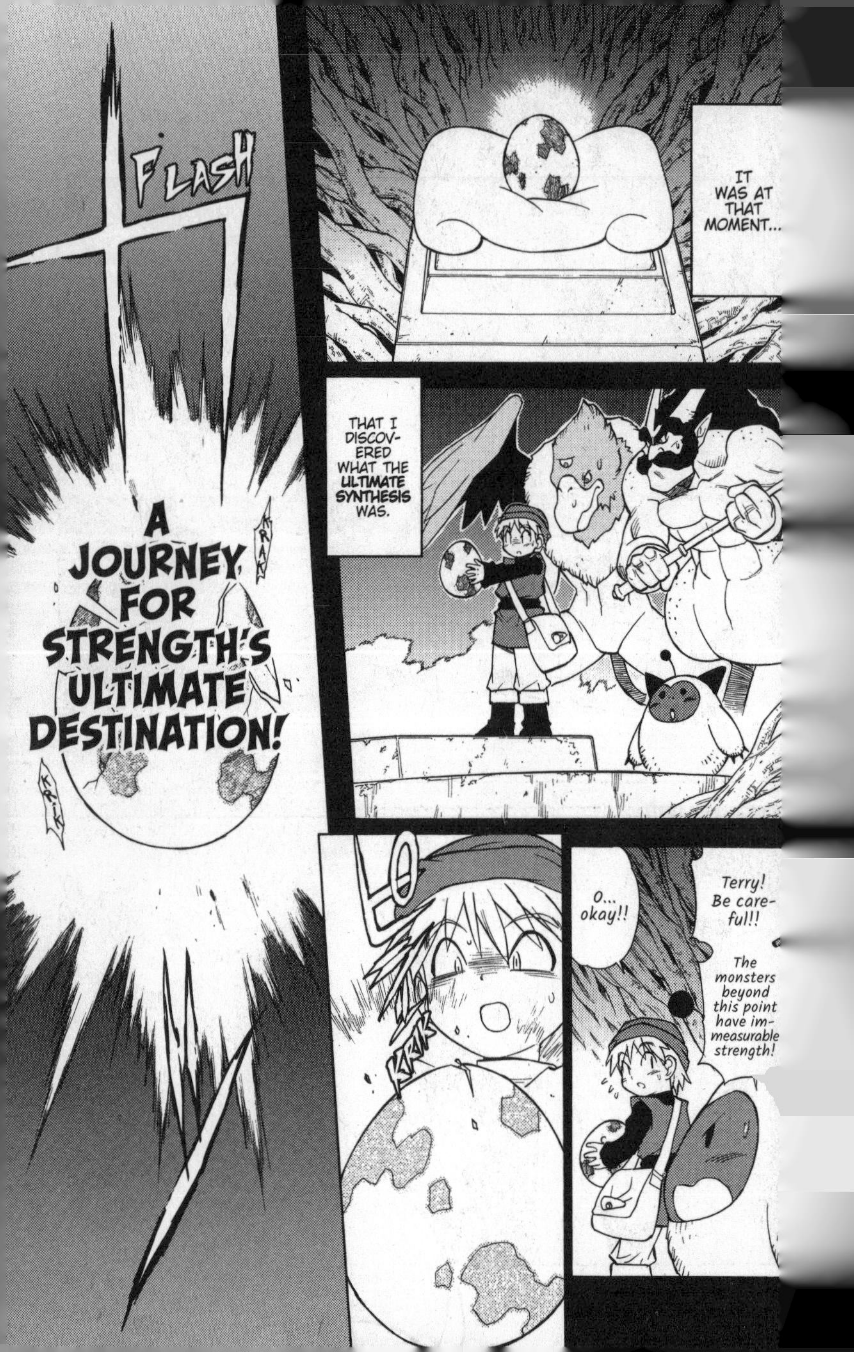
IT WAS AT THAT MOMENT...
THAT I DISCOVERED WHAT THE **ULTIMATE SYNTHESIS** WAS.
Terry! Be careful!!
The monsters beyond this point have immeasurable strength!
O... okay!!
KRAK
FLASH
A JOURNEY FOR STRENGTH'S ULTIMATE DESTINATION!
KRAK
KRIK

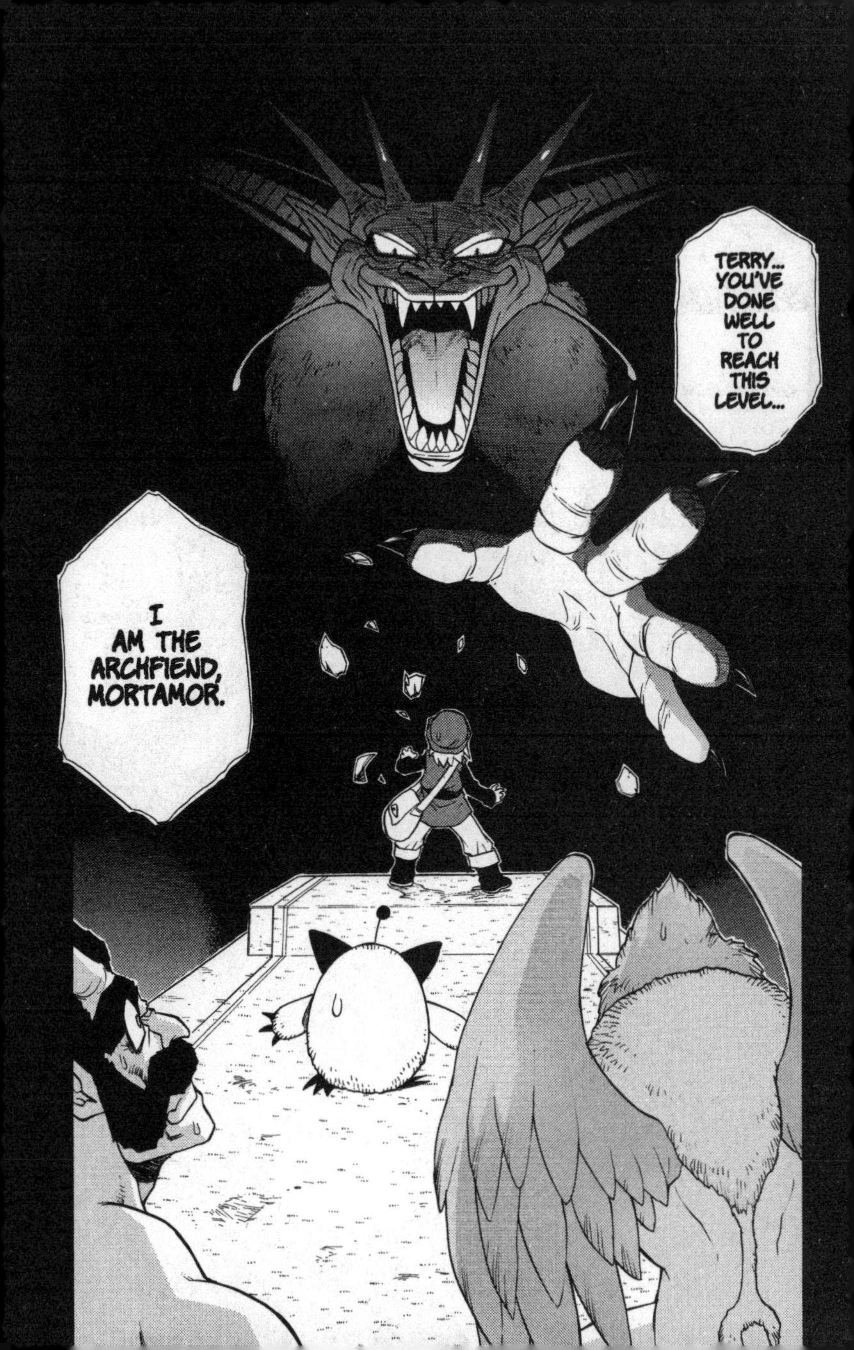
TERRY... YOU'VE DONE WELL TO REACH THIS LEVEL...
I AM THE ARCHFIEND, MORTAMOR.

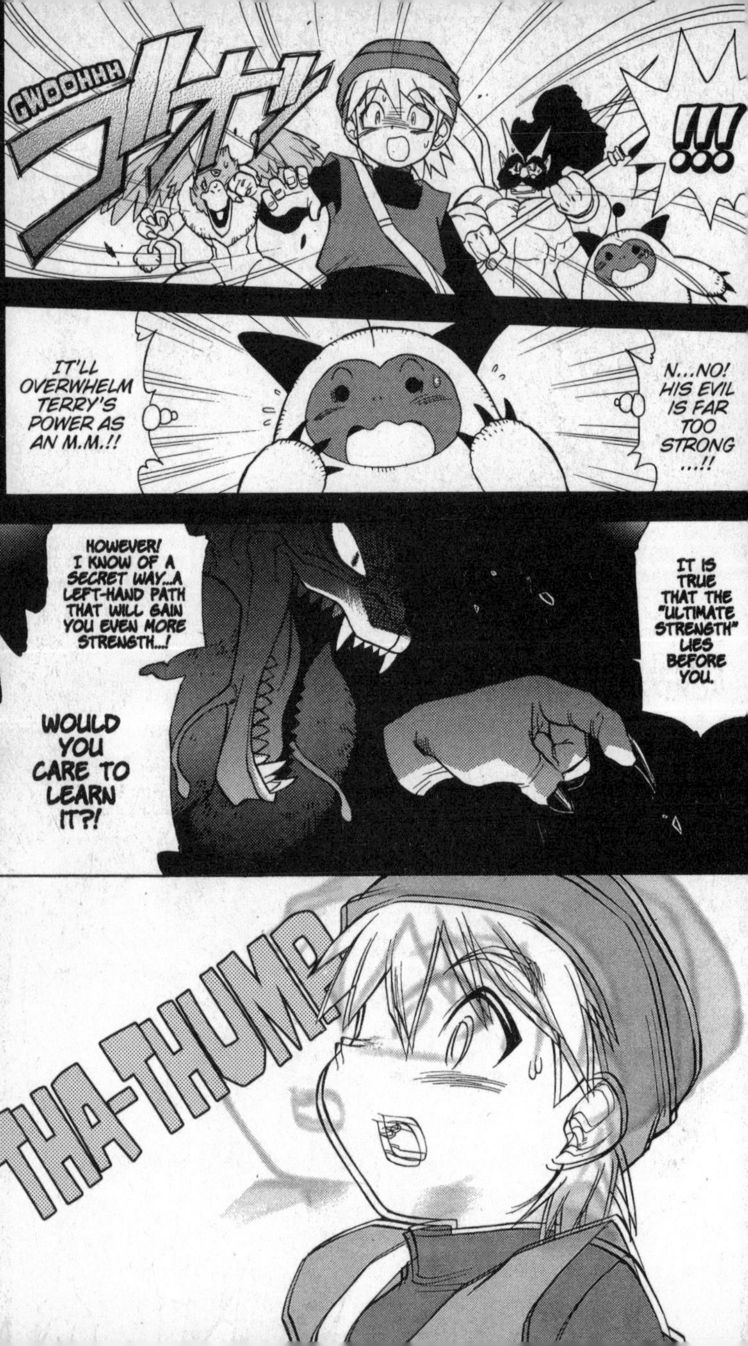
!!!
GWOOHHH
N...NO! HIS EVIL IS FAR TOO STRONG ...!!
IT'LL OVERWHELM TERRY'S POWER AS AN M.M.!!
IT IS TRUE THAT THE "ULTIMATE STRENGTH" LIES BEFORE YOU.
HOWEVER! I KNOW OF A SECRET WAY...A LEFT-HAND PATH THAT WILL GAIN YOU EVEN MORE STRENGTH...!
WOULD YOU CARE TO LEARN IT?!
THA-THUMP

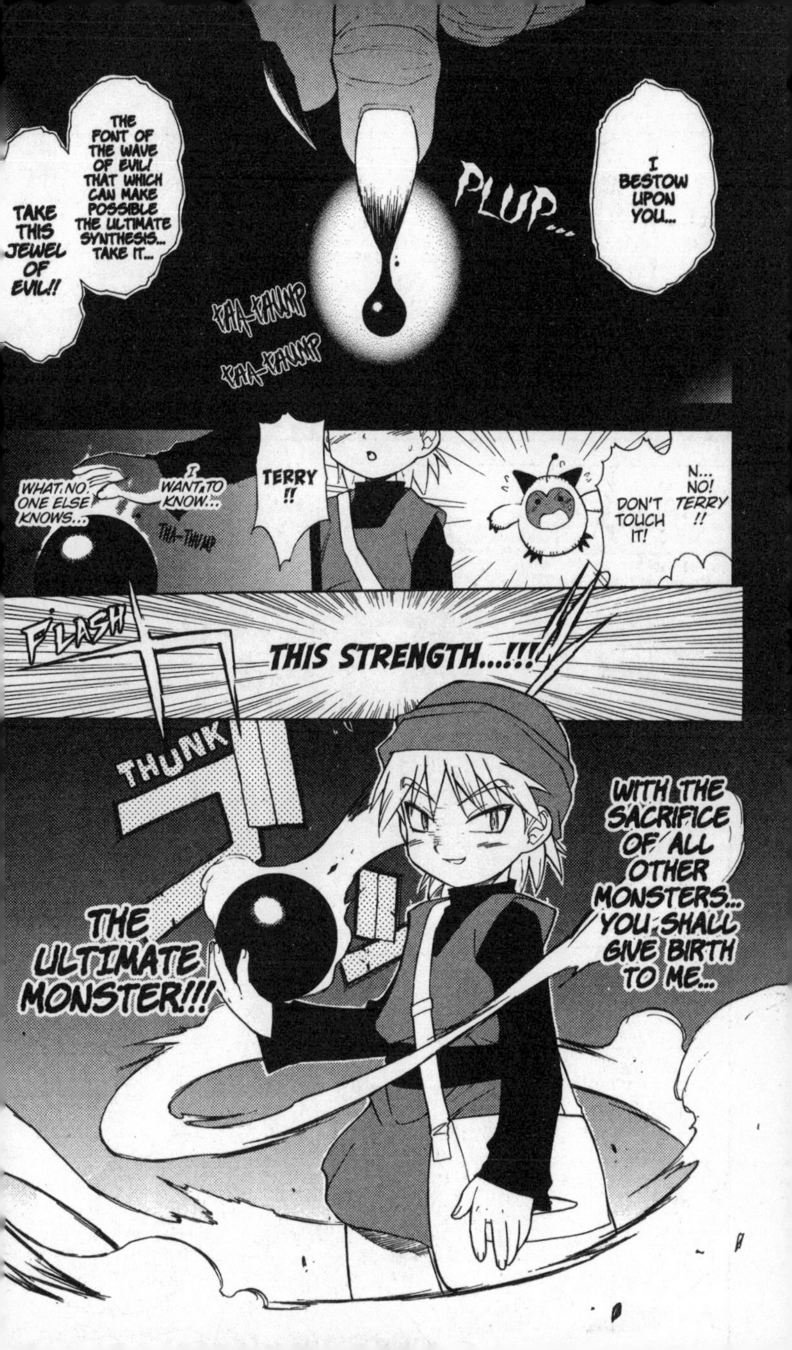
I BESTOW UPON YOU...
PLUP...
THE FONT OF THE WAVE OF EVIL! THAT WHICH CAN MAKE POSSIBLE THE ULTIMATE SYNTHESIS... TAKE IT...
TAKE THIS JEWEL OF EVIL!!
KAA-KAUMP
KAA-KAUMP
N... NO! TERRY!!
DON'T TOUCH IT!
TERRY!!
I WANT TO KNOW...
WHAT NO ONE ELSE KNOWS...
THA-THUMP
FLASH
THIS STRENGTH...!!!
THUNK
WITH THE SACRIFICE OF ALL OTHER MONSTERS... YOU SHALL GIVE BIRTH TO ME...
THE ULTIMATE MONSTER!!!

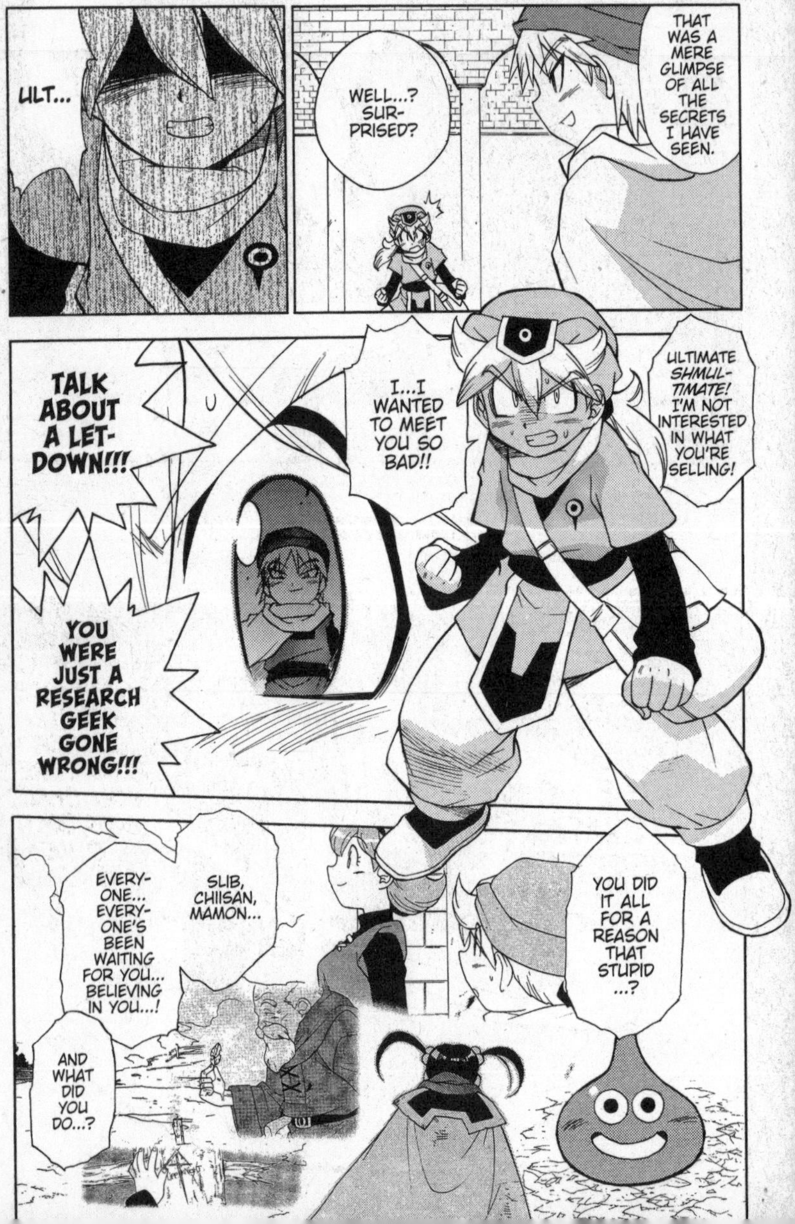
THAT WAS A MERE GLIMPSE OF ALL THE SECRETS I HAVE SEEN.
WELL...? SUR-PRISED?
ULT...
ULTIMATE SHMUL-TIMATE! I'M NOT INTERESTED IN WHAT YOU'RE SELLING!
I...I WANTED TO MEET YOU SO BAD!!
TALK ABOUT A LET-DOWN!!!
YOU WERE JUST A RESEARCH GEEK GONE WRONG!!!
YOU DID IT ALL FOR A REASON THAT STUPID ...?
SLIB, CHIISAN, MAMON...
EVERY-ONE... EVERY-ONE'S BEEN WAITING FOR YOU... BELIEVING IN YOU...!
AND WHAT DID YOU DO...?

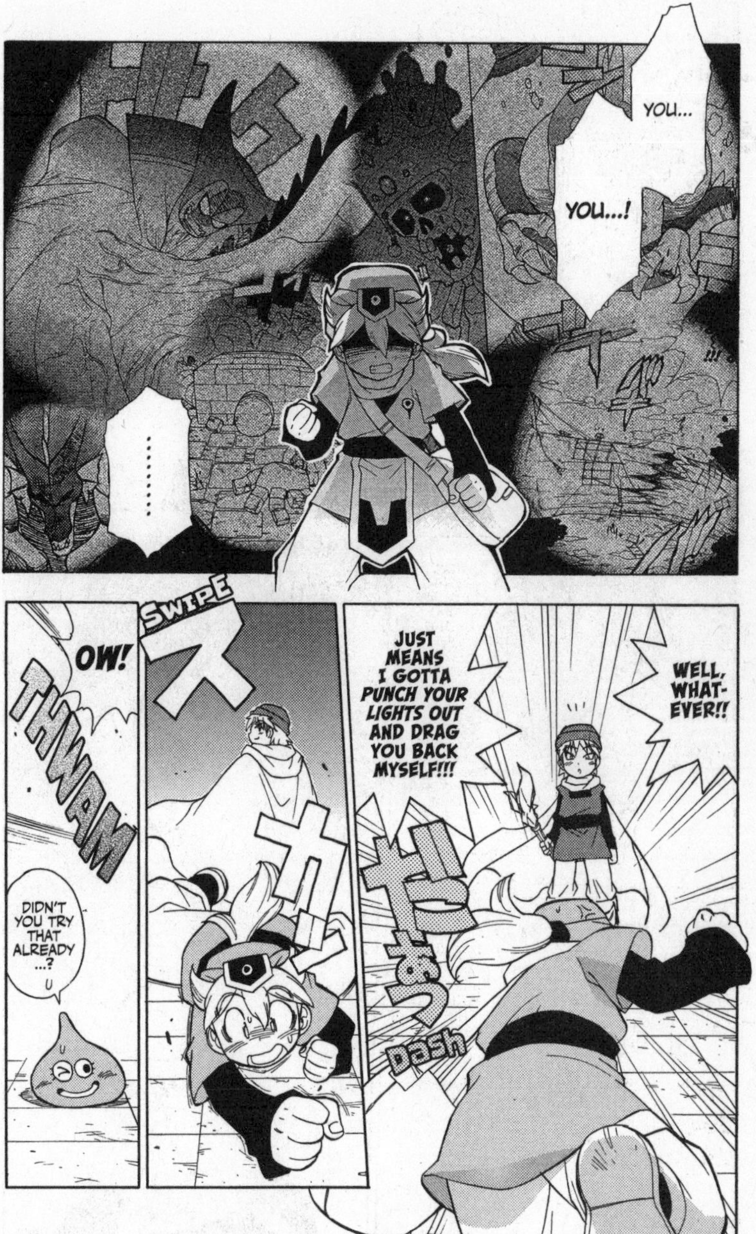
YOU...
YOU...!
......
WELL, WHAT-EVER!!
JUST MEANS I GOTTA PUNCH YOUR LIGHTS OUT AND DRAG YOU BACK MYSELF!!!
DASH
SWIPE
OW!
THWAM
DIDN'T YOU TRY THAT ALREADY ...?

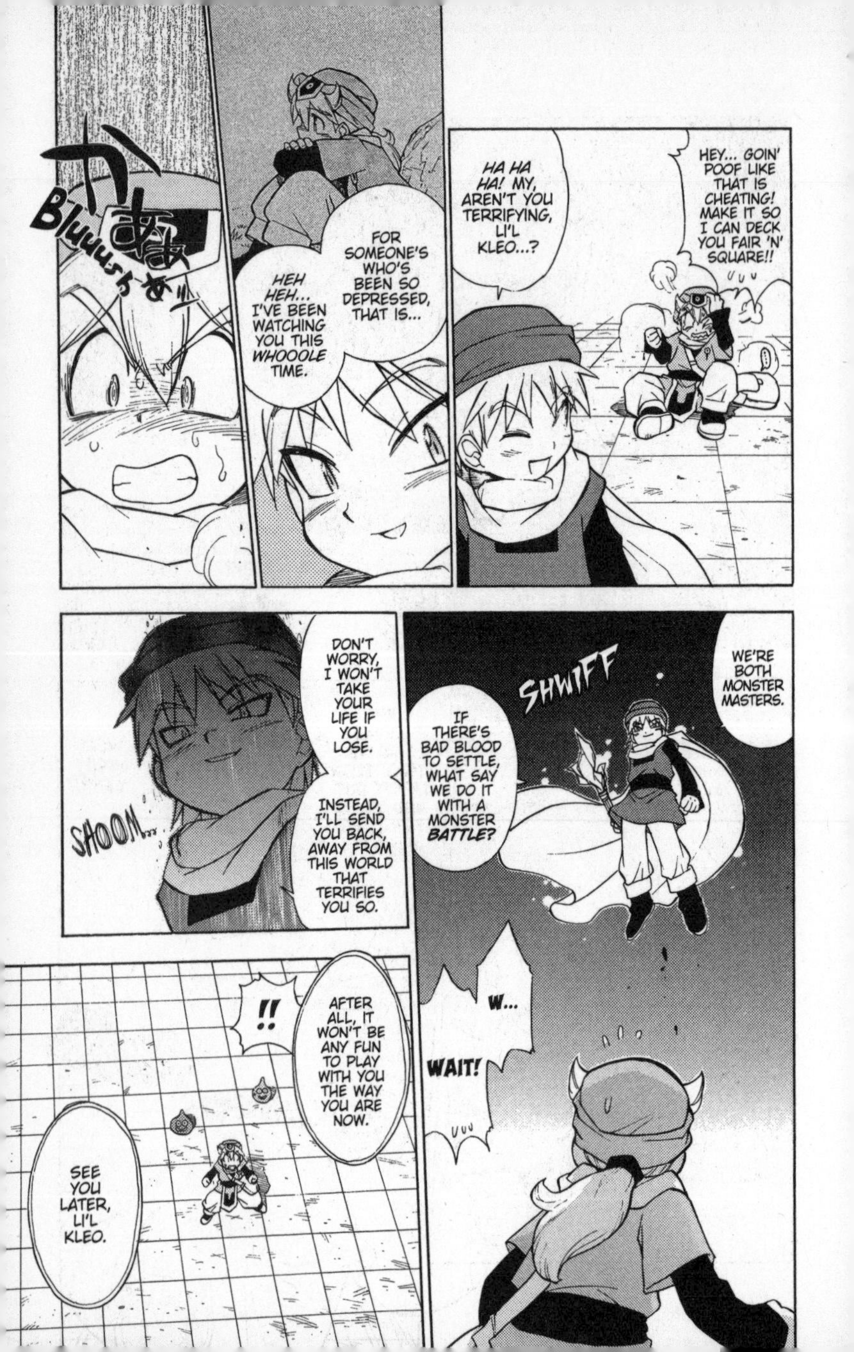
HEY... GOIN' POOF LIKE THAT IS CHEATING! MAKE IT SO I CAN DECK YOU FAIR 'N' SQUARE!!
HA HA HA! MY, AREN'T YOU TERRIFYING, LI'L KLEO...?
FOR SOMEONE'S WHO'S BEEN SO DEPRESSED, THAT IS...
HEH HEH... I'VE BEEN WATCHING YOU THIS WHOOOLE TIME.
Bluuush
WE'RE BOTH MONSTER MASTERS.
SHWIFF
IF THERE'S BAD BLOOD TO SETTLE, WHAT SAY WE DO IT WITH A MONSTER BATTLE?
W...
WAIT!
DON'T WORRY, I WON'T TAKE YOUR LIFE IF YOU LOSE.
INSTEAD, I'LL SEND YOU BACK, AWAY FROM THIS WORLD THAT TERRIFIES YOU SO.
SHOOM...
!!
AFTER ALL, IT WON'T BE ANY FUN TO PLAY WITH YOU THE WAY YOU ARE NOW.
SEE YOU LATER, LI'L KLEO.

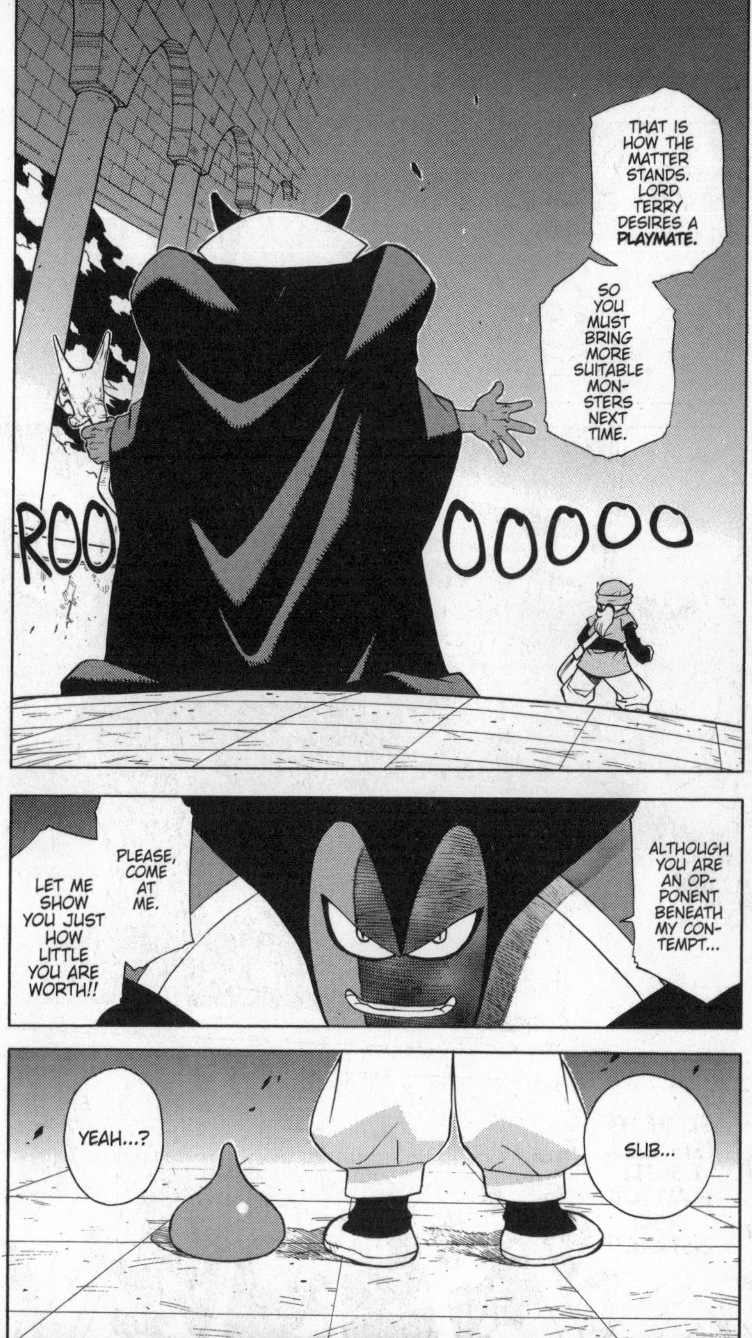
THAT IS HOW THE MATTER STANDS. LORD TERRY DESIRES A **PLAYMATE.**
SO YOU MUST BRING MORE SUITABLE MONSTERS NEXT TIME.
ROO OOOOO
ALTHOUGH YOU ARE AN OPPONENT BENEATH MY CONTEMPT...
PLEASE, COME AT ME.
LET ME SHOW YOU JUST HOW LITTLE YOU ARE WORTH!!
SLIB...
YEAH...?

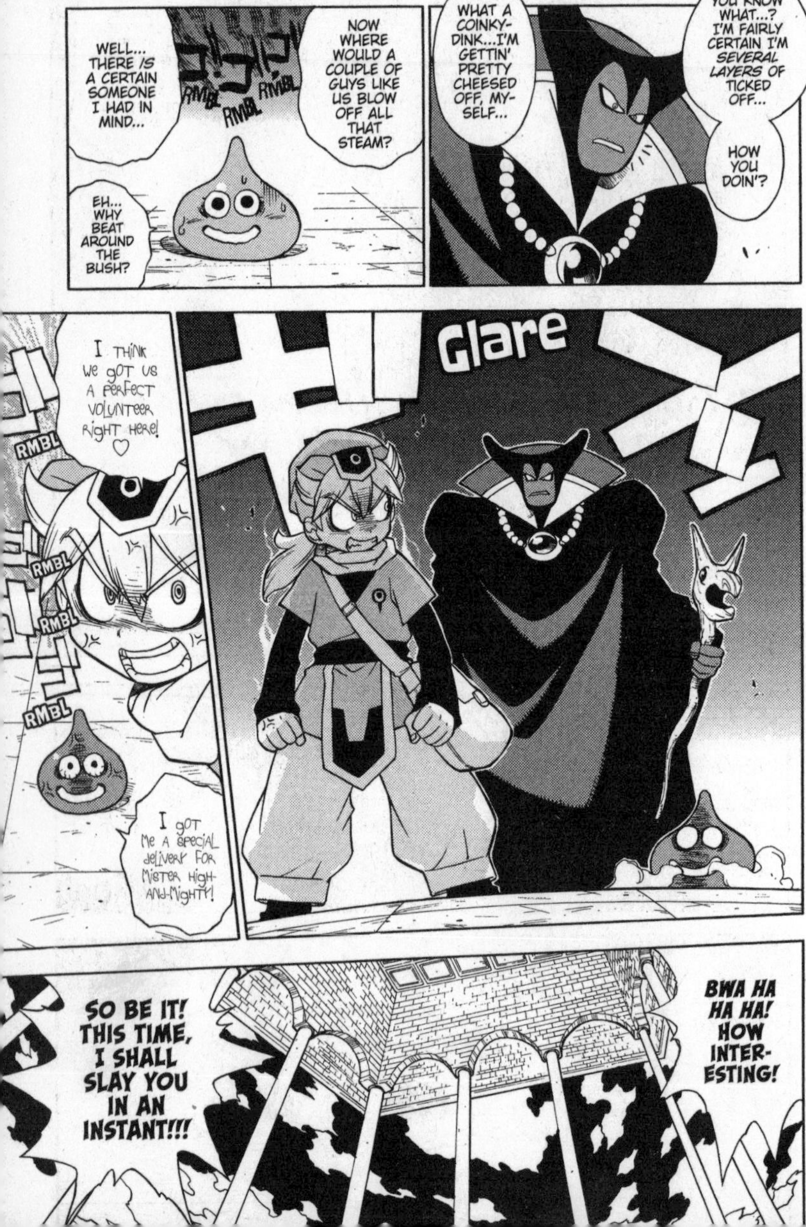
YOU KNOW WHAT...? I'M FAIRLY CERTAIN I'M SEVERAL LAYERS OF TICKED OFF...
WHAT A COINKY-DINK...I'M GETTIN' PRETTY CHEESED OFF, MY-SELF...
HOW YOU DOIN'?
NOW WHERE WOULD A COUPLE OF GUYS LIKE US BLOW OFF ALL THAT STEAM?
RMBL RMBL RMBL
WELL... THERE IS A CERTAIN SOMEONE I HAD IN MIND...
EH... WHY BEAT AROUND THE BUSH?
Glare
I THINK WE GOT US A PERFECT VOLUNTEER RIGHT HERE! ♡
RMBL
RMBL
RMBL
RMBL
I GOT ME A SPECIAL DELIVERY FOR MISTER HIGH-AND-MIGHTY!
BWA HA HA HA! HOW INTER-ESTING!
SO BE IT! THIS TIME, I SHALL SLAY YOU IN AN INSTANT!!!

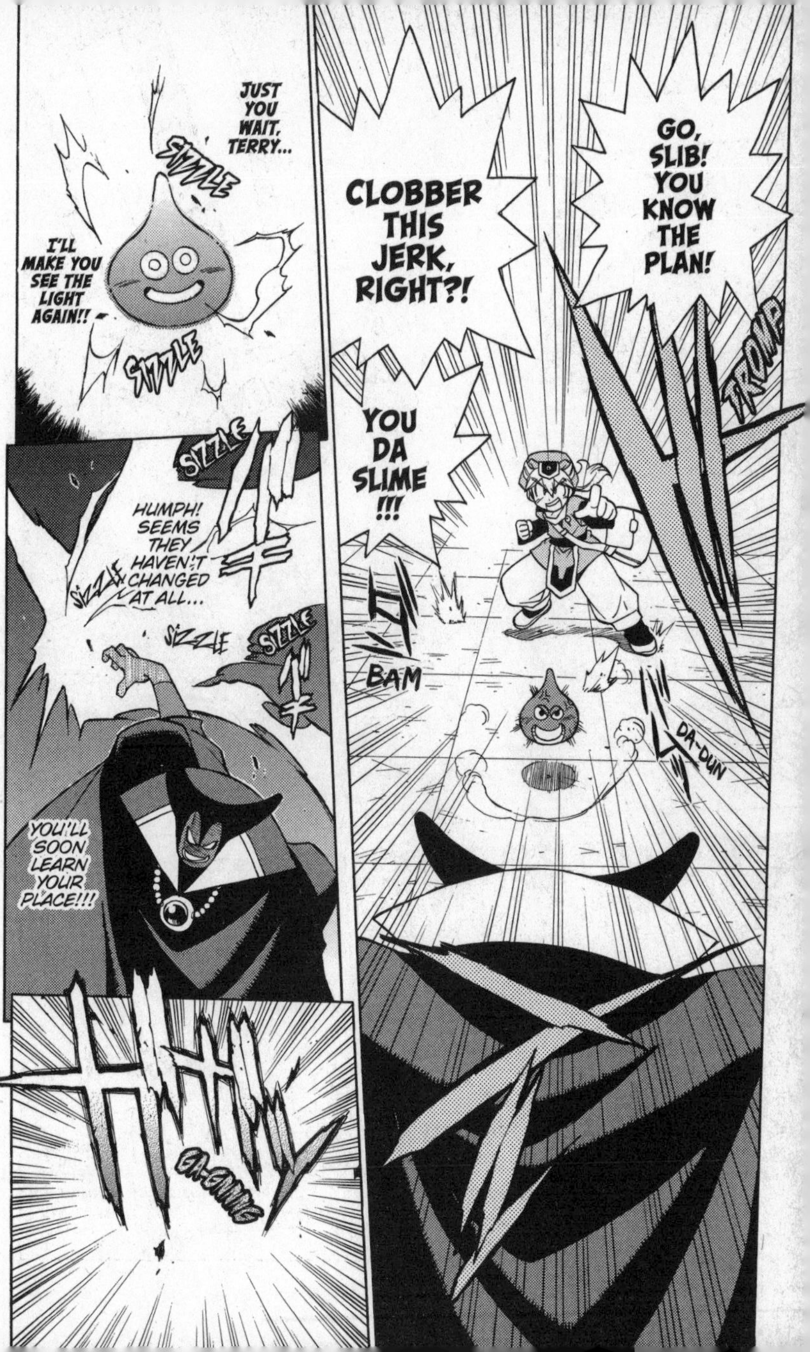
GO, SLIB! YOU KNOW THE PLAN!
CLOBBER THIS JERK, RIGHT?!
TROMP
YOU DA SLIME!!!
BAM
DA-DUN
JUST YOU WAIT, TERRY...
SIZZLE
I'LL MAKE YOU SEE THE LIGHT AGAIN!!
SIZZLE
SIZZLE
HUMPH! SEEMS THEY HAVEN'T CHANGED AT ALL...
SIZZLE
SIZZLE
SIZZLE
YOU'LL SOON LEARN YOUR PLACE!!!
GA-CHING

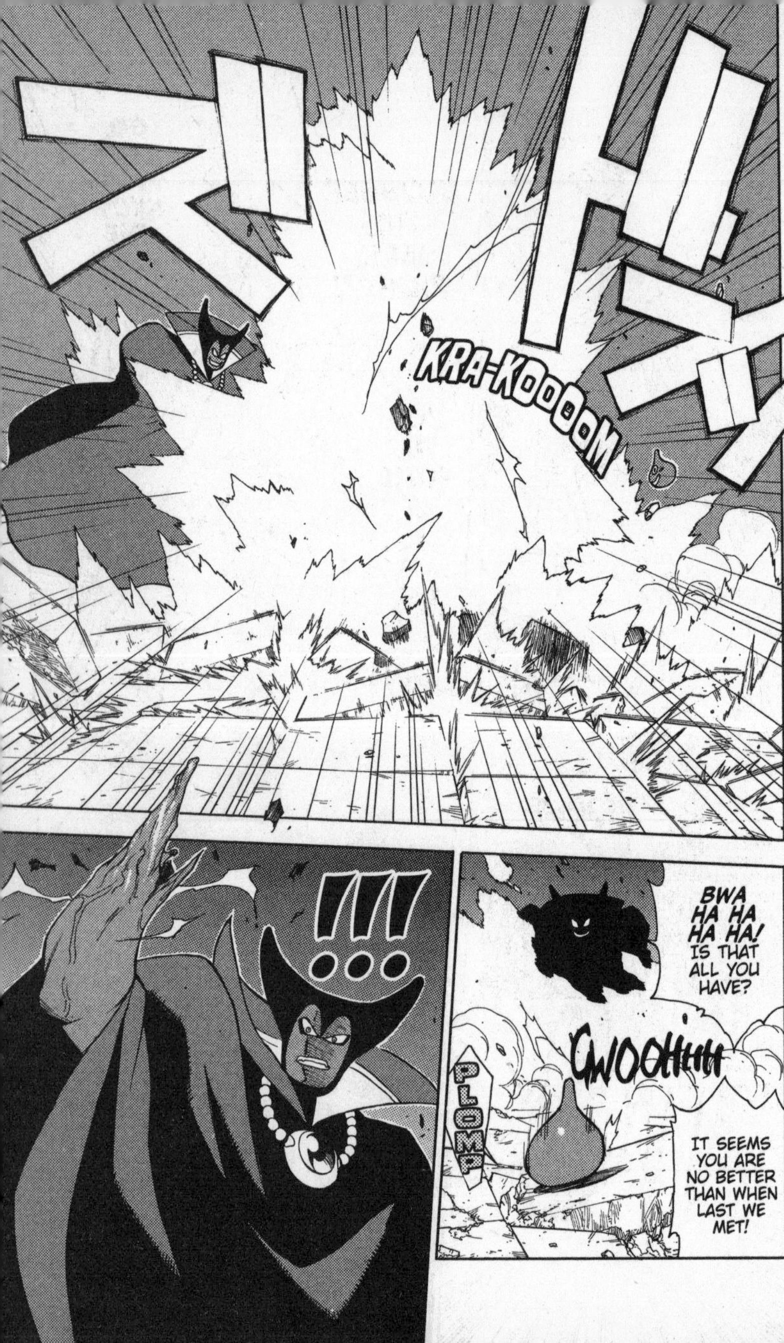
KRA-KOOOOOM
BWA HA HA HA HA! IS THAT ALL YOU HAVE?
GWOOHHHH
PLOMP
IT SEEMS YOU ARE NO BETTER THAN WHEN LAST WE MET!
!!!...

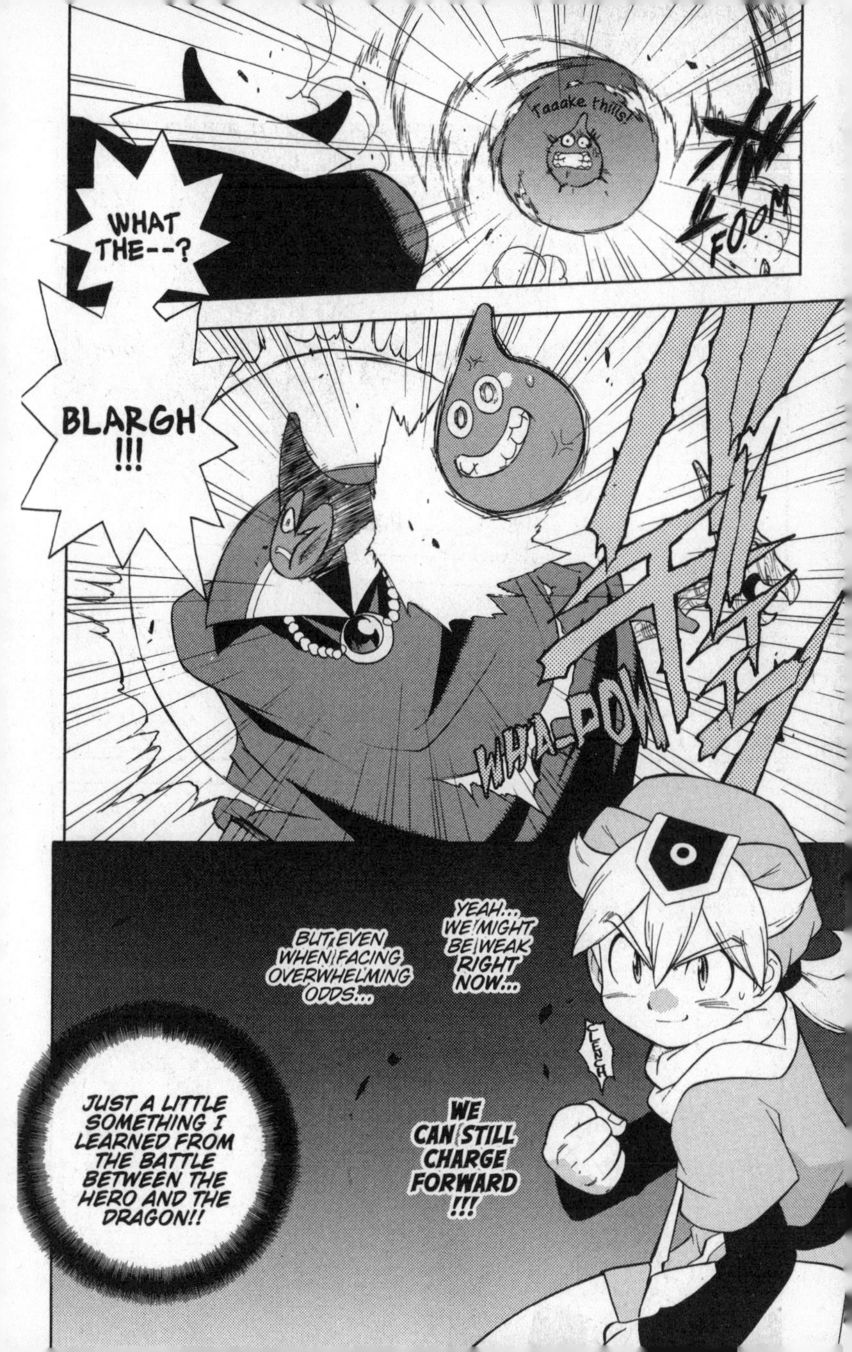

Taaake this!
FOOM
WHAT THE--?
BLARGH!!!
WHA-POW
YEAH... WE MIGHT BE WEAK RIGHT NOW...
BUT EVEN WHEN FACING OVERWHELMING ODDS...
LENCH
WE CAN STILL CHARGE FORWARD!!!
JUST A LITTLE SOMETHING I LEARNED FROM THE BATTLE BETWEEN THE HERO AND THE DRAGON!!

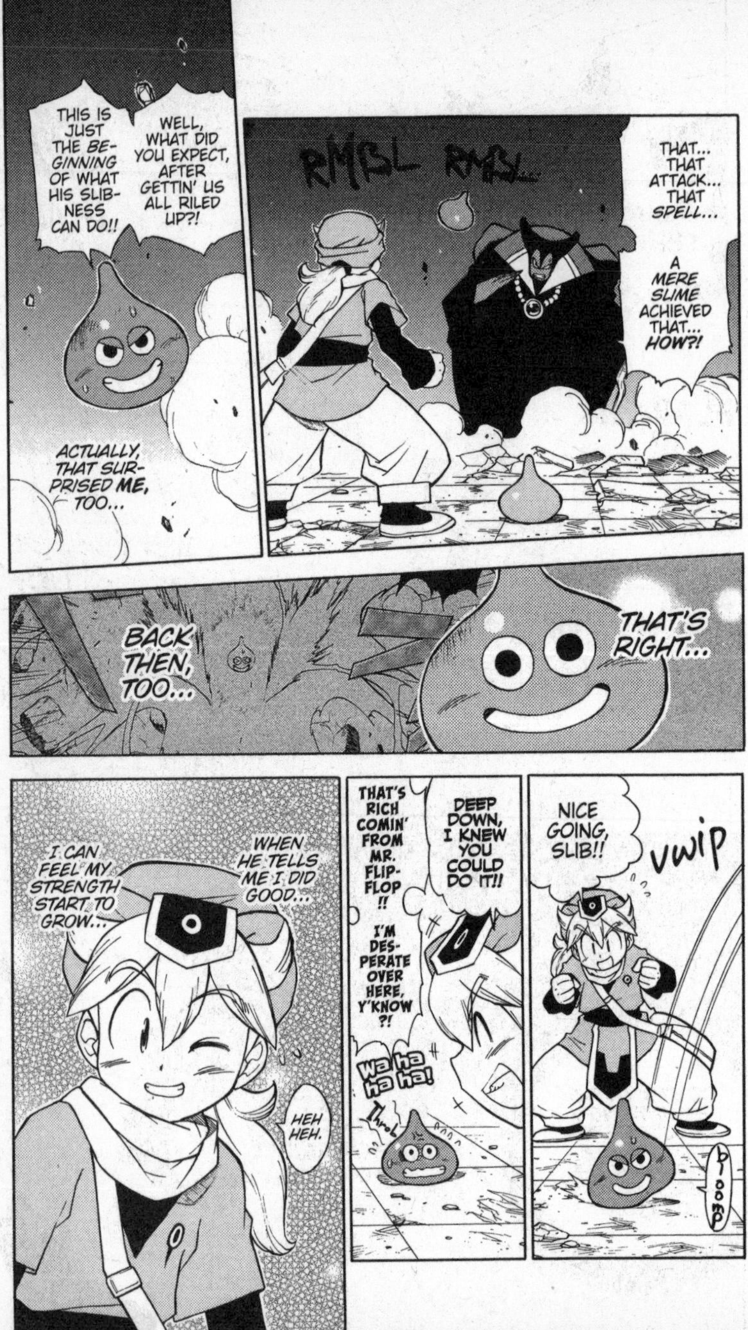
RMBL RMBL...
THAT... THAT ATTACK... THAT SPELL...
A MERE SLIME ACHIEVED THAT... HOW?!
WELL, WHAT DID YOU EXPECT, AFTER GETTIN' US ALL RILED UP?!
THIS IS JUST THE BEGINNING OF WHAT HIS SLIBNESS CAN DO!!
ACTUALLY, THAT SURPRISED ME, TOO...
THAT'S RIGHT...
BACK THEN, TOO...
NICE GOING, SLIB!!
VWIP
bloomp
DEEP DOWN, I KNEW YOU COULD DO IT!!
THAT'S RICH COMIN' FROM MR. FLIP-FLOP!!
I'M DESPERATE OVER HERE, Y'KNOW?!
wa ha ha ha!
Throb
WHEN HE TELLS ME I DID GOOD...
I CAN FEEL MY STRENGTH START TO GROW...
HEH HEH.

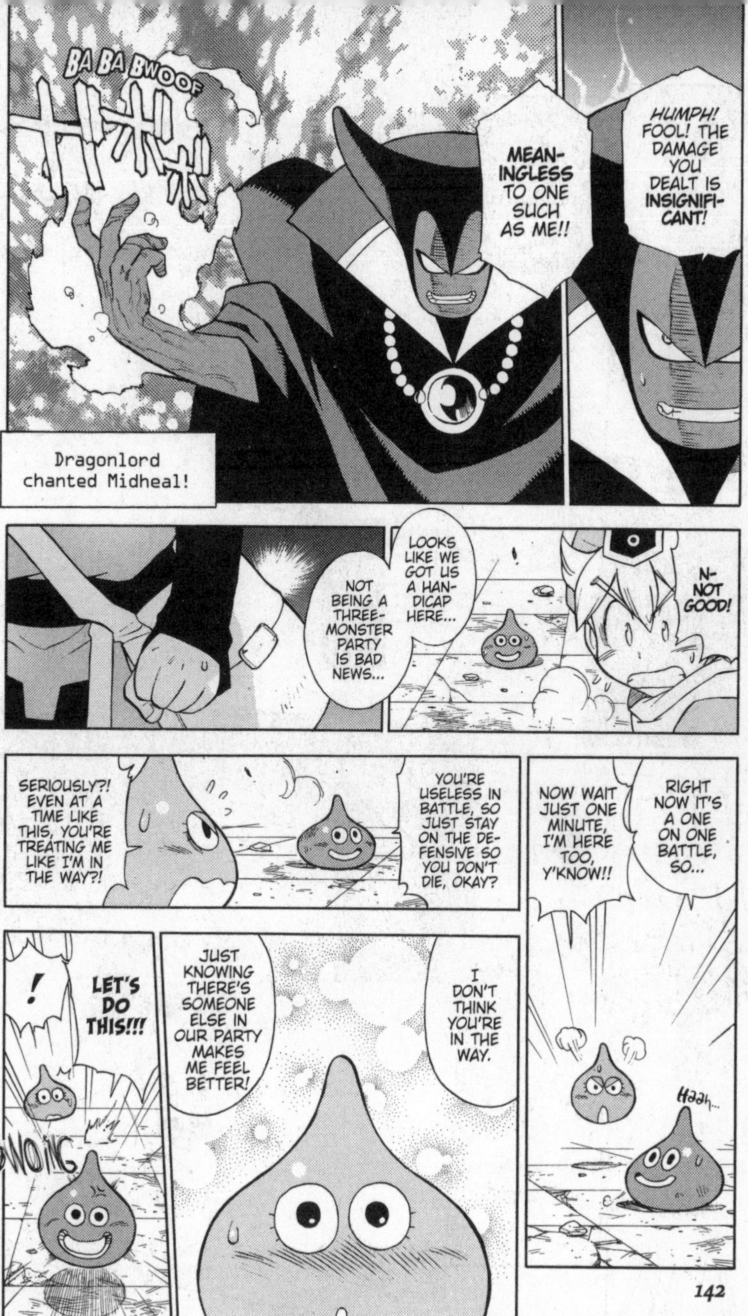
HUMPH! FOOL! THE DAMAGE YOU DEALT IS INSIGNIFICANT!
MEAN-INGLESS TO ONE SUCH AS ME!!
BA BA BWOOF
Dragonlord chanted Midheal!
N-NOT GOOD!
LOOKS LIKE WE GOT US A HAN-DICAP HERE...
NOT BEING A THREE-MONSTER PARTY IS BAD NEWS...
RIGHT NOW IT'S A ONE ON ONE BATTLE, SO...
NOW WAIT JUST ONE MINUTE, I'M HERE TOO, Y'KNOW!!
Haah...
YOU'RE USELESS IN BATTLE, SO JUST STAY ON THE DE-FENSIVE SO YOU DON'T DIE, OKAY?
SERIOUSLY?! EVEN AT A TIME LIKE THIS, YOU'RE TREATING ME LIKE I'M IN THE WAY?!
I DON'T THINK YOU'RE IN THE WAY.
JUST KNOWING THERE'S SOMEONE ELSE IN OUR PARTY MAKES ME FEEL BETTER!
!
LET'S DO THIS!!!
BNOING

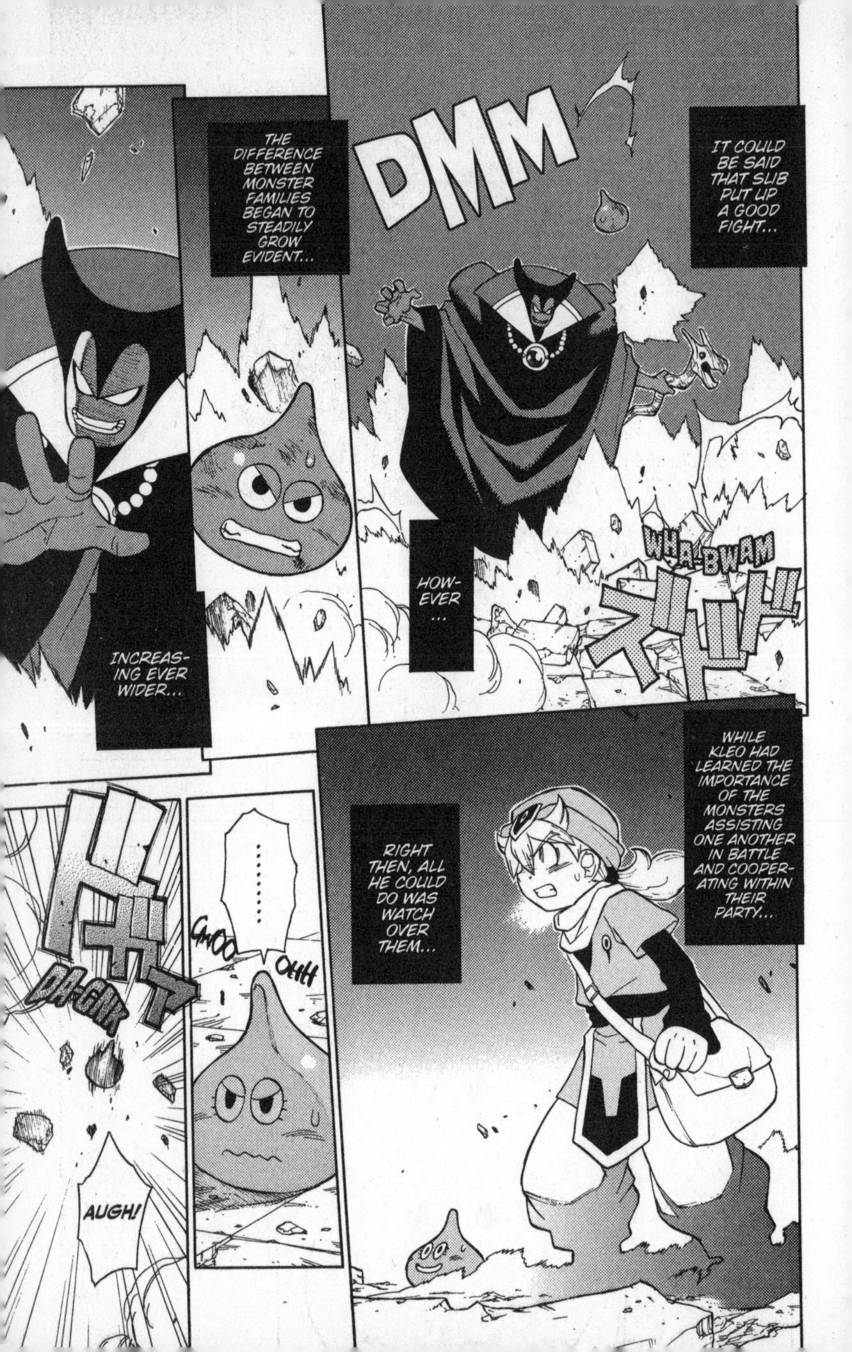

IT COULD BE SAID THAT SLIB PUT UP A GOOD FIGHT...
DMM
WHA-BWAM
HOWEVER...
THE DIFFERENCE BETWEEN MONSTER FAMILIES BEGAN TO STEADILY GROW EVIDENT...
INCREASING EVER WIDER...
WHILE KLEO HAD LEARNED THE IMPORTANCE OF THE MONSTERS ASSISTING ONE ANOTHER IN BATTLE AND COOPERATING WITHIN THEIR PARTY...
RIGHT THEN, ALL HE COULD DO WAS WATCH OVER THEM...
......
GWOOOHH
DA-GAK
AUGH!

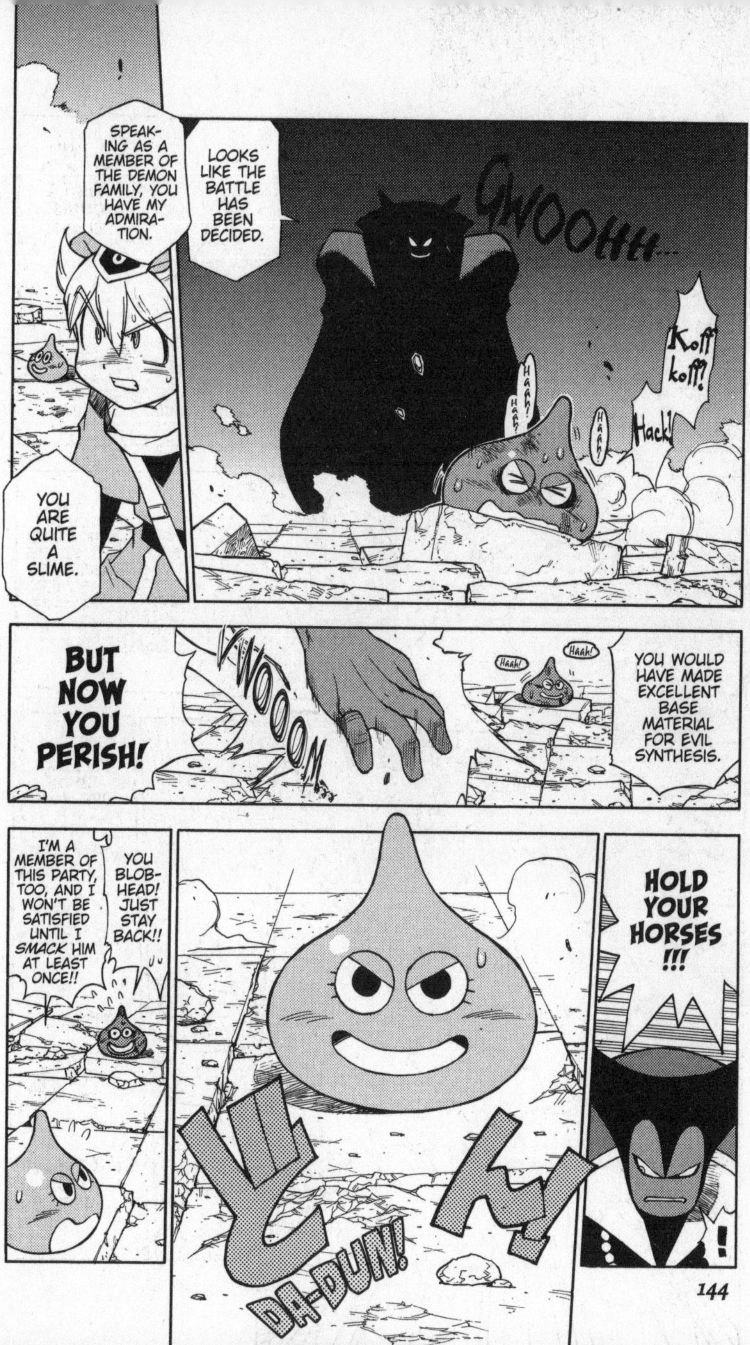
LOOKS LIKE THE BATTLE HAS BEEN DECIDED.
GWOOHHH...
Koff koff!
Hack!
Haah!
Haah!
Haah!
SPEAKING AS A MEMBER OF THE DEMON FAMILY, YOU HAVE MY ADMIRATION.
!
YOU ARE QUITE A SLIME.
YOU WOULD HAVE MADE EXCELLENT BASE MATERIAL FOR EVIL SYNTHESIS.
Haah!
Haah!
WOOOOOM
BUT NOW YOU PERISH!
HOLD YOUR HORSES!!!
!
DA-DUN!
YOU BLOB-HEAD! JUST STAY BACK!!
I'M A MEMBER OF THIS PARTY, TOO, AND I WON'T BE SATISFIED UNTIL I SMACK HIM AT LEAST ONCE!!

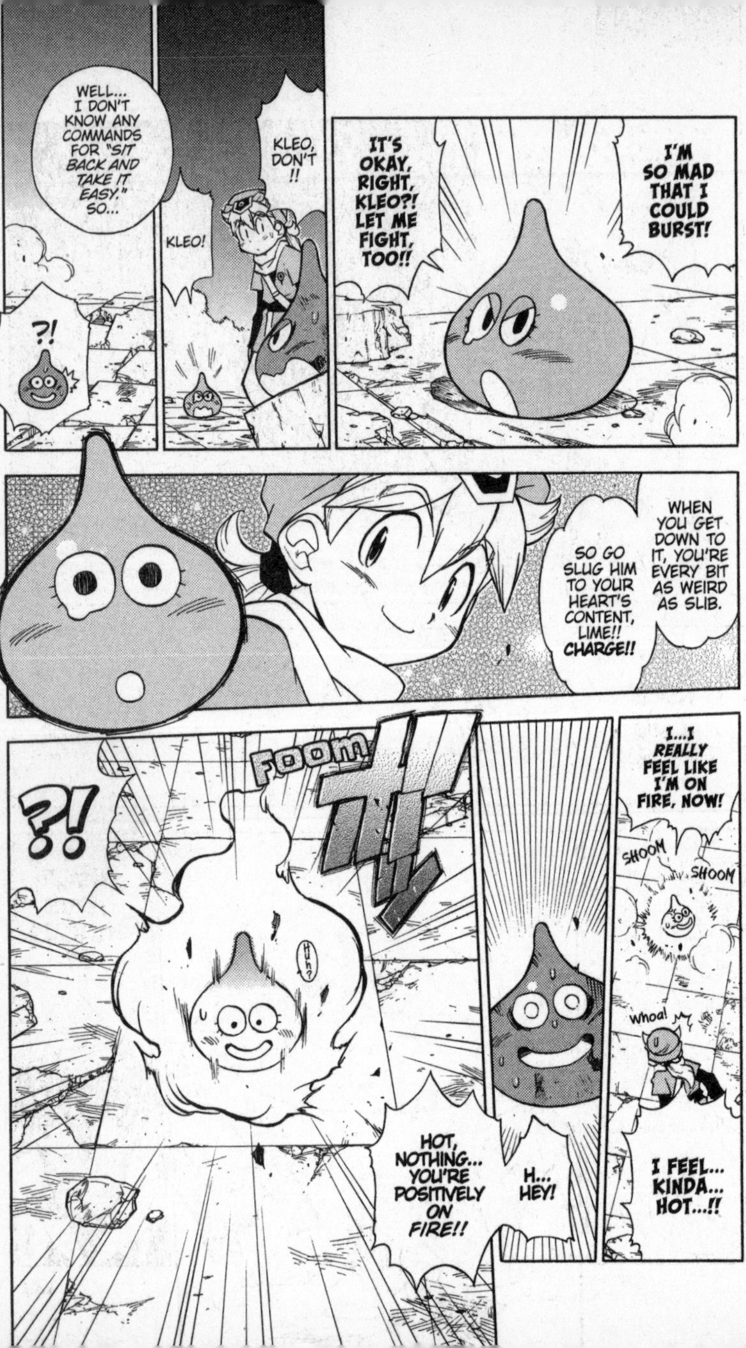
I'M SO MAD THAT I COULD BURST!
IT'S OKAY, RIGHT, KLEO?! LET ME FIGHT, TOO!!
KLEO, DON'T !!
KLEO!
WELL... I DON'T KNOW ANY COMMANDS FOR "SIT BACK AND TAKE IT EASY." SO...
?!
WHEN YOU GET DOWN TO IT, YOU'RE EVERY BIT AS WEIRD AS SLIB.
SO GO SLUG HIM TO YOUR HEART'S CONTENT, LIME!! CHARGE!!
I...I REALLY FEEL LIKE I'M ON FIRE, NOW!
SHOOM
SHOOM
Whoa!
I FEEL... KINDA... HOT...!!
H... HEY!
HOT, NOTHING... YOU'RE POSITIVELY ON FIRE!!
FOOM
?!
Huh?

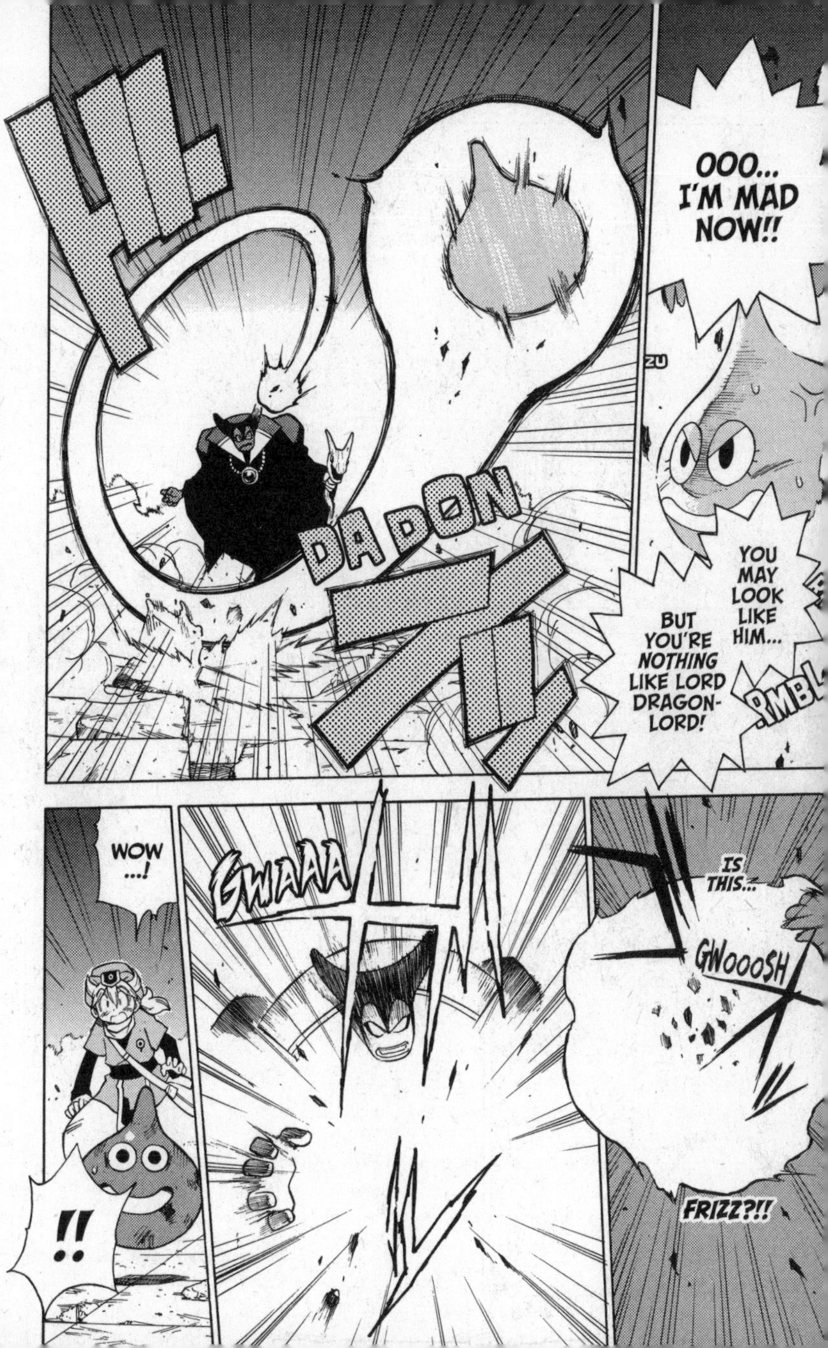
OOO... I'M MAD NOW!!
ZU
YOU MAY LOOK LIKE HIM...
BUT YOU'RE NOTHING LIKE LORD DRAGON-LORD!
DA DON
IS THIS...
GWOOOSH
FRIZZ?!!
GWAAA
WOW ...!
!!

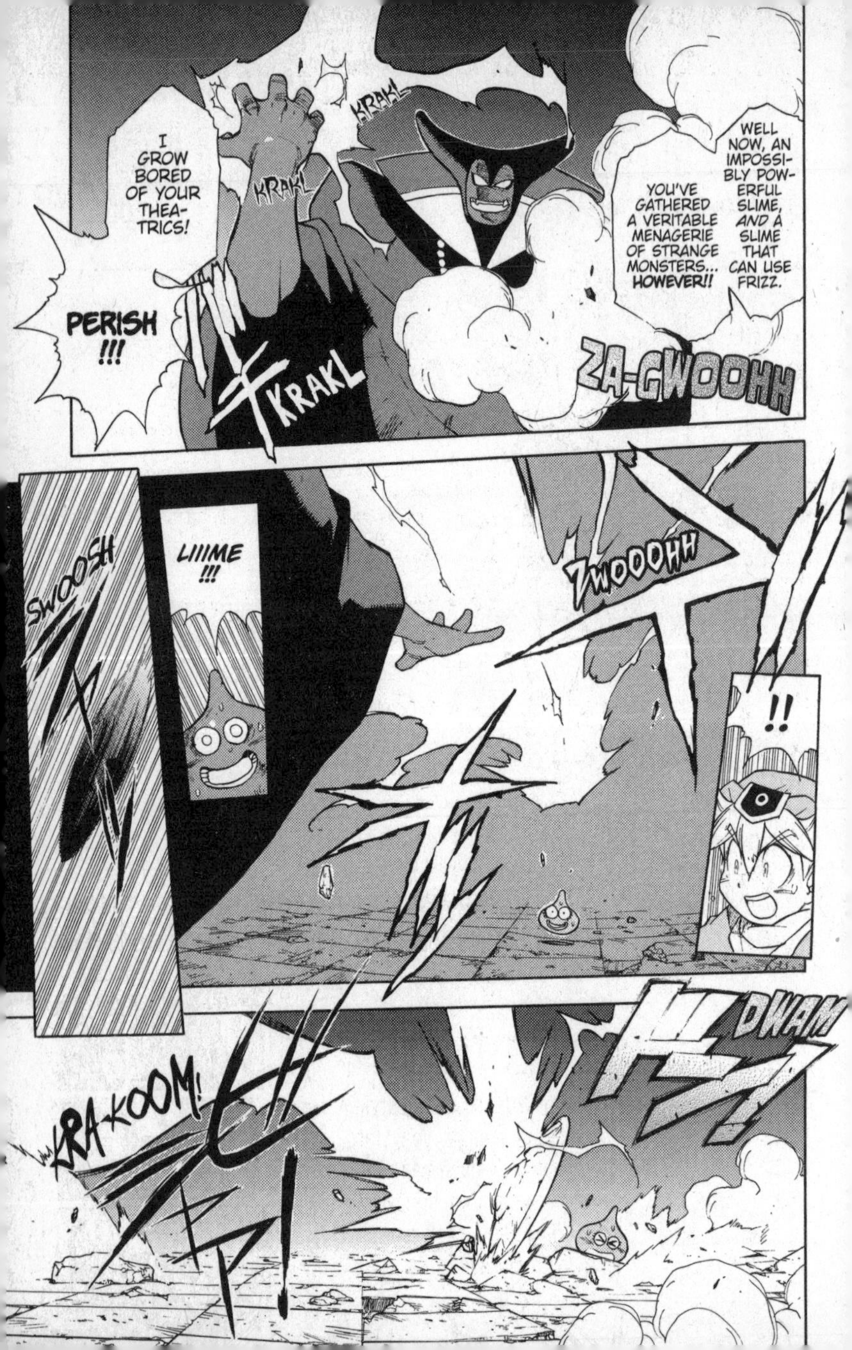

WELL NOW, AN IMPOSSIBLY POWERFUL SLIME, AND A SLIME THAT CAN USE FRIZZ.
YOU'VE GATHERED A VERITABLE MENAGERIE OF STRANGE MONSTERS... HOWEVER!!
ZA-GWOOHH
KRAKL
KRAKL
I GROW BORED OF YOUR THEATRICS!
PERISH!!!
KRAKL
!!
ZWOOOHH
LIIIME!!!
SWOOSH
DWAM
KRA-KOOM!

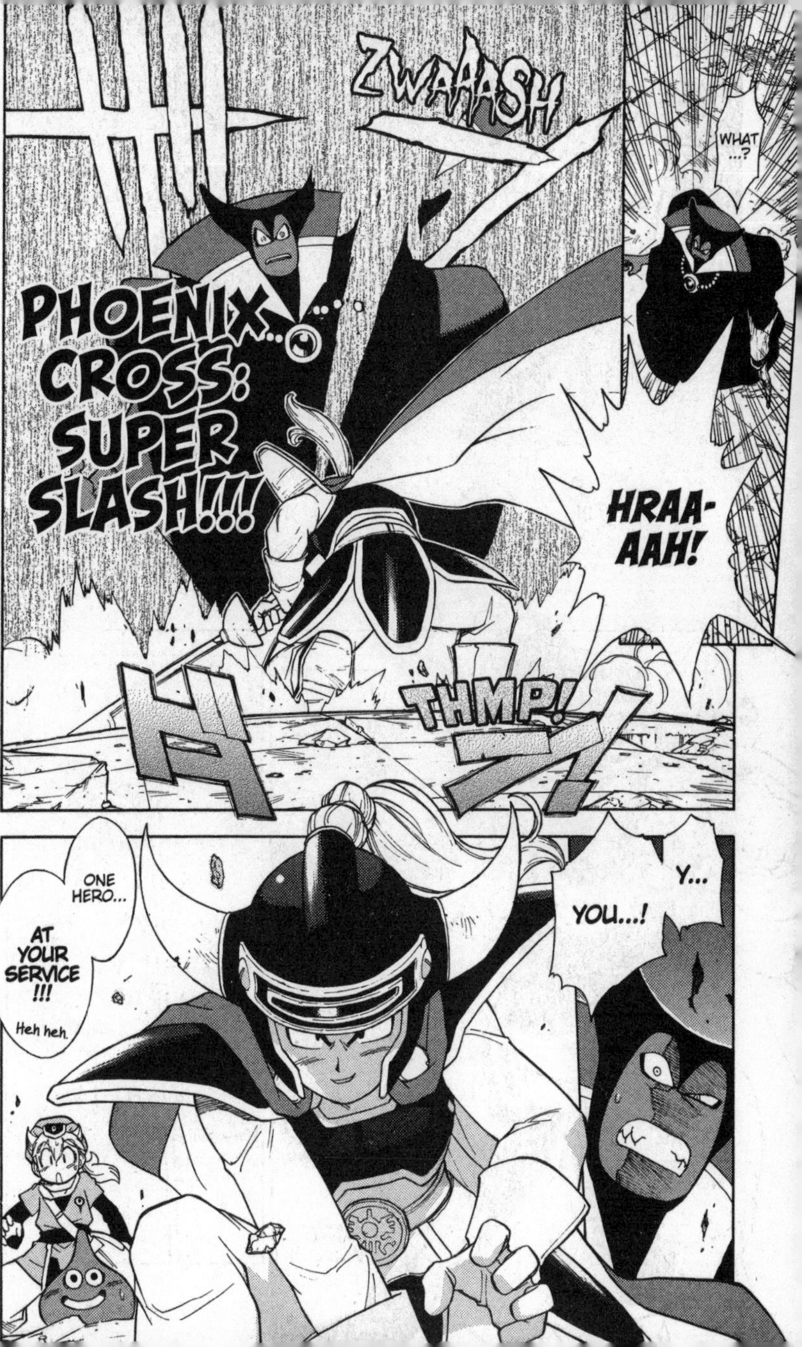
WHAT ...?
ZWAAASH
PHOENIX... CROSS: SUPER SLASH!!!
HRAA-AAH!
THMP!
Y...
YOU...!
ONE HERO...
AT YOUR SERVICE !!!
Heh heh.

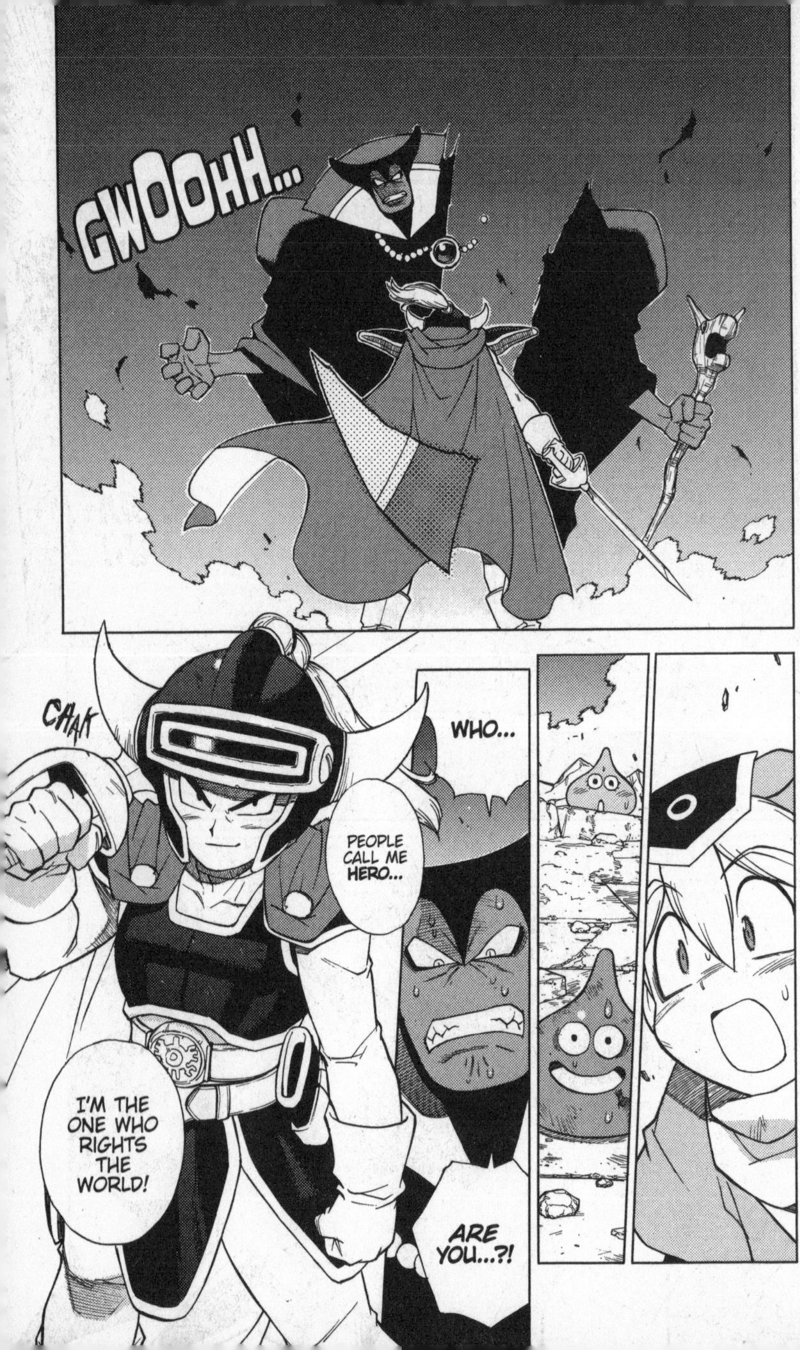
GWOOHH...
WHO...
ARE YOU...?!
CHAK
PEOPLE CALL ME HERO...
I'M THE ONE WHO RIGHTS THE WORLD!

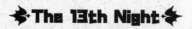

The 13th Night

If I Could Save the World...

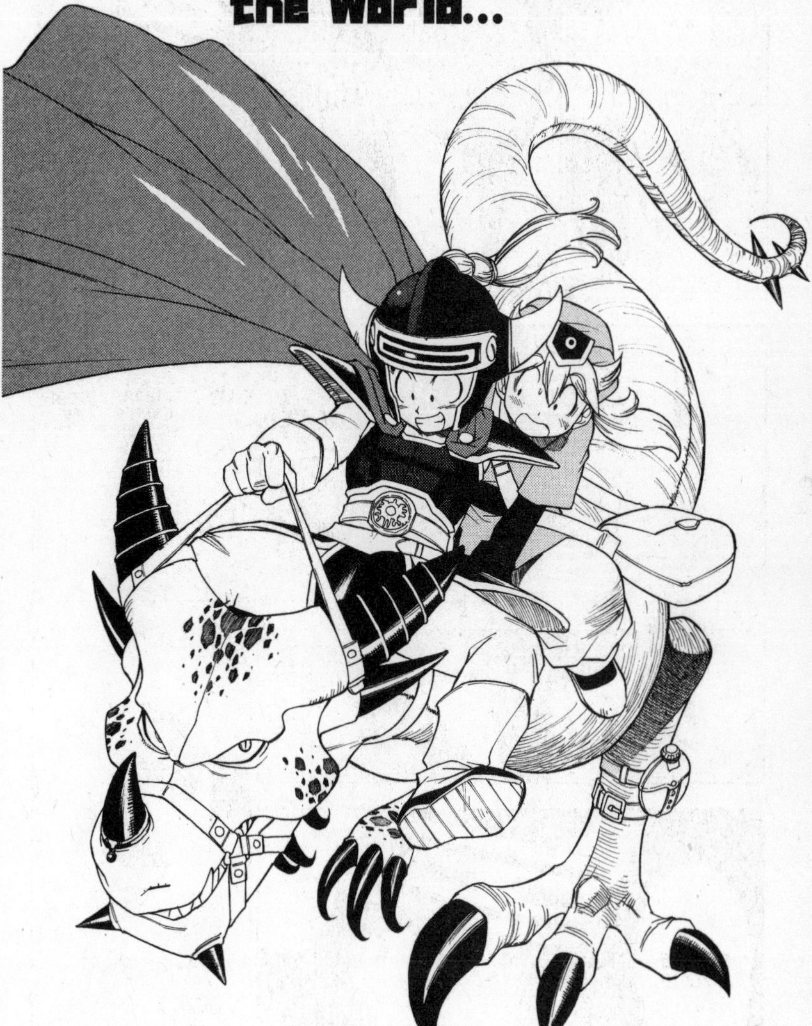

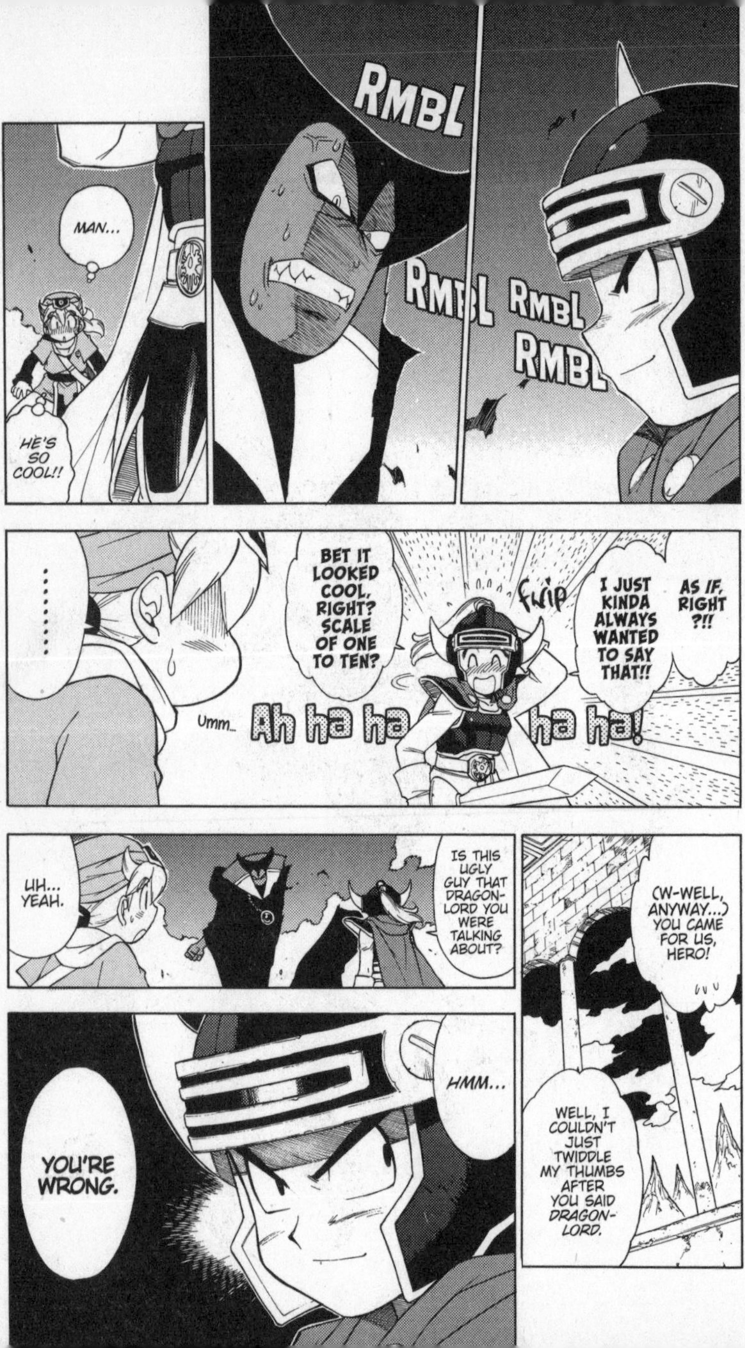
RMBL
RMBL RMBL
RMBL
MAN...
HE'S SO COOL!!
AS IF, RIGHT?!!
I JUST KINDA ALWAYS WANTED TO SAY THAT!!
fwip
BET IT LOOKED COOL, RIGHT? SCALE OF ONE TO TEN?
Ah ha ha ha ha!
Umm...
......
(W-WELL, ANYWAY...) YOU CAME FOR US, HERO!
WELL, I COULDN'T JUST TWIDDLE MY THUMBS AFTER YOU SAID DRAGONLORD.
IS THIS UGLY GUY THAT DRAGONLORD YOU WERE TALKING ABOUT?
UH... YEAH.
HMM...
YOU'RE WRONG.

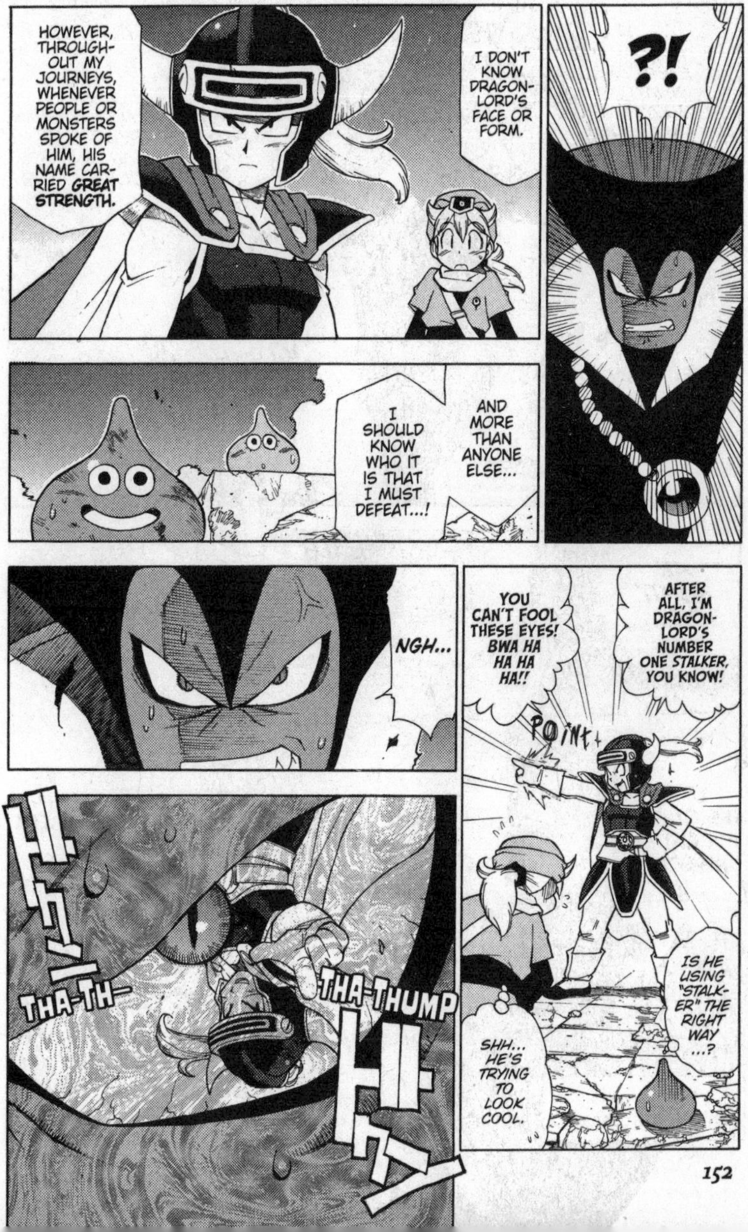
?!
I DON'T KNOW DRAGON-LORD'S FACE OR FORM.
HOWEVER, THROUGH-OUT MY JOURNEYS, WHENEVER PEOPLE OR MONSTERS SPOKE OF HIM, HIS NAME CAR-RIED **GREAT STRENGTH.**
AND MORE THAN ANYONE ELSE...
I SHOULD KNOW WHO IT IS THAT I MUST DEFEAT...!
AFTER ALL, I'M DRAGON-LORD'S NUMBER ONE STALKER, YOU KNOW!
YOU CAN'T FOOL THESE EYES! BWA HA HA HA HA!!
POINT
IS HE USING "STALK-ER" THE RIGHT WAY ...?
SHH... HE'S TRYING TO LOOK COOL.
NGH...
THA-TH-
THA-THUMP

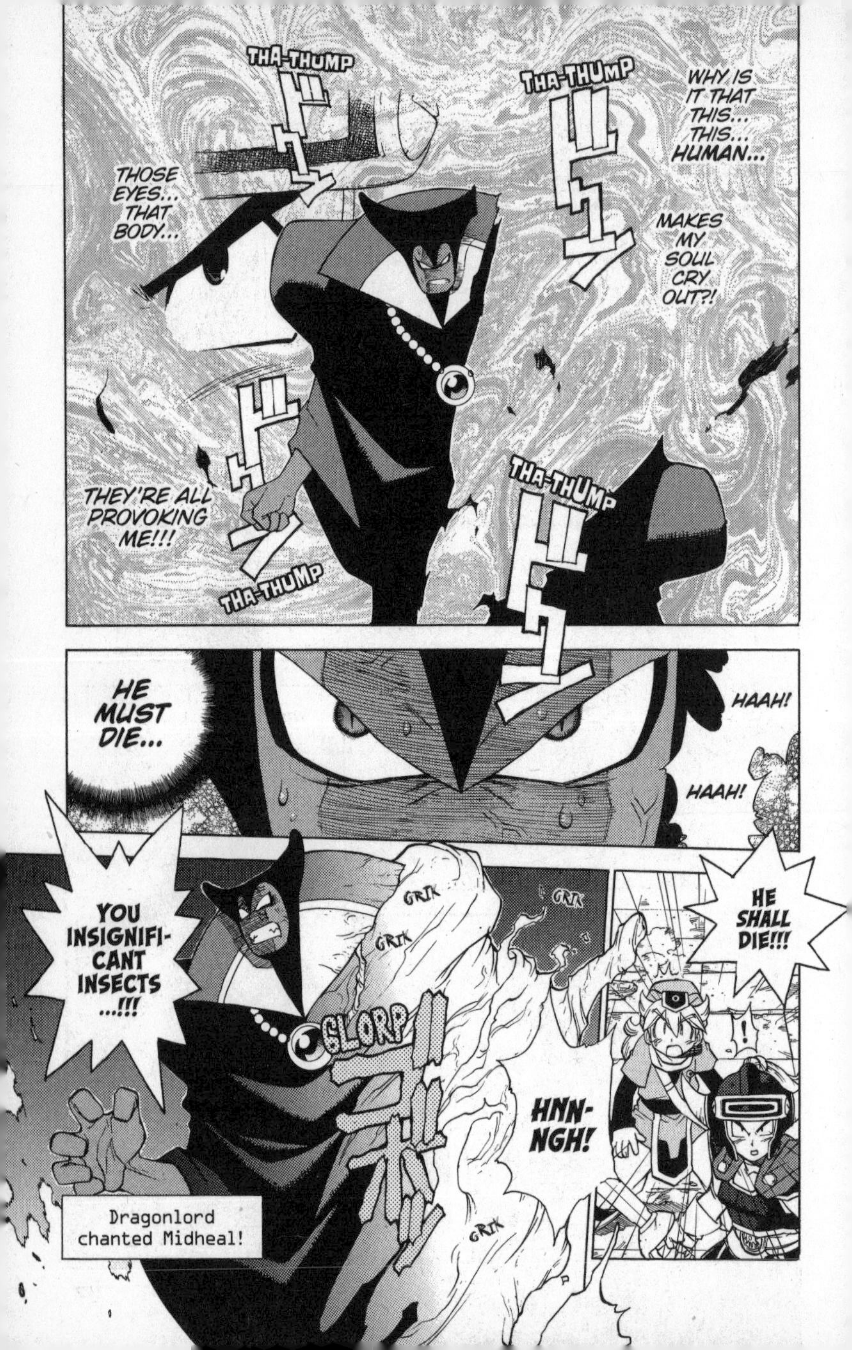
WHY IS IT THAT THIS... THIS... HUMAN...
THA-THUMP
MAKES MY SOUL CRY OUT?!
THA-THUMP
THOSE EYES... THAT BODY...
THA-THUMP
THEY'RE ALL PROVOKING ME!!!
THA-THUMP
HAAH!
HAAH!
HE MUST DIE...
HE SHALL DIE!!!
GRIK
GRIK
GRIK
YOU INSIGNIFICANT INSECTS...!!!
GLORP
!
HNN-NGH!
GRIK
Dragonlord chanted Midheal!

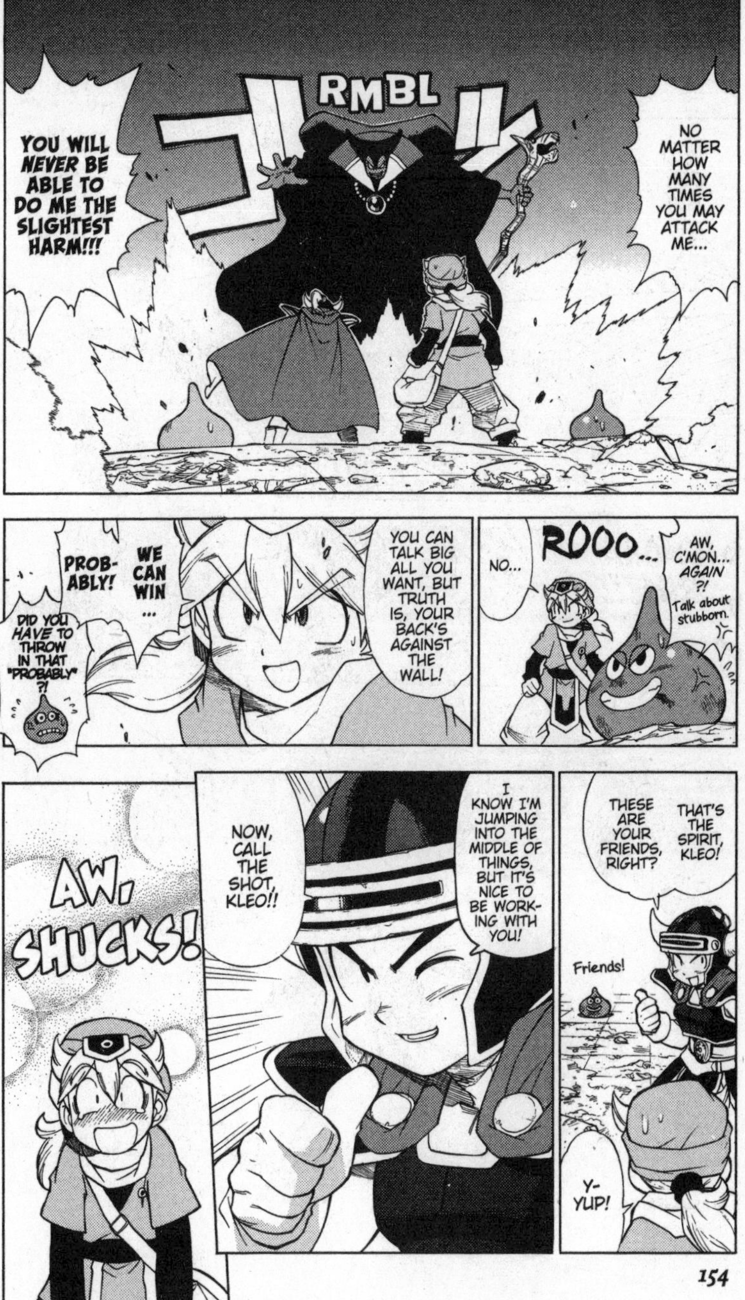
NO MATTER HOW MANY TIMES YOU MAY ATTACK ME...
RMBL
YOU WILL NEVER BE ABLE TO DO ME THE SLIGHTEST HARM!!!
AW, C'MON... AGAIN?!
Talk about stubborn.
ROOO...
NO...
YOU CAN TALK BIG ALL YOU WANT, BUT TRUTH IS, YOUR BACK'S AGAINST THE WALL!
WE CAN WIN...
PROB-ABLY!
DID YOU HAVE TO THROW IN THAT "PROBABLY"?!
THAT'S THE SPIRIT, KLEO!
THESE ARE YOUR FRIENDS, RIGHT?
Friends!
Y-YUP!
I KNOW I'M JUMPING INTO THE MIDDLE OF THINGS, BUT IT'S NICE TO BE WORK-ING WITH YOU!
NOW, CALL THE SHOT, KLEO!!
AW, SHUCKS!

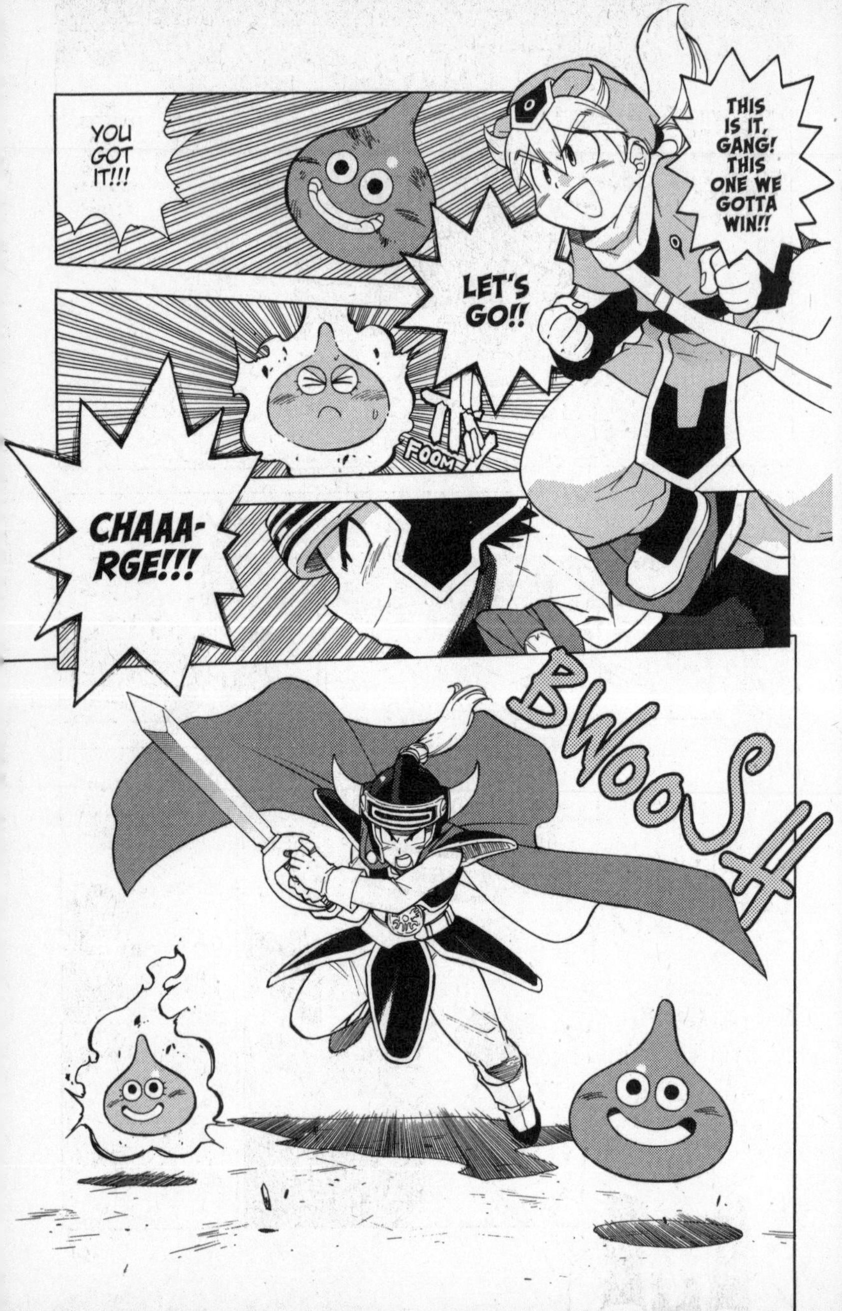
THIS IS IT, GANG! THIS ONE WE GOTTA WIN!!
YOU GOT IT!!!
LET'S GO!!
FOOM
CHAAA-RGE!!!
BWOOSH

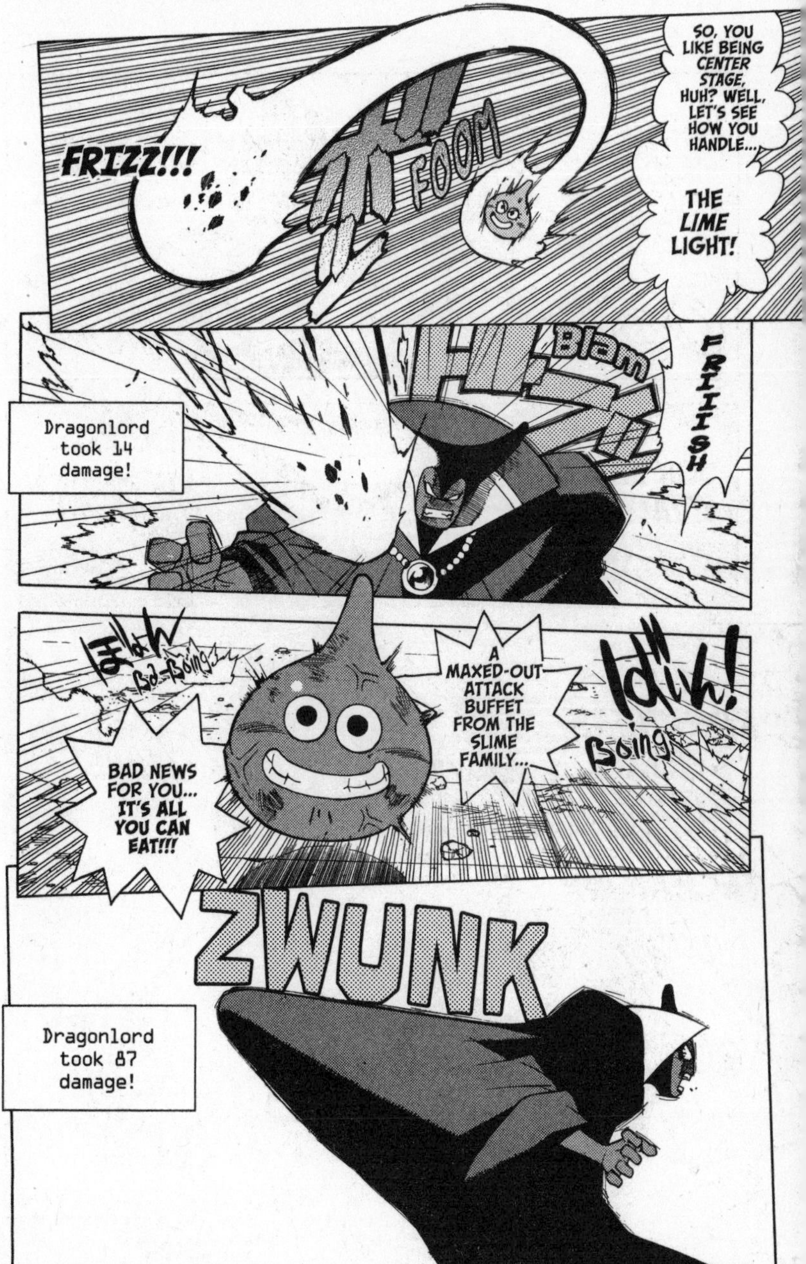
SO, YOU LIKE BEING CENTER STAGE, HUH? WELL, LET'S SEE HOW YOU HANDLE...
THE LIME LIGHT!
FOOM
FRIZZ!!!
FRIIISH
Blam
Dragonlord took 14 damage!
Boing
A MAXED-OUT ATTACK BUFFET FROM THE SLIME FAMILY...
Ba-Boing
BAD NEWS FOR YOU... IT'S ALL YOU CAN EAT!!!
ZWUNK
Dragonlord took 87 damage!

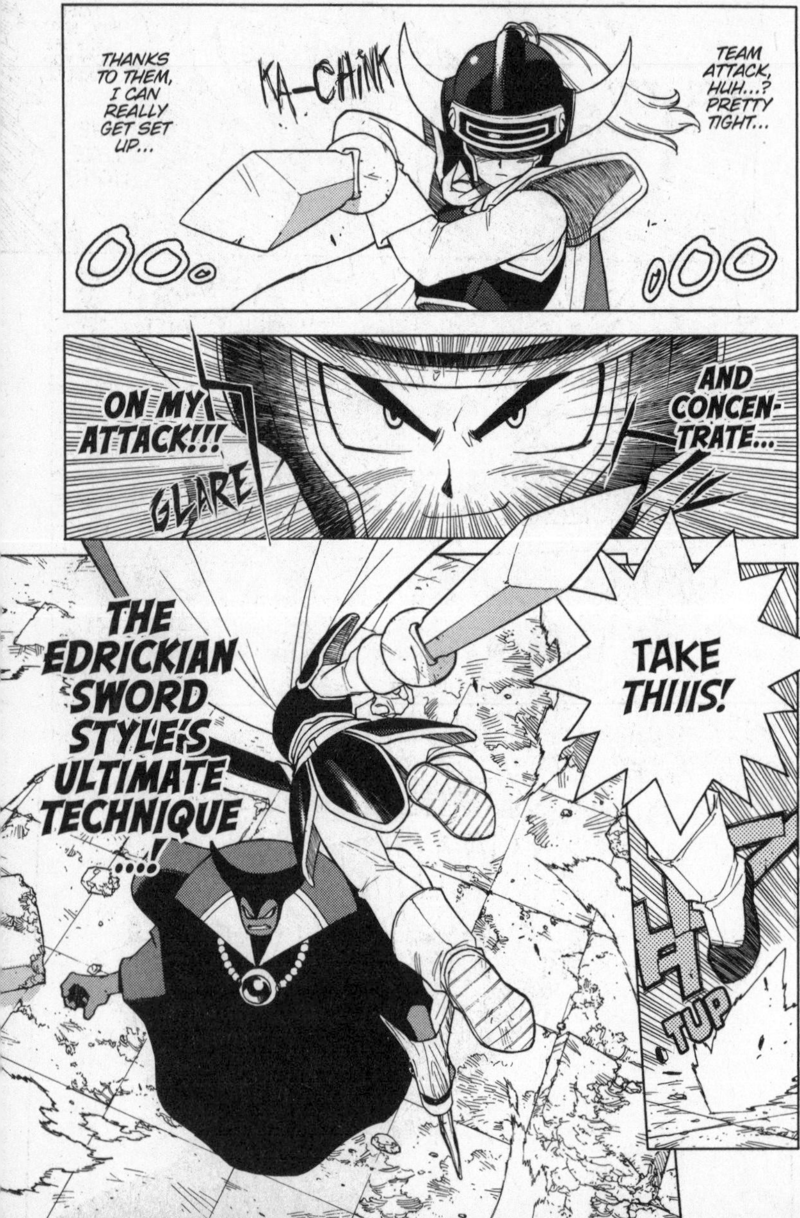
TEAM ATTACK, HUH...? PRETTY TIGHT...
KA-CHINK
THANKS TO THEM, I CAN REALLY GET SET UP...
AND CONCENTRATE...
ON MY ATTACK!!!
GLARE
TAKE THIIIS!
HA
TUP
THE EDRICKIAN SWORD STYLE'S ULTIMATE TECHNIQUE...!

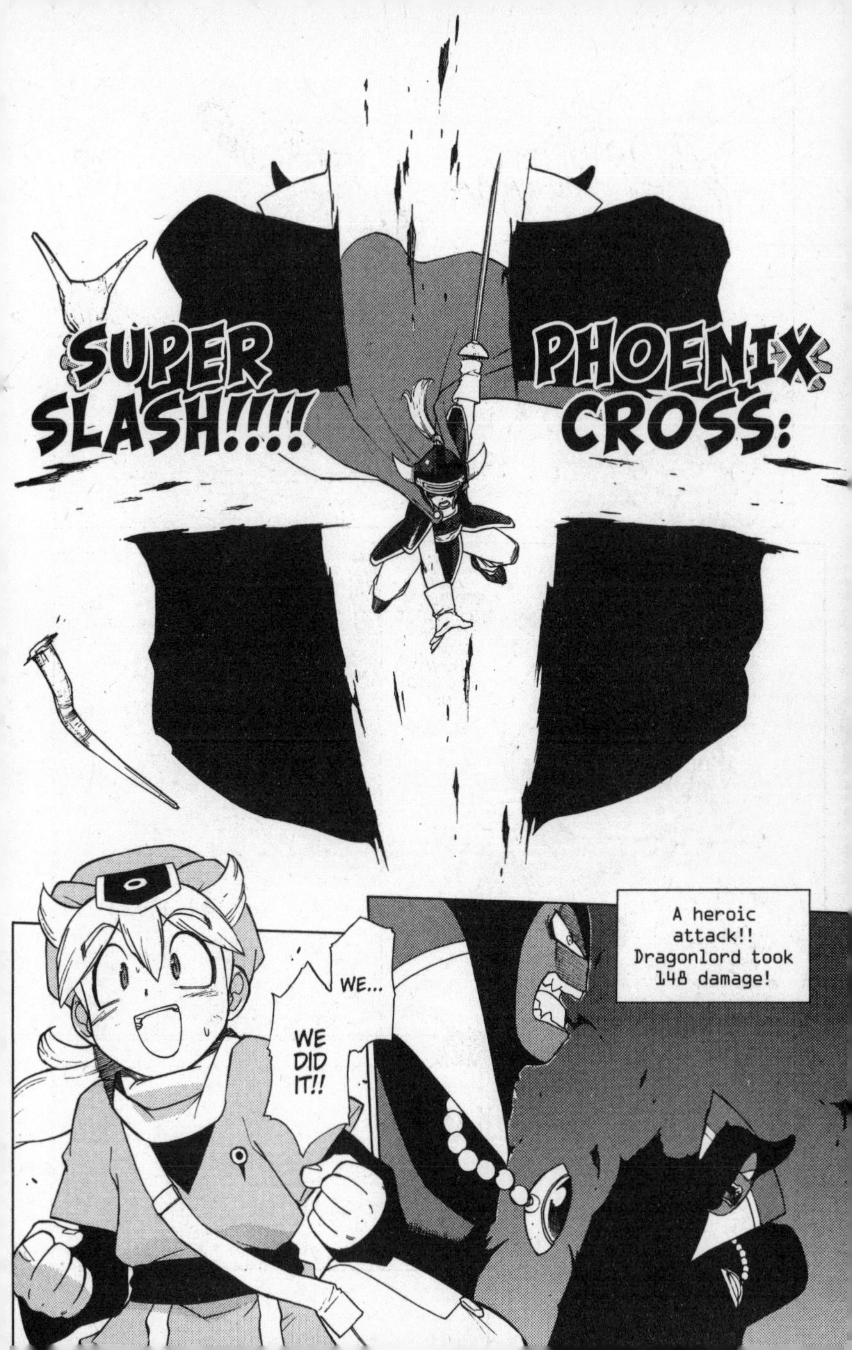
PHOENIX CROSS:
SUPER SLASH!!!!
A heroic attack!! Dragonlord took 148 damage!
WE...
WE DID IT!!

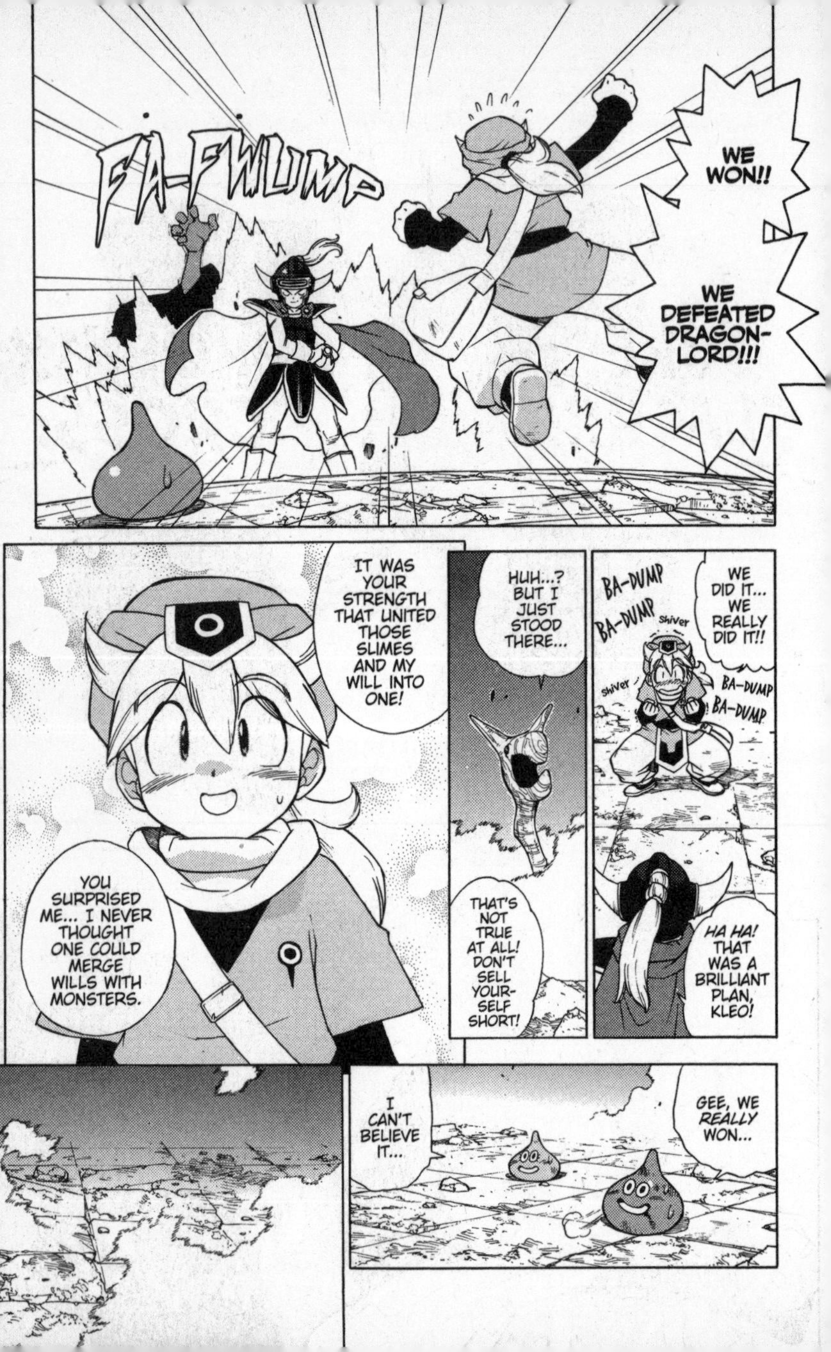
WE WON!!
WE DEFEATED DRAGON-LORD!!!
FA-FWUMP
WE DID IT... WE REALLY DID IT!!
BA-DUMP
BA-DUMP
Shiver
Shiver
BA-DUMP
BA-DUMP
HA HA! THAT WAS A BRILLIANT PLAN, KLEO!
HUH...? BUT I JUST STOOD THERE...
THAT'S NOT TRUE AT ALL! DON'T SELL YOUR-SELF SHORT!
IT WAS YOUR STRENGTH THAT UNITED THOSE SLIMES AND MY WILL INTO ONE!
YOU SURPRISED ME... I NEVER THOUGHT ONE COULD MERGE WILLS WITH MONSTERS.
GEE, WE *REALLY* WON...
I CAN'T BELIEVE IT...

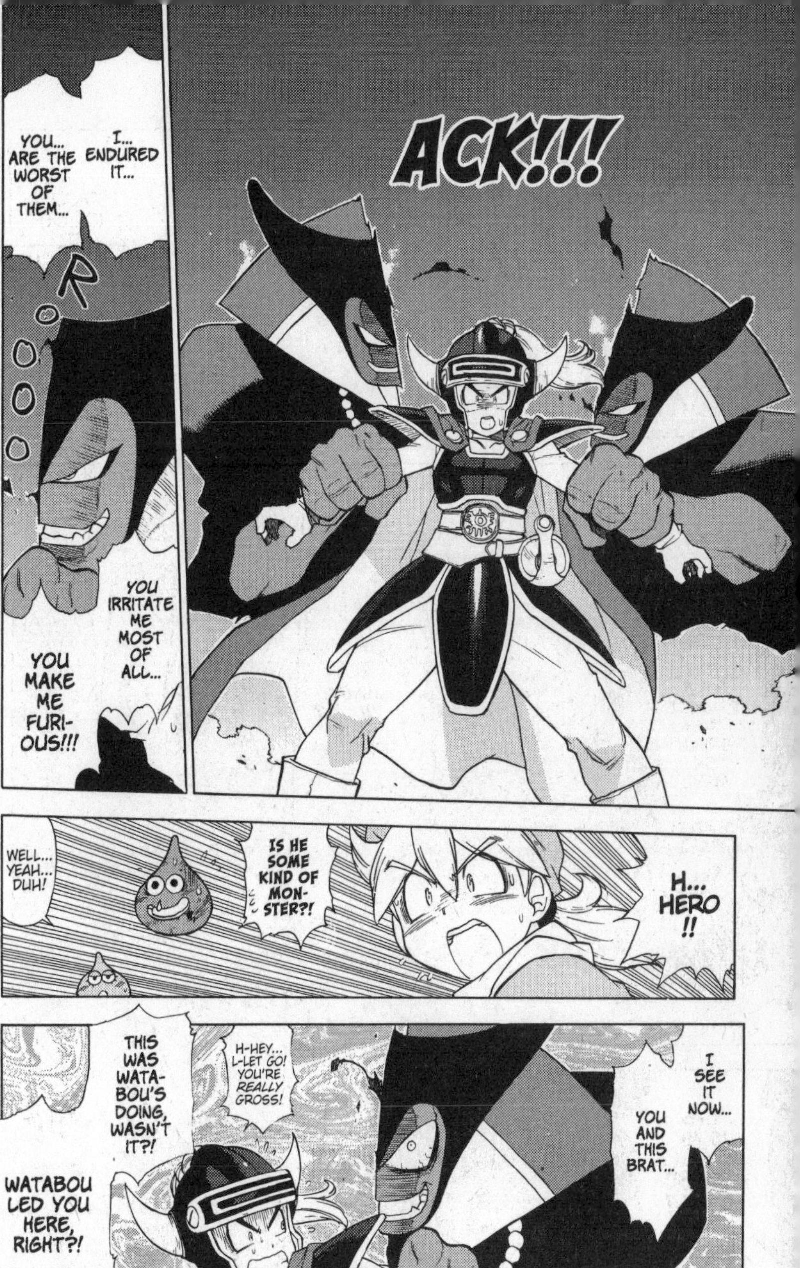
ACK!!!
I... ENDURED IT...
YOU... ARE THE WORST OF THEM...
ROOOO
YOU IRRITATE ME MOST OF ALL...
YOU MAKE ME FURI-OUS!!!
H... HERO !!
IS HE SOME KIND OF MON-STER?!
WELL... YEAH... DUH!
I SEE IT NOW...
YOU AND THIS BRAT...
H-HEY... L-LET GO! YOU'RE *REALLY* GROSS!
THIS WAS WATABOU'S DOING, WASN'T IT?!
WATABOU LED YOU HERE, RIGHT?!

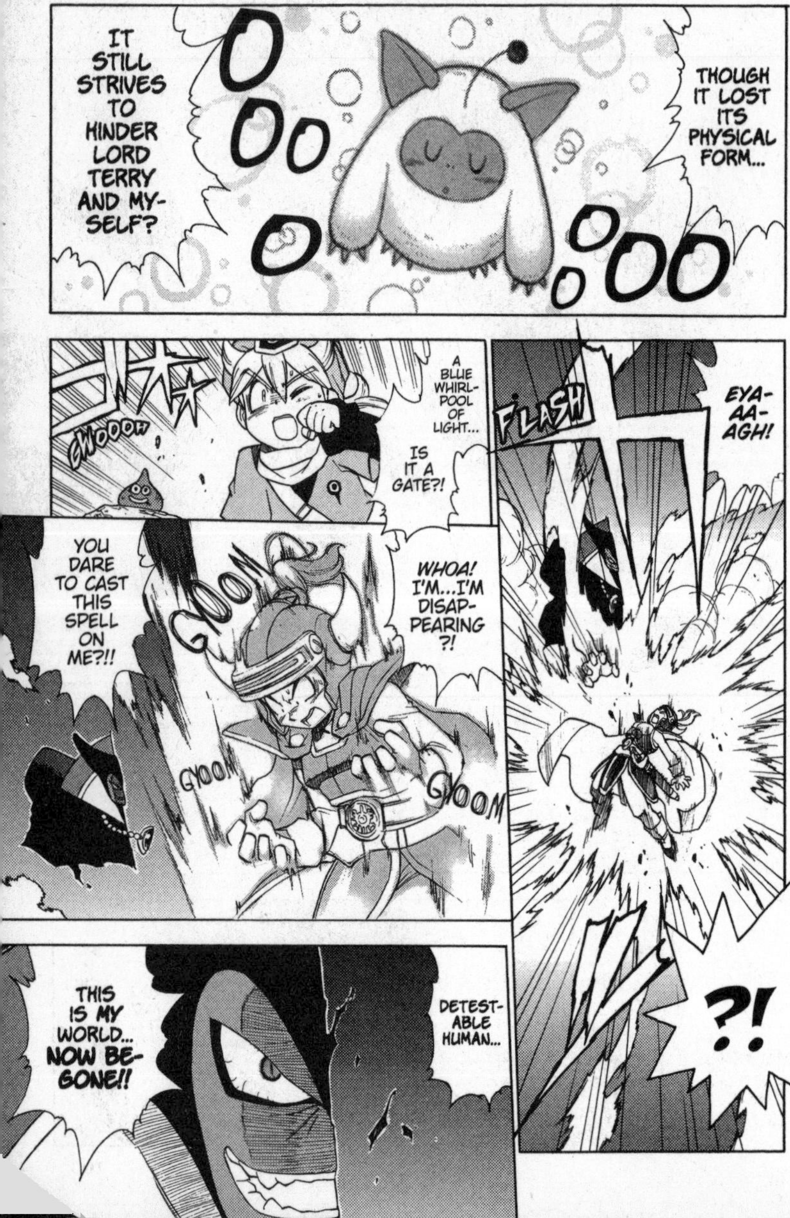
THOUGH IT LOST ITS PHYSICAL FORM...
OOOOOOOO
IT STILL STRIVES TO HINDER LORD TERRY AND MY-SELF?
EYA-AA-AGH!
FLASH
?!
A BLUE WHIRL-POOL OF LIGHT...
IS IT A GATE?!
GWOOOW
WHOA! I'M...I'M DISAP-PEARING?!
GOOON
YOU DARE TO CAST THIS SPELL ON ME?!!
GYOOM
GYOOM
DETEST-ABLE HUMAN...
THIS IS MY WORLD... NOW BE-GONE!!

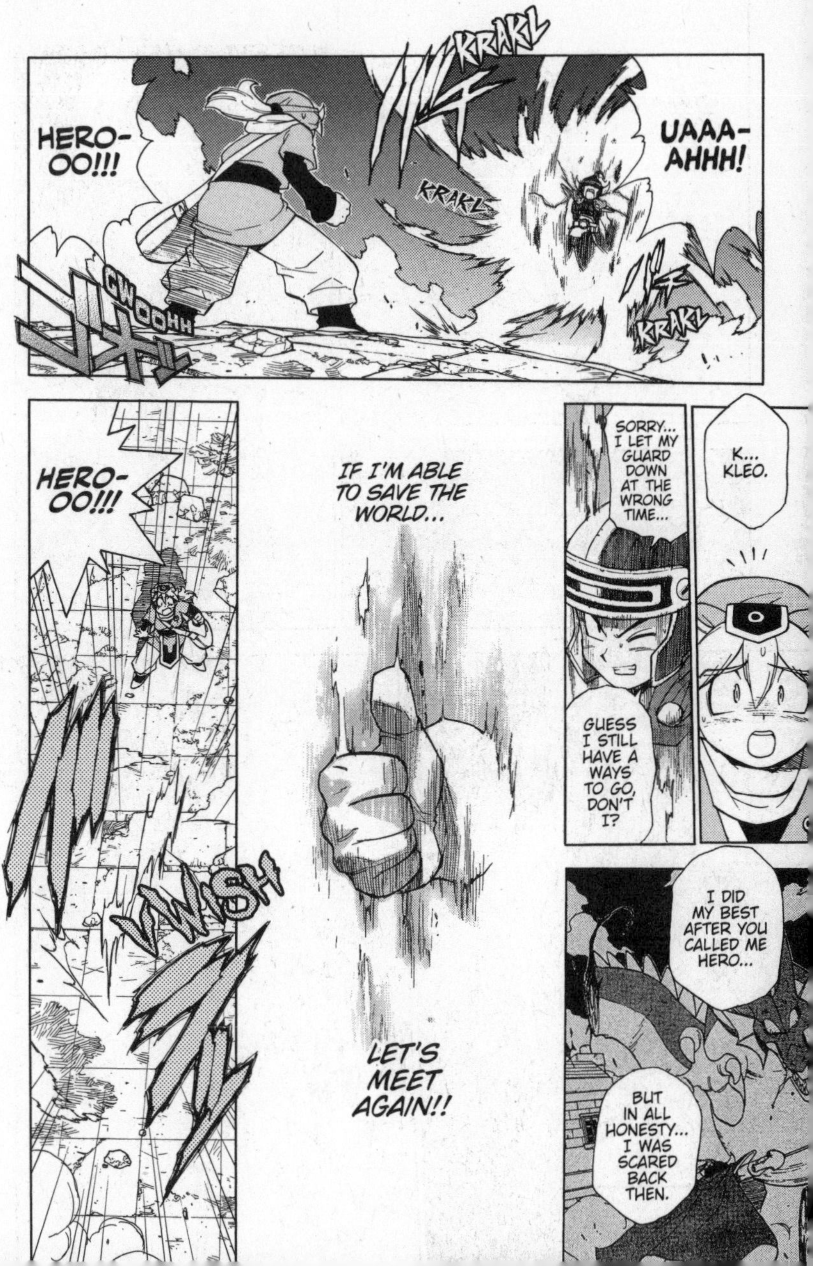
UAAA-AHHH!
KRAKL
KRAKL
KRAKL
HERO-OO!!!
GWOOHH
K... KLEO.
SORRY... I LET MY GUARD DOWN AT THE WRONG TIME...
GUESS I STILL HAVE A WAYS TO GO, DON'T I?
I DID MY BEST AFTER YOU CALLED ME HERO...
BUT IN ALL HONESTY... I WAS SCARED BACK THEN.
IF I'M ABLE TO SAVE THE WORLD...
LET'S MEET AGAIN!!
HERO-OO!!!
WWISH

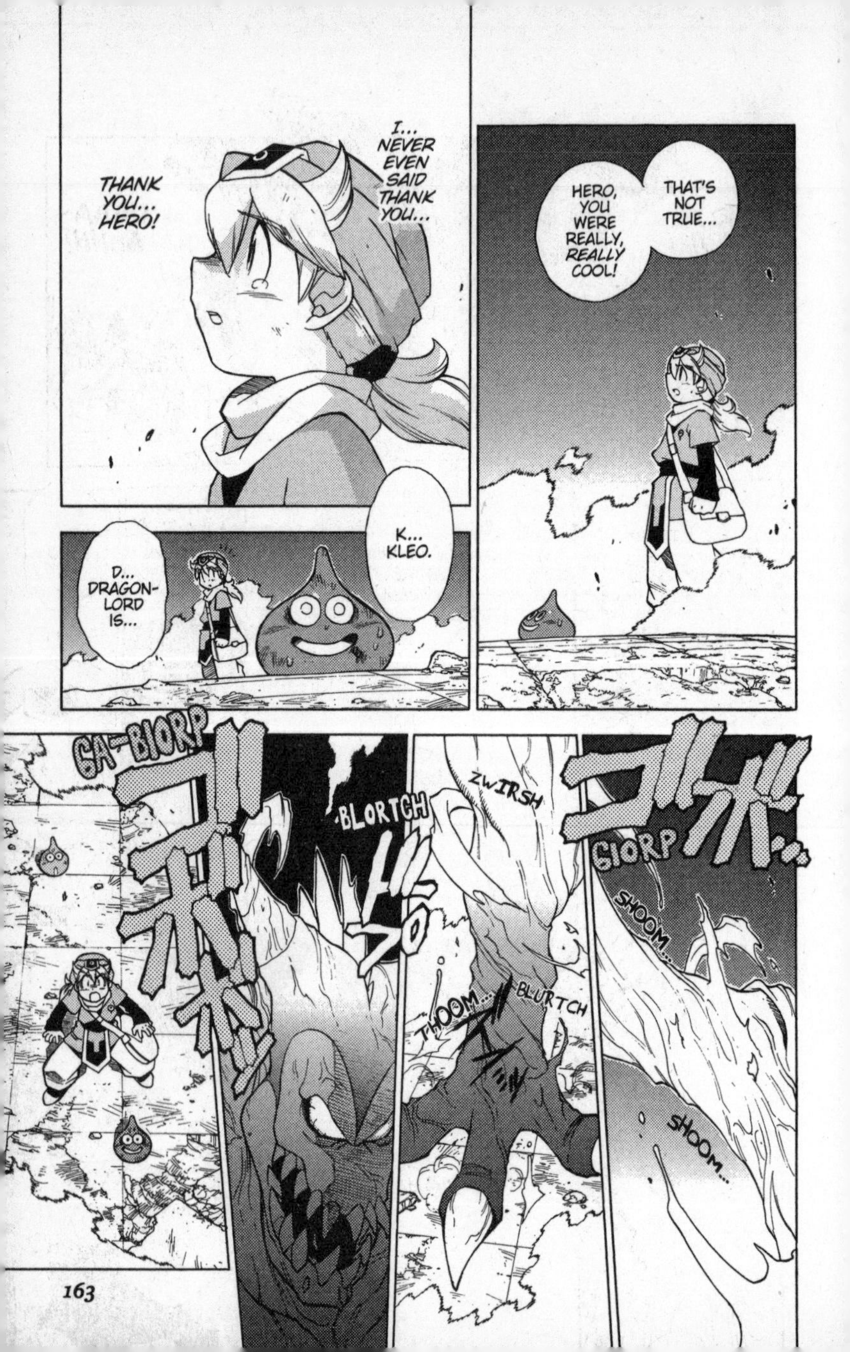
THAT'S NOT TRUE...
HERO, YOU WERE REALLY, REALLY COOL!
I... NEVER EVEN SAID THANK YOU...
THANK YOU... HERO!
K... KLEO.
D... DRAGON-LORD IS...
GIORP
SHOOM...
SHOOM...
ZWIRSH
BLURTCH
THOOM...
BLORTCH
GA-BIORP

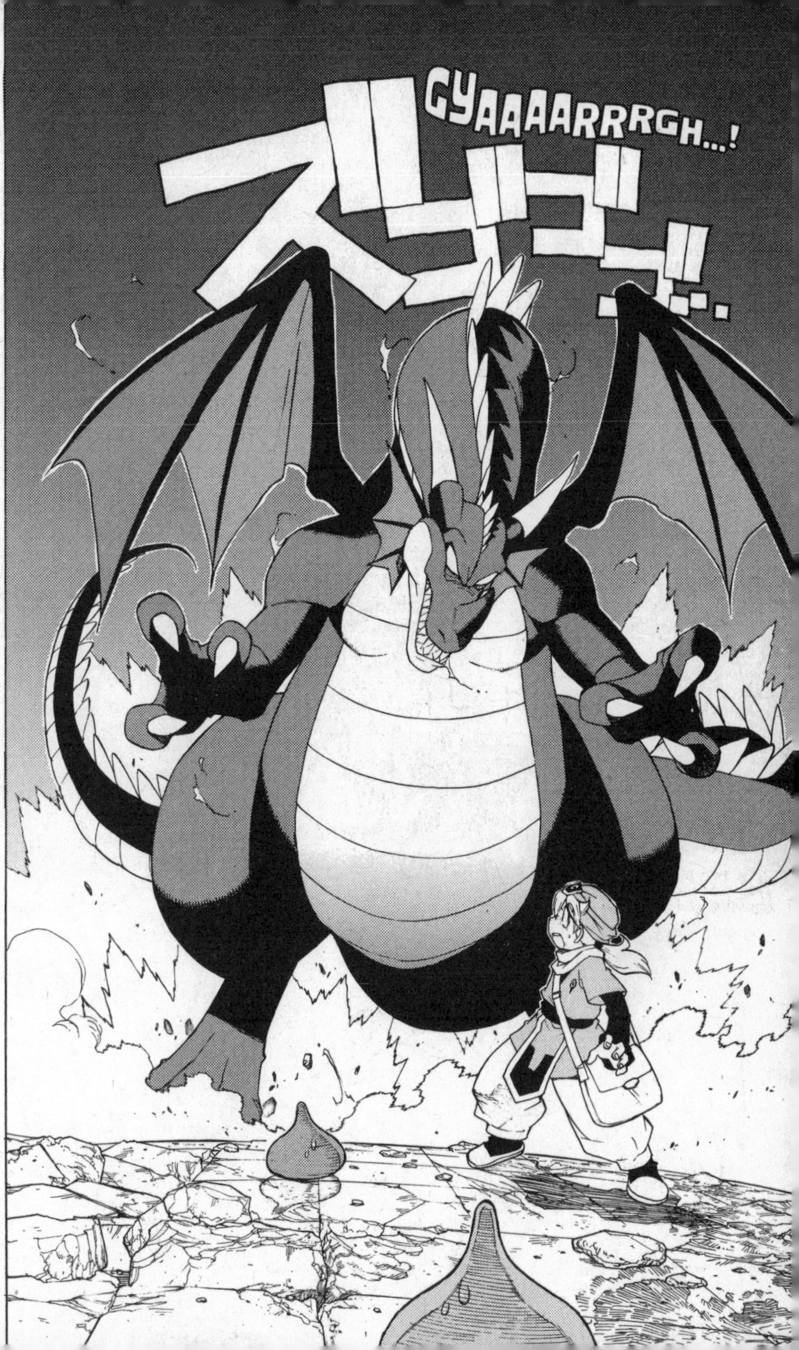
GYAAAARRRGH...!
ズゴゴゴ..

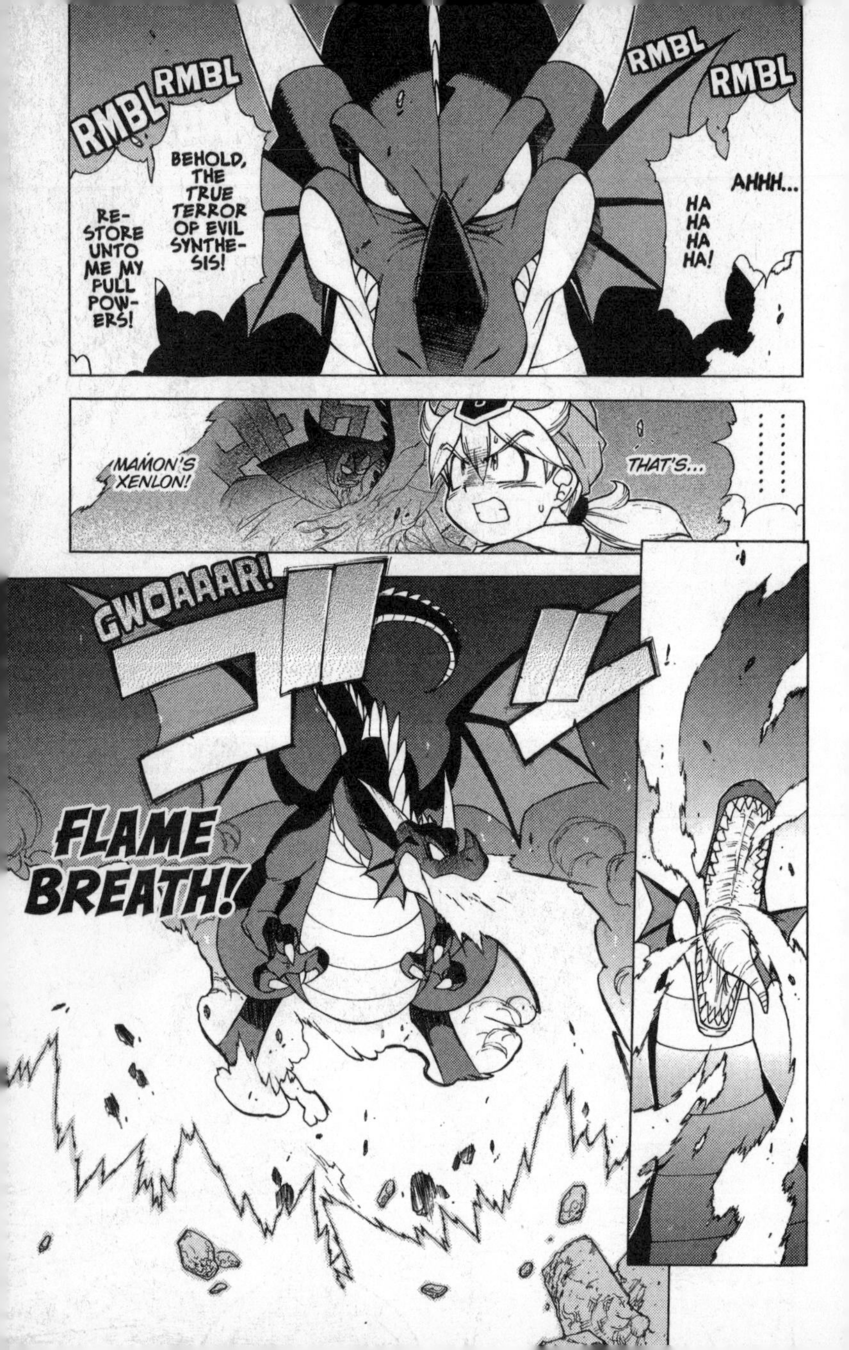
RMBL
RMBL
AHHH...
HA HA HA HA!
BEHOLD, THE TRUE TERROR OF EVIL SYNTHESIS!
RE-STORE UNTO ME MY FULL POW-ERS!
RMBL
RMBL
......
THAT'S...
MAMON'S XENLON!
GWOAAAR!
FLAME BREATH!

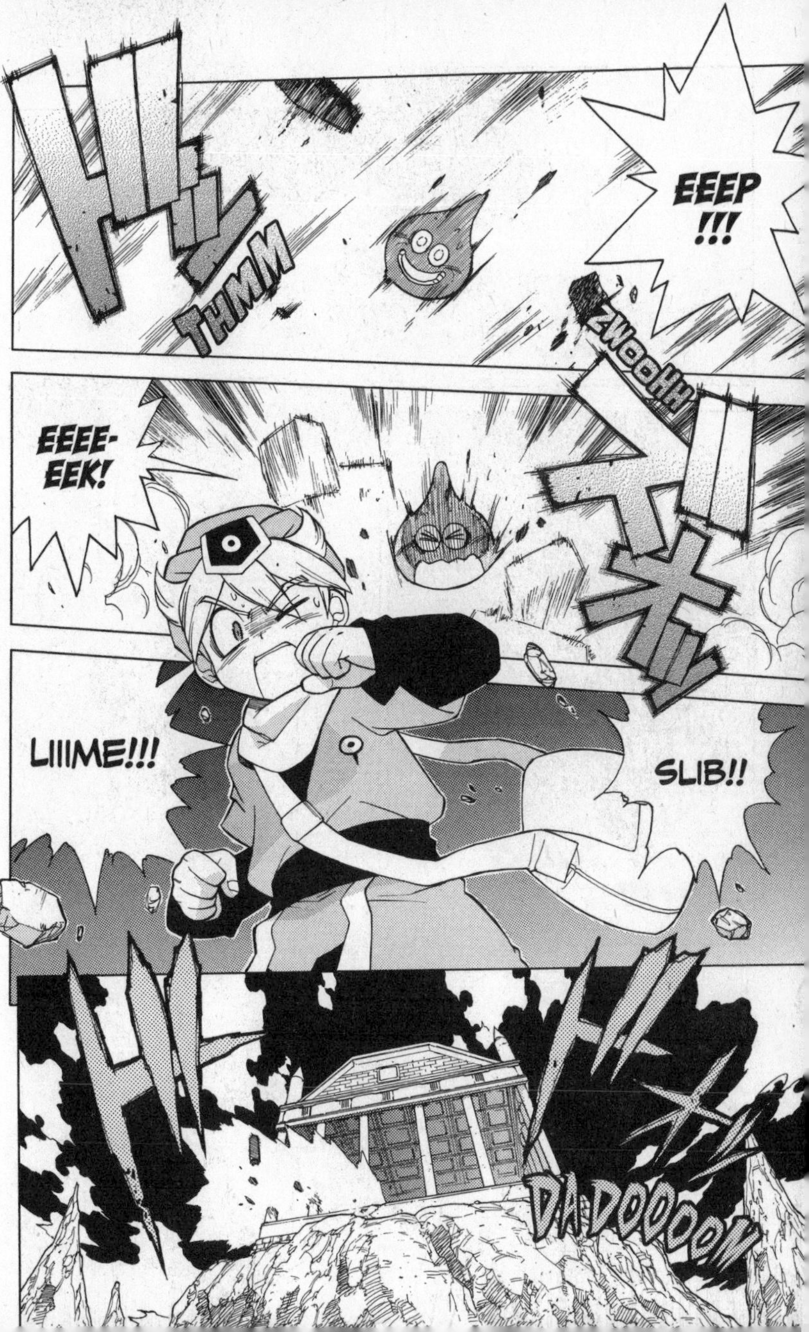
EEEP !!!
THMM
ZWOOHH
EEEE-EEK!
SLIB!!
LIIIME!!!
DADOOOOON

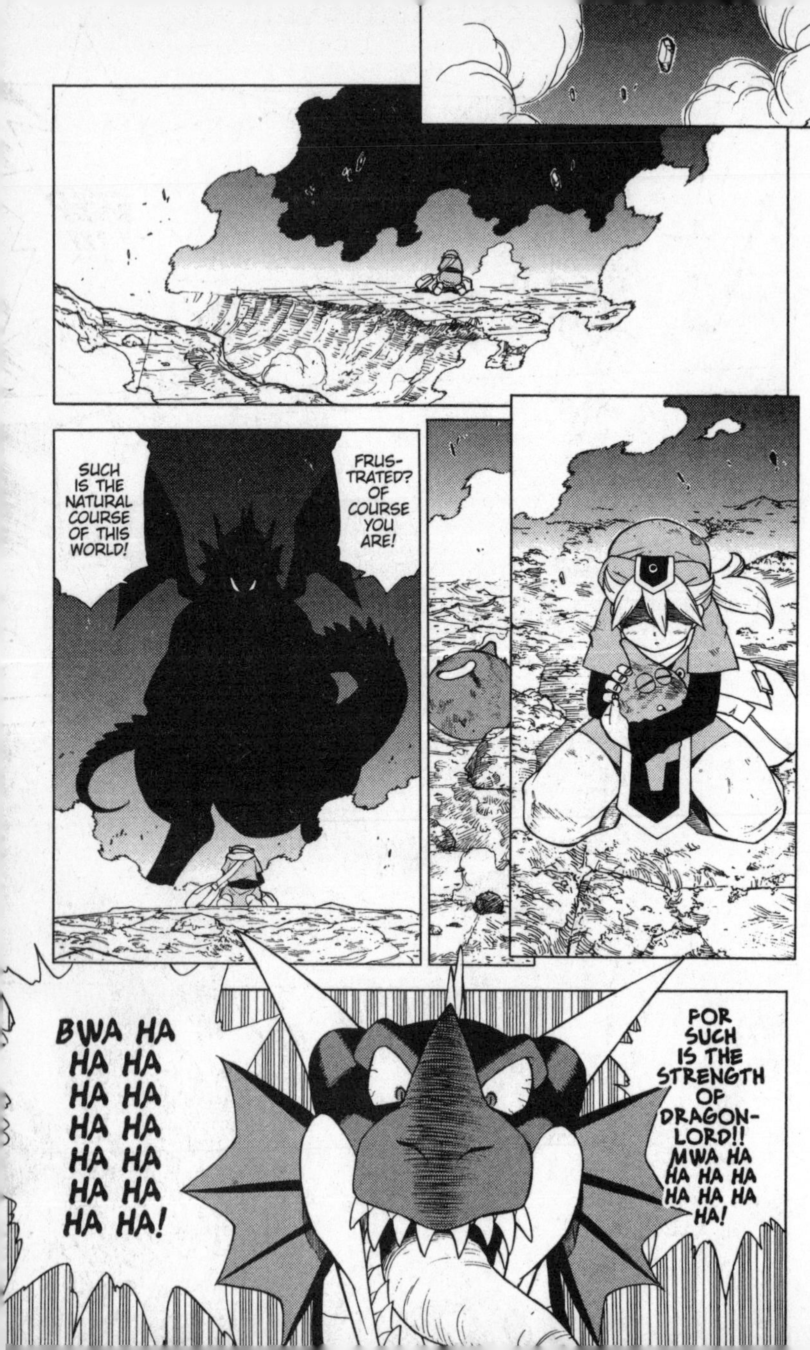
FRUS-TRATED? OF COURSE YOU ARE!
SUCH IS THE NATURAL COURSE OF THIS WORLD!
FOR SUCH IS THE STRENGTH OF DRAGON-LORD!! MWA HA HA HA HA HA HA HA HA!
BWA HA HA HA HA HA HA HA HA HA HA HA HA HA!

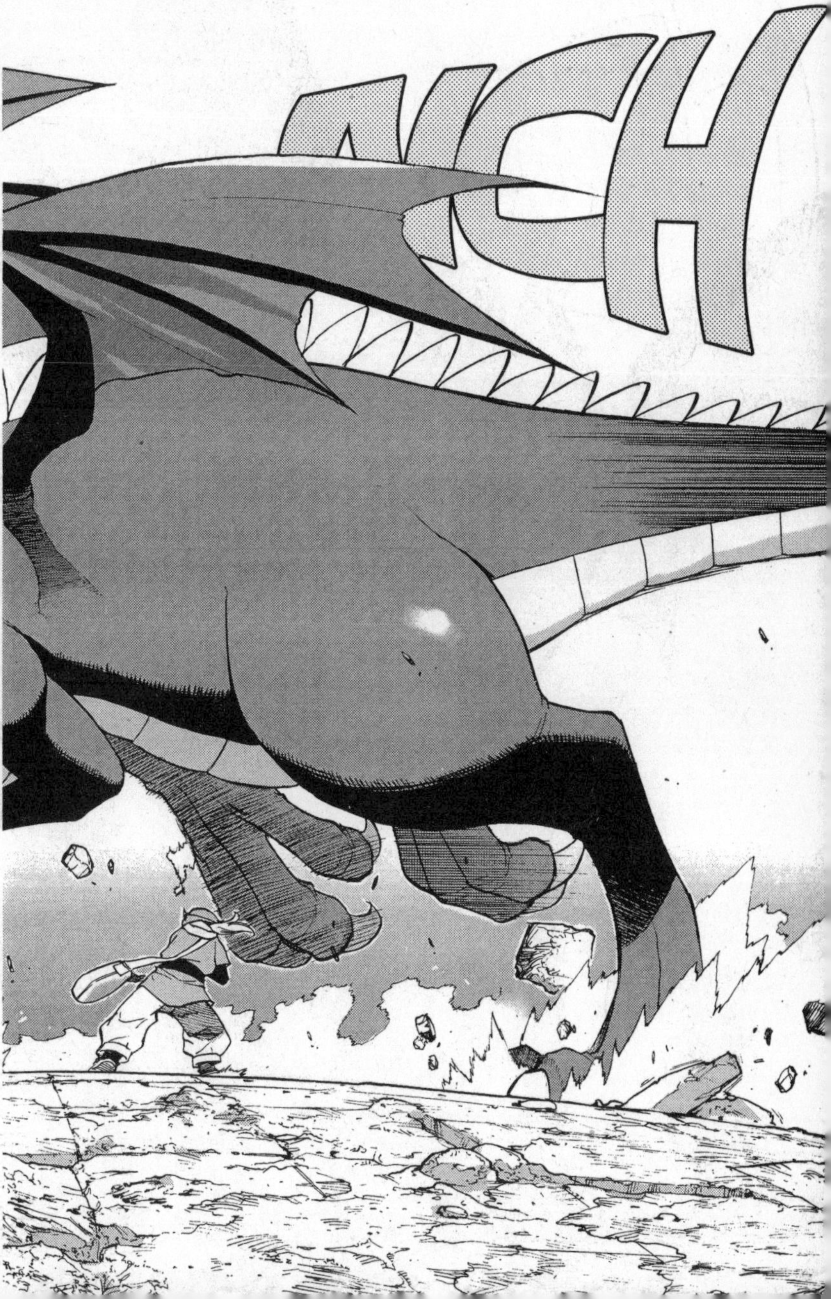
AICH

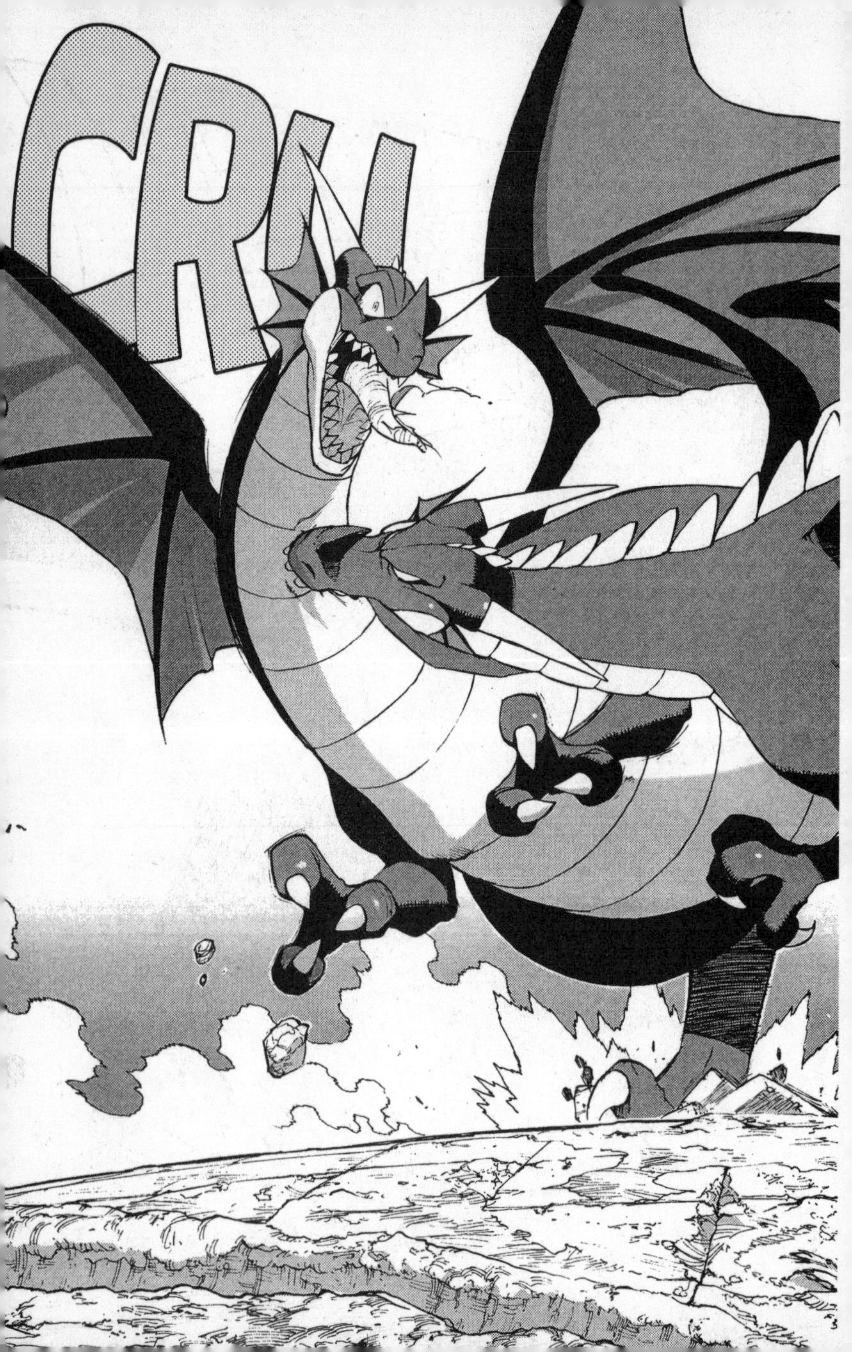
GRN

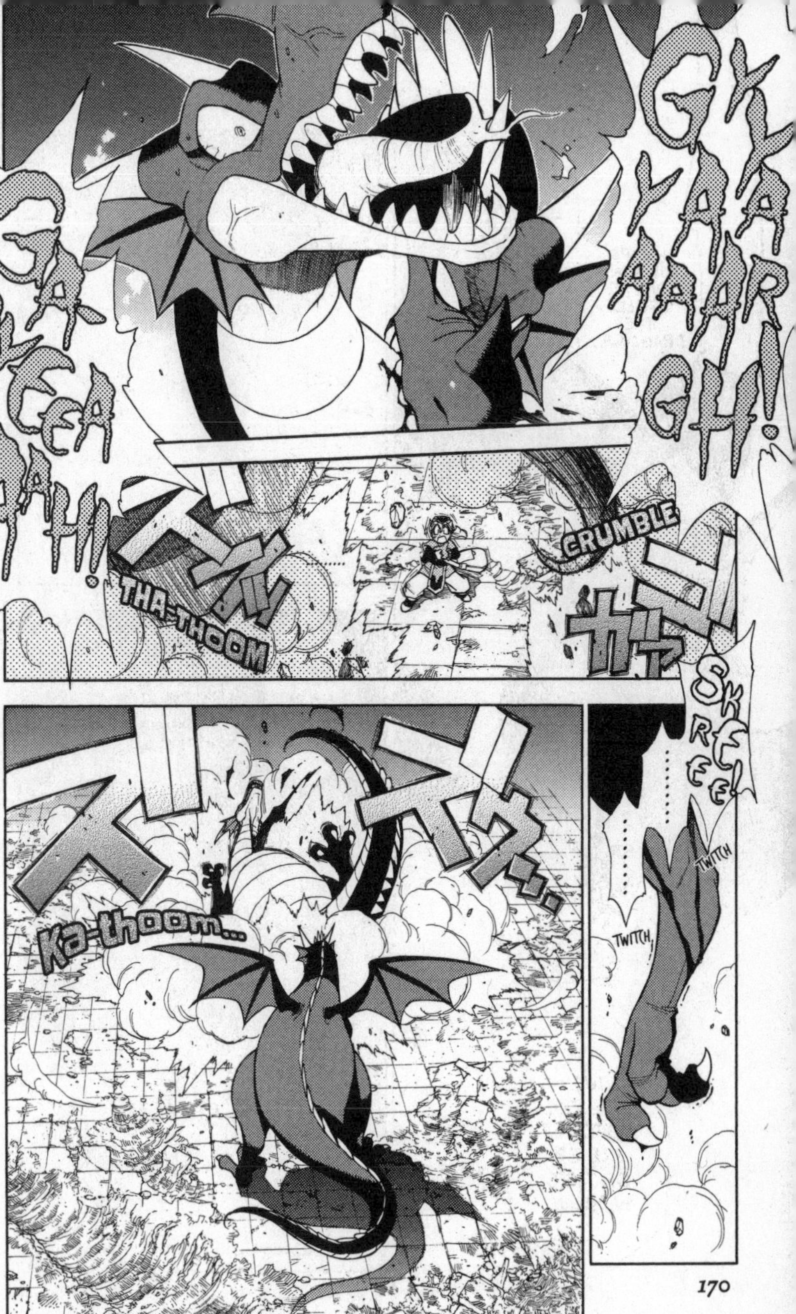
GKYAAAAARGH!
GA-GYEEAAAH!
CRUMBLE
THA-THOOM
SKREEE!
TWITCH
TWITCH
Ka-thoom...

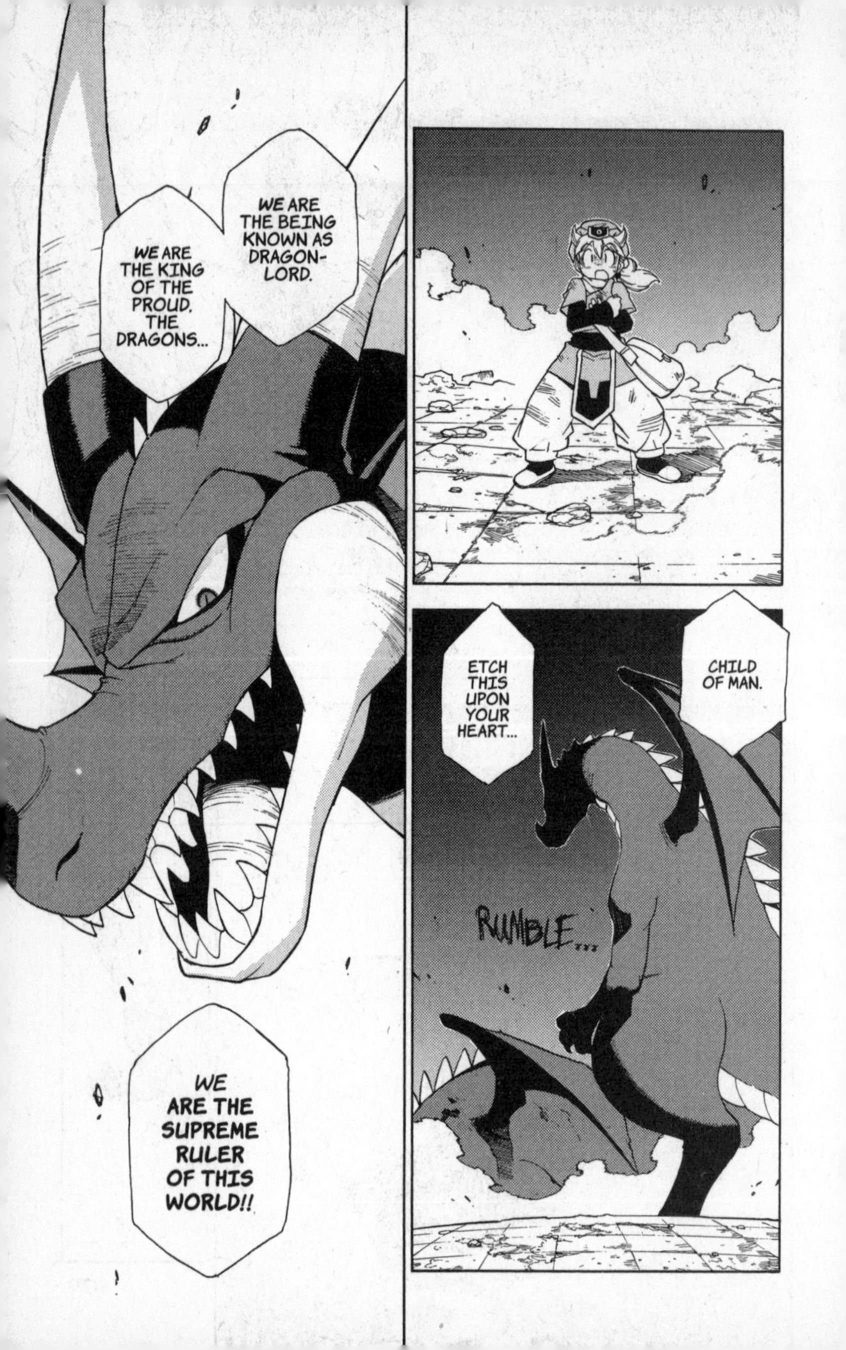
CHILD OF MAN.
ETCH THIS UPON YOUR HEART...
RUMBLE...
WE ARE THE BEING KNOWN AS DRAGON-LORD.
WE ARE THE KING OF THE PROUD, THE DRAGONS...
WE ARE THE SUPREME RULER OF THIS WORLD!!

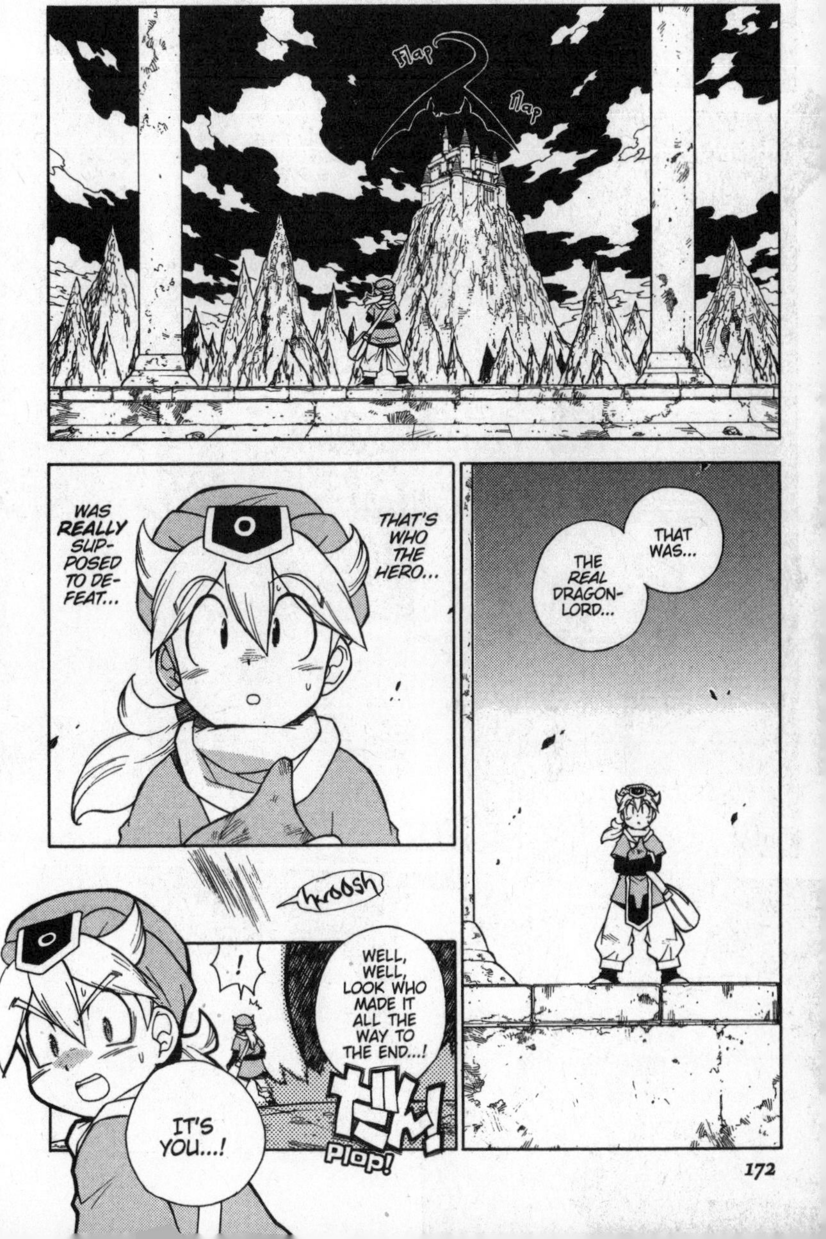
Flap
flap
THAT WAS...
THE REAL DRAGONLORD...
THAT'S WHO THE HERO...
WAS REALLY SUPPOSED TO DEFEAT...
hwoosh
WELL, WELL, LOOK WHO MADE IT ALL THE WAY TO THE END...!
!
IT'S YOU...!
Plop!

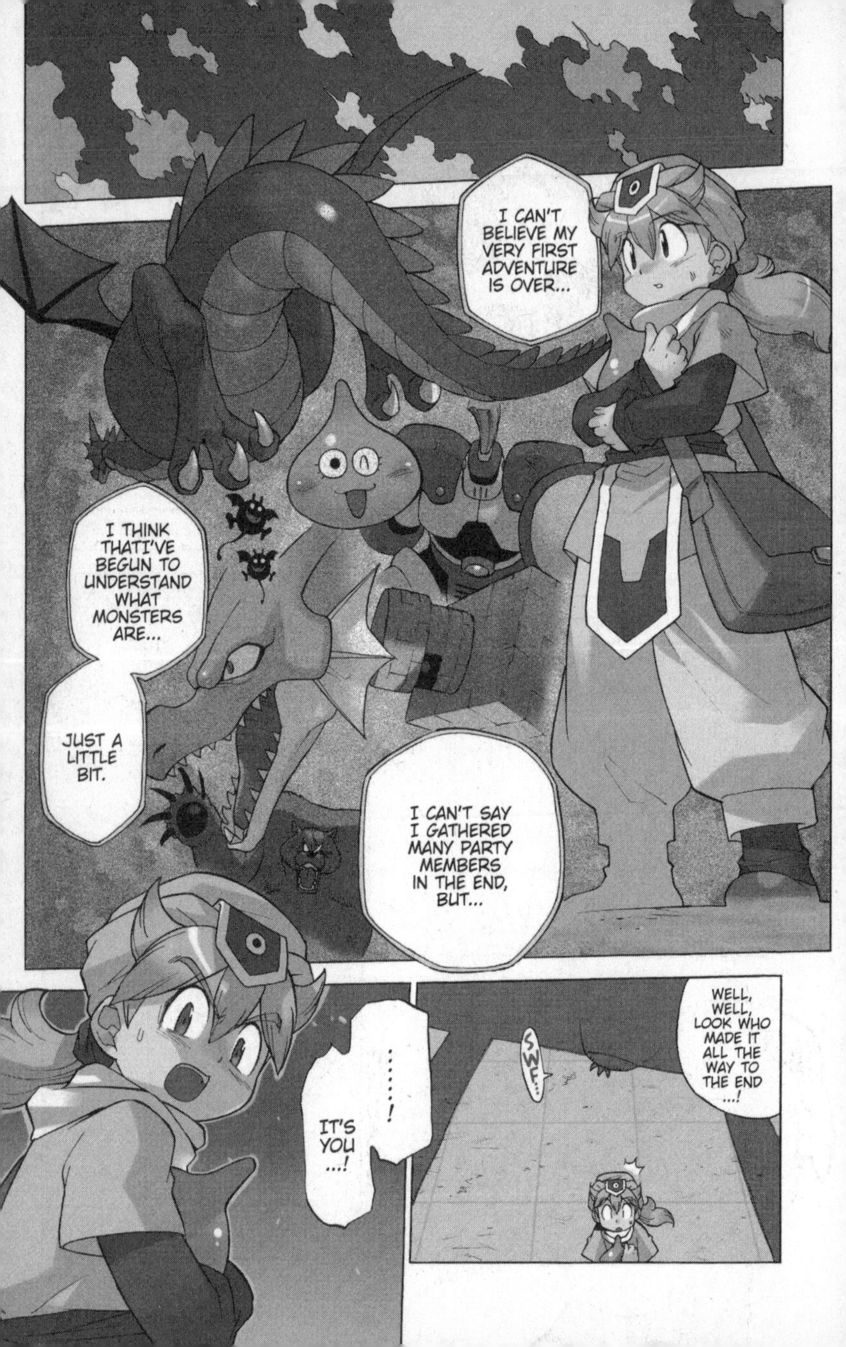
I CAN'T BELIEVE MY VERY FIRST ADVENTURE IS OVER...
I CAN'T SAY I GATHERED MANY PARTY MEMBERS IN THE END, BUT...
I THINK THATI'VE BEGUN TO UNDERSTAND WHAT MONSTERS ARE...
JUST A LITTLE BIT.
WELL, WELL, LOOK WHO MADE IT ALL THE WAY TO THE END ...!
SWF...
......!
IT'S YOU ...!

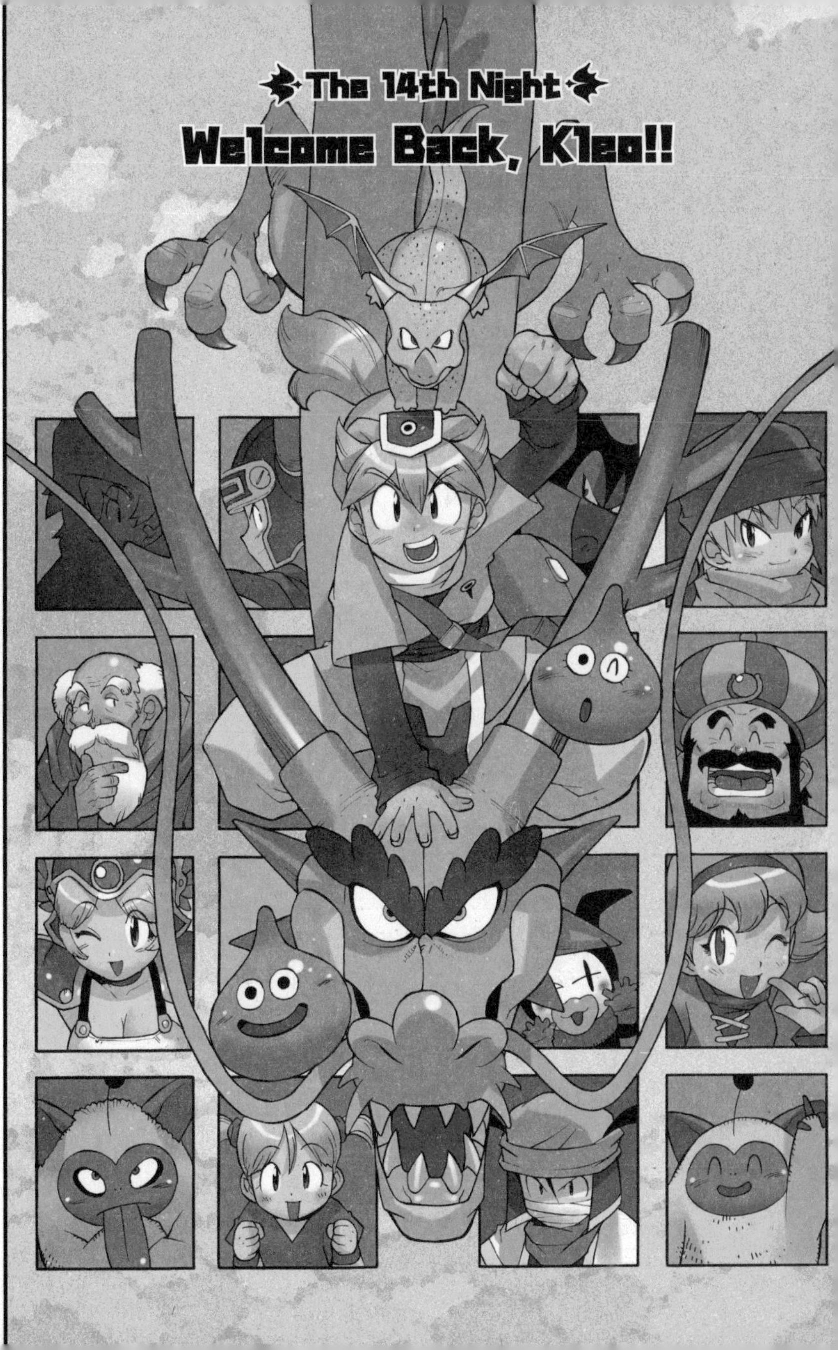
The 14th Night
Welcome Back, Kleo!!

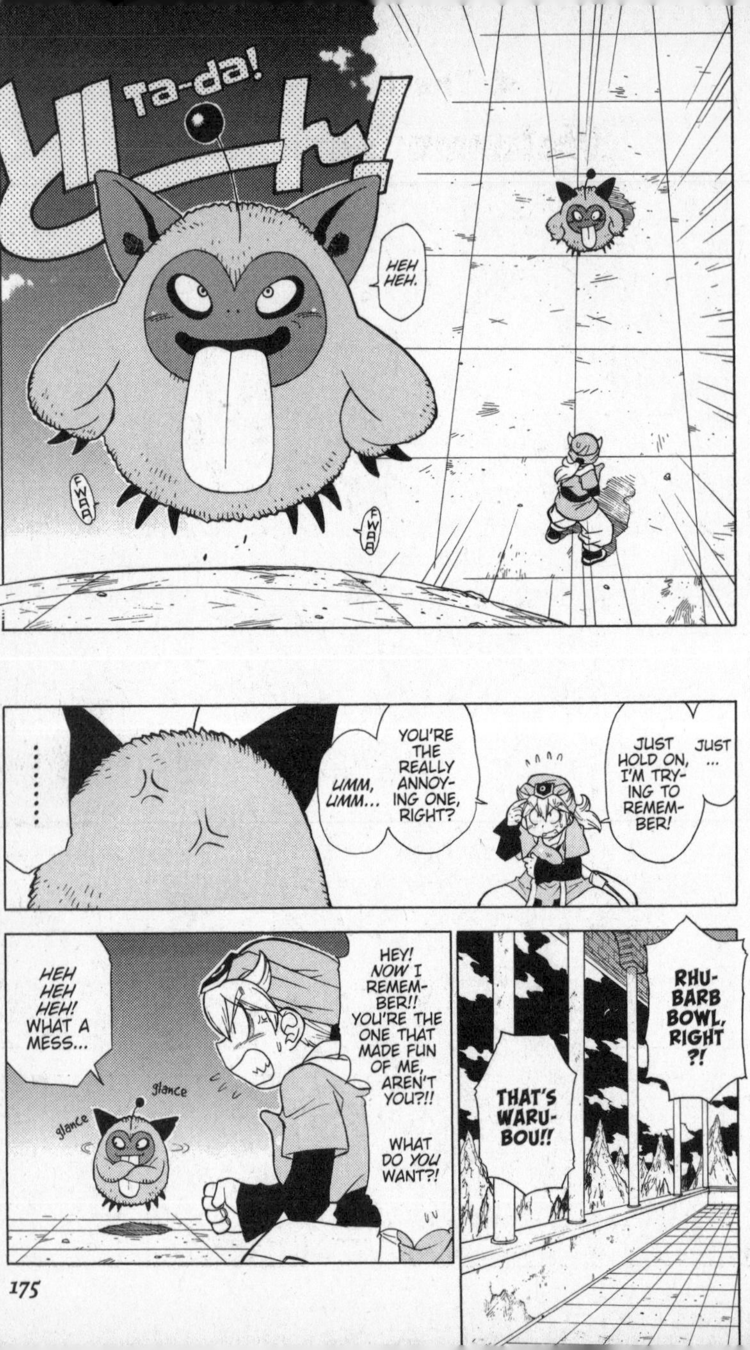
HEH HEH.
TA-DA!
FWAA
FWAA
JUST ...
JUST HOLD ON, I'M TRYING TO REMEMBER!
YOU'RE THE REALLY ANNOYING ONE, RIGHT?
UMM, UMM...
......
RHUBARB BOWL, RIGHT?!
THAT'S WARUBOU!!
HEY! NOW I REMEMBER!! YOU'RE THE ONE THAT MADE FUN OF ME, AREN'T YOU?!!
WHAT DO YOU WANT?!
HEH HEH HEH! WHAT A MESS...
glance
glance

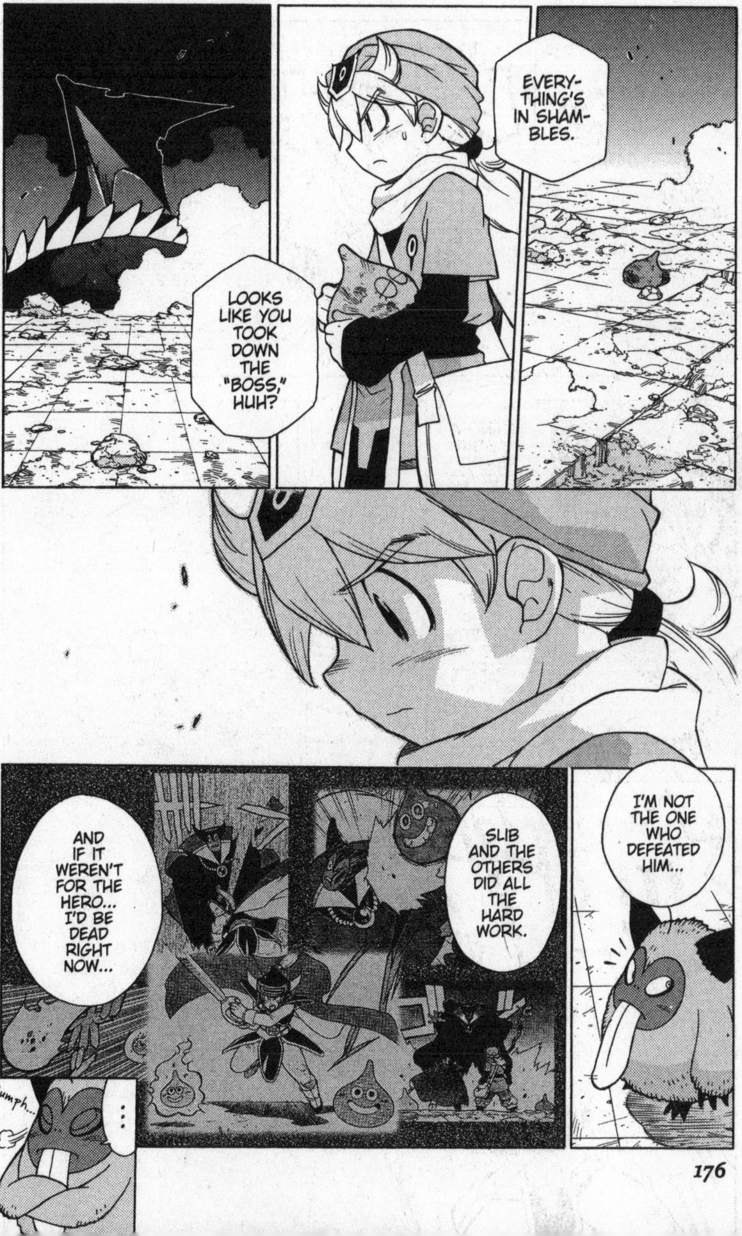
EVERY-THING'S IN SHAMBLES.
LOOKS LIKE YOU TOOK DOWN THE "BOSS," HUH?
I'M NOT THE ONE WHO DEFEATED HIM...
SLIB AND THE OTHERS DID ALL THE HARD WORK.
AND IF IT WEREN'T FOR THE HERO... I'D BE DEAD RIGHT NOW...
Humph...
...

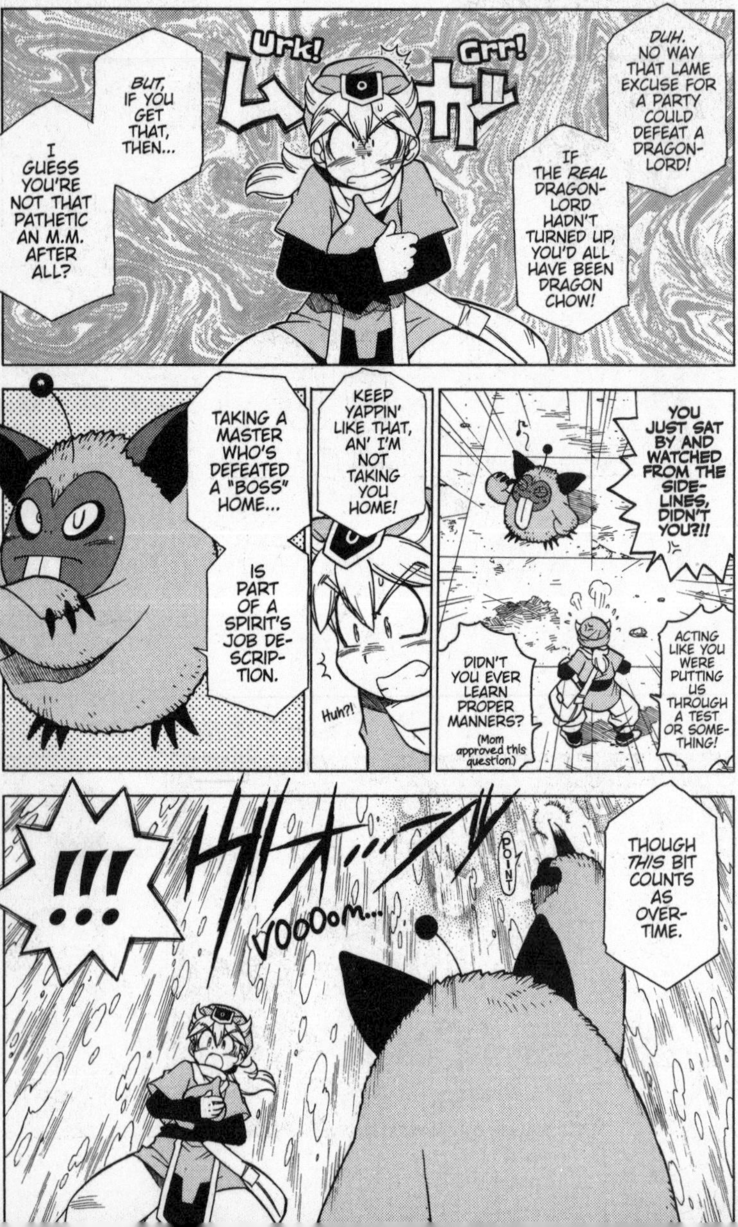
DUH. NO WAY THAT LAME EXCUSE FOR A PARTY COULD DEFEAT A DRAGON-LORD!
Grr!
IF THE *REAL* DRAGON-LORD HADN'T TURNED UP, YOU'D ALL HAVE BEEN DRAGON CHOW!
Urk!
BUT, IF YOU GET THAT, THEN...
I GUESS YOU'RE NOT THAT PATHETIC AN M.M. AFTER ALL?
YOU JUST SAT BY AND WATCHED FROM THE SIDE-LINES, DIDN'T YOU?!!
ACTING LIKE YOU WERE PUTTING US THROUGH A TEST OR SOME-THING!
DIDN'T YOU EVER LEARN PROPER MANNERS?
(Mom approved this question.)
KEEP YAPPIN' LIKE THAT, AN' I'M NOT TAKING YOU HOME!
Huh?!
TAKING A MASTER WHO'S DEFEATED A "BOSS" HOME...
IS PART OF A SPIRIT'S JOB DE-SCRIP-TION.
THOUGH *THIS* BIT COUNTS AS OVER-TIME.
POINT
VOOOom...
!!!
...

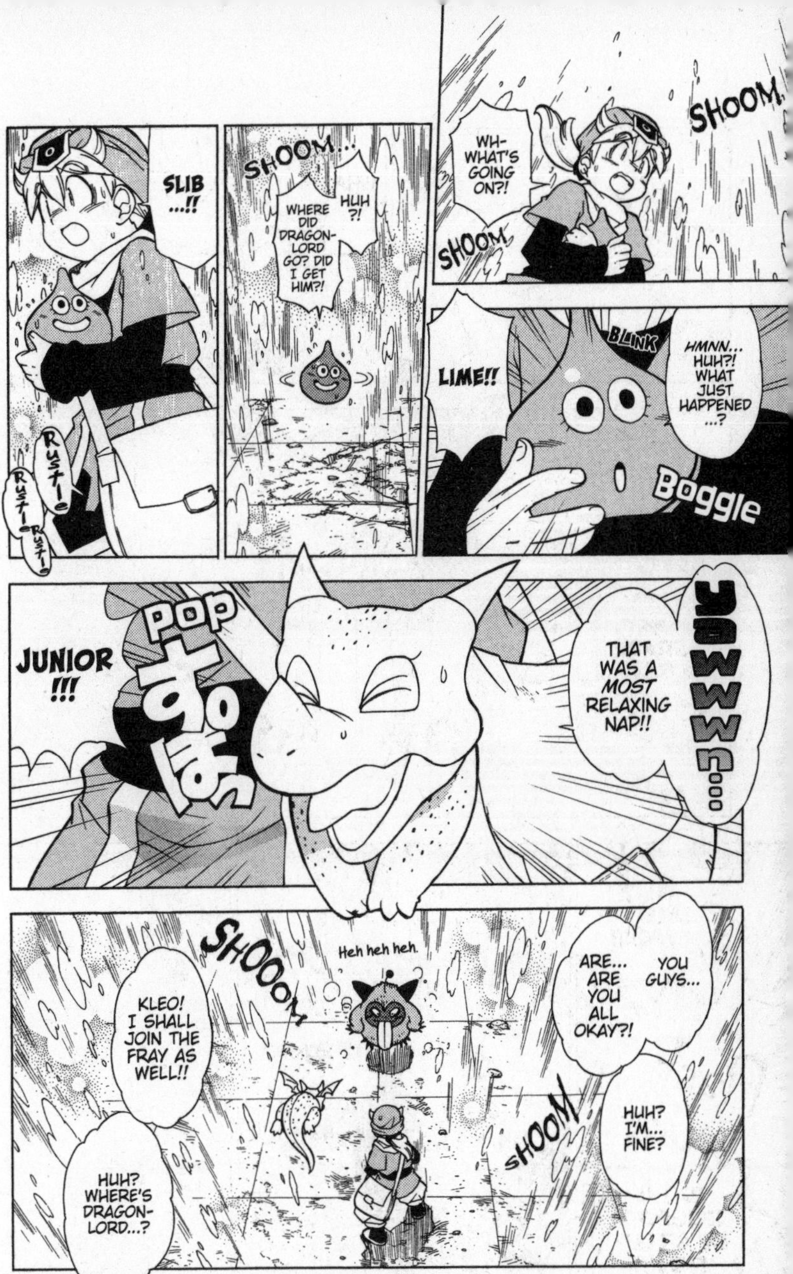
SHOOM
WH-WHAT'S GOING ON?!
SHOOM
HMNN... HUH?! WHAT JUST HAPPENED...?
BLINK
LIME!!
Boggle
HUH?!
WHERE DID DRAGON-LORD GO? DID I GET HIM?!
SHOOM...
SLIB...!!
Rustle
Rustle Rustle
YAWWWWn...
THAT WAS A MOST RELAXING NAP!!
pop
すぽん
JUNIOR!!!
YOU GUYS...
ARE... ARE YOU ALL OKAY?!
HUH? I'M... FINE?
Heh heh heh.
SHOOOOM
SHOOM
KLEO! I SHALL JOIN THE FRAY AS WELL!!
HUH? WHERE'S DRAGON-LORD...?

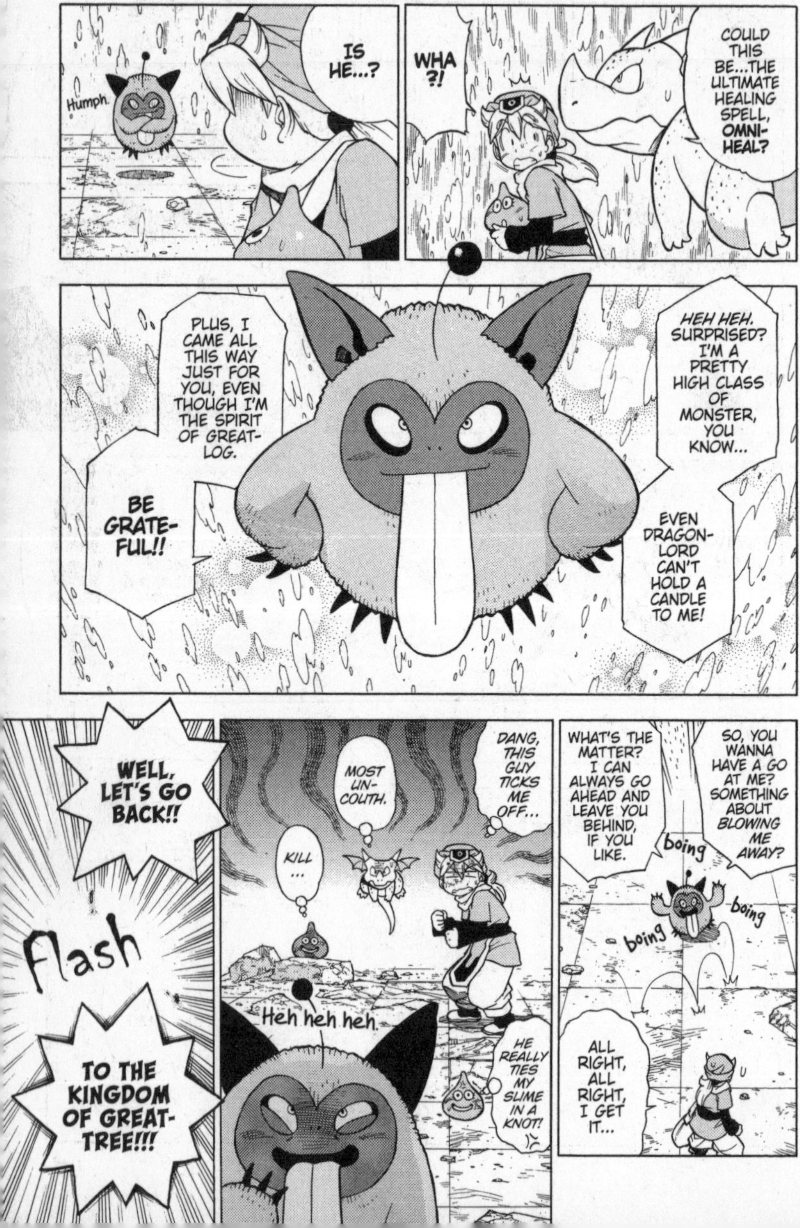
COULD THIS BE...THE ULTIMATE HEALING SPELL, OMNI-HEAL?
WHA ?!
IS HE...?
Humph.
HEH HEH. SURPRISED? I'M A PRETTY HIGH CLASS OF MONSTER, YOU KNOW...
EVEN DRAGON-LORD CAN'T HOLD A CANDLE TO ME!
PLUS, I CAME ALL THIS WAY JUST FOR YOU, EVEN THOUGH I'M THE SPIRIT OF GREAT-LOG.
BE GRATE-FUL!!
SO, YOU WANNA HAVE A GO AT ME? SOMETHING ABOUT BLOWING ME AWAY?
WHAT'S THE MATTER? I CAN ALWAYS GO AHEAD AND LEAVE YOU BEHIND, IF YOU LIKE.
boing
boing
boing
ALL RIGHT, ALL RIGHT, I GET IT...
DANG, THIS GUY TICKS ME OFF...
MOST UN-COUTH.
KILL ...
Heh heh heh.
HE REALLY TIES MY SLIME IN A KNOT!
WELL, LET'S GO BACK!!
Flash
TO THE KINGDOM OF GREAT-TREE!!!

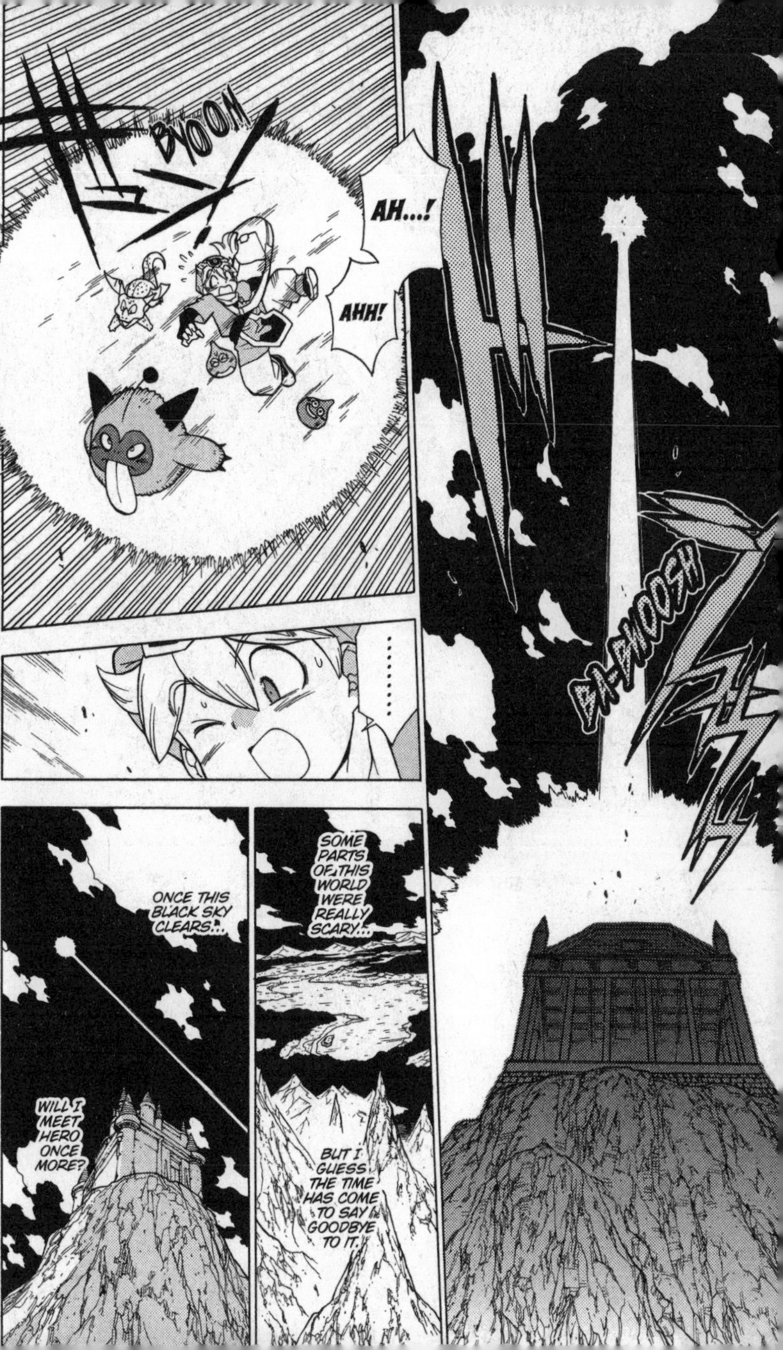
BA-DHOOSH
BYOOOM
AH...!
AHH!
......
SOME PARTS OF THIS WORLD WERE REALLY SCARY...
BUT I GUESS THE TIME HAS COME TO SAY GOODBYE TO IT.
ONCE THIS BLACK SKY CLEARS...
WILL I MEET HERO ONCE MORE?

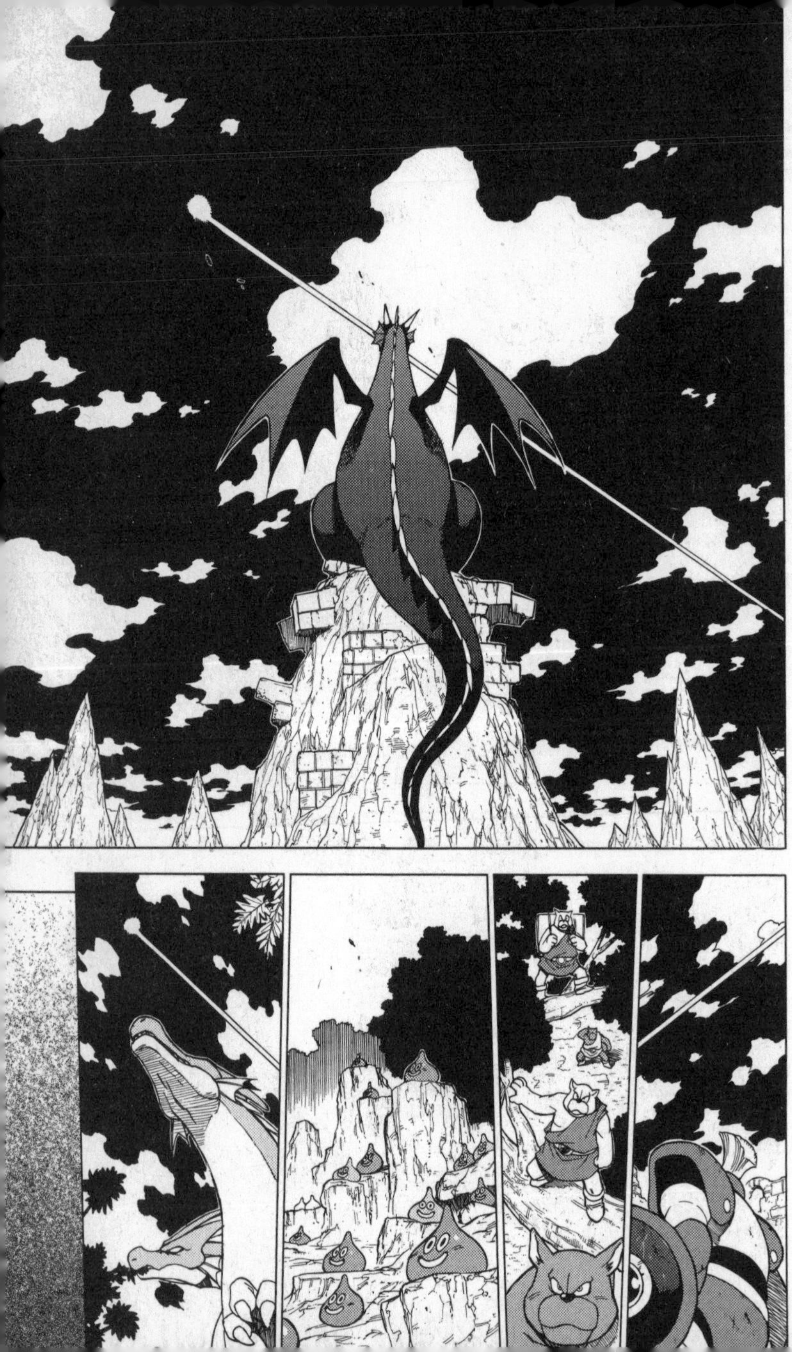

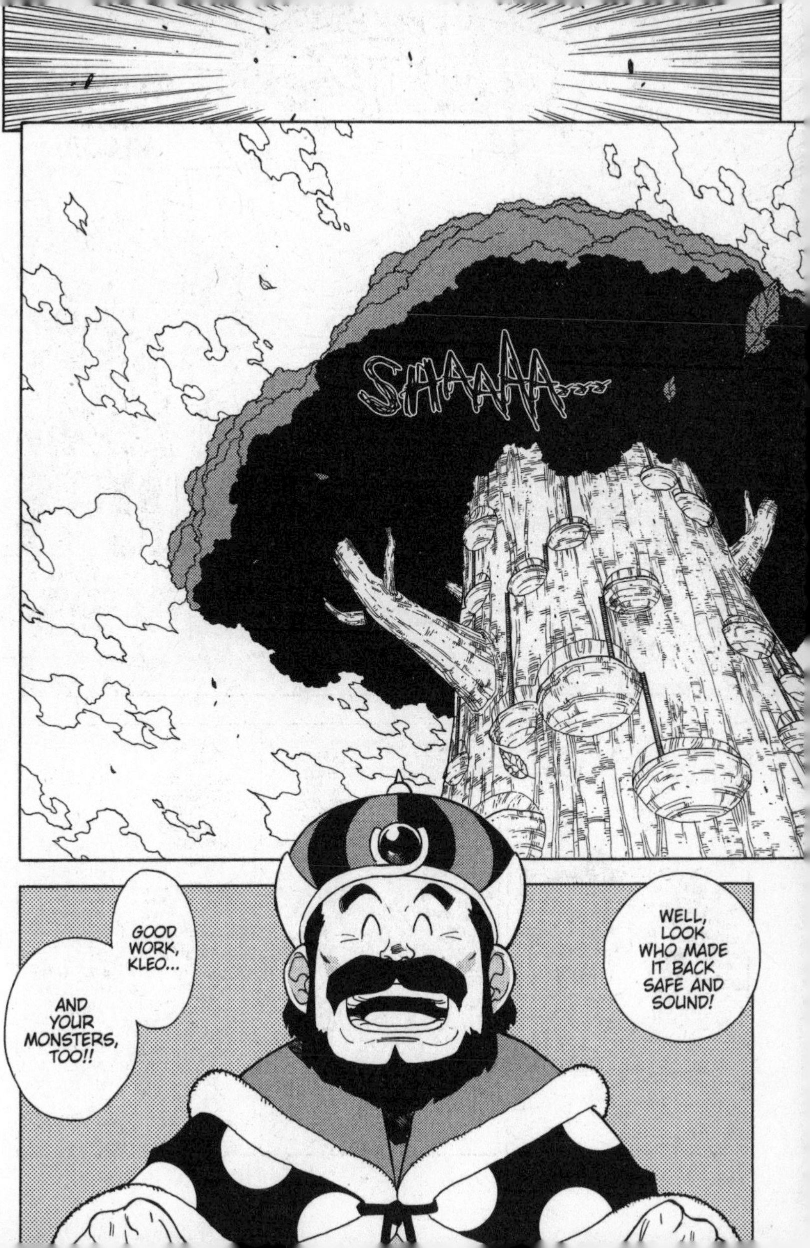
SHAAAA
WELL, LOOK WHO MADE IT BACK SAFE AND SOUND!
GOOD WORK, KLEO...
AND YOUR MONSTERS, TOO!!

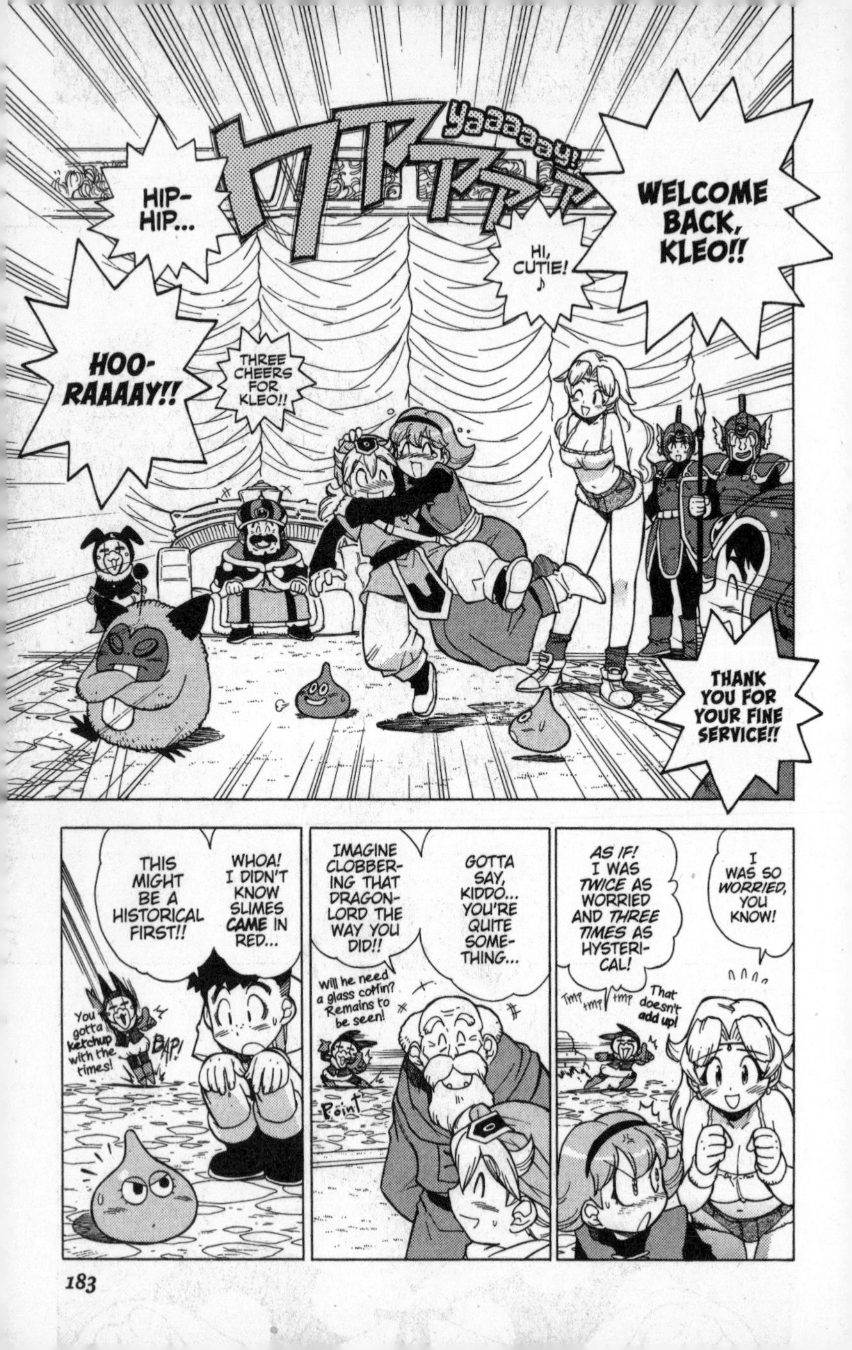
WELCOME BACK, KLEO!!
HI, CUTIE! ♪
yaaaaaay!
HIP-HIP...
THREE CHEERS FOR KLEO!!
HOO-RAAAAY!!
THANK YOU FOR YOUR FINE SERVICE!!
I WAS SO *WORRIED*, YOU KNOW!
AS IF! I WAS *TWICE* AS WORRIED AND *THREE TIMES* AS HYSTERICAL!
That doesn't add up!
tmp tmp tmp
GOTTA SAY, KIDDO... YOU'RE QUITE SOMETHING...
IMAGINE CLOBBERING THAT DRAGONLORD THE WAY YOU DID!!
Will he need a glass coffin? Remains to be seen!
Point
WHOA! I DIDN'T KNOW SLIMES **CAME** IN RED...
THIS MIGHT BE A HISTORICAL FIRST!!
BAP!
You gotta ketchup with the times!

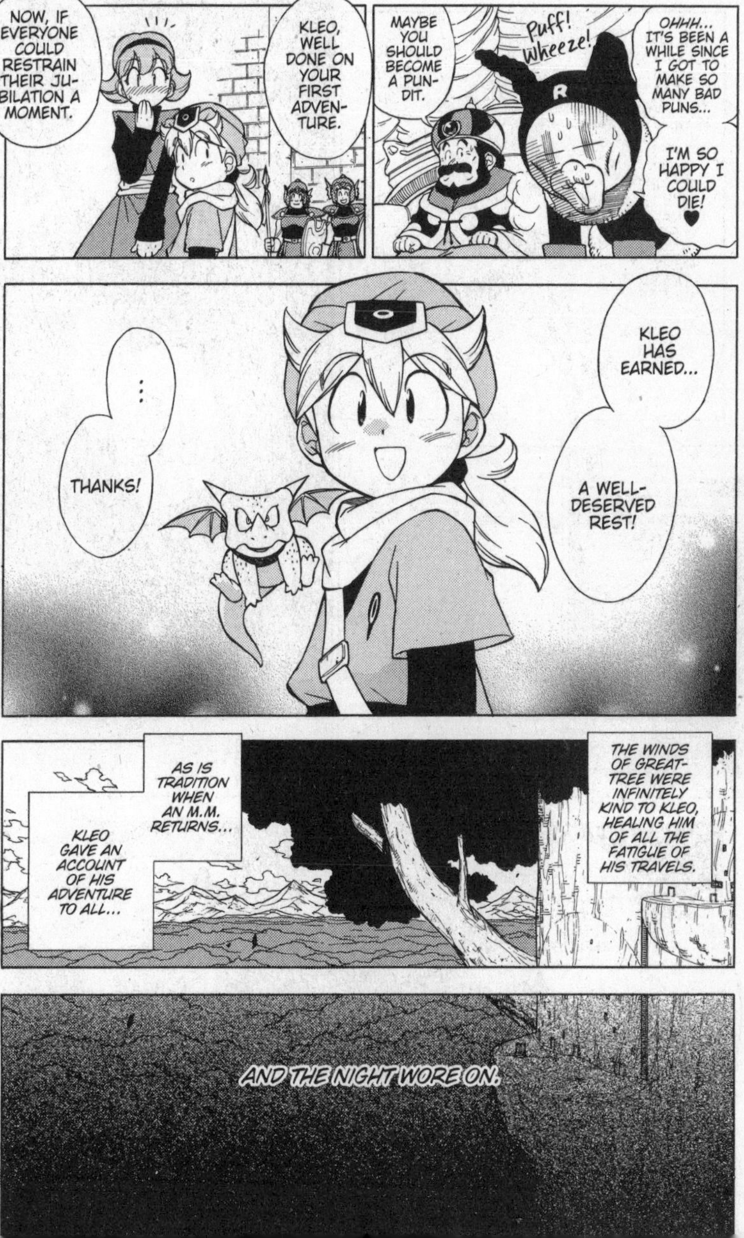
OHHH... IT'S BEEN A WHILE SINCE I GOT TO MAKE SO MANY BAD PUNS...
I'M SO HAPPY I COULD DIE! ♥
Puff! Wheeze!
MAYBE YOU SHOULD BECOME A PUN-DIT.
KLEO, WELL DONE ON YOUR FIRST ADVEN-TURE.
NOW, IF EVERYONE COULD RESTRAIN THEIR JU-BILATION A MOMENT.
KLEO HAS EARNED...
A WELL-DESERVED REST!
...
THANKS!
THE WINDS OF GREAT-TREE WERE INFINITELY KIND TO KLEO, HEALING HIM OF ALL THE FATIGUE OF HIS TRAVELS.
AS IS TRADITION WHEN AN M.M. RETURNS...
KLEO GAVE AN ACCOUNT OF HIS ADVENTURE TO ALL...
AND THE NIGHT WORE ON.

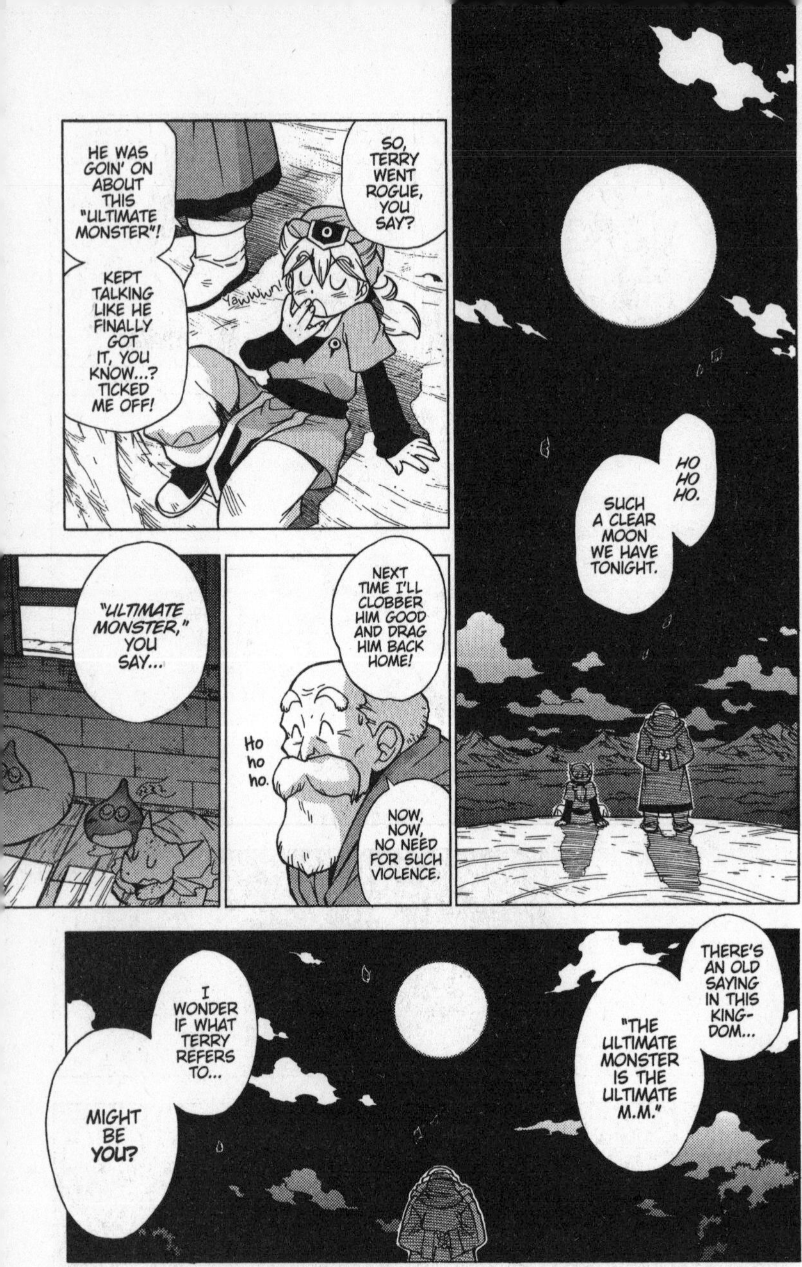
HO HO HO.
SUCH A CLEAR MOON WE HAVE TONIGHT.
SO, TERRY WENT ROGUE, YOU SAY?
YAWWWN!
HE WAS GOIN' ON ABOUT THIS "ULTIMATE MONSTER"!
KEPT TALKING LIKE HE FINALLY GOT IT, YOU KNOW...? TICKED ME OFF!
NEXT TIME I'LL CLOBBER HIM GOOD AND DRAG HIM BACK HOME!
Ho ho ho.
NOW, NOW, NO NEED FOR SUCH VIOLENCE.
"ULTIMATE MONSTER," YOU SAY...
THERE'S AN OLD SAYING IN THIS KING-DOM...
"THE ULTIMATE MONSTER IS THE ULTIMATE M.M."
I WONDER IF WHAT TERRY REFERS TO...
MIGHT BE YOU?

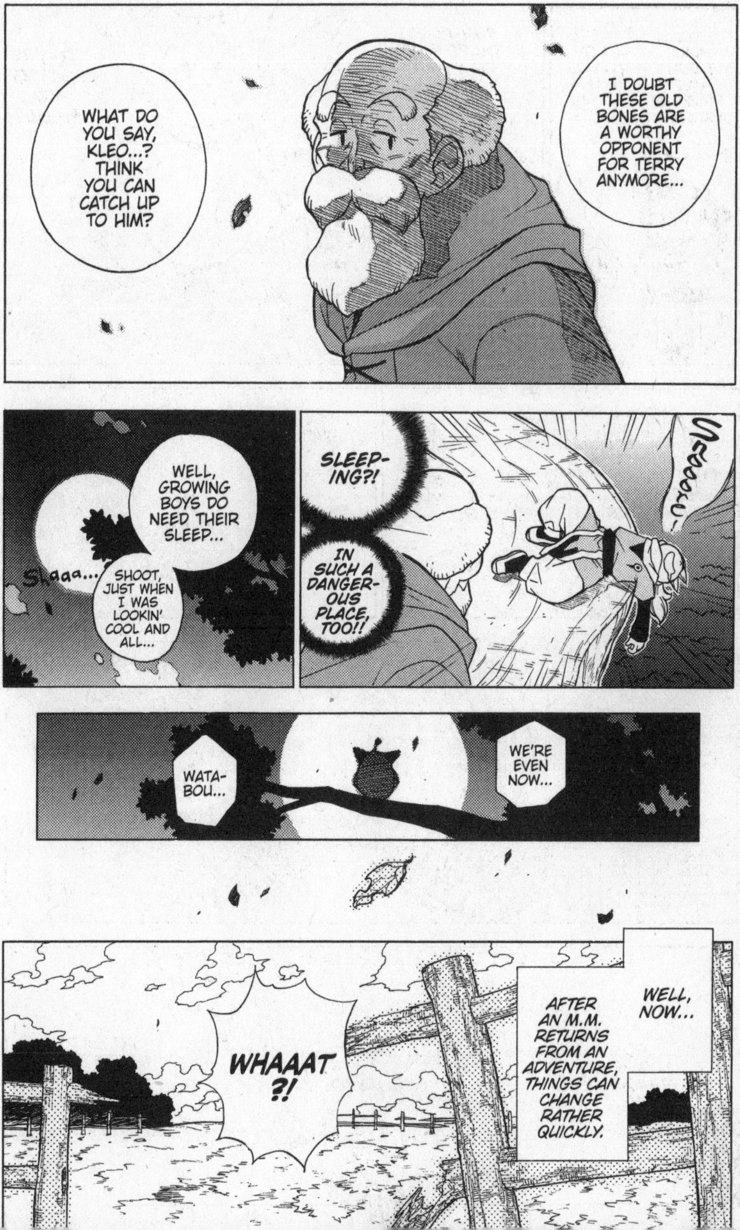
I DOUBT THESE OLD BONES ARE A WORTHY OPPONENT FOR TERRY ANYMORE...
WHAT DO YOU SAY, KLEO...? THINK YOU CAN CATCH UP TO HIM?
SLEEP-ING?!
IN SUCH A DANGER-OUS PLACE, TOO!!
WELL, GROWING BOYS DO NEED THEIR SLEEP...
Shaaa...
SHOOT, JUST WHEN I WAS LOOKIN' COOL AND ALL...
WE'RE EVEN NOW...
WATA-BOU...
WELL, NOW...
AFTER AN M.M. RETURNS FROM AN ADVENTURE, THINGS CAN CHANGE RATHER QUICKLY.
WHAAAT?!

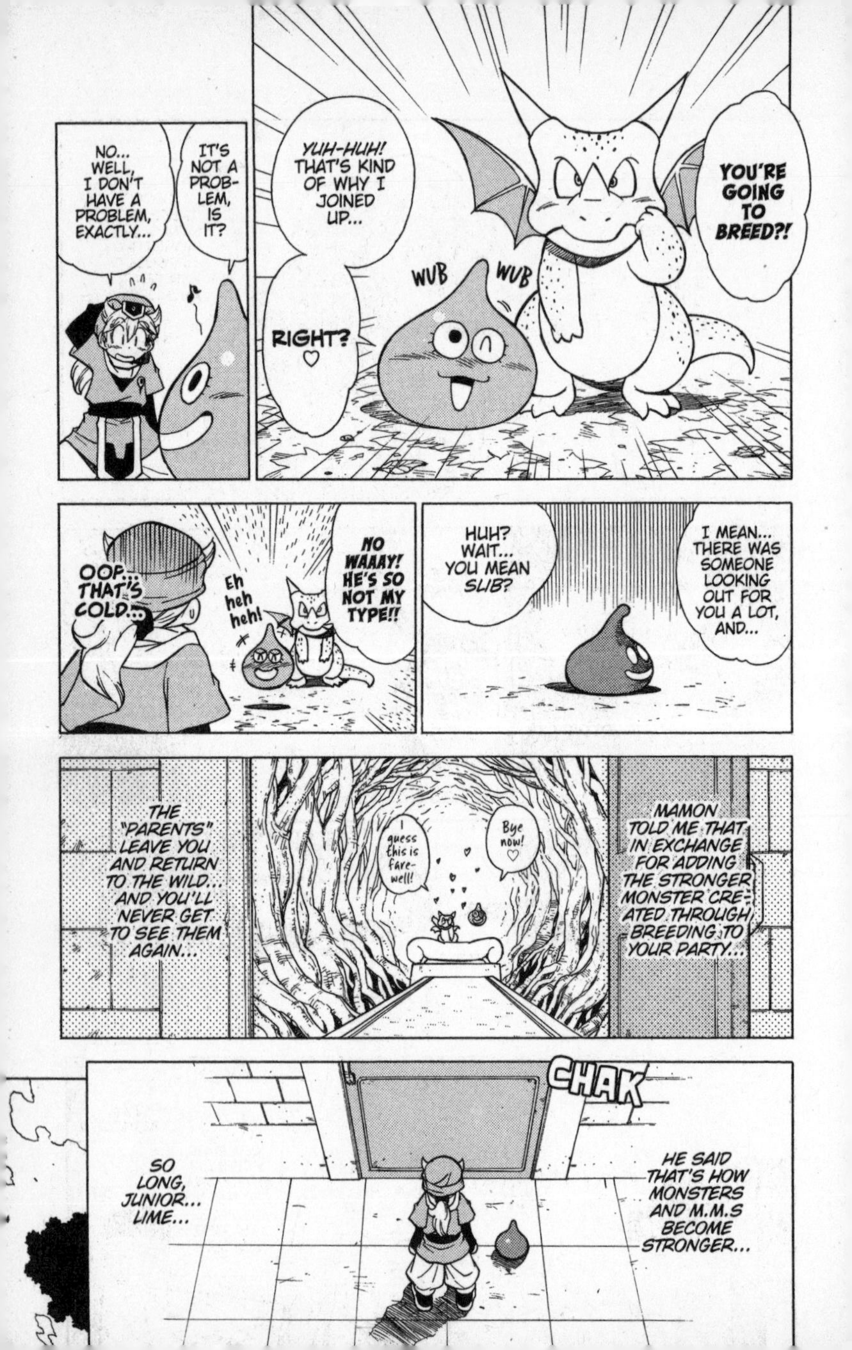
YOU'RE GOING TO BREED?!
YUH-HUH! THAT'S KIND OF WHY I JOINED UP...
WUB WUB
RIGHT? ♡
IT'S NOT A PROBLEM, IS IT?
NO... WELL, I DON'T HAVE A PROBLEM, EXACTLY...
I MEAN... THERE WAS SOMEONE LOOKING OUT FOR YOU A LOT, AND...
HUH? WAIT... YOU MEAN SLIB?
NO WAAAY! HE'S SO NOT MY TYPE!!
Eh heh heh!
OOP... THAT'S COLD...
MAMON TOLD ME THAT IN EXCHANGE FOR ADDING THE STRONGER MONSTER CREATED THROUGH BREEDING TO YOUR PARTY...
Bye now! ♡
I guess this is fare-well!
THE "PARENTS" LEAVE YOU AND RETURN TO THE WILD... AND YOU'LL NEVER GET TO SEE THEM AGAIN...
CHAK
HE SAID THAT'S HOW MONSTERS AND M.M.S BECOME STRONGER...
SO LONG, JUNIOR... LIME...

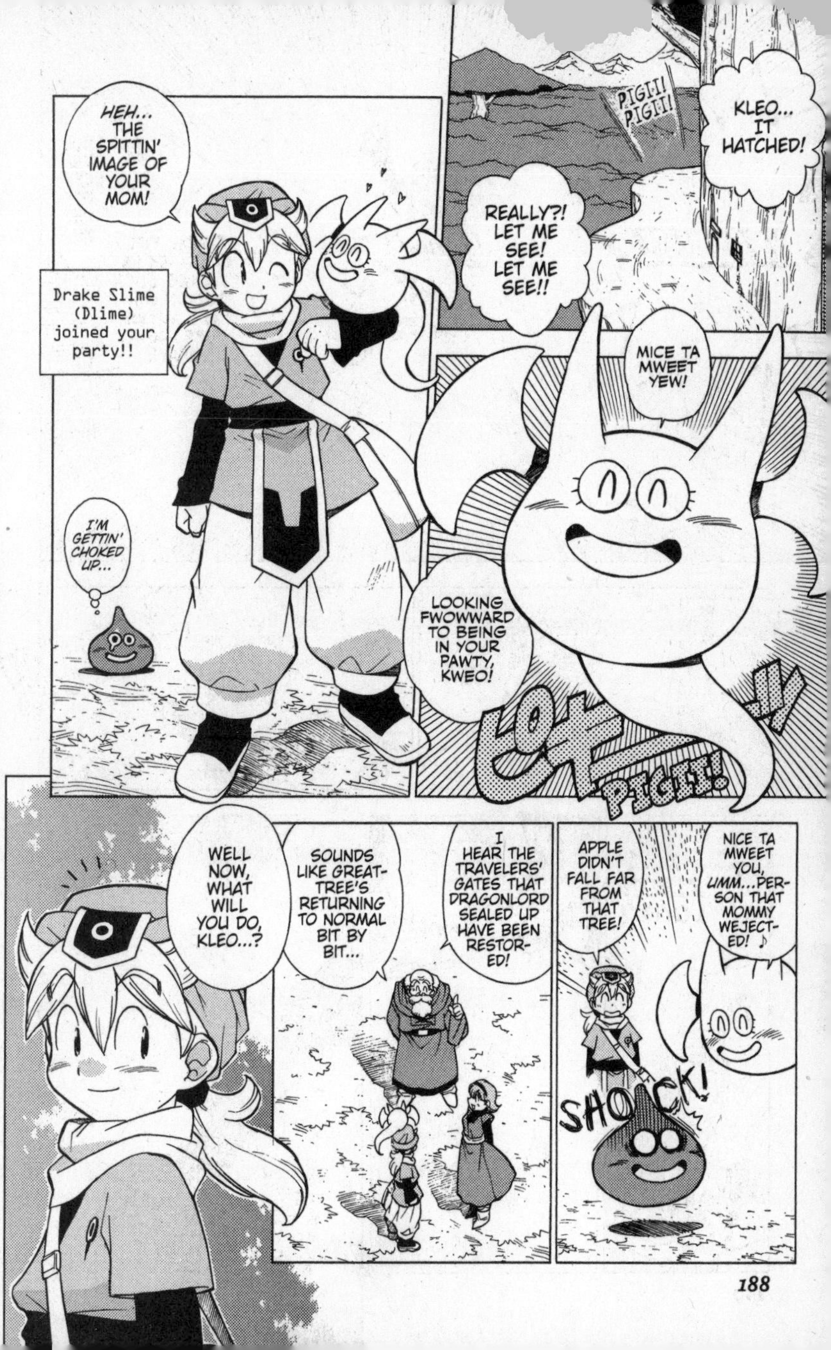
PIGI!! PIGI!!
KLEO... IT HATCHED!
REALLY?! LET ME SEE! LET ME SEE!!
MICE TA MWEET YEW!
LOOKING FWOWWARD TO BEING IN YOUR PAWTY, KWEO!
PIGI!!
HEH... THE SPITTIN' IMAGE OF YOUR MOM!
Drake Slime (Dlime) joined your party!!
I'M GETTIN' CHOKED UP...
NICE TA MWEET YOU, UMM...PERSON THAT MOMMY WEJECTED! ♪
APPLE DIDN'T FALL FAR FROM THAT TREE!
SHOCK!
I HEAR THE TRAVELERS' GATES THAT DRAGONLORD SEALED UP HAVE BEEN RESTORED!
SOUNDS LIKE GREAT-TREE'S RETURNING TO NORMAL BIT BY BIT...
WELL NOW, WHAT WILL YOU DO, KLEO...?

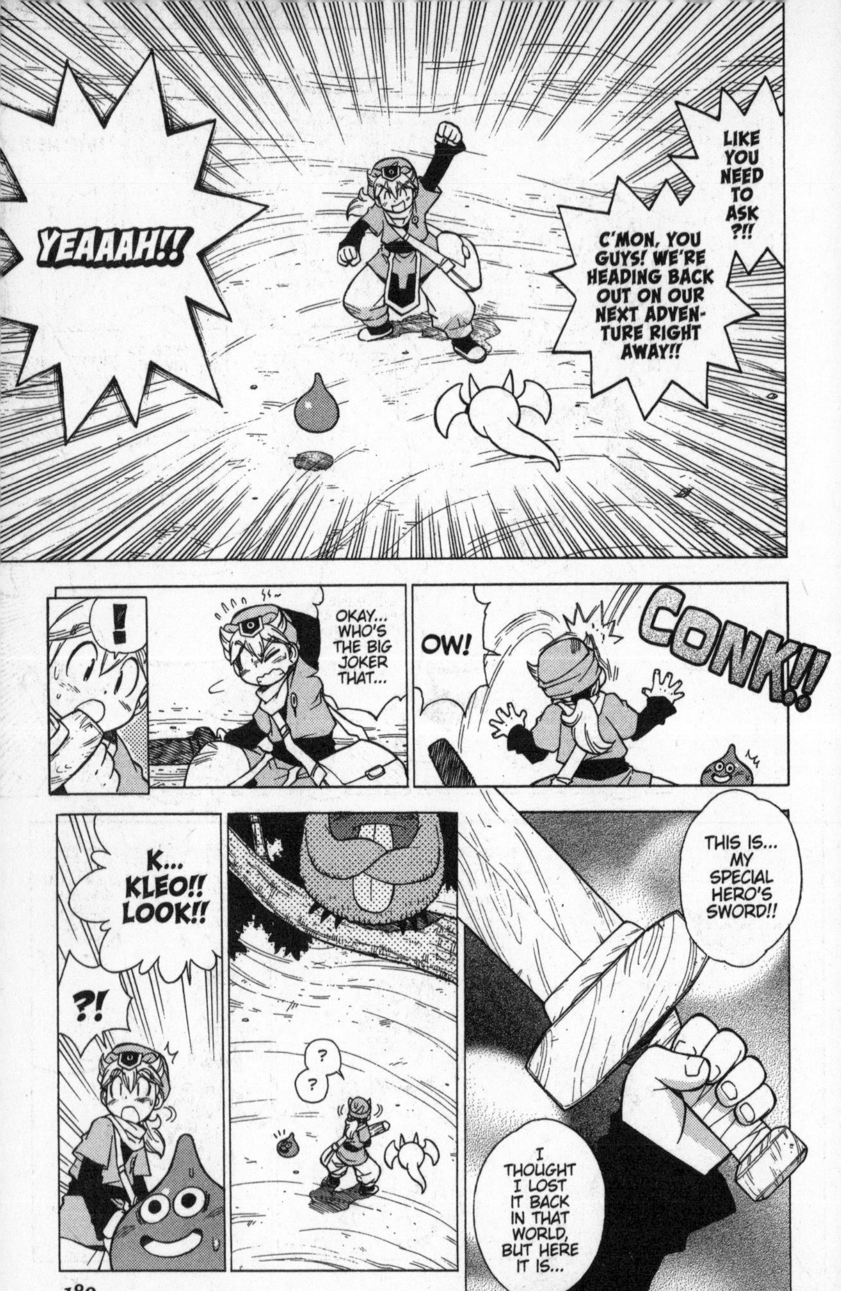
LIKE YOU NEED TO ASK?!!
C'MON, YOU GUYS! WE'RE HEADING BACK OUT ON OUR NEXT ADVENTURE RIGHT AWAY!!
YEAAAH!!
CONK!!
OW!
OKAY... WHO'S THE BIG JOKER THAT...
!
THIS IS... MY SPECIAL HERO'S SWORD!!
I THOUGHT I LOST IT BACK IN THAT WORLD, BUT HERE IT IS...
?
?
K... KLEO!! LOOK!!
?!

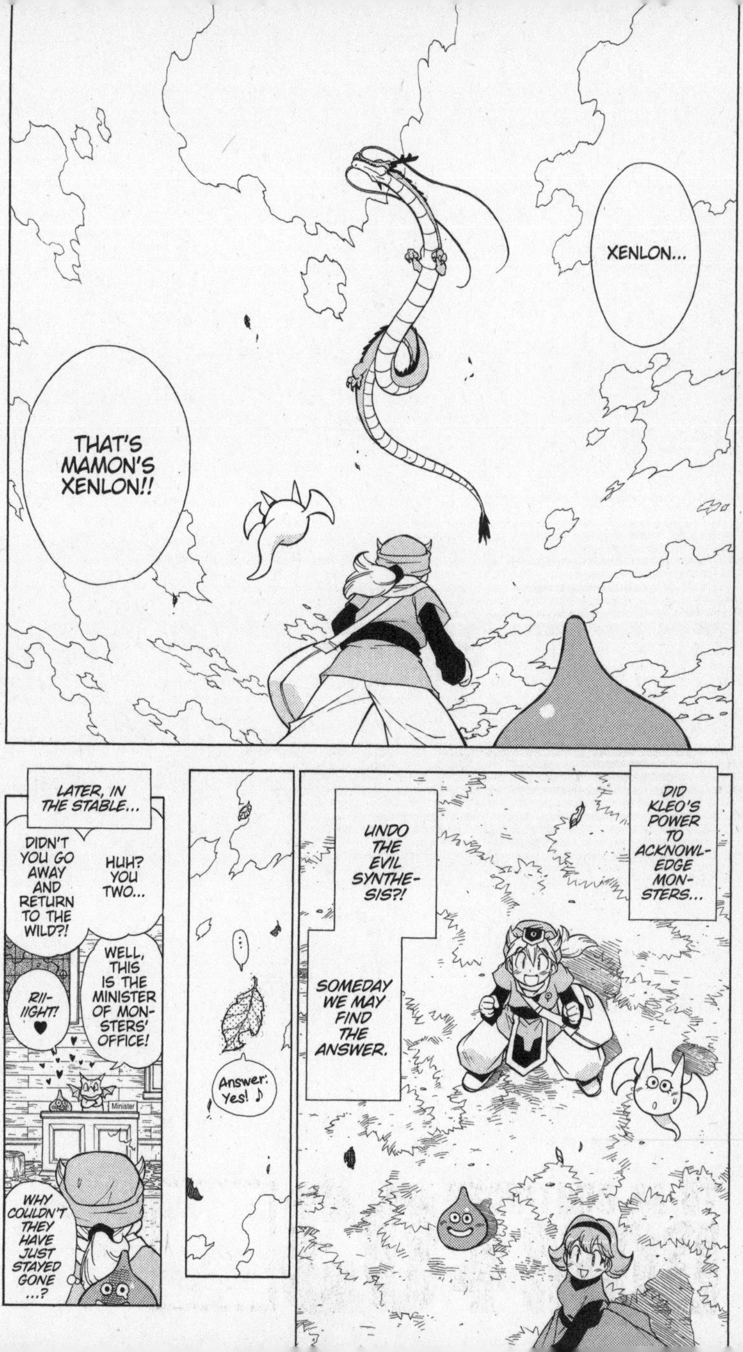
XENLON...
THAT'S MAMON'S XENLON!!
DID KLEO'S POWER TO ACKNOWL-EDGE MON-STERS...
UNDO THE EVIL SYNTHE-SIS?!
SOMEDAY WE MAY FIND THE ANSWER.
...
Answer: Yes! ♪
LATER, IN THE STABLE...
HUH? YOU TWO...
DIDN'T YOU GO AWAY AND RETURN TO THE WILD?!
WELL, THIS IS THE MINISTER OF MON-STERS' OFFICE!
RII-IIGHT! ♥
Minister
WHY COULDN'T THEY HAVE JUST STAYED GONE ...?

TO BE CONTINUED

DQM+03

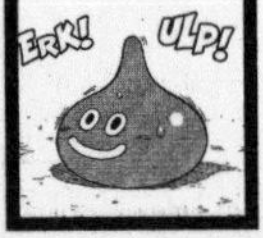
ERK!
ULP!

Monster Encyclopedia Vol.2

Who are the monsters that await on Kleo's journey...?! Let's have a look at the ones who appear in this volume.

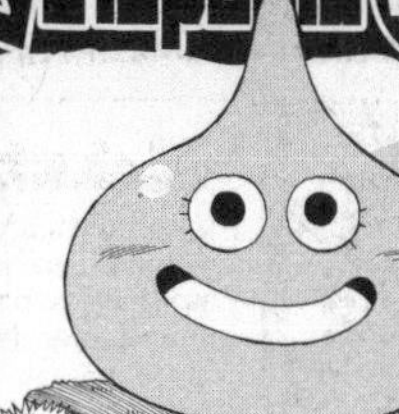

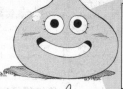

She-Slime
[Lime]

She's a weirdo who wanted to join Kleo's party of her own accord ♀. It would appear she's not very assertive when it comes to battle.

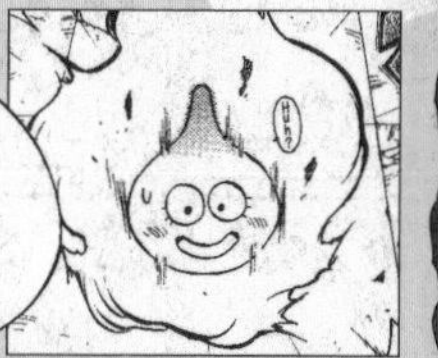

▲ Influenced by the party's valiant efforts during the battle with Dragonlord, she erupted with the chant Frizz.

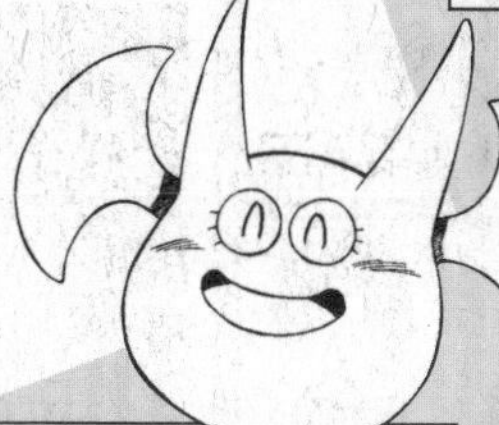

Drake Slime
[Dlime]

This monster is the result of Lime and Jr.'s breeding. It looks and acts like Lime...?!

LYCANT

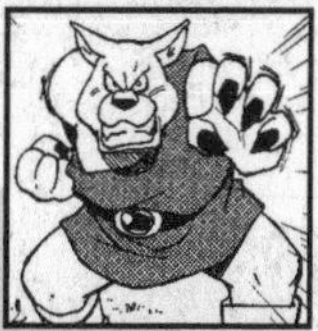

▲Bewarewolf

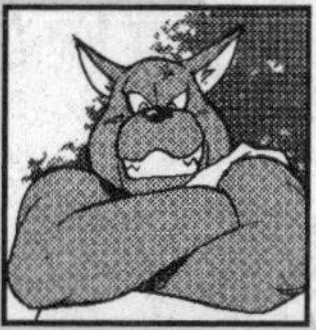

▲Scarewolf

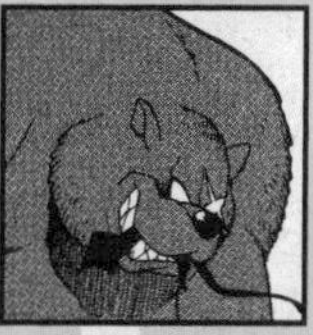

▲Ursa Mega

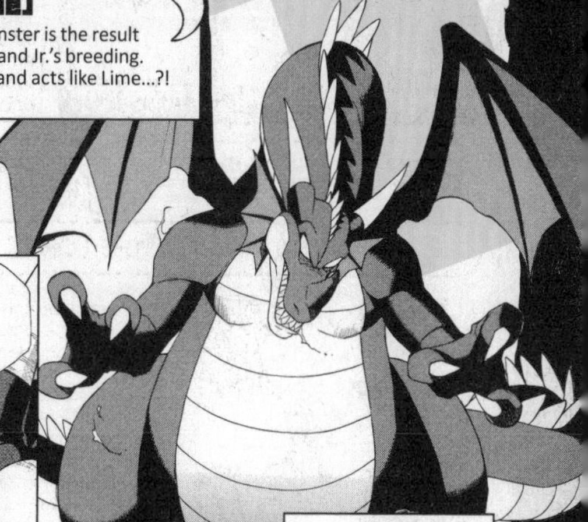

Dragonlord

This dragon drenched in evil power was born through Terry's Evil Synthesis.

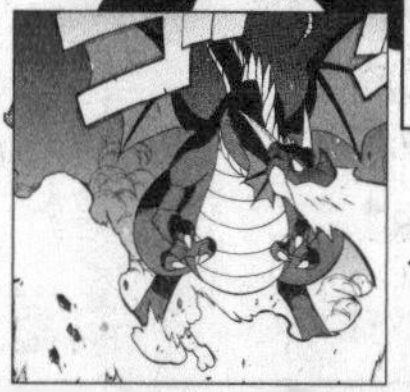

◀ It is capable of Flame Breath, the high-level attack from the fire breath category that easily defeated Slib and company in one puff.

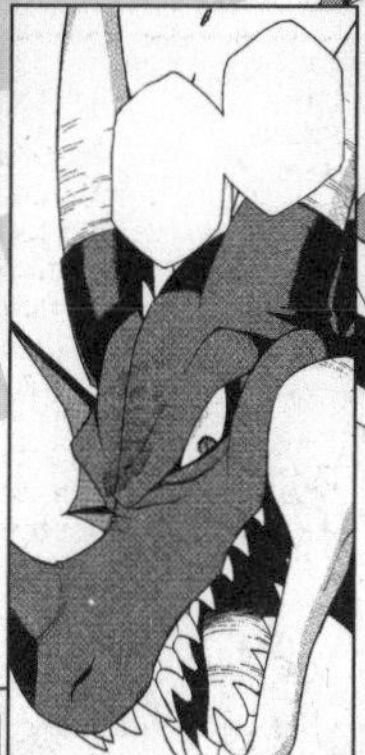

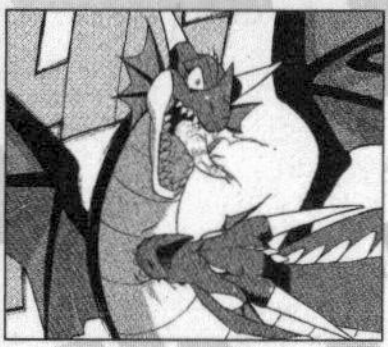

▲ Though they are both "Dragonlord," the difference in power is unmistakable.

Dragonlord

He is the Hero's arch-enemy and Supreme Ruler of all the world's monsters. His power is incomparable to that of the Dragonlord born of Evil Synthesis.

AND OTHER MONSTERS

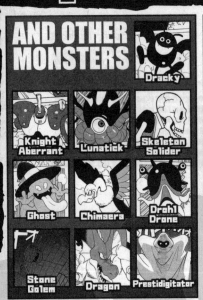

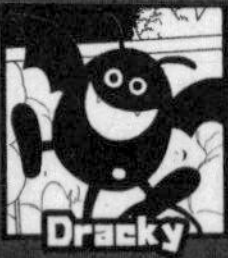
Dracky

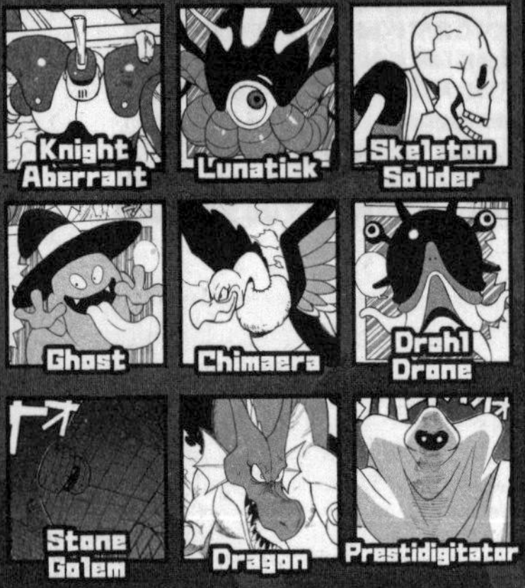
Knight Aberrant
Lunatick
Skeleton Solider
Ghost
Chimaera
Drohl Drone
Stone Golem
Dragon
Prestidigitator

Jinkster

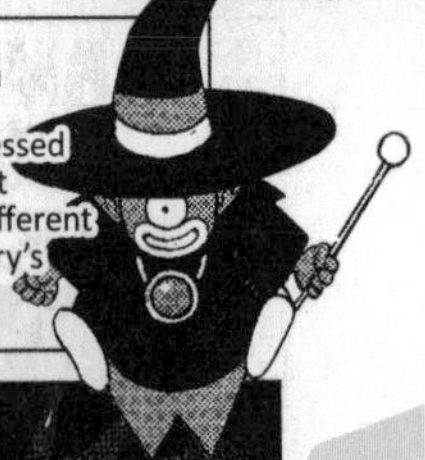

This monster is obsessed with Evil Synthesis. It synthesizes many different monsters under Terry's direction.

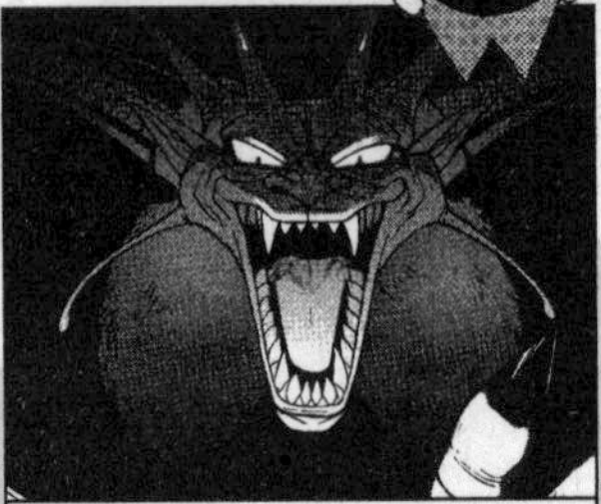

Mortamor (Final Evolution)

This demon lord appeared to Terry when he stumbled upon the ultimate synthesis. He bestowed upon Terry the Jewel of Evil, the source of the Wave of Evil.

DQM ✚ Secrets Revealed!

MaMon's SHRINE OF ANSWERS

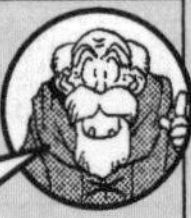

I'LL TELL YOU ALL THE LORE I KNOW.

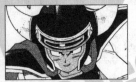

▶ "Phoenix Cross: Super Slash" deals deadly injuries to one's opponent.

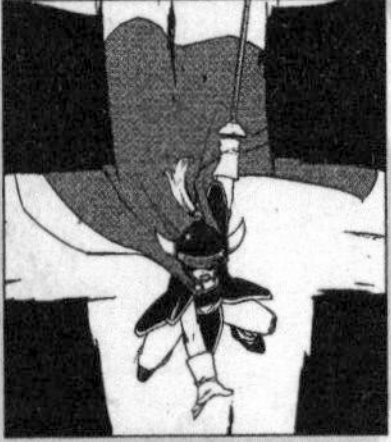

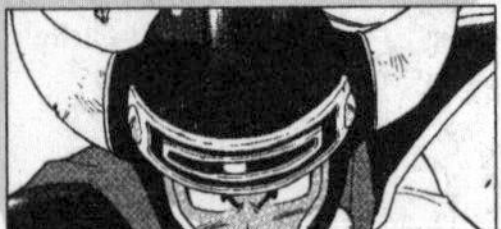

▲Only this Hero could have belted out such a fine blow...he's pretty powerful!!

You remember the spell Dragonlord used to dispatch the Hero...? What really happened was that he created his own tiny "Traveler's Gate" to blow the target away into another world. It's the ancient spell "Bazoom."

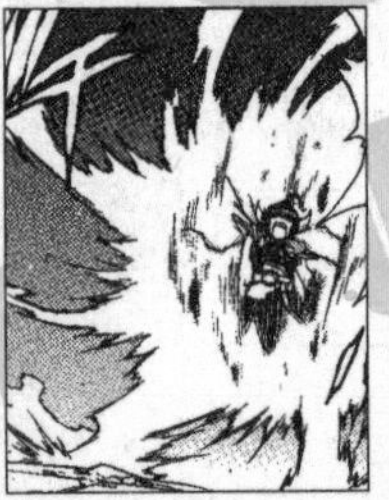

The Lycants began to wear clothes after a certain period in their evolution. The Ursa Mega, who don't wear clothes, are the few remaining with an elder-like status among the Lycants. There used to be many Ursa Mega, but not these days...

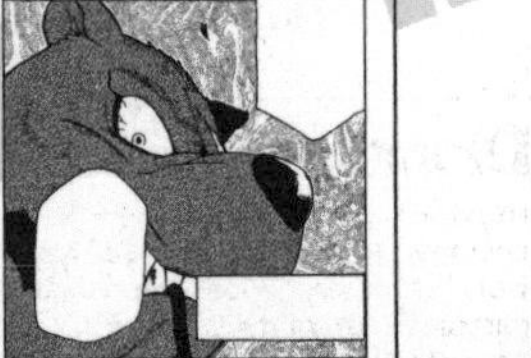

SEVEN SEAS ENTERTAINMENT PRESENTS

DRAGON QUEST MONSTERS+

story and art by MINE YOSHIZAKI

VOL. 2

...RE ENIX

...LTD.

...CO., LTD. and

...Mori Agency, Inc.

Carolina Hernandez Mendoza

COVER DESIGN
Nicky Lim

PROOFREADER
Brett Hallahan
Danielle King

EDITOR
J.P. Sullivan

PRODUCTION MANAGER
Lissa Pattillo

MANAGING EDITOR
Julie Davis

EDITOR-IN-CHIEF
Adam Arnold

PUBLISHER
Jason DeAngelis

Seven Seas books may be purchased in bulk for promotional, educational, or business use. Please contact your local bookseller or the Macmillan Corporate and Premium Sales Department at 1-800-221-7945, extension 5442, or by e-mail at MacmillanSpecialMarkets@macmillan.com.

Seven Seas and the Seven Seas logo are trademarks of Seven Seas Entertainment, LLC. All rights reserved.

ISBN: 978-1-642750-48-5

Printed in Canada

First Printing: March 2019

10 9 8 7 6 5 4 3 2 1

FOLLOW US ONLINE: www.sevenseasentertainment.com

READING DIRECTIONS

This book reads from **right to left**, Japanese style. If this is your first time reading manga, you start reading from the top right panel on each page and take it from there. If you get lost, just follow the numbered diagram here. It may seem backwards at first, but you'll get the hang of it! Have fun!!

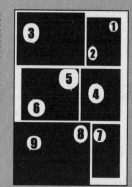

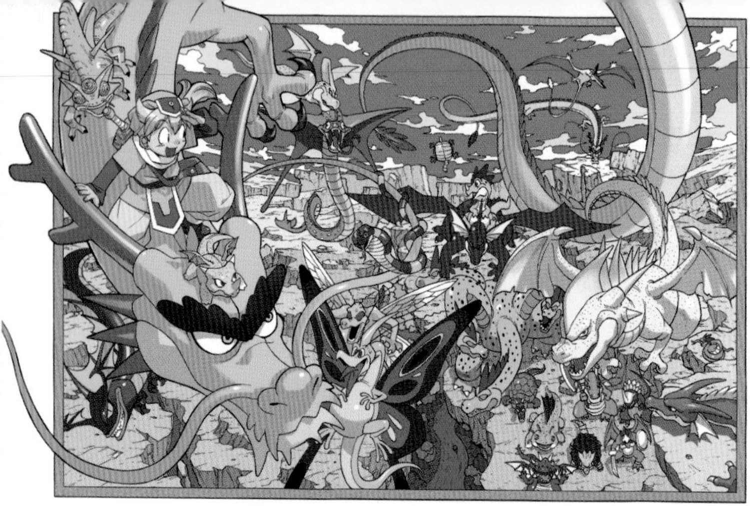

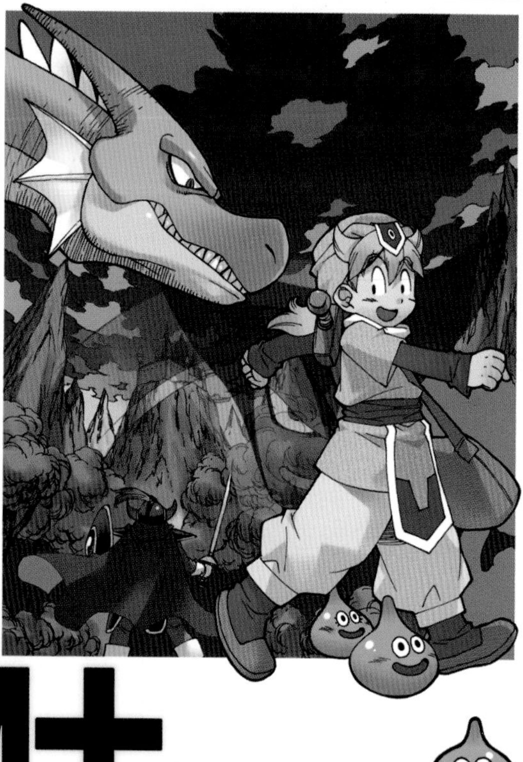

DQM+

DRAGON QUEST MONSTERS

Illust Gallery

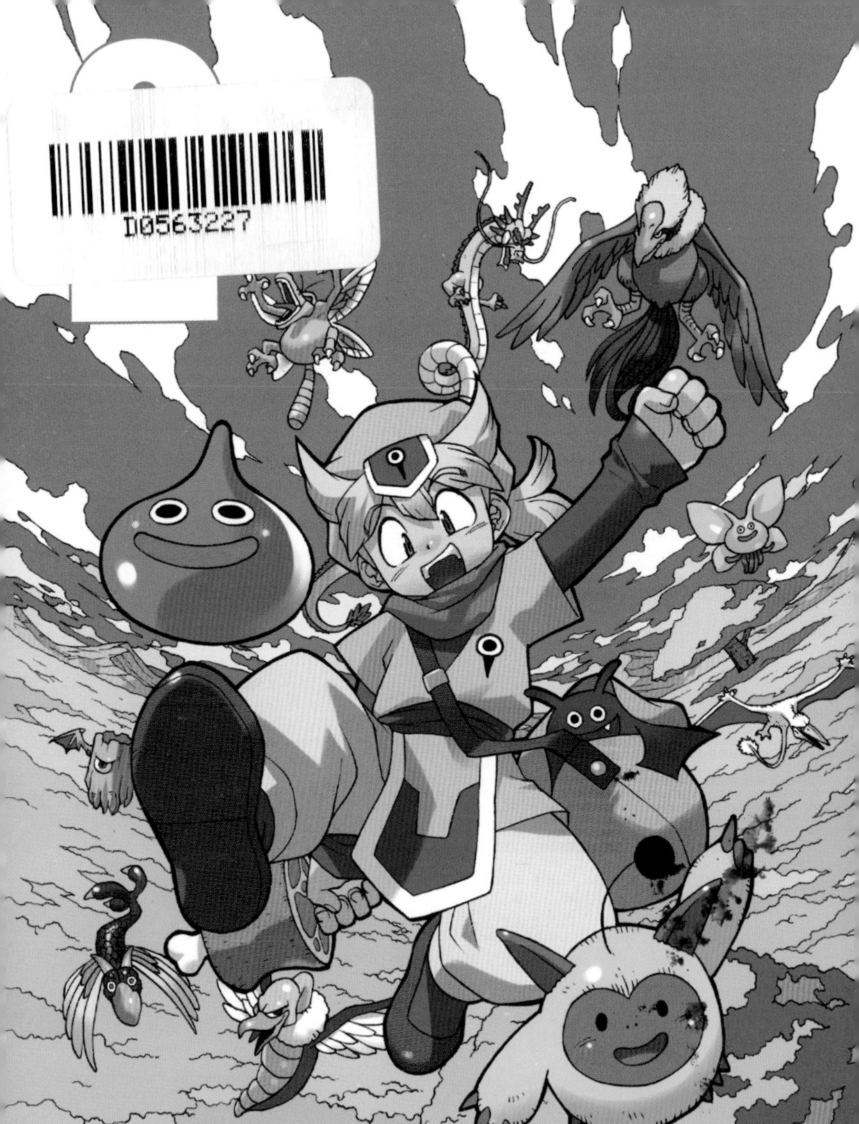

MINE YOSHIZAKI

DRAGON QUEST MONSTERS+